THE FAMILY IN RENAISSANCE FLORENCE

THE FAMILY IN RENAISSANCE FLORENCE

A translation by Renée Neu Watkins of
I LIBRI DELLA FAMIGLIA
by Leon Battista Alberti

With an Introduction by the translator

UNIVERSITY OF SOUTH CAROLINA PRESS

Columbia, South Carolina

CONTENTS

THE FAMILY IN
RENAISSANCE
FLORENCE

INTRODUCTION

A Monument of Attitudes

The wealthy prodigal lives surrounded by fair-weather friends. "You have seen the water swarming with fish while the bait's afloat; when the bait is gone, all is deserted and empty." The sentiment is attributed to Giannozzo Alberti, a Florentine *pater familias.* The image is Leon Battista's own, reflecting both his interest in nature and his implacably allegorical eye.

Leon Battista Alberti is read in Italy as a classic of the national literature, a voice from the Florence of the Medici. He defended the Italian vernacular in a time of narrow classicism, when the language of Dante was being forsaken for that of Cicero. Burckhardt devotes some glowing pages to his manly grace and universal abilities; even among the many forceful persons who crowd *The Civilization of the Renaissance in Italy,* he stands out as a kind of benevolent titan. Alberti was courtier, athlete, scientist, architect, musician, and theorist of the arts, but one of his most consistent roles was that of humanist. He was one of those who distilled classical reading and personal observation to offer posterity a variety of poems, plays, and treatises. He favored the dialogue form, and among his dialogues, *Della Famiglia* is the one that seems most closely to represent actual conversation. It is, as R. R. Bolgar put it, "that revealing work where Alberti paints the Florentine merchant class in the fullness of its good sense and sober ostentation." [1]

Upon closer scrutiny *Della Famiglia* does not, of course, present a single, homogeneously bourgeois outlook. As a dialogue it expresses conflicting points of view. It is a monument of attitudes. It enables us to relive social and moral conflicts which troubled early capitalist society. Ponderous and slow of speech, delighting in heavy ironies and elaborate insinuations, Alberti's personages confront much of what it means to be

---

[1] R. R. Bolgar, *The Classical Heritage and its Beneficiaries,* Cambridge, 1954, 281.

consciously urban—to experience social mobility, to recognize the psychological as well as the practical importance of purchased commodities, to wish in vain for stable families and firm public authority amid fluctuating fortunes and alliances. They debate these subjects on the basis of ethical assumptions derived from Christianity but under the no less pervasive influence of classical models. For, to cite Bolgar again, "Where the twelfth century had seen the Greeks and Romans as paragons of learning, the fifteenth saw them as paragons of human excellence." [2] To all that they learn from the classics, moreover, Alberti's personages add a ubiquitous Renaissance quality, a commitment to action, and this is why they seem implicitly optimistic. Reason is their source of policy, policy their means to achievement. Such a view of thought itself was a new thing.

Publishing History

In the *Vita anonyma*, Alberti's disguised autobiography, we are told something of the composition of *Della Famiglia*.[3] The first three books were drafted before he had reached his thirtieth year, hence before 1434. He was at this time a secretary in the Papal Curia. The books were produced quickly, begun and finished in Rome in ninety days. He first circulated them among his own family. His relatives doubtless scented the sharp criticism of themselves on these pages, and their hostility, he says, "decided him to destroy [the books] by fire." He was moved to preserve the work only by the interference of "certain princes." [4] A fourth book appeared in 1437, dealing primarily with the theme of friendship. Since this was also accepted as the theme of a literary contest which Alberti helped to organize in Florence in 1441, he then and there presented *Della Famiglia* IV to the Florentine Republic. In 1443 he reviewed the whole book with the help of two friends, a fellow Florentine humanist, priest, and papal secretary, Leonardo Dati, and a younger friend named

[2] *Ibid.*

[3] Renée Watkins, "The Authorship of the *Vita anonyma* of Leon Battista Alberti," *Studies in the Renaissance*, IV (1957), 101–12.

[4] Leon Battista Alberti, *Vita anonyma*, in L. A. Muratori, ed., *Rerum italicarum scriptores . . .* , Milan, 1723–1751, XXV, 295–304.

Tomaso Ceffi. The two readers urged, interestingly enough, that Alberti make his classical citations explicit. Thus we owe to them the relative ease with which we can follow the play of the author's erudition. The book was then to be sent to "Sicily," probably to Alfonso the Magnanimous, newly crowned that year as king of the Two Sicilies.

Thirteen fifteenth-century manuscripts of *Della Famiglia,* one of them a complete copy with the author's revisions in his own hand, are preserved today. Girolamo Mancini, Alberti's learned biographer of the late nineteenth century, observed that the work was cited by eight scholars of the sixteenth and seventeenth centuries. It was not printed at all, however, until 1734. Even at that date, only the third book was presented to the public. It masqueraded under the name of another fifteenth century Florentine, Agnolo Pandolfini—a mistake that went uncorrected for a hundred years. In the 1840's at last, after some controversy, Antonio Corso and others traced the error to a senator of Tuscany, Filippo Pandolfini, who, at the end of the sixteenth century, had found the work among the remains of his ancestor's library. In his inherited copy Pandolfini names had been substituted for the Alberti names of the interlocutors. Clearly a printed version with the original interlocutors and the attribution to Alberti was called for.

Such an edition, of Book III alone, saw the light in 1843 in Naples. In 1845 Anicio Bonucci in Florence published all of the first three books of *Della Famiglia* in the first volume of his collection of Alberti's *Opere Volgari.* Girolamo Mancini re-edited all of *Della Famiglia* in 1908. It became a classic used in Italian schools and was several times reprinted with new notes. In 1960 Cecil Grayson made a modern and truly critical text the first in a series of Alberti's *Opere Volgari,* which is superseding Bonucci's edition.[5] Grayson's work forms the basis of the present translation.

Aims of the Translation

In rendering one language into another quite remote in its cultural context, many compromises are necessary. I have tried to suggest the

[5] Leon Battista Alberti, *Della Famiglia,* in *Opere Volgari,* I, Cecil Grayson, ed., (Scrittori d'Italia, no. 235), Bari, 1960.

solemnity, occasional pathos, and sly humor of the original by use of a rhetoric inevitably quite different from the Latinistic Italian one. To convey specific meanings, single words could not be matched by single words. For *virtu,* for example, I frequently used virtue, virtues, nobility, excellence, qualities, and character, to name only a few. For readability's sake, I have cut Alberti's elaborate periods and unparagraphed flow of sentences into many shorter sentences forming paragraphs. Perhaps an English kind of fluidity replaces the close-knit unity of his constructions. In view of the leisurely and repetitious character of Alberti's text, I have compressed occasionally the redundant phrasing that was an embellishment in the eyes of his contemporaries but not in ours.

Immediate Origins and Purposes of Della Famiglia

Alberti's own family was both subject and object of *Della Famiglia.* He was a scion of one of the oldest, wealthiest, and most politically prominent merchant clans of Florence. The privileged status that he inherited, however, was severely limited. Since his family had offended the ruling Florentine group in the 1390's, he was born in exile and was not legally able to enter his father's city before 1428. Battista, who only later adopted the dignified name of Leo or Leon, was born in 1404, the second illegitimate son of a liaison between Lorenzo Alberti and a lady of the Genoese patriciate, Bianca di Carlo Fieschi, widow of a Grimaldi.[6] Their father not only recognized his sons and gave them his name, but he removed them from Genoa at the time of a plague in 1406 that killed their mother. He afterward raised them in Venice and Padua. While Battista never mentions the fact of his illegitimacy, it may well have stimulated in him the assertive sense of family membership which he expresses in *Della Famiglia.* Unlike his older brother, he seems never to have married or passed on the family name. He took orders and held benefices from the Curia. When he died in 1472 he established, by his will, a residence and stipend for members of the Alberti family who might wish to study at Bologna.

This final disposition reflects an important experience of Battista's

[6] Carlo Ceschi, "La Madre di Leon Battista Alberti," *Bolletino del Arte,* XXXIII (1948), 191–92.

youth—his years of study and poverty. He received at the school of the humanist Gasparino Barzizza in Padua an unusually good literary education in Latin. He continued his education at the University of Bologna, where he studied law and prepared himself to earn a living. In May of 1421, however, his first year there, Lorenzo Alberti died. The occasion of that last illness, when many of the family were gathered in his father's house, later furnished Battista with the setting of *Della Famiglia*. The loss of his father was soon followed by that of his father's brother and partner, Ricciardo. His cousins, Benedetto and Antonio, took over the branch of the firm formerly managed by Lorenzo and Ricciardo. In the tax registers of Florence for 1430, they state that they had paid over less than half the inheritance of Battista and Carlo, left in their trust nine years before. It would appear, partly from the emphasis on these themes in *Della Famiglia*, that they were also reluctant either to employ or to support younger members of the family. They claimed to the tax officials that they had spent large sums (almost half the eight thousand gold florins left by Lorenzo) on the boys' education. They also claimed to have incurred heavy losses in the trade with Bruges, and ten years later, in fact, the Alberti firm suffered general financial collapse.[7]

In his writings Battista often looks back with indignation on the poverty of his student years, when he was ill and even, for a time, suffered a partial loss of memory. As he laments in the *Vita*, friends proved kinder at this time of trial than did his cruel relatives. Money was not the only issue, for "after the death of his father, Lorenzo Alberti, some of his relatives viciously resented his incipient, nearly established, reputation." Members of his family even plotted his death by the hand of a hired assassin, he says. (This episode, however, may have been a result rather than a cause of his writing *Della Famiglia*.) As he sums up in the *Vita* his view of the situation: "When he had tried again and again to win over his wicked relatives with many favors and every sort of kindness, he would remark that, actually, he knew full well that another knot won't fix a rotten gangplank."

He kept at least one good friend among the Alberti, his cousin Francesco d'Altobianco, who worked with him in the Papal Chancery. He was a partner of Benedetto and Antonio from 1427, but was already

---

[7] See Roberto Cessi, "Gli Alberti di Padova," *Arch. stor. ital.*, ser. 5, XL (1907), 233–84; Girolamo Mancini, *Vita di Leon Battista Alberti*, rev. 2nd ed., Florence, 1911, 51–54; and G. A. Holmes, "Florentine Merchants in London, 1343–1450," *Economic History Review*, Second Series XIII (1960), 193–208, for evidence on this family quarrel.

being sued by them in Venice in 1436. In 1443 he in turn sued Benedetto's heirs in Florence. He wrote poetry for the Florentine public contest of 1441, and to him Battista dedicated Book III of *Della Famiglia*.

Certain pious affectionate scenes in the dialogue seem to veil ironic reproaches. Lionardo, chief speaker of Books I and II, suggests that to help poor members of the family establish their own families, richer ones should contribute to a kind of charitable fund. "You feed and clothe both foreigners and slaves, not so much to enjoy the fruit of their labor as to have a large company in your household. To contribute to a single charity which would support your own kinsmen would cost you far less." He shows special interest in Battista's studies, praising and encouraging his growing classical eloquence. In granting his request to talk about the family and teach the boys something, he says, "Even if I were called to other occupations, I would always think this something that ought to come first—to satisfy your praiseworthy desires and wholly honorable ambition." He almost outlines Battista's future when he says, "Literary endeavors also depend on a thousand chances. Sometimes a man has no father, his relatives are envious, hard, and inhumane, and poverty strikes him down or he suffers some accident." Fortunately, he assures Battista, "No member of our family ever broke faith in his business dealings or failed to pay his honest debts." In view of documentary evidence that this same Lionardo engaged Benedetto as his agent in the purchase of land in 1422, it seems safe to assume he was at least friendly with the senior partner of the Paduan firm at the time of the financial manipulations and social neglect that offended Battista so deeply. Our author is probably reminding him of former friendship and broken promises.

If the occasion was personal, the theme was not unusual. Like Foligno de' Medici in his book of Ricordanze (1373) or like the London printer William Caxton in his preface to an edition of Cato (1483), Alberti deplores the decline of many great merchant families. As Caxton put it, "the children . . . encreace and prouffyte not lyke theyr faders and olders." [8] Or, as Foligno rather prematurely remarked of the Medici, "the status acquired by our ancestors, which is great, and was still greater in the past . . . began to decline as a result of the lack of valiant men." [9] Like Foligno, Alberti dwells on the fact of declining numbers due to late

[8] William Caxton, *The Prologues and Epilogues*, W. J. B. Crotch, ed., London, 1928, 77.

[9] Quoted by Gene A. Brucker, "The Medici in the Fourteenth Century," *Speculum*, XXXII (1957), 1.

marriages and high mortality rates; like Caxton, he thinks the chief ailment was factions and quarreling. Alberti suggests that prudence can deal with all these problems. He says that the family is like the community, even like the Roman empire, in the causes of its ascent and decline. In all cases, virtue, not physical chance alone, accounts for greatness, and lack of it for decadence. The writer's task is to inculcate such virtue as will save the family. Alberti's conception of his task, though essentially conventional, is wider, richer, and more systematic than that of others. He intends to map out on a large scale those laws of prudent conduct that may save family character, wealth, and public image. So much is clear from the first prologue.

The prologue to the third book justifies Alberti's choice of Italian rather than Latin for the entire work. Book III attempts a more natural and colloquial style than Books I and II. In its finished form it is the fruit of Alberti's return to his native city, when the Curia found refuge there from rebellious Rome in 1434. Alberti then learned to write, as he says in the *Vita,* with "purity of diction and elegance." He also engaged in the current debate on the origins of Italian and Latin. Had Latin really been at one time a spoken vernacular? Was Italian the product of a gradual transformation of Latin? On these questions, Alberti took the affirmative for reasons that do credit to his historical imagination. They are set forth in the prologue to Book III, and also serve to explain the value of writing in the vernacular. If Latin had once been a spoken language, Tuscan too might with cultivation become a medium for the highest flights of thought and eloquence. By writing in Tuscan he does no more nor less than the respected classical authors, who likewise wrote for their widest possible public. By his own time, as Alberti observed, many people had only a superficial understanding of Latin, for all their grandiose claims to education. They could not respond to either style or content in Latin as well as in the vernacular. He promises that *Della Famiglia* will introduce them to Greek as well as Latin ideas, apothegms, and stylistic devices— especially to the noble simplicity of Xenophon—all in Tuscan. In another manuscript Alberti also took the logical step of devising a grammar of Italian, the first modern grammar of a living European language.[10]

Florence was bursting with cultural competition. In 1441, when Alberti had established close ties with the artists, the intellectuals, and the rulers of the city, he was among the organizers of a formal public contest

[10] Cecil Grayson, *Leon Battista Alberti: La Prima Grammatica della Lingua Volgare,* Bologna, 1964.

presenting new Italian poetry. The pompously named *Certame coronaria* showed how classicizing tastes could remodel the rustic tongue. While *Della Famiglia* IV could not be read aloud on the occasion as were Alberti's poems, the author may have hoped to receive the laurel crown for both. Near the end of the book, Adovardo, its central figure, reflects, "When we compete for such prizes as the favor and grace of the people can bestow, I think it is hardly right, once engaged in the contest, to think our own judgment less fallible than public opinion. If we have taken the position that those who confer the dignity are competent and are guided by reason and reflection, it is a matter of honor and a sign of self-discipline to accept their judgment." The author has accepted the burden and the risks of the contest.

Though that particular crown was not bestowed on anyone at all by the cautious judges, Alberti won in his lifetime increasing general fame. He gained patrons as well as wide repute in Florence, Rimini, Ferrara, and Mantua, and his name was built on his writings as much as on his architectural activity. Three years after his death in 1472, his young friend Cristoforo Landino wrote a philosophical dialogue called *Disputationes Camaldulenses,* choosing Lorenzo de' Medici to represent the active life, and Leon Battista Alberti to represent and to defend the contemplative. While this role reflects the platonizing, retiring outlook of some of Alberti's moral speculations, Landino is also paying tribute to the total intellectual stature and dedication of the man. The tribute is too limited, however, for Alberti had been practical as well as philosophical in his writings, had preached a civic morality as well as a morality of philosophical resignation, and of course he had worked artistically as well as philosophically in the world. In *Della Famiglia,* with the vigor of youth, he put forth the rationale for a wise conduct of practical affairs. He would not rest, nor let others rest, in eloquence, rationality, or wit alone.

Major Themes

The talk in *Della Famiglia* begins with the problem of paternal responsibility (Book I), then shifts to the bond underlying family relationships, conjugal love. In Book II Alberti envisages happy marriage as a special case of bonds of close affection, and attempts to define such bonds. The focus of Book III is the material basis of family prosperity, the wise management of the household. Marriage must be considered again, now as a special problem in the wise division of labor. Book IV, although added after some years, is closely linked in substance to what has gone before. The question under discussion is the proper handling of the external relations of the head of the family: what kinds of friendship lie open to him, how can he avoid enmities and exile, how govern his relations with powerful men.

Interlocutors and Their Special Themes

On the afternoon and evening of a single day in May, 1421, the persons of the dialogue encounter each other in a house in Padua, where they are attending the dying Lorenzo Alberti, the author's father. His children, Battista and Carlo (the latter here seems younger, but documents show he was two years older), receive not only his own last wishes concerning them but a great deal of valuable advice from their elders. The dialogue moves at long intervals from one main speaker to another. Each represents not so much a philosophical position as a certain sort of education and a certain practical position in life. They illustrate the point that thought does not occur in a vacuum, but grows out of life. Lorenzo gives a mature and powerful statement of his troubled situation. He grieves that he cannot now nurture and protect his children, in whom he knows he has sowed the seed of honorable character and zeal for knowledge. The pleasure he has taken and would take in their achievements is as clear as his grief.

Thereupon Adovardo and Lionardo Alberti engage in a kind of debate on the burdens versus the privileges of fatherhood. Adovardo was in fact forty-five years old, married to his cousin Caterina di Ricciardo degli Alberti, and the father of three girls and a boy; he has raised his children in exile and knows both the anxieties and the affection of a parent. Lionardo appears as a young bachelor, one whom everyone urges to marry. He was in fact twenty-nine. Adovardo seems to view him as a valuable and erudite person, but also as a slippery fellow. After Adovardo expounds the delights and worries of fatherhood, Lionardo philosophically praises the gratifications it brings and minimizes the troubles as unnecessary. He is something of a Stoic, and he draws richly on Cicero, Xenophon, Plutarch, and others. The two men interact in a form of duet rather than a duel. One represents the practical, the other the theoretical side of the question; the former is older, the latter younger. This kind of relationship prevails in all three remaining books as well, though different interlocutors play the roles.

Battista, though a mere student of seventeen, is also able to uphold a position, and does so in Book II. It is a position appropriate to his age but foreign to his actual wisdom. He declares here that there is nothing better or more powerful than the "amatory passion." His argument is filled with conscious sophistry, biting misogynism, and clever misuse of the classics. Battista makes able use of irony. Sex must be a vile and despicable force indeed, if it can make kings sacrifice their thrones, men their honor, and women their homes. His argument is not entirely empty of positive points, however. He calls our attention to "nature—the creator of all things." Such is the role Alberti assigns to his youthful self. As he argues with Lionardo, it is Lionardo who shows ripeness, moderation, practical awareness of the subtleties of real situations. Yet Battista has the grace to apologize frequently, to play at his role rather than fall wholly into it, and to blush modestly at what he undertakes to defend. He fully shares the misogyny of Lionardo, moreover: the love of women only tempts men to bestiality or weakness.

To the power of lust, Lionardo opposes the charms of honorable friendship. Friendship, he points out, is one of the few things really vital to the family. He enters then upon a solemn lament for the exile and subsequent sufferings of the Alberti family. Thereafter he is persuaded to embark on a discussion of the few essential things he has hinted at: numbers, wealth, and reputation. Such are the subjects he takes up; his underlying theme in respect to all of them, however, is the power of the human will. Lionardo says, "What a man wants to do, they say, that he can do." One of Alberti's best poems speaks of the way excess of will can disable a man. The warrior trembles and weeps with anger; the lover, too stricken, cannot weep or sigh; the starved man cannot eat; overfull sails capsize the boat; and the overswift hound misses his prey. Nature gave man a measure of power to which excessive force of will is ill fitted.[11] What he teaches and celebrates through Lionardo in Book II of *Della Famiglia* is a will that has been shaped by reason and tempered by education and self-discipline.

In speaking of the preservation of numbers in the family, Lionardo

[11] *Opere Volgari*, II, 1.

advises young men to marry (notwithstanding his own failure in this respect) and suggests what features distinguish a good wife. He speaks of the importance of conceiving one's children while in a sober and healthy state. He deals—and with great seriousness—with the problem of health. While he strongly favors watchful care for the ailing, he recommends one flee from the plague-stricken, for inhumane as this may seem, it can save the family. Sentiments, whether Stoic or Christian, which made men like the older humanist, Salutati, reject all counsel to flee in such cases, are implicitly condemned; because they endanger the family, they interfere with the economy of life. Alberti lost his mother in a plague, and in a letter of his schoolmaster, Barzizza, we hear of the boy's being unable to sleep and weeping with concern over his father's remaining in Venice during a plague. In Lionardo's speech, then, Alberti's anxiety has been transformed by his power to reason and to plan.

While Battista in his role in Book II speaks of nature as instilling lust, Lionardo describes it as a model of fecundity, economy, and beauty. Nature functions; therefore, in his view, it labors, it offers man a good example. Lionardo eulogizes work, and glorifies man: man was created by "nature, that is, God," to make use of his capacities, not, he says, to suffer for his sins. He must bear witness to the excellence of his creator by his own excellence.

Work must be distinguished, of course, from mere drudgery. The important opposition is not made, as one might have expected, between manual and mental labor or between mental labor and the mixture of both that Alberti says is art. Rather, the crucial opposition is between free and unfree work. Every career is more noble, according to him, the more it depends on skill and the less on fortune; you can swim away from a shipwreck with your skill, he points out. Commerce is rated neither high nor low, but commerce on a large scale is decisively preferred to small scale commerce, for only grand commerce can bring real wealth, and real wealth can bring both freedom and honor. Another aspect of freedom lies in the social purposes of work. "The minimum of enslavement, then, is work performed for love, and not for payment. One would rather work for one's own family than for others, rather for friends than for strangers, rather for good men than for such as are not good. One's own country, of course, has more right to command one than any other person."

Lionardo stresses the power of society for good. Education is based on the opposed alternatives of shame and honor. By fear of shame and hope of honor, men of basically good disposition are drawn toward greatness.

Less good men emulate them from envy. As to variations in human ability and intelligence, these need not lead anyone to renounce some degree of honor. It is only essential to choose a career in which one *will* be able to excel. It is necessary not merely to appear good, but to be good. This maxim (to be reversed for princes by Machiavelli) is based on social effectiveness, not on some inward compulsion. Lionardo gives the amusing example of a fool who boasts of his ability to swim when he cannot. He almost drowns and has to be rescued by a silent and modest fellow with the real skill. Need he elaborate on which one is more admired by the crowd?

In Book III, as in Book I, Lionardo again plays the younger and more bookish interlocutor. He is now, however, almost as humble as the silent Carlo. The venerable figure of Giannozzo—probably the most memorable character of *Della Famiglia*—dominates the scene. Giannozzo was a distant relative of Lorenzo, for their great grandfathers were brothers, and was sixty-four years old in 1421. He speaks of himself as an old man, but one proudly vigorous for his years. He leads an orderly life, including a certain amount of exercise every day, and some kind of activity at the *palazzo* of the government. Today he is pleading for a friend with some official of the city. While this particular errand cannot be a daily activity, it is suggested that he is ever engaged in some sort of charitable counseling and that he has had long experience of business. The charm of his healthy countenance and his temperate ways is so distinctly conveyed that we remember the remark in Alberti's *Vita:* "He would see old men of venerable aspect, health and vigor, and never tire of looking at them; this he considered part of his love of the beauties of nature." Giannozzo gives his prescription for maintaining health and youthful appearance: cleanliness, chastity, a moderate diet, and, most important, exercise.

Giannozzo's views seemed to Werner Sombart, a social historian and theorist who rivaled Max Weber in the scholarly controversies over the origins of capitalism, to represent the very essence and first articulation of "the spirit of capitalism." In his large work on that subject, he matches Leon Battista Alberti, actually seen through Giannozzo in Book III of *Della Famiglia,* with Benjamin Franklin as the latter appears in his *Autobiography;* and it is not possible to deny the many-sided resemblance. There is, for example, the same economic vision of moral life, the Stoic self-discipline, the non-Stoic activism, the emphasis on thrift, sobriety, cleanliness. It is probably fair to say that Franklin is at once more talkative and more repressive about his passions for food and women.

Both stress the masterful role of the male. It is certain that Franklin is a free and easy eclectic reaching out to books from an assumed foundation of innate reasonableness. Giannozzo, as one might expect, draws and depends on family tradition, on the teaching of venerable elders.

Book III becomes a hymn to *masserizia*—economy, thrift, good management. Giannozzo extends this concept to all things, first applying the notion to those things which "truly belong to us": the body, the soul, and time. These, Giannozzo says, are the only real possessions. Returning to the discussion of practical experience, Giannozzo describes an ideally balanced private economy including the citizen's private house in the city, his shop, and his villa or farm in the country. Giannozzo considers questions of manufacture, of food storage and sale, of managing tenants and employees, of buying cheap and selling dear. He discusses the training of a spouse (where he borrows heavily from Xenophon's *Oeconomicus,* but also gives us vivid glimpses of the Florentine home). He is keenly aware of the close relationship between wealth and status. He knows that external social factors are what determine both wealth and status; these are the "friendships" outside the family that we have already heard are essential to its welfare. He discusses the wise choice of neighbors, preferring good, respectable people. He considers the problem of giving loans or standing surety, where he recommends all sorts of tactics of evasion. Although Giannozzo demands at times a Stoic indifference to fortune's cruel tricks, he, more than any other of the interlocutors in *Della Famiglia,* resolves the pervasive *virtu-fortuna* problem (the problem, in modern terms, of self against the absurd) by keeping up a continual dance of adaptation.

Many basic virtues are amply praised by Giannozzo. He detests waste, whether it comes about through prodigality or through irrational stinginess. He demands a total rationalization of the household economy, and of its relation to the surrounding world. He admires self-discipline, true thrift, moderation of the passions. He demands a strong sense of time. He asks the merchant to keep written accounts of everything and he admires the merchant with inky fingers. He is reliable, this merchant, far-seeing, honest, benevolent, generous with relatives, friends, sometimes even with strangers (to make an impression), but he is never impetuous or unrestrained. Giannozzo's view of human relations is one that came into its own in the sixteenth century literature of economic ethics. It indicates "the devaluation of the demands of friendship," as Benjamin Nelson describes it.[12] Polonius is a later Giannozzo, with his "Neither a lender nor a bor-

[12] Benjamin N. Nelson, *The Idea of Usury,* Princeton, 1949, 155.

rower be" and, as Nelson suggests, his outlook ("To thine own self be true") "can easily be harnessed to the service of a self-regarding capitalist morality."

The "inky fingers" of Giannozzo's ideal merchant have led to some speculation about the quality and quantity of his literacy. Sombart took them as a sign that the bourgeois of 1420 was still a clumsy fellow with his pen. Armando Sapori, an eminent Italian economic historian, assures us, to the contrary, that these inky fingers belonged to men of considerable fluency. They were accustomed to write their thoughts as well as their accounts. Alberti himself illuminates this issue as he repeatedly contrasts Giannozzo, the practical fellow, empty of Latin and therefore of literary erudition, with the young but learned Lionardo. Lionardo listens with reverence to every word old Giannozzo utters, and always flatters him when he speaks of feeling inadequate before "learned men" or before "you and your books." Occasionally, however, Giannozzo lets his real pride show: "Thus you young men profit by asking your elders about your problems and hearing their advice. Many things in this world are better understood by experience than by speculation and theory."

Alberti's view of Giannozzo is certainly not one of unalloyed admiration. He gives him a strong role as practical counselor, but there is a touch of malice toward both sides in exchanges between Lionardo and Giannozzo where the former offers effusive reverence and the latter false modesty. When Giannozzo discusses the problem of lending money, or rather of not lending money, he plays the not altogether savory part of sly old fox. There is also a lively discussion with Lionardo on the question of political participation, a delicate question in Cosimo de' Medici's newly tamed Florence. Giannozzo firmly rejects all unnecessary involvement with public affairs. Public life is full of "pretence, vanity, and lies"; it involves one in cruelty; it leads to unpopularity, for "whether you follow popular thought in its errors or rely on the arrogance of a leader, you are disgraced as though the mistake were your own; even if you labor to serve others, when you please one, you displease a hundred." "A man wants to live for himself, not for the community." Lionardo, who distinguishes between mere powerlust and true public spiritedness, seems to give a judicious reply: "Like you, I would say that a good citizen loves tranquillity, but not so much his own tranquillity as that of other good men, rejoices in his private leisure, but does not care less about that of his fellow citizens than about his own. He desires the unity, calm, peace, and tranquillity of his own house, but much more those of the country and of the republic."

In Book IV, Giannozzo has retired from the scene. His place is taken by another older man, Piero. Piero is not the slippered sage, but rather the polished old diplomat. He illumines the subject of friendship by telling of his smooth handling of three great Italian princes of the opening of the century, Gian Galeazzo Visconti, Ladislas of Naples, and Pope Giovanni XXIII. Piero was born in 1357 so that he was in his forties and fifties at the time of the attendance on princes he describes. He seems to look back from his present age of sixty-four to a time when he was strong, agile, and athletic. His life in Milan, Naples, and Rome is presented with the charm of a good story. The three stylized portraits of rulers are as deft as most in Renaissance historical literature. Piero shows what it meant to be a Machiavellian courtier before the time of Machiavelli and Castiglione. As Lionardo and Adovardo point out when he has finished, moreover, it turns out that he has cleverly given a historical illustration of Aristotle's three kinds of friendship—for virtue (with the wise duke), for pleasure (with the gallant king), and for utility (with the avaricious pope).

The remainder of Book IV is a disquisition by Adovardo on the subject of friendship. Adovardo, whom we remember for his paternal sentiments in Book I, again claims to be a man of experience rather than a man of theory. He picks out the weakness of all theory, which lies in its vagueness; a very complete theory, he says, would be an excellent thing. Moral philosophy stands, however, in the position of a man who would attempt astrological prediction on the basis of knowing the influences of the separate constellations alone, but not their interaction. He then speaks in everyday terms and uses daily situations to illustrate his points, making some remarkable ethical observations on the scope of friendship (analogous, he says, to marriage as the Church sees it) and enmity. He explores, indeed, the foundations of human society.

Lionardo had earlier proposed that "God established in the human mind a strong tie to bind together human beings in society, namely justice, equity, liberality, and love." Lionardo had also put forward the idea that variations in "humors" and in abilities were created to reinforce this tendency. In this way "I should have need of you, and you of him, he of another, and some other of me. In this way one man's need for another serves as the cause and means to keep us all united in general friendship and alliance." Giannozzo ended his talk by going off on a charitable errand, not so much because of personal friendship with the recipient of his help but because "Even if you do not know them personally, you should always love and help good and virtuous men." Adovardo, in Book IV, builds on the concept of an emotional bond that men naturally accept, one that they wish and even need to feel. Honorable competition within a framework of amity builds up societies and enables them to achieve civic life; war between individuals or factions is a monster that, once unleashed, uncontrollably and unpredictably destroys men. He goes beyond the ethical conceptions of the others, to take a very generous, pacific view of relations within society at large. In contrast to the younger Lionardo, he is firmly opposed to the pursuit of vengeance, which is reminiscent of the remark of Alberti's *Vita:* "He was scarcely able to tolerate anyone's surpassing him in good will toward men." Adovardo Alberti is kind, urbane, temperate, and eager to impart the fruit of both reading and experience. In age he represents a generation between Piero and Giannozzo on one side, Lionardo, Battista, and Carlo on the other. In sentiments he represents the author most closely, for he corrects the weaknesses of the others and exalts an arduous and subtle magnanimity.

Elements of a Bourgeois Ethic

If Adovardo Alberti is something of a model moralist and humanist, we may ask whether he also exemplifies the outlook of his social class. Is Alberti presenting in him, perhaps, a fuller realization of the bourgeois ethic than in Giannozzo, the old merchant? There are some indications that this is so, especially in the argument on economics recounted toward the end of Book III. Giannozzo had built a picture of economics in which all commodities were (as Riccardo and Marx were to expound) the result of labor applied to fortune's gifts. The merchant's markup is the payment of his labor. Some commodities are primarily gifts of fortune, especially if they are direct fruits of the soil; others are primarily services. All bring profit if and only if properly managed. Giannozzo, cheerfully contradicting the theologians, makes money another commodity, essentially one that carries the service of exchange. According to him it breeds profit as naturally as cows by the gift of fortune produce calves. In both cases good management is essential.

For Giannozzo, however, as Adovardo remarks with amazement, money has no special role. It is a commodity like any other, to be managed like any other. To Adovardo it is something special, the key to all other commodities. Well managed, unlike any other gift of fortune or product of labor, it is practically contingency-proof. In a world of perishables, only money is an abstract form of wealth which keeps profit coming in. Adovardo suggests the philosophy of bankers, as distinct from Giannozzo's general merchant philosophy. Lionardo, youngest of them all, had already explained in Book II that large profits only come from large investments in large-scale commerce. All three admire hard work, seeing labor—mainly the labor of management—as the source of value. Adovardo stresses that wealth should be fluid. Lionardo knows that capitalism requires the ability to take great risks with equanimity: gambling without passion.

In Adovardo's love of peace, the vision of amity we described earlier, there is a bourgeois correction of chivalric ideals. Giannozzo had loved warlike sports and tournaments when he was a boy but had learned eventually the wisdom of his elders, who saw that fighting, though aristocratic, was useless, expensive, and dangerous. Does Adovardo speak from the same kind of experience when he refuses to admire homicidal rage and suicidal love of liberty? He praises patience and endurance as ways of avoiding contention and an unpredictable flow of catastrophes; if one does allow oneself to fight, at least let it be on the basis of the most painstaking calculation of one's chances. If such ideas fit bourgeois experience, as they do, one must remember they are also in line with the scholastic arguments concerning the just war. Scholastic precedent likewise condemned suicide in private life and even suicidal courage in the pursuit of liberty and happiness. Explicitly, Adovardo draws not on this Christian tradition, but on its ancient beginnings, Platonic and Stoic. He thus makes a judicious choice of authorities to support a philosophy which also corresponds to strong practical motives.

At every turn ideas in *Della Famiglia* derive from classical thought. This is true when Lionardo celebrates the generosity of nature and the powers of man for work and action, when he views man as engaged in the cultivation of his own character for the achievement of virtue and glory, when Adovardo considers the various ends which are served by human friendship, and when he celebrates the golden mean of proper and fitting conduct. At all times ideas are substantively selected, however, to fit the needs of contemporary civic life. And the Renaissance city, as Max

Weber observed, differed from the ancient city-state in being primarily a city of merchants rather than of farmer-warriors.

There is a further great difference from the thinking of Xenophon, Plutarch, and Cicero in the method of Alberti. Alberti strives to show moral norms and questions as they appear in specific historical situations. He uses ideal examples only to suggest conduct in a specific and varying environment. His ancient sources generally make even historical environments into abstract types of the human condition—hence the clear notions conveyed to us by the names of Athens, Sparta, Roman Republic. To Alberti, however, the value of rhetoric seems to have been its power to make the ideal actual, to influence the imagination of active men, to apply moral principles to practical situations. The empirical world is not merely the starting point for ethical speculation, but also its ultimate testing ground.

Alberti undertakes to give a set of precepts for dealing with human beings, precepts in the moral tradition, of course, but chiefly precepts tested and found to work. Like Machiavelli later, he claims to assure worldly success. Such prudence can be learned only when remote literary authorities are matched to an immediate knowledge of the practical world. At least once, through Giannozzo, he dismisses the high philosophical ideal of friendship simply because such friendships are rare or nonexistent. In general, he avoids mere theory and deals with bonds of mutual advantage, shared tastes, admiration, and sympathy such as one meets in daily life. The method affects the substance of his teaching. Like Machiavelli, he asserts that ultimately the individual owes no one anything: man is born for his own happiness. This is the only sound foundation for moral aims; for his own happiness he will work, and even work unselfishly, to acquire inner tranquillity and outer glory. Machiavelli, of course, did not keep such a reconciliation of the moral and the actual.

Virtue (*virtu*) is a key word for Alberti as for Machiavelli, but with a different meaning. It is consistently linked in *Della Famiglia* to an ideal of aesthetic balance and harmony, as well as to the ideal of ethical unity among men, service from each to all. Though Alberti certainly meant his *virtu* to correspond to the Greek *arete* and the Latin *virtus,* it is looser and more pragmatic than the connotation of those words in Plato and Cicero. Plato makes sharp definitions of the good, leading us away from ordinary experience toward a transcendent object of contemplation. What the mass of men value is given up for a more rigorous theory of ends and means. Alberti tried to resolve the tension between any such theory and socially determined standards of the good. His speakers, after deliberation, conclude that men generally admire and reward real virtue. This virtue embodies a curious combination of the success that men admire with the qualities of soul that provide an easy conscience. His chief means to the description of virtue is to point to the familiar reality of Florentine psychological experience: the bourgeois sense of honor.

"Civic humanism," as Eugenio Garin and Hans Baron have described it, suited the Florentines by corresponding partly to their practice and partly to their half-articulated notions of good conduct. The Florentines were widely admired for their shrewdness and their powers of intellect. They were also widely pitied for the instability of all their arrangements. It is, of course, for stability, that one takes to formulating and believing principles. Alberti, with his amalgam of classical and native sense, held out, on condition, an explicit hope of stability to great merchants in their insecure splendor. The bourgeois ethic as he transmuted it transcended the market place, and the merchant, to be a good man by these standards derived from his own habitual sayings and wishes, would surely have to be more consistently philosophical, after all, than the merchant usually was.

For the patriciate themselves much of the charm of *Della Famiglia* may have been that in articulating their code it portrayed them as a kind of aristocracy. If it was ill received by some of the Alberti, others within the family, notably Francesco d'Altobianco, appreciated it. Piero de' Medici, son of Cosimo, must have liked the work to have accepted the dedication of the fourth book at the Certame. Agnolo Pandolfini, a distinguished citizen and art patron, passed down that copy which in due time led to a Pandolfini version of the third book. There is little doubt that the blending of popular ideas with those of classical authorities represented a feat of rhetoric to humanist admirers. In the *Vita anonyma,* Alberti boasts that his fellow Florentines borrowed felicitous phrases from *Della Famiglia* for their speeches in the Signoria—a tribute to a man born in exile.

The essential convictions running through *Della Famiglia* brought Alberti into the Florentine world. To that agonistic society built around commercial capitalism, he offered three major consolations and rationalizations for the inevitable damage done by fierce competition. First, he assured them that competition itself was for the betterment of all participants. Second, he asserted that the family, the fundamental social unit, would not be destroyed in the universal contest; on the contrary, by functioning effectively, it would tend to preserve itself as well as its members. Third, whether success were fast or slow in coming, the freedom and dignity, the self-convinced autonomy of the individual was guaranteed by his *virtu*—his self-respect. The ethic postulated a little more than the possible of society's discretion in rewarding the good and of human character in maintaining autonomy. That perhaps made it only the more dignified. Alberti was illegitimate, without business experience, and celibate. His work did not truly express the daily outlook of merchants, but it drew from their social existence the terms of a finer life.

Selected

BIBLIOGRAPHY

of Works in English on Civic Humanism
and L. B. Alberti

HANS BARON, "Franciscan Poverty and Civic Wealth," *Speculum,* XIII (1938), 1–37. The civic spirit of the Florentine patriciate, according to Baron, finds a literary voice in the first decades of the fifteenth century, particularly through Lionardo Bruni and Matteo Palmieri. Alberti's position is interesting. He does not remain with the earlier humanist asceticism, nor does he, like Bruni, "share the proud belief of the wealthy merchants on the Arno that rich external possessions are a condition for the full development of the moral life." He revives the "true, the premedieval Seneca" with a philosophy that takes riches into the house, but not into the heart.

HANS BARON, *The Crisis of the Early Italian Renaissance,* Princeton, Princeton Univ. Press, 1955, (2 vols.) rev. ed. 1966 (1 vol.). Republican ideas dominated the moral attitudes as well as the directly political opinions of Florentine humanists from 1402 to the 1440s due to the impact of the Milanese threat to Florentine liberty. Alberti is an outsider who contributed to the patriotic movement in some ways.

JACOB BURCKHARDT, *The Civilization of the Renaissance in Italy,* New York, Harper Torchbooks, ed., 1958. This essay of 1860 is still enlightening as well as stimulating. Burckhardt asserted the existence of a unified Renaissance civilization involving political, moral, and intellectual patterns. The humanists found personal ideals in the classics, accepted a variety of pagan philosophies without abandoning Christianity, and internalized their religion. Alberti appears as *uomo universale,* ideal product of the new well-rounded education.

DELIO CANTIMORI, "Rhetoric and Politics in Italian Humanism," *Journal of the Warburg Institute,* I (1937–38), 83–102. Seen as part of the background of Machiavelli and Guicciardini, the humanists' approach to politics is described as "a faith, sincere though still somewhat ingenuous and crude, in virtue, in passion, in dignity." This critical essay sheds light indirectly on the intent of Alberti's rhetoric.

EUGENIO GARIN, *Italian Humanism*, New York, Harper and Row, 1967. Profound but selective philosophical reading of the humanists. Garin sees Alberti, like other civic humanists of the Florentine Quattrocento, giving the active life value on metaphysical grounds over the contemplative. Alberti, as Garin emphasizes, believed that "virtue always defeats fortuna," and thought man's dignity could be found "in work—and only in work."

CECIL GRAYSON, "The Humanism of Alberti," *Italian Studies*, XII (1957) 37–56. Though brief, this is the best introduction to Alberti available in any language. Early in his life, Alberti confronted the difference between the values of a commercial society and those of a disinterested scholar and man of letters. He reconciled the two most closely in *Della Famiglia*. As Grayson shows, "the impregnability of the individual intellect" was Alberti's precious and central conviction, sometimes intensified by his disillusionment with the way society worked. In his later work, Alberti suggests that an enlightened prince provides the best chance for the autonomous self to fulfill its need to explore nature and to benefit humanity.

PAUL OSCAR KRISTELLER, *Renaissance Thought*, II, New York, Harper Torchbook ed., 1965. In this and earlier studies, Kristeller gives a learned analysis of humanist literature. He accepts the reality of a group of particularly civic-minded humanists. He stresses, however, that the humanists generally had only a pedagogical, narrowly cultural ideal in common. The functions of that ideal are only partially clarified, in my opinion, by his survey and assessment of their explicit philosophies. These are less important than their literary loyalties and methods, reflecting their concept of rhetoric and hopes for its effects.

LAURO MARTINES, *The Social World of the Florentine Humanists*, Princeton, Princeton Univ. Press, 1963. A statistical profile of the humanists, based on biographical facts, supports the thesis that they belonged to and served the highest order of the Florentine patriciate. On their thought, Martines is less informed than on their lives and less convincing. Simplifying the thesis of Baron, he suggests that both humanists and patriciate were responsible and interested in self-government in the early decades of the quattrocento, falling into contemplative detachment or hedonism in the second half of the century. The application of this thesis to Alberti, however, short-circuits understanding of his actual development.

JERROLD E. SEIGEL, " 'Civic Humanism' or Ciceronian Rhetoric," *Past and Present,* No. 34 (July 1966), 3–48. An interesting attempt to refute Baron's thesis in *Crisis of the Early Italian Renaissance.* Seigel's notes serve as a guide to the current controversy on the sociological and traditional roots of humanism. Hans Baron replied to this article in "Leonardo Bruni," *Past and Present,* XXXVI. (1967), 21–37. He showed, in rebuttal of Seigel, Bruni's periodic attachment to Florence and his interest in formulating political and moral ideals relevant to Florentine realities.

VON MARTIN, ALFRED, *The Sociology of the Renaissance,* London, Kegan Paul, 1944, N.Y. Harper Torchbook, 1944. Builds on Burckhardt, Sombart and others but also on close knowledge of the humanist writings, to portray Florentine society in the fifteenth century as a structure of classes with class ideologies. Von Martin effectively suggests how "bourgeois" values differed from those of the "intelligentsia," and how both sets of values changed under different pressures.

WERNER SOMBART, *The Quintessence of Capitalism,* New York, E. P. Dutton, 1915. Inspite of his impressionism and careless scholarship, Sombart still provides an incisive picture of the "capitalist ethic," which he traced to the Italian merchant particiate. He detected it particularly in Alberti's *Della Famiglia.*

PROLOGUE

I call to mind what ancient records and the recollection of our elders, as well as our own experiences, can teach us. Many families in Italy and elsewhere have been seen first at the height of fortune and honor, then lying prostrate, reduced and exhausted. Often I have marveled and sorrowed that fortune's cruelty and ill will seemed to have such power over men. Fortune's fickleness and imprudence actually seemed able to seize families rich in heroes, abounding in all that is precious, dear, and most desired by mortal men, endowed with honor, fame, high praise, authority, and public favor, and to cast them down into poverty, desolation, and misery. They were reduced from a great number of ancestors to a very few descendants, from unmeasured riches to strait necessity, and hurled from the brightest splendor of glory. They were drowned in calamity, plunged into obscure, oblivious, tempestuous adversity. How many families do we see today in decadence and ruin! It would not be possible to enumerate and describe all the most noble families among the ancients, like the Fabii, Decii, Drusii, Gracchi, and Marcelli and others. They stood in our land for the public good, for the maintenance of liberty, and for the conservation of authority and dignity in peace and in war. They were modest, wise, and fortunate families, feared by their enemies, but loved and revered by their friends. Of all these families not only the magnificence and greatness but the very men, not only the men but the very names are shrunk away and gone. Their memory, almost every trace of them, is wiped out and obliterated.

For these reasons I have always thought the question worth asking whether fortune really has such power over human affairs. Is the supreme license hers in fact, by her inconstancy and instability, to plunge the greatest and most admirable families into ruin? I think about this matter objectively, with a mind detached and free of passion, and consider, O, young Albertis, our own Alberti family. I consider the great calamities to which it has now for so long opposed a noble fortitude, and integrity of heart and intellect. Thus have our Albertis been able to throw off or endure with constancy bitter misfortunes and furious blows from a cruel fate. I see clearly then that fortune has too often been unjustly blamed. I observe that many who have fallen on evil days by their own folly have accused fortune. They complain of being buffeted by her stormy seas when they themselves, most foolishly, threw themselves into the flood.

If anyone undertakes to investigate the nature of those things which exalt and increase the family, and to see how it is maintained at a high level of honor and happiness, he soon discovers that men are most inclined to view themselves as cause of their own good or poor estate. They will never attribute so much influence to anything as to deny, in the end, that praises, greatness, and fame are won more by character than by fortune. If we think about the republics and principalities of the past, we shall find that to acquire and augment power and glory, to preserve and keep them once won, fortune was never more important for any state than good and pious traditions of conduct. Who would deny it? Just laws, virtuous princes, wise counsels, strong and constant actions—these are effective. Love of country, fidelity, diligence, highly disciplined and honorable behavior in the citizens—these have always been able, even without the help of fortune, to earn and kindle fame. With fortune's help, they have enabled countries vastly to extend their domain, to expand with increased glory, mightily to commend themselves to posterity, to immortality.

Fortune favored the Macedonians and made them prosper as long as they maintained the use of arms together with the love of virtue and the desire for glory. True it is that after the death of Alexander the Great, as soon as the Macedonian kings began to pursue only their private good and to care not for the public empire but for their own kingdoms, discord arose and burning flames of hate were kindled among them. Their spirits were consumed with greed and fury. They longed to do harm and to take vengeance. Then those same arms and triumphant hands which had seized and subjected the liberty and the strength of innumerable peoples, which had built so great an empire, by which the name and fame of Macedonia had become world famous, these same undefeated arms, serving the private appetites of a few hereditary tyrants, were the ones to tear up and scatter every law, every justice and excellence they had instituted. They cut through every tendon of their once feared strength. Thus the Macedonians destroyed, not by fortune but by folly, the happiness they had attained. Soon they found themselves without empire and without glory. Greece kept her victory, glory, and empire just as long as she was zealous and vigorous in ruling, eager to govern and discipline the minds of her citizens, not just to crown herself with delights and lord it over others with pompous ceremonies.

Is not our Italian situation clearly of the same kind? For a long time we observed our best and most hallowed traditions. We labored to make ourselves the equals of our ancestors and even to outshine the glory of their past achievements. Our citizens thought that they owed to their country all labor, diligence, and art, that all they had should serve the public welfare and provide reward and sustenance for the whole community. Our possessions, blood, and life were willingly poured out to maintain the authority, majesty, and glory of the Latin name. Was there any people anywhere, even the most savage nation of barbarians, which did not fear and obey our edicts and laws? This marvellous empire without limits, this lordship over all peoples acquired by our Latin forces, obtained by our diligent efforts, increased by our Latin armies, can it be said to have been granted us as a gift of fortune?

Shall we admit that what our character won for us we owe to fortune? Shall we ascribe to fortune the prudence and moderation of Fabius, whose delaying and passive tactics saved our almost captured Latin liberty? What of the justice of Tarquin, who, to maintain military discipline, refused a pardon to his son? What of the purity of a man who, content with a farmer's life, preferred honesty to any amount of gold? What of the stern justice of Fabritius, the temperance of Cato, the fortitude of Horatio Cocles, the sufferings of Mutius, the faith and piety of Regulus, the patriotism of Curtius? What of the other remarkable, excellent, and incredible virtues of soul that were praised and honored among the ancients? Shall we ascribe to fortune sacred qualities which worked no less than iron and violence to let our noble Italian ancestors subdue the peoples of every barbarous region? With these did they subjugate the proud and stubborn barbarian enemies of Latin liberty, glory, and name.

Shall we view fortune, then, as the teacher of morals, the moderator of conduct, and the guardian of our most sacred traditions? Shall we consider subject to fortune's fickle and arbitrary will these standards which men, with mature wisdom and with hard and painful efforts, set up for themselves? How can we say that fortune, with her equivocal ways and her inconstancy, can ruin and destroy the very works which we most want to subordinate to our own watchfulness and reason, and not to another's whim? How shall we admit that what we fervently and laboriously strive to maintain belongs to fortune rather than to us? It is not in fortune's power, it is not as easy as some foolish people believe, to conquer one who really does not want to be conquered. Fortune has in her hand only the man who submits to her.

At Cannae, Trebbia, Trasimenus, in the Gauls, in Spain, and elsewhere, fortune in various ways rose up to fight against the Latin armies with no less cruelty and inhumanity than our most savage enemies. She exerted all her might to crush us and stamp out our empire, our glory, and all Italy. Nonetheless the empire grew from day to day by a wondrous series of rapid and numerous triumphs. Who can count exactly how often, then and later, fortune herself was wicked and hostile? She certainly raised up the envy of peoples, of kings, and of nations against us and provoked spite and enmity toward us in all the world. Her furious and bestial attacks could never daunt the courage of the good Roman patrician senators. They fought down and transcended every danger to become the lords and masters of all proud peoples. They divided the world into provinces. They set the bounds of the Latin empire outside the very limits and borders of the earth.

Our Latin forefathers, then, were able to oppose and to sustain every attack of fortune. Their noble spirits never gave up the will, and with the will the power, and with the power the ability to achieve expansion and glorious success. Though the course of their great triumphs was often interrupted by envious fortune, their history was never lacking in high heroism. As long as they considered good works and the strict moral traditions of their fatherland the ornament and the enduring strength of their empire, fortune, too, always proved favorable in the end. They continued to enjoy both imperial glory and good fortune as long as they possessed lofty and pious spirits, grave and mature counsel, perfect faith and loyalty toward the fatherland—as long as concern for the public good outweighed with them the pursuit of private ends, as long as the will of the state overruled the individual's desires.

As soon as lust for personal power and individual pleasures, as soon as unjust desires counted for more in Italy than good laws and the hallowed habits of restraint, the Latin empire grew weak and bloodless. It lost its grace and splendor and all its original strength. Latin glory, which once had shed its light beyond the very bounds of Ocean and lighted all the world, became cloudy and obscure. You, O noble Italy, were the crown and citadel of all the world while you were united, agreed, harmoniously determined on the preservation of your high virtues and on the achievement of renown and increase of glory. You used all your zeal and skill to conquer proud peoples and to govern nations with humanity and justice once you had subjected them. You bore every adversity with a proud and upright spirit. You thought it more praiseworthy to suffer and win in some hard and arduous enterprise than to disdain such painful labors. You showed your enemies your strength, your friends your loyalty, and your subjects your mercy. Thus you overcame fortune and rose above all mortal men. You proclaimed sacred laws and appointed governors in all the nations of the earth. To the very borders of India you were able to erect shining monuments to your immeasurable, divine, and well-earned glory. For your excellent qualities, for your magnificent, courageous, and mighty spirit, were you like gods revered and loved and feared.

After this you suddenly began to decline from your former majesty. Your Latin altars, temples, and theaters were long the scene of games and banquets and of rejoicing, long laden to groaning with the tribute of enemies, the votive offerings of victors, the triumphant laurels. Suddenly all these began to witness sorrow and misery, to be washed with tears and to resound with mourning and lamenting. The barbarian nations, distant slave peoples which formerly put aside pride and anger to tremble when they heard your venerated name, O Italy, now they were puffed up with boldness. They burst into your very heart, most sacred Italy, to burn the nest, the ancient seat of the empire of empires.

Other nations have usurped our empire by our negligence and laziness, or we have shed and abandoned our once deserved glory. Now who would dare hope ever to recover our lost imperial scepter, or expect to see again the purple and the diadem restored to their sacred and most happy home here in Italy. To our reproach they have here been long and sorely missed. Who could fail to conclude that the great glory of the Latin name was removed from its natural setting through no other fault than our own? What multitude of people could have opposed the power that all the world obeyed?

We know, then, that fortune is weak and powerless when it comes to taking away the least part of our character. Nobility of soul, we cannot but recognize, is itself sufficient to ascend and to possess the highest peaks: glorious praise, eternal fame, immortal glory. It seems undeniable that nothing is easier to acquire than this nobility, if only you seek it and value it. Only he who does not want it is without virtue. Character, discipline, and manly labor are available to men as much as they want. Good counsel, wisdom, strong and constant and persevering spirits, reason, order, method, good arts and skills, equity, justice, diligence, and zeal permeate and animate the greatest empire and overcome the might of deceitful fortune to achieve the highest degree, to take the last fortresses of glory. O young Albertis, how can any of you think to convince me, by appealing to the frequently observed fickleness and brittleness of impermanent things, that the noble character, which cannot be denied to men as long as they use judgment and will to seize and to hold that which is by nature a true possession of men, can be easily taken away from zealous and vigilant possessors, from proud and strong defenders? We shall always believe that in political affairs and in human life generally reason is more powerful than fortune, planning more important than any chance event. I believe it is your own opinion as well, for you are all prudent and wise. Nor have I ever thought a man wise or prudent who put his faith in chance situations rather than in character. Men must see that industry, skill, persevering labors, wise counsel, honest activity, just demands and reasonable expectations do maintain and defend both republics and principalities. With these any empire can rise to glory, while without them it inevitably remains empty of majesty and honor. When one realizes that laziness, inertia, lust, deceit, cupidity, iniquity, the raw appetites and unrestrained passions of men are what infects, subverts, and undermines every solid and well founded human endeavor, one must also, I think, see that these truths apply as much to families as they do to kingdoms. One is forced to admit that families rarely fall into decrepitude through any other cause than their own lack of wisdom and energy.

This much I know, that fortune's cruel floods quickly submerge and destroy the family that throws itself upon those waves either by abandoning restraint and moderation in prosperity or by lacking a firm posture and a prudent self-control in the face of hostile storms. I also have no doubt at all that by good management, careful and diligent rule by the father, good habits, and the utmost integrity of conduct, culture, courtesy, and responsibility, the family can become great and fortunate. I have undertaken, therefore, to investigate with all seriousness and diligence what might be the wisdom, applicable to the conduct and education of fathers and of the whole family, by which a family may rise at last to supreme happiness. Thanks to such wisdom it should under no circumstances have to yield to cruel and merciless fortune.

All the time I have been able to take from my other duties, I have been happy to spend going through the ancient authors to find whatever right and relevant thoughts they have left us to further the welfare, honor, and greatness of our families. Since I did find many excellent lessons there, I took it upon myself to compile and order them in such a way that you might come to know them with little trouble. Having come to know them, you might take them to heart. I think, too, that when you have reviewed with me the sayings and authority of the great writers of antiquity and considered the excellent customs of our own Alberti ancestors, you will conclude, as I have done, that your fortune, along with your character, depends on you. You will also be pleased, as you read me, to discover what were the noble ancient ways and beliefs of our Alberti house. When you see that the counsels and remembered customs of the older members of the family are all excellent and highly applicable, you will admire and follow them yourselves. You will learn how the family may multiply to live happily and well. You will see what practices bring the family favor, popularity, and friends. It will be clear by what kind of conduct the family gains a wide reputation, fame, and glory. You will see how the family name may achieve everlasting glory and immortality.

Let no one suppose, however, that I have the impudence to consider myself your teacher in matters of such importance, as if your own reason and discretion did not fully instruct you. I have always realized that everyone of you far surpasses me in intelligence and in learning and in knowledge of great and high matters. I admit that to you there is little I could teach, and that there is less I could remember that you do not know and remember better than I. Still it may not be a vain ambition which has prompted me to give many a day to this laborious endeavor. I hope to be of some use at least to the younger members of the family who will be coming along. In truth I should like my efforts to please you no little. I should hope that even if this work were not to be as useful to the Alberti family as it will be, it would be my great honor to be frequently read by you. This would be my greatest possible reward. It would especially satisfy me if you understand what I am so eager to convey, that all my desire and expectation is aimed at nothing but making myself as well liked by you as I can. Indeed I hope to be much better liked and accepted by you.

I have convinced myself that Battista cannot but please you. As far as possible I have applied my imagination and energy to make myself better from day to day, more useful to you, and more dear to your hearts. This will also give me incentive to labor on with still greater vigor and zeal. I shall keep still more vigils, exercise still more painstaking care, in order one day to delight your judgment and fulfill your hopes with some more perfect, more polished work. This is what I shall do, indeed, if I see that you appreciate, as I think you ought to appreciate, the lessons given us by our Alberti ancestors. These you will find most noble and worthy of memory. I shall be encouraged if you esteem me also for being most eager to keep alive the true honor and well-founded glory of our Alberti family. It has always merited appreciation and praise, and to its name I have always devoted all my efforts, my labors, my thoughts, my intellect and will. Never, as long as there is art or power in me, will I spare myself fatigue or exertion or any strenuous effort that may prove good or useful to the Alberti family. I shall labor the more happily, eagerly, and industriously if only I see them glad to receive my work. So I ask you young Albertis to join me in what I know you are doing already: seek the well-being, increase the honor, magnify the fame of our house. Listen, also, to what our Alberti ancestors thought that learned, educated, culti-vated persons owed to the family. See what they remind us should be done. Read me and take me to your hearts.

BOOK ONE

The First Book on the Family: of the Duties of the Old toward the Young and of the Young toward Their Elders, and of the Education of Children

ur father, Lorenzo Alberti, who lay ill in Padua of the illness which eventually took him from us, had for some days been longing to see his brother, Ricciardo Alberti, when he heard that Ricciardo was expected at any moment. He was greatly cheered by the news, sat up in bed for the first time in a long while, and expressed his satisfaction in various ways. We, in turn, who were constantly at his side were all encouraged by his contentment, and we were filled with joy at signs which seemed to offer us hope. We saw Lorenzo restored beyond what he had been for some time. Adovardo and Lionardo Alberti were there, men of sensibility and refinement, to whom Lorenzo spoke in words very like this:

I cannot express to you in words how much I look forward to seeing our brother, Ricciardo Alberti, both to discuss some practical matters with him concerning our family, and to recommend to his care these two boys of mine, Battista and Carlo. They do somewhat burden my mind, not that I have the slightest doubt that Ricciardo will be very anxious and eager to do all he can to help them in every way, but because it still does worry me that I cannot fully discharge the responsibility which falls on us fathers. I am sorry to leave this worthy and demanding task undone. I shall depart this life free of that burden when I have asked each of you, and most of all Ricciardo, to help these boys to become good men, and to do for their education and guidance what you would want done for your own children in case of need.

Then Adovardo, who was older than Lionardo, replied:

Lorenzo, how much do these things you are saying move my heart! I see in you the love and fatherly concern for your sons which often spurs me on, myself. I see clearly that you want all the others of our house to show the same love for each member of the family, the same concern and active care for the welfare and honor of the whole family, that you yourself have always shown. It also seems to me that you rightly recognize the good faith and integrity of your brother Ricciardo, who is after all your brother not only in body but in his responsible outlook, his sensibility, and his character. There is no one kinder than he, no one more discreet, no one more self-restrained. But have no doubts about the rest of us; as far as possible we all feel the same way. We want everyone to see that we are good and faithful kinsmen, in all that pertains to the needs and honor of the least member of this house no less than to your sons, who are not the last among those we love. If friendship has more power than kinship, we shall act as friends, true and straight. The things that are dear to you, the concerns of Lorenzo, whom each of us loves as much as he does himself, will be as close to our hearts and as directly under our care as you have wished and as we find possible.

Any of us will be glad to do it in case of need, all the more because it will be a light and pleasant task to guide toward praise and honor the lives of these boys. They have already had an excellent beginning from you and a model in the way to gain fame and noble character. We see, too, that they are not unsuited by intelligence and temperament to make something of themselves. This means that whoever helps them in their education will have his own reward and satisfaction in the results. But may God give you back to us well and happy, Lorenzo. You must not persuade yourself, Lorenzo, that this and any other good thing life has to offer will not be available to you once again. It seems to me you are looking much better, and I hope you will be able to take care of your own children and to do for others as much as you have always been accustomed to do.

Lorenzo: What? It would be a shame if I did not trust you, Adovardo, and you, Lionardo, as I should trust my dear kinsmen and good friends. How could I, in honesty, doubt that my concerns were truly the concerns also of those who are joined to me by blood and whom I have always, all my life, labored to join me by kindness and love as well. Truly I would prefer not to have to leave you the burden of raising my children. Though dying itself troubles me little, still the delight of living, the pleasure of being and talking with you and with friends, the charm of seeing the things that are mine, makes me sad to give it all up. I would not wish to be deprived of all this before my time. Perhaps it would be a less painful and hardly bitter thing to lose so much if I could say of myself, with Julius Caesar, that as to age and happiness, I had lived enough. But I am not of an age such that death would no longer be bitter to me. Nor am I in such a fortunate state that I would not hope, by going on living, to see my condition improve. What a fulfillment of all my desires would it be, what extreme joy would be mine, if I could be in my father's house, in my own country, if not to live there with some honor, then at least to die there and be buried among my ancestors. If fortune does not grant me this, or if nature here pursues its course, or if I was simply born to suffer these hardships, I suppose it would hardly be the part of wisdom to rebel against necessity. I should indeed be happier, my boys, not to leave you at this age, and it would trouble me less to die at a less young age simply because I could then go on working according to my custom for the welfare and honor of our house. But if another destiny calls this my spirit, I neither should nor would view it as an evil. I would not oppose my soul to what I cannot prevent by not wishing it. God's will be done of me.

Adovardo: I think perhaps it is a help, in overcoming any fear of death, to think on the fact that every mortal has always had to come to the end of his life. But when one is ill and weak one should not definitely expect death. To expect it does help conquer the fear and shadow of death, but to be worried hurts the peace and tranquillity of one's spirit. And I think, having arrived at this state of mind, perhaps I would be unavoidably worried concerning those whom I would be leaving behind, and how I might arrange matters, and to whom I might recommend the affairs most dear and precious to me. These concerns are so vital I do not know who could help having his mind on them. Yet I think they would not help one to sustain the burden of the illness itself. Therefore, Lorenzo, it would be admirable if you could be of better cheer. Do as I suggest, then, and take comfort. Hope for the best from fortune, and especially from your own condition. Believe as we do that, unless we are gravely mistaken, these sons of yours will certainly grow up to be such that you can be well pleased with them.

Lorenzo: My sons, it has always been no small reward of goodness that it compels praise. You see how these men think well of you and how much they promise you. It will be to your honor to strive with all your might and skill to become such as they hope you are. Usually, in a naturally good disposition, any excellence increases with the encouragement of praise. Perhaps, Adovardo and Lionardo, you say things that are not really true; but a father may be allowed to overestimate the virtues of his sons; nor will I be called unwise if, to encourage them in the love of virtue, I show in their presence how much it delights me and how pleased I would be to see them achieve excellence. Every bit of praise they receive naturally seems important to me.

I have always applied my efforts and my intellect, it is true, to make myself more loved by all than feared. I have never wished to appear as a master to those who viewed me as a father. So these children have always been voluntarily obedient and respectful, and have listened to my words and followed my commands, and I have never found any contumacy or discovered any vice in them. I have rejoiced in every good habit they developed. I have thought that I might hope and expect to see still more from day to day. But who does not know the dubious ways of the young? If they have some vice, they keep it covered up and hidden from parents or elders for fear or shame. Only later it is revealed and expressed. The more young people lack awe and reverence, the more various vices grow in them from day to day. Sometimes they are depraved and corrupted by their own native inclinations, sometimes inspired to evil and wholly ruined by the bad conversation and customs around them. A thousand ways exist to make a good person into a scoundrel. We have seen it both elsewhere and in our own country, when sons of excellent citizens who appeared most promising as children, with a very pleasant manner and appearance, full of gentleness and good manners, grew up to be disgraceful people. I believe it happened through the negligence of those who did not restrain them.

Here, however, I am reminded of our father, Benedetto Alberti, a man of wisdom and authority, and of a fame that was not vulgar. He was diligent in all things, but especially in pursuing and carefully tending the fortune and honor of our family. When he was encouraging other members of the Alberti family of that time to be, as they certainly were, careful and industrious in all they did, he used to speak in the following words:

"The duty of a father is not only, as they say, to stock the cupboard and the cradle. He ought, far more, to watch over and guard the family from all sides, to check over and consider the whole company, to examine all the practices of every member, inside and outside the house, and to correct and improve every bad habit. He ought preferably to use reasonable rather than indignant words, authority rather than power. He should appear to give wise counsel where this would help more than commands, and should be severe, rigorous, and harsh only where the situation really calls for it. He ought in every thought always to put first the good, the peace, and the tranquillity of his entire family. This should be a kind of goal toward which he, using his intelligence and experience, guides the whole family with virtue and honor. He knows how to steer according to the wind's favor, the waves of popular opinion, and the grace given him by his fellow citizens, toward the harbor of honor, prestige, and authority. He also knows how to remain afloat there, how to strike and furl the sails, and how, in storms and in such misfortunes as have unjustly afflicted our house these last twenty-two years, to restrain the spirits of the young men. He must neither let them yield to the blows of fortune nor leave them to lie in defeat. He must never allow them to try something irresponsible and wild, either for revenge or to satisfy some youthful and frivolous optimism.

"When fortune is tranquil and goodnatured, but still more when the times are stormy, the good father never departs from the pilot of reason and the careful conduct of life. He remains alert, foresees from a good distance every mist of envy, every storm cloud of hate, every lightning stroke of enmity threatening on the faces of his fellow citizens. Encountering any contrary wind, any shoal and danger which may confront the family, he acts the part of the experienced expert sailor. He recalls with what winds others have sailed, how they rigged their ships and how they sighted and avoided every danger. He never forgets that in our country no one ever spread all his sails, even though they might not be the greatest of all, without having to take them down again, not whole any longer but ripped and torn. Also he knows that there is more harm done by one badly navigated voyage than good by the successful accomplishment of a thousand. Envy vanishes where modesty, not pomp, shines forth; hate falls aside where courtesy, not pride, flourishes; enmity is quelled and extinguished where you arm and fortify yourself not with indignation and spite but with civility and gentleness. To all these things the elders of families ought to open their eyes and minds, to stretch out their intellects and hearts. They ought to stand ever prepared and ready to foresee and to know everything. For these duties they must undergo fatigue and anxiety, exerting the greatest care and effort in making their young people from day to day more upright, more excellent, and more dear to our fellow citizens.

"Let fathers realize that excellent sons rejoice and support their parents at every age. In the father's watchfulness lies the son's character. Laziness and sloth corrupt and disgrace the family; anxious and responsible fathers restore it to honor. Greedy, lascivious, wicked, and proud men load the family with ill fame, misfortunes, and troubles. The good ones, however gentle, moderate, and humane they may be, ought to realize that if they are not also very concerned, diligent, foresightful, and active in correcting and restraining the young, when any part of the family falls, they too will be ruined. The more greatness and wealth and rank was theirs in the family, the greater will be their downfall. The top stones in the wall shatter most when they fall.

"Therefore let the elders be ever alert and busy for the well-being and honor of the whole family, counseling, correcting, and keeping a firm hold, as it were, on the bridle of the whole family. For it is nothing if not an honorable, pious, and blessed labor to rein in with words and courtesy the appetites of the young, to wake up the lazy spirits, to enflame the wills that are cold, at the same time doing honor to oneself and glorifying one's country and one's house. Nor does it seem to me less than a very noble and pleasant work for fathers of families to contain and to restrain with seriousness and moderation the excessive license of youth. Anyone who wants to deserve well of the young will most appropriately maintain in himself the jewel of old age, which consists, I believe, in nothing else than authority and reverence.

"The old cannot more appropriately acquire, increase, and conserve great authority and dignity than by caring for the young. They must draw them toward virtue and make them every day more learned and more charming, more loved, and more valued. Thus must they draw them toward the greatest and highest ambitions, keep them to the study of the best things and those of highest esteem, quiet any disordered desire of theirs and every small shameful vexation of spirit, and so extirpate every root of vice and reason of enmity. They must fill them with good counsel and lessons.

"They must not do like certain old men used to do who were perhaps given to avarice. These, when they meant to make their children thrifty, made them unhappy and servile. They appreciated money more than honor, and so they taught them ugly and low occupations. I do not praise that sort of liberality which would be harmful unless rewarded by fame or friendship, but I do condemn extremely every form of stinginess. I have also always found every sort of excessive pomp displeasing.

"The old, then, should be common fathers to all the young. Indeed they are mind and soul to the whole body of the family. And just as having dirty naked feet brings dishonor on the face and on the whole man and is a disgrace, so the old, any of the elders, should realize that neglecting the least member of the house brings justified blame on them. They are to blame if they have allowed any part of the family to fall into misery or dishonor. Let them keep in mind that the first duty of the elders is to work for everyone of the house, like those good ancient Lacedaemonians who considered themselves fathers and tutors of every young person. Each of them corrected all the errors of any young citizen that might be, and his closer, more immediate kinsmen were glad and fully accepted the improvement produced by others. It brought honor to fathers that they showed gratitude and thanks to whoever had made their youth more reasonable and more responsible in carrying out any undertaking. Because of this good and most useful system of moral discipline, their land was glorious and honored with immortal and well-earned fame. There was no enmity among them. Anger and hostility were immediately rooted up and overthrown. There was but a single will among the citizens, and that directed to making the country virtuous and disciplined. Such were the goals for which everyone labored, exerting energy, mind, and will. The old offered their counsel, their memories, and their good example, while the young gave their obedience and imitation."

These things and many others that Messer Benedetto used to mention are indeed the duties of fathers of families. If the young should really receive care not only from their fathers but also by the merit of others, surely no one can question the justice of my efforts, like other fathers, to apply every argument, cnsideration, and art to assure my own very dear sons of being well recommended and as cherished as possible by their own kinsmen and by everyone's good faith and piety.

I conclude, my children, that the duty of the young is to love and obey the old, to respect age, and to have toward all their elders the same attitude as toward their father, showing them all the required submissiveness and reverence. In the accumulation of years there is long experience of things, and the knowledge of many sorts of conduct, of many ways, and of many human souls. The old have seen, heard, and thought through innumerable practical solutions and excellent and noble answers to every condition of fortune. Our father, Benedetto, this man of whom I think at all times, as I should do since he tried at all times to be our wise and cultivated guide, happened to be on the island of Rhodes with some friends, and they discussed the cruel and bitter sufferings of our family. They came to the conclusion that our Alberti family had been too greatly abused by fortune. He, then, seeing perhaps some flame of envy and unjust hatred kindled in one of our fellow citizens, predicted in the course of discussion many things that would happen in our country and which we have since seen largely fulfilled. Then, since to his listeners it seemed a very remarkable thing that he should clearly predict what it was hard for the others even to understand when he spoke, they asked him please to reveal whence he derived his long-range predictions. He then smilingly uncovered the top of his head and pointed to his white hair, saying, "These hairs have made me wise and given me knowledge."

Indeed who could doubt that in great age there is a vast memory of the past, long experience of things, intelligence practiced in predicting and in assessing the causes, purposes, and results of things. There is the knowledge of how to relate present affairs to those of yesterday so as to foretell what may become of them tomorrow. The old, therefore, give by their foresight sure and highly relevant counsel. By their counsel they provide the best solutions to maintain the family in a tranquil and honorable state. With faith and diligence may they always protect it from any sudden ruin, and with strength and virility of soul guide and restore it if it has already been in part shaken or bent by fortune's blows. The intelligence, wisdom, and knowledge of the old together with their diligence constitute the very means to maintain the family in a flourishing and happy state of fortune and to ornament it with splendor and praise. What do the old deserve, then, who have the power to do this for their people, to keep them fortunate, to strengthen their resistance to misfortune, to support them in a life not deprived of adornment and pleasure? Do they not deserve great respect?

The young should respect the old, but more especially their own fathers. To these both for their age and for other reasons the young owe all too much. From your father you have your being and many principles to guide you in acquiring excellence of soul. Your father, with his sweat and zeal and hard work, made you the man you are. He gave you your years, your fortune, your condition. If you owe something to him who helps you in necessity and trouble, certainly to him who as far as he was able never allowed you to suffer the least need, to him you owe much indeed. If you ought to share every thought, every possession, every gift of fortune with your friend, and to suffer discomfort, fatigue, and strain for one who loves you, still more should you do for your father to whom you are dearer than anyone and to whom you owe almost more than to yourself. If your friends ought to enjoy a good portion of your possessions and goods and wealth, far more ought your father, from whom you have received, if not your goods, still life itself, and not only life but nurture for so long a time, and if not nurture, still being and name. Therefore ought young people to refer every wish, thought, and plan of their own to their fathers and elders and to take counsel with them about everything, especially with those to whom they know they are dearer than to the others. They should listen eagerly to them as to very wise and experienced men, and gladly submit to the guidance of men of judgment and age. Nor let the young be slow to help any of their elders in their old age and infirmity. Let them hope for the same humanity and sense of duty in their juniors that they have shown to their elders. Let them be quick and eager, then, to give them, in the staleness of old age, comfort, contentment, and repose. Nor let them imagine that any contentment or joy of the old surpasses that of seeing the young turn out well and worthy of love. Surely nothing can be a greater comfort to the old than to see those on whom they have long lavished their hope and expectation, those for whom they have been ambitious, rise through their conduct and character to attain general esteem, love, and honor. Very happy will be the old age which witnesses all the young people directed toward or engaged upon a peaceful and honorable life. A life which is well conducted will always be peaceful; a life guided by virtue will always be honorable. Nothing is such a source of anxiety in human life as vice.

Your duty, then, young men, is to try to satisfy your fathers and all your elders by your character in general, and particularly by doing things which bring praise and fame to you and, to your kinsmen, happiness, pleasure, and delight. So, my sons, follow virtue, flee from vice, respect your elders, act so as to be well liked, to live in freedom, to be happy, honored, and loved. The first step toward being honored is to make yourself liked and loved; the first step toward acquiring good will and love is to make one's goodness and honorableness apparent; the first step toward acquiring that grace of virtue is to feel a horror of vice and to flee from the vice-ridden. One should keep oneself ever worthy of the praise and love of good men. Never should one depart from those who give one good examples and the sort of teaching that tends toward the attainment and full development of character and good conduct. These you must love and respect. You should delight in having all of them accept you as a man without blame. Be not difficult, hard, obstinate, frivolous, or vain. Be most courteous, tractable, versatile, and, as far as your age permits, thoughtful and grave. Trying with all your might to please everyone, show yourself, particularly toward your elders, full of respect and obedience. Civility, gentleness, restraint, and modesty usually win no little praise. Respect from the young toward their elders has always been a sure source of satisfaction and a sorely wanted thing.

I do not say this to boast, but to give you a familiar example which you may be more inclined both to take to heart and to keep in mind than a remote one. I cannot recall a place where our brother Ricciardo was present, or any of the others older than I, where I ever wished to be seen seated or to stand without clear signs of my deference. No one ever saw me among other people or in a public place not standing straight and alert to do my elders' bidding. Wherever I saw them, I always rose and took off my hat to do them reverence. Wherever I encountered them my habit was to leave at once any pleasure or company I might be engaged with in order to join my elders, honor them, and attend on them. Nor would I ever retire from their company and return to my young friends without first asking their permission as though from a father. I was not considered faulty for such submissiveness either by my elders or by young people either. In my own opinion I merely fulfilled my duty, so that to have done the opposite, in other words to have failed to please, to love, and to submit to my elders, would have seemed to me a disgrace and a fault. I also felt it my duty to be entirely open in everything with Ricciardo; I sought his counsel and viewed him as a father, such was the dignity and honor which I knew was due to age.

I charge you, then, be very reverent toward your elders, and do your best to show the powers of your character. Nor should you hesitate, my sons, if the face of virtue seems hard and forbidding, while erroneous ways seem at first sight inviting and delightful. In fact the difference which lies between them is this: vice brings you more remorse than satisfaction, more sorrow than pleasure, and more waste on all sides than utility. Virtue, on the other hand, is just the opposite; happy, gracious, and gentle, virtue will always satisfy you. It will never bring sorrow, never satiation. From day to day it grows more pleasant and useful. The more you practice right conduct and excellence of character, the more will good men appreciate you, praise and truly love you. At this you will rejoice inwardly. What virtue alone can do is to make man blessed and happy as he devotes himself in thought and deed to carrying out those lessons and precepts that keep men far from vice and make them flee every ugly habit and unworthy act.

I am of those, my sons, who would rather leave you virtue than riches as a heritage, but this is not within my power. All that seemed possible was to start you off as best I could to help you and guide you toward the goals of praise, public grace, and honor. It is up to you to make use of the intelligence you have by nature, which I think is neither small nor feeble. You must improve it by study and by practice in worthwhile areas. It is up to you to devote yourselves unstintingly to arts and letters. The fortune that I leave to you, you must use and distribute in such a way as to make you dear to your own kinsmen and to other men too. It seems likely to me that at times you will wish that you had me alive again, my children. You will perhaps undergo anxieties and privations which would have less power over you if I were still alive. I am not unacquainted with the way fortune can hound the years of weakness and the inexperienced minds of young people without guidance and help. Our house is an example to me; abounding in wisdom, intelligence, and experience, firmness, virility, and constancy of spirit, it truly knows in these our times of trouble how much fortune with its fury and wickedness can do even to the soundest judgment and most firmly competent mind.

But be of strong and unbroken spirit. Adversities are the material of which character is built. Whose unshakeable spirit, constant mind, energetic intelligence, indefatigable industry and art can show its full merit in favorable and quiet situations? Where fortune is easy and tranquil, who can win such praise and reputation as the man who faces a hostile and difficult fate? Conquer fortune with patience, therefore, and conquer the wickedness of men by the pursuit of virtue. Adapt yourselves to such needs as arise, adjust to the times with reason and wisdom, and accept the usage and custom of men with modesty, civility, and discretion. Above all, seek with all your intelligence, art, zeal, and labor, first to be and second to appear men of noble character. Let there be nothing more dear to you, nor more eagerly sought, than virtue. Be sure you have decided within yourselves to place knowledge and wisdom before any other thing. You will then see the conveniences fortune can give as small advantages. Let honor alone claim first place in your desires. Let fame stand first, and never subordinate reputation to riches. In the attainment of honor and reputation nothing, no matter how arduous or laborious, will seem too much for you to attempt and to carry through. You will be satisfied with the sole reward of public appreciation and high reputation. Do not doubt that a man who has excellence sooner or later sees his work bear fruit. Never lose faith in the persevering and assiduous study of the noble arts, in the continual searching out of rare and highly honorable things, in learning and following good teachings and labors. Often it is the slow debtor who pays at last with ample interest.

It is a matter of no small satisfaction to me that at your present young and tender age you have had some training in strengthening yourselves to bear the blows of human misfortune with firm and undaunted spirit. I leave you in exile, fatherless, outside your country and your house. It shall redound to your praise, my sons, if at your tender and weak years you set yourselves to overcome, if not wholly at least in part, the hard and bleak situation that confronts you. If you have been able, in every sort of situation, to disdain the malevolence and overcome the onslaughts of fortune, it will stand as a true triumph for you when you grow to a less vulnerable age. Be guided from now on by the thought that the less you fail in diligence, in zeal, and in love of honorable and noble things, the less will you miss my presence, and still less the help of others. He who has virtue within has but few outer necessities.

Ample the riches, great the possessions, and abundant the good fortune of him who knows how to content himself with inner excellence alone. Blessed the man who appears virtuous in his conduct, strong in friendships, abounding in the favor and affection of his fellow citizens. No one will have greater, firmer, or more solid honor than he who dedicates himself to the renown and lasting fame of his country, his fellow citizens, and his family. He alone deserves to have his name praised and famous and immortal among his descendants who, rightly despising every transient and perishable thing, loves virtue alone, seeks wisdom, desires only pure and righteous glory. It will be your duty, my sons, to show what you can do in the noble arts and in the higher studies not to disappoint, through your own fault, the high hopes of these friends. Seek, then, in every honorable way, with all possible labor and ardor and effort and persistence, to merit their praise and favor. Seek to deserve also the good will, dignity, and authority which other men can bestow upon you. Leave among the young, including those still to be born, the memory of yourselves and of your remarkable words, actions, and works.

Now cheer up. Here are Adovardo and Lionardo. Ricciardo will soon be here, to whom I hope you will stand recommended. I know every

member of our Alberti family has an affectionate nature, and I believe
they will not wish to be thought so hard and unfeeling as to leave
unaided such kinsmen as show a high character. Thus do I pray you,
Adovardo, and you, Lionardo, look at the age of these boys—you know
the dangers of youth, you value the welfare and honor of our house. Then
be watchful. Take on yourselves, you two, this great task. It is everyone's
duty to labor for the education of the members of our house toward
excellence and fame. It is thought good to honor with sepulchers those
already fallen from life, and to give to their passing the decorum of
funeral festivities though these are useless to the deceased. Why is this so,
if not because it brings the living appreciation and approval for their
tender feelings and dutiful conduct? If this is clear, do you not see that it
is necessary to honor and exalt the living far more by means of timely
assistance? It is necessary to come to their aid when need arises, to push
them forward until they, representing the whole family, stand in an
elevated and honorable place. Do not let it be said that I spoke in this
way out of an inordinately high opinion of my two boys. Rather let it be
your responsibility to show that my commendation of them to you while I
was still alive did serve them after I had gone.

Thus spoke Lorenzo. Adovardo and Lionardo stood by, listening atten-
tively in silence. The discussion was interrupted when the doctors arrived
and advised Lorenzo to rest for a while. This he did. In his absence, when
we had left the room, Adovardo said:

Who would believe, except by the experience of his own feelings, how
great and intense is the love of a father toward his children? Every kind
of love seems to me no small matter. Many have been known to risk all
their possessions, to give time and fortune, to undergo terrible hardships,
dangers, and troubles only to display their loyalty and the quality of their
love for a friend. And it is said that there have been men who, for desire
of things loved which they thought they had lost, refused to continue
living. Histories and memories of men are full of these powers, and the
affections of the human spirit have been experienced by many men. But
I am sure that no love is more unshakable, more constant, more
complete, or more vast than the love which a father bears to his children.
I willingly admit to Plato that his four madnesses have a powerful and
intense effect on the human mind and spirit, the madnesses of prophet,
minister, poet and love. And the passion of Venus in itself seems to me
much the most mad and savage that there is. Yet not infrequently do we
see this passion shrivel up and perish as a result of offense, negligence, or

a new desire, and almost always it leaves behind ill feeling in its place. Nor would I deny to you that true friendship binds with a whole and mighty love. Yet if you don't object I cannot believe there is a greater, a more active and ardent affection of the spirit than that which by nature is rooted and born in a father's mind.

Lionardo: It is not for me to judge how great is the affection of fathers toward their children, for I do not know what it is to have children, whatever pleasure or sweetness it may bring. But from what I gather at a distance by conjecture, it seems to me I can fairly join you in your opinion and say that the father's love is in many ways immense. Other evidence aside, here we see how zealously and with what tenderness Lorenzo has just been recommending his sons to us. It is not, I think, that he thought he had to make us care for them, since he knows that we care very much for them already. Rather, perhaps, the fervor of paternal love carried him away. It seemed to him that no man could watch over the children of another, however solicitous, interested, and wise he might be, with as much care and good counsel as would satisfy a father's love.

To tell the truth, those words of Lorenzo moved me most when I saw how right and reasonable it is to consider and to give anxious attention to the youthful wards of a family. At times, indeed, I could not refrain from tears. I saw you standing all abstracted, and it seemed to me you were perhaps thinking within yourself well beyond what was passing through my own mind.

Adovardo: That's how it was. Every word Lorenzo said compelled me both to a sense of duty and to compassion. You know that I am a father myself, and that these are the sons of a friend who is my good and affectionate kinsman. If for these boys, who should be dear to me by blood and the more dear for having been commended to our care, I did less or felt differently than I would for my own sons, truly Lionardo, I would be neither a good kinsman nor a true friend. You would have to view me rather as a man without feeling, a traitor and a man of the lowest type. For this I should stand condemned, I should be infamous. Wouldn't anyone have feelings for those in his care? Could anyone help having constantly before his eyes the father of these orphans, this same friend of yours? Could anyone not find these last words engraved on his heart, words with which a kinsman, both relative and friend, leaves his sons, his dearest concern to your care? Having faith in you, he leaves them to your bosom, to your arms.

My sentiments in this are such, Lionardo, that before I would let these children experience the least discomfort, I should suffer my own children to lack everything. My own family's poverty I alone know, but the inadequate care given to those commended to me would concern every good and charitable person of judgment. It is our duty here to satisfy reputation, honor, good custom, and morality. My belief is that where someone is fitted by nature and birth to reach high honor in the world and a man lets him go to waste through avarice or neglect, that man deserves not mere condemnation but a truly terrible punishment. It is hardly a handsome act to keep an ox or a mare uncared for, unclean and out of condition. It is actually bad to let the animal die through neglect, even if the beast is no use to anyone. Certainly, then, he who would keep a human mind sunk in miseries and sorrows, bereft of honor, he who disdains that mind and, through sloth and stinginess, allows it to suffer and perish, what does he deserve if not the gravest judgment? Should we not consider him unjust and utterly inhuman? Does he not deserve much odium among good men, and deepest infamy? Oh, let him beware of acting with such cruelty, let him fear the vengeance of God. Let him listen to the wise and true saying, "You let the other's children go, your own son's beard will never grow."

Lionardo: I am beginning to understand what a worry it is to be a father. Lorenzo's words, I think, troubled you more profoundly than I realized at the time. These arguments of yours now indicate to me what I believe you feel concerning your own children. While you were speaking I found myself wondering at last which is actually greater, the responsibility and anxiety or the pleasure and satisfaction in raising offspring. There is no doubt in my mind about the labor involved, but I think that this is itself the cause of the love you fathers bear your children. I have noticed that by nature almost everyone loves his own works. The painter, the writer, and the poet all do. The father, I suppose, feels even more so, since the labor demanded of him is long and drawn out. All try to make their works widely pleasing, to win praise, and to gain as much immortality as they can.

Adovardo: Yes. Certainly what has cost you much labor is all the more dear. But there is by nature something in a father—I don't know exactly what—a kind of greater need, so strong is the desire to have and to raise children and afterward to take delight in seeing them express his very image and likeness. Here he focuses all his various hopes, and therefore trusts that he will find them a kind of fortress in his old age and a refuge in the weary and feeble years.

If you think it all over for yourself and meditate upon it, you will find that many different sorrows crop up in the process of raising children, and you will note how fathers are ever in a state of suspense, like good old Mizio in Terence waiting for his son to come home. What were his thoughts? What suspicions crossed his mind? What fears oppressed his spirit? He was afraid his son might be lying somewhere fallen, broken, or crushed in some part. But face it, there it is—if a man takes it into his head to love something more than himself, this is the result. We are always worried and timid in the present, and with our thoughts we are ever running ahead a long way, alert and fearful, looking for any road by which we may steer our family toward good fortune. If nature itself did not demand this kind of anxiety and concern from fathers, few, I think, would not regret having had children. You see the birds and other animals, who obey only the commands of nature, laboriously constructing the nest, brooding, and hatching. Punctiliously and conscientiously they guard, defend, and preserve their newborn, flying about anxiously to gather food and feed the helpless young. All these essentially great and heavy tasks are made light for them because they are debts to nature. What seems to you a troublesome and sordid burden likewise appears an acceptable, fitting, and fortunate task to us fathers, because it is almost a necessity of nature.

Why speak especially of children rather than of other things? I know of nothing in man's life that does not contain as much bad as good. Riches are generally thought useful and desirable, yet experience shows how many worries and sorrows they cause. A prince's power is revered and feared, and yet it is obvious how burdened he is with suspicions and fears. Everything seems to have its corresponding opposite: for life, death; for light, darkness; nor can you have one without the other. So also with children there is no hope but is accompanied by many disappointments, nor is there any solace or delight without some sorrow and bitterness. The older they grow, I won't deny it, the greater the joy your children give you, but also the more the griefs. And in the human spirit, sufferings are more sharply perceived than happiness, pleasure and delight less than sorrow and bitterness, because the latter beat and oppress you violently, while the former caress you more gently. Children of any age necessarily cause you concern. They do so when still in swaddling clothes, and more seriously as they grow older, and much, indeed infinitely, more labor arises as they become bigger boys. Still more care and effort are required when they reach a riper age. So have no doubt,

Lionardo, being a father is not only a worry, it is a situation overflowing with griefs.

Lionardo: I can imagine that with fatherhood it is as with other things. Nature, as I have always observed, labors to make everything that is procreated preserve itself. Everything receives nourishment from what produced it, and is helped to survive and develop. I see that in plants and bushes the roots draw up the nourishment and distribute it to the trunk, the trunk to the branches, and the branches to the leaves and fruit. Hence one ought perhaps to view it as the natural thing that fathers neglect no means of nourishing and preserving those who are issued from them and born by means of them. I admit, too, that it is your duty as fathers to care for and worry over your offspring.

I shall not ask you now whether this concern which fathers do show is a necessity of nature or whether it springs and grows from the enjoyment of those charms and hopes which fathers derive from the actions and the personality of their children. I know it is by no means unusual to see a father prefer one son to another. He may give the one who seems more promising more handsome adornments and more liberty and indulgence of his wishes. Another kind of father one sees every day hardly cares whether his son wanders in distant and foreign lands, is ragged in the stables, suffers need and danger and perhaps, which ought to worry the father more, falls into vice and incorrigible ways. Let us not make it our present aim, however, to investigate the origins, the growth, or the ends of each kind of love. Nor shall we search out whence it is that fathers show some disparity in their love. There you might answer me by pointing out that some men become evil by the corruption of nature and the depravity of their mind. Nature herself, perhaps, seeking in all things to produce what is fitting and perfect, detaches those corrupt children from the true love of the father and deprives them of his entire charity. Then, too, a father may prefer to see some specific achievement in his sons rather than to keep them at home in the lap of domestic ease and leisure. I think it would take a long discussion for you to explain to me your opinion on this question.

Here let me say something, not to contradict you, but just to clarify for myself what you said about children and how, from the time of swaddling clothes on, they cause their father much anxiety. I am not convinced that a wise father would burden his soul or even concern himself at all with certain things, especially those which are women's domain and properly fall to the nurse and the mother much more than to the father. It seems to me that this whole tender age is more properly assigned to women's quiet care than to the active attention of men. As for me, I am one of those who would certainly never torment the little ones or wish to see, as I sometimes have seen, babies tossed too freely in the air by their fathers. People are fools not to realize the danger to a baby in his father's hard hands. At that age the least thing can strain or twist those tender little bones. One can hardly squeeze or handle them without the greatest gentleness, lest a limb be turned or thrown out of joint, as a result of which some are left twisted and crooked. So let that earliest period be spent entirely outside the father's arms. Let the child rest, let him sleep in his mother's lap.

The age which follows this one is full of delight and is accompanied by general laughter. The child begins to make known his wishes and partly to express them in words. The whole family listens and the whole neighborhood repeats his sayings, not without joyful and merry discussion, interpreting and praising what he says and does. Already in this springlike age there seems to be a sparkle and promise in the child's face, manner, and words. On his ways infinite hopes are founded, wonderful evidence is seen of subtle intelligence and keen memory, and so everyone says that small children are the comfort and delight of their fathers and of the old people of the family. I do not think there is a father so tied down with responsibilities and burdened with cares that the presence of his children does not give him great pleasure. Cato, that good man of ancient times, who was given the epithet "the Wise" and who was reputed, as indeed he was, most unbending and severe in all things, yet often in the course of the day used to interrupt his great public and private doings to go home and see his little children, so little bitterness and sorrow did he find in children, and so much solace and pleasure did he gain from the sight of their laughter, the sound of their words, the enjoyment of all those simple and sweet childish charms scattered on the brow of that pure and lovely young age. If this is true, Adovardo, if the worries of a father are but slight and accompanied by much delight, if fatherhood is full of love and high hopes, of laughter, joy and amusement, those sorrows you were speaking of—tell me, where are they? I should be glad to be able to think more clearly about this.

Adovardo: I should be most pleased if you, like me, could partly base your thinking about it on experience. It grieves me to see so many of you younger Albertis without an heir, not having done what you could to increase the family and make it numerous. What do I mean by this? I mean that according to a count I took a few days ago not less than twenty-two young Albertis no younger than sixteen or older than thirty-six are now living alone and without a female companion, since they have no wife. This grieves me. I see clearly the great harm it will do our family if all the number of sons who might have been expected from you young men continues not to appear. I think we should gladly bear all the discomforts and unpleasant burdens in the world rather than allow our family to stand desolate, with none to succeed in the place and name of the fathers. I particularly hope that you, first among the others, will adorn and increase the Alberti family, not only as now with your fame and renown but also with sons like yourself.

I am very much afraid, therefore, to persuade you of something which might make you doubt and hold back. Yet I think I might soon show you that with children of every age, a father has not a few troubles. They are not slight, but serious and acute. You can quickly realize that, from their birth, children not only bring joy and laughter to their affectionate father, but often also sorrow and tears. You would not deny that great emotion and heavy concern beset the father long before his children give him laughter or solace. He must think far ahead to find a good nurse, and he must with much effort get hold of one who will be ready in time. He must check that she is sick or of immoral character. He must expend much thought and labor to be absolutely sure that she is free, clear, and clean of those vices and defects which infect and corrupt the milk and the blood. Still more, he must be sure she is not the sort who will bring scandal or shame to the house. It would take a long time to tell you how careful we fathers have to be about these things, and how much trouble there is each time before one has found an honest, good, and competent nurse. Nor would you believe, perhaps, how much anxiety, trouble, and remorse of spirit results if she is not found in time or if she is not adequate. Yet this sort of person always seems to be unavailable just when you need her most. You know, at the same time, how great is the danger with a sick or immoral girl, for leprosy and epilepsy and other serious diseases are passed on by the breast, it is said. You know, too, how rare is a good nurse and how much in demand.

But why am I telling you all these little details, since I would much rather have you think, as is also the truth, that children are a great comfort to their father? He sees the little ones happy around him, marvels at all that they do and say, considers everything very full of meaning, and cherishes rather high hopes for them. One thing, perhaps, may overshadow all these delights and fill your mind with far greater and more ardent apprehensions. Consider, you who hate to see them cry when they have fallen and hurt their hands, how much anguish it is to a father to think that more children perish at this age than at any other. Imagine the painful waiting from hour to hour in expectation of losing so great a happiness. In fact this first period of life seems to me the one that particularly causes many and great sorrows. It seems to be almost nothing but attacks of smallpox, measles, and rose rash. It is never free of stomach trouble, and there are always periods of debility. Those little ones are often weighed down with some illness which you do not know yourself and which they are unable to explain to you. Every little sickness seems a major illness to you, the more so since you cannot tell how to give correct and useful treatment to an unknown ailment. Even the little pains of children thus keep the soul of the father in agony.

Lionardo: You would be all too pleased, Adovardo, if I could no longer say, like one who utters a happy thought, "Never have I had a wife." You well know whether in these things I have good and strong desires. I think it does not bother you at all that many people, all too often, scald my ears about it. I think it's clear that you don't care if everyone who has nothing better to say to me, lacking conversation or an argument, begins to babble about providing me with a wife. Here great streams of eloquence flow as they undertake to prove to me the necessity and excellence of the conjugal state, society taking its origin from this primeval institution, the procreation of a line of hereditary succession, the growth and increase of the family. They urge me to "take this one or that one"—"you can't say she does not have adequate dowry, or beauty, or a good family." Often enough, with their overwhelming presumption, as they try to kindle in me a wish no longer to remain free as I am, they spark instead some righteous indignation. Yet I would soon wish not to lack a wife, and would like to have children, so that you might not have so great an advantage over me now. Then I might not be unable to answer your authority with as much evidence as logic. God knows, and you know it too, how ardent is my good will and how often we have tried together, with you and with the others, to find the right thing. But it only leads to disaster every time—that weights on me as a certainty. The maidens who suit your taste would not please me. Those who perhaps would not offend me, never seem to suit the rest of you. So my spirit remains athirst, not so much to avoid having my place and name in the family extinguished and blank after my own passing, as just to escape the pestering of all those friends and acquaintances who cavil, I know not through what envy, at my liberty in being without a wife. But I am afraid it is with me as with that sacred fountain in Epirus, which the ancients describe, in which a flaming brand was extinguished and one that was burnt out and cold rekindled. Perhaps it would be best if you let me satisfy you with the fire kindled in me by me. Otherwise, if you really think your speaking could do me some good, wait at least, I suggest, until my own ardent desire of foolish woman is cooled.

But we have laughed enough. Even if I had children, I should not take on myself the trouble of finding any other nurse for them than their own mother. I am reminded of Favorinus, that philosopher mentioned by Aulus Gelius, and of the other ancient writers who praise the milk of the mother above any other's. Perhaps these doctors nowadays will assert that giving the breast weakens the mother and makes her sterile for a time. But I find it easier to believe that nature has made adequate provision for all. It is probably not by coincidence, but for excellent reasons, that pregnancy is accompanied by the springing up and increase of an abundance of milk, as though nature herself were preparing us for the need and telling us how much we may expect the mother to do for the children. I would take this license if the mother were weakened by some accident: then I would provide, as you say, a good, knowledgeable, and moral nurse. I would not do this to give the lady more leisure, or to relieve her of that duty she owes to her children, but only to give less unhappy nourishment to the child.

I think it is true that besides those illnesses which you say can be passed on by bad milk, still more the worthless, immoral nurse can injure the character of the child. She can incline him toward vices and fill his spirit with savage and bestial passions of anger, fear, terror, and similar evils. I think that if the nurse is aflame, by nature or by the use of too heady or too undiluted wines or other stimulants, and her blood is kindled and burned up, it may well be easy for him who has taken his nourishment thus kindled and scorched at the source to become temperamentally inclined and prepared for anger, cruelty, and savagery. Likewise the wetnurse who is discontented, full of resentment and heaviness of spirit, can make a child languid, dispirited, and timid. So it goes, with similar causes producing their effects in this first period of life. If a small tree is deprived of the right soil to give it proper nourishment and lacks the abundant air and moisture it requires, you will find it limp and dry ever after. And you will see that a small bruise does more harm to a tender

little branch than two great cuts in an aged trunk. Therefore one should
make every effort to provide the best possible nourishment at that tender
age. If a nurse is necessary, let one be found who is happy, clean, free of
any heat or turbulence of blood or spirit; let her live moderately, nor be
intemperate or improper in any way.

If, as you say, nurses seldom meet these requirements, then you must
admit also that the mother herself, as she is more modest and of better
character than other nurses, offers more suitable and much more practical
nourishment to her own children. I shall not go on to describe which of
them takes care of the child with more love, more constancy, diligence,
and zeal, the one who does it for pay or the mother herself. I shall not
show you at length that the mother's love toward her child is fostered and
strengthened while he grows and is nourished in her bosom. Even if, as
rarely happens except in the absence of a mother, it really is necessary to
find a nurse, however, and to concern oneself with these things, it does
not seem such a heavy task to me. I seem to see many men gladly exhaust
themselves in labors less worthy than this one. This is for the health of
the children, an honorable and highly necessary responsibility.

But you know, to be as anxious as you seemed to be, and worried
because so many children die in those first years, does not seem commend-
able to me. As long as there is breath in a child, one should hope for the
best rather than fear the worst. The illnesses of childhood are not all as
serious, either, as they seem. Yesterday you saw him lying utterly limp
and as if lifeless; today he appears lively and strong and the whole thing
has passed over. And if at some point in the course of childhood it pleases
God to end your child's days, I think it is the father's duty rather to recall
and to render thanks for the many joys and delights which the children
have given him than to sorrow because the one who lent them to you has
in his own time claimed them again. Rightly is the reply of Anaxagoras
admired, for, like a prudent and wise father, when he heard that his son
had died, he spoke with as patient and rational a spirit as he could. He
said that he knew that he had begotten a mortal. It did not appear intolerable to him that one who was born to die should have died already.
But what simpleton could you find so ignorant and foolish as not to know
for sure that just as anything that is called dead must first have been alive,
so nothing is alive but awaits the payment of its debt to death.

And perhaps I should go further, Adovardo, and say to you that a
father ought to feel, I won't say content, but certainly far less troubled, if
his children die without further corruption and without experiencing the

many anxieties of mortal life. There is nothing more wearisome than living. Fortunate those who depart from so many trials and end their days young in the house of their fathers in our country. Fortunate those who do not know our sufferings, have not gone wandering through the lands of others without dignity, without authority. They have not been scattered, far from relatives, friends, and dear ones. They have not been scorned, despised, expelled, and hated by those who used to receive from us honorable and courteous treatment. Oh, great is our misfortune, for in our adversity we have found help and refuge in every foreign country, our calamity awoke pity and compassion in every foreign people, but our own citizens have long hardened their hearts against mercy. Proscribed without reason, persecuted without cause, we have been abandoned and execrated without mercy. But what was I saying? Every age, not only infancy, has its great and serious illnesses, unless you find that adults and old people with their gout, their catarrhs, their hips and sciaticas are light and free, or unless you think that fevers, pains, and diseases cannot afflict strong and healthy young men as well as children. Even if some age is more often subject to fatal illness, is that a reason to condone the father who does not show a fitting moderation and wisdom? Does it seem small folly to you to harbor fear and anxiety in your heart when there is no further remedy for you to apply?

Adovardo: Anyway, I do not want to argue with you or quarrel over fine points. I am satisfied that you consider unwise whoever continues to fear what he cannot cure. You should hardly judge me mad, however, for all that I frequently cannot help worrying about my children. If you do, you must consider all fathers utterly foolish, for you cannot find one who does not struggle mightily and is not filled with fear at the threat of losing those who are dearest to him. If you blame them for this, you condemn fatherhood itself.

But, Lionardo, I must now say this. Let us suppose, if possible, that a father knows his sons will live to a great old age in health and prosperity; that he lives to see the grandchildren of his grandchildren, as it is written of Augustus Caesar the Divine. Let us suppose that he need fear no serious illness, which are sometimes not less terrible and unbearable than death, and that he hopes to be like Dionysius, the tyrant of Syracuse, who at sixty had never had occasion to attend the funeral of any of the children of his three wives or of any of his grandchildren. Let us suppose he has the power of life and death over his sons, to give long life or brief, as happened when the gods granted to Altaea that her son, Meleager, would live as long as a certain branch remained whole and safe, but she, in her anger, threw it into the fire, and as the wood was consumed, Meleager's life ebbed away. Granted all this, I say that children would be to a father nothing if not a source of abundant griefs.

Lionardo: From you, since you don't want to quarrel, this, I suppose, is a statement one had better accept. From anyone else one would be inclined to ask for an explanation before one agreed. Perhaps I see where you are tending, however. Perhaps you have in mind the father of but small wisdom who wears himself out and hammers out his whole life in heavy labor, who goes from hard travel to hard work in endless discomfort and servitude in order to leave his heirs an abundance of leisure, luxury, and pomp.

Adovardo: You know I don't see myself as one of those who spend their time collecting for their children that which fortune can snatch away in a moment, not only from the heirs but even from those who acquired it. I do certainly say that I would rather leave my children rich and fortunate than poor. I heartily desire by working as hard as I can to leave them in such a state of fortune that they need seldom ask for anyone's charity. I am not unaware what misery it is to be forced in one's need to call on the hands of others for help. But don't imagine that a father who need fear neither death nor poverty for his children is free of trouble. Whose is the burden of shaping their character? The father's. The task of having them taught letters and morals? The father's. The immeasurable responsibility of making them learn various sorts of knowledge, art, and science? The father's too, as you well know. To this add the anxious decision which falls upon a father concerning the particular art, science, and career most suited to the temperament of his son, the status of his family, the customs of his country, the circumstances, times, situation, opportunities, and expectations of his fellow citizens.

Our country will not tolerate from one of its citizens an overgreat success in the career of arms. This is wise, for it would endanger our ancient liberty if one in our republic, instead of gaining his will by winning the approval and love of the citizens, could by threat and force of arms go wherever his spirit carried him, wherever fortune seconded him, and wherever times and conditions allowed and beckoned him. Nor does our country admire literary men too much, rather it seems all bent on profit and avid for wealth. Whether because of the nature of the region or because of the character and customs of its past inhabitants, everyone seems bred to the cultivation of profit. Every discussion seems to concern economic wisdom, every thought turns about acquisition, and every art is expended to obtain great riches.

I do not know whether we Tuscans have this character from the heavens, as they said in antiquity that because Athens had a clear bright sky, men there were subtle and sharp of mind. Thebes had a cloudier sky, and so the Thebans were slower and less clever. Some said that the Carthaginians, because their land was sterile and dry, were forced by necessity to visit and to entertain many neighbors and foreigners, as a result of which they became knowledgeable and clever in wiles and tricks. Perhaps for our citizens, too, the experience and the ways of their ancestors have been a framework and an influence. As Plato, that prince of philosophers, says that the Lacedaemonians were in all their customs inspired by the will to victory, so I think in our country the heavens produce minds acute in seeking out profit. The place and its customs urge them on, not primarily to glory but to the acquisition and preservation of goods. They learn to desire riches. With these they believe they are more able to confront necessity and also to attain power and status.

If it be thus, how worried a father will be when he thinks that his children have more aptitude for letters or for arms than for the collecting and heaping up of money! Will he not suffer a conflict of spirit between his wish to follow the customs of the country and his desire to fulfill their greatest promise? Will it be a matter of small annoyance to a father to have to give up the convenience and honor of his children and of his family? Will he not be heavy of heart if, to avoid the spite and envy of his fellow citizens, he cannot direct his son, as he would wish to do and as it would be good to do, toward one or another sort of achievement or honor? I cannot soon call to mind all our troubles, and perhaps it would be too much labor and too exacting a task to try to list them one by one. You should be able already to see that children are the source of innumerable griefs and sorrows to their father.

Lionardo: What sense would it make, Adovardo, if I claimed to you that a father did not suffer trials. Every life, as Chrysippus said, is painful and laborious. There is no mortal whom sorrow does not touch. Illness, poverty, and griefs press down on him; to bury children, friends, and relatives; to lose and build again; to wait for and strive to obtain the things we need for our infinite requirements. And this further pain seems to be the lot of anyone who lives, that he tells over the blows of fortune. Men grow old in their houses with tears, mourning, and black garments. Thus if a father were more free than other mortals from those laws decreed for us by nature, and were safe from those incursions and attacks, released from the many anxieties and concerns destined for all men, ever shrouding the heart of anyone who is not a complete fool, then I would indeed think a father more happy and blessed than other men.

I will not deny that, as you say, the father more than anyone must labor with hands and feet, with every nerve, with zeal and wisdom, for he must attempt to make his children moral and upright. Thus may they serve the advantage of the family—moral character being no less precious in a young man than wealth—and be an ornament and credit to their family, their country, and themselves. Children whose character is excellent are a proof of the diligence of their father, and an honor to him. It is generally thought better for a country, if I am not mistaken, to have virtuous and upright citizens rather than many rich and powerful ones. And surely children whose character is poor must be a terrible sorrow to any father who is not insensible and utterly foolish. Not only will the ugly and disgusting acts of the son be distasteful to him, but, as everyone knows, every errant child in many ways brings shame on his father. This only shows that everyone knows and believes it is up to the father of the family to make the young behave with honesty, restraint, and nobility. I do not believe that anyone would deny that a father can do with his sons as much as he wills to do. A good and careful trainer can make a colt gentle and obedient, while another, less alert and more neglectful, will not be able to break him. The father, too, can make his children educated and modest by the exercise of care and skill. The father of sons who do not behave well but go wild and vicious, therefore, is not without great guilt for his negligence.

Therefore, as Lorenzo was saying before, the first thought and care of the older members of the family should be to see that the youth be as rich in good qualities and moral character as possible. For the rest I would counsel the father that he should rather pursue the good of his family in dealing with his children than listen to vulgar opinion. In fact it appears that virtue almost never lacks for a welcome and a place, for it finds a place anywhere it is praised and loved. I would do, therefore, as did that Apollonius of Alabanda, a teacher of rhetoric, who, if he found that the young people in his charge did not seem to have the aptitude for eloquence, shifted them to some occupation to which they were by nature more suited. He did not let them waste their time.

It is written that those Gymnosophists, Oriental peoples respected for their wisdom among the Indians, raised their children, not according to the will and desire of the fathers, but according to the decision and judgment of certain public sages. It was their job to observe the birth and physiognomy of everyone and to decide the extent and character of everyone's talents, and thus the parents worked according to the recommendations of these wise old men. But if a child were weak and unable to achieve anything, no one wanted to waste money and effort on his education: the sages told his parents to throw him away, and sometimes they drowned him. Thus should a father use the aptitudes of his children, in accordance with the famous oracle of Apollo which gave to Cicero the reply, "With labor and industry, follow where nature and your own genius call you." If the children are ready to develop a noble character, to perform manly deeds, to study the higher sciences and arts, to pursue military victory and glory, let them take up these things. Let them train themselves and learn. Let someone make an effort to accustom them to such things from an early age. Whatever practice is taught to children, they grow up with. If perhaps they lack the capacity, the intelligence, the strength, and the health to undertake the more formidable things, let them be given lesser and lighter training, but always let there be set before them work that is as noble, manly, and honorable as they are able to do. If they are not talented and clever enough to do the things that win most praise, and if they are useless for anything else, let the father do like those Gymnosophists, let him drown these children in greed. Let him make them into moneygrubbers, let him kindle in them the desire not for honor and glory but for gold, riches, cash.

Adovardo: This is another of our troubles, Lionardo, we do not know for certain what career will be easiest for our offspring. We do not easily discern the good road to which nature destines them.

Lionardo: Personally I think a watchful father who really looks will discover without too much difficulty what sort of work fits his son's inclinations and what sort of achievements lie within his scope. What could be more difficult than to find those things which tend to remain most hidden, the things nature keeps covered up under the earth? Yet these, as we know, have been discovered and reached by industrious craftsmen. Who told avaricious and greedy men that down there such metals as silver and gold might be found? Who cleared the hard and obscure way for them? Who assured them that these ores contained precious metals rather than lead? There were signs, there were clues which led men to investigate. Thus these metals came to men's attention and went into use. The industry and diligence of man was so potent a thing that now none of these very well hidden things is unknown to us.

There are also architects who want to build a well or a fountain. First they look for signs, and then they dig, but not everywhere, because it would be a waste of money to dig where there was no good, clean, and rapid stream. They apply their minds to see on the earth's surface what lies underneath, inside, hidden below ground. Where they see the terrain is bumpy, dry, and sandy they do not waste their efforts. Where they see young shoots, soft grass, and myrtle or similar plants, there they hope that their labor will not be in vain. Not without some clues do they begin to establish a structure. They build, moreover, in a way that may best suit the conditions they have been led to expect.

Let the father act in much the same way. Let him note from day to day the ways his son adopts, the desires that persist or recur in him, what he does with most zeal and what he must be persuaded to do against his will. These, in fact, will be ample and clear indications to give and even confirm a complete picture. Don't imagine that the clues to other secrets are more reliable than those contained in the behavior and physiognomy of men. Men are by nature social, willing and eager to associate together, happy among men and averse to solitude. They dislike isolation, and it makes them unhappy. You are certainly mistaken if you think that being thus disposed they give less signs and permit less certainty than other things which are not only deeply hidden but entirely without any need of human acquaintance, presence, and understanding. Nature, the best of builders, not only made man to live exposed in the midst of others, but also seems to have imposed a certain necessity on him to communicate and reveal to his fellows, by speech and other means, all his passions and feelings. Rarely does she permit a thought or deed to remain so well hidden that no other man knows it in some way.

Nature herself also seems to have bonded and incorporated in things, from the first day that they see the light, clear indications and manifest signs by which they fully declare their character. Men are able, therefore, to recognize and use them according to the uses for which they were created. In the mind and intellect of mortal man, nature has placed the seed and kindled the light of a knowledge, an insight, into the remotest, most secret reasons for the clear and present causes of things. He knows whence and for what end things were born. To this nature added a divine and marvelous capacity for distinguishing and discriminating between what is good and what is harmful, between injurious and salutary, useful and useless. As soon as any plant appears above ground, the expert and interested observer recognizes it; and the man with less experience does so somewhat later. Surely everything is recognized before it begins to decline, is put to use before it disappears.

Likewise, I think, did nature deal with men. She did not give to children such hidden and dark ways of acting, nor to fathers such callow and inexpert judgment that they could not, from a variety of evidence, learn the direction of their sons' interests. From the first day that a child begins to manifest some particular desire, the father notes at once what is his inclination. I remember hearing from doctors that if a baby hears you snap your fingers like this, and responds with delight and alert interest, he is showing that his temperament will be suited to manly exercises and arms. If he prefers the doggerel and the songs which people use to soothe him and put him to sleep, this shows that he is born for a life of contemplation and leisure filled with letters and science.

A diligent father learns from day to day, he thoughtfully interprets his sons' every little action, word, and gesture. It is written of the rich farmer, old Servius Oppidius, that when he saw that one of his little sons was always carrying nuts in his apron and playing with them and giving them away to various people, while the other son sat very quiet, mute and sullen, counting the nuts he received and putting them in certain crannies, he knew by this sign alone what sort of mind and nature each boy had. When he lay dying, therefore, he called them and said he would divide their heritage between them lest, seized by some madness, they might have cause to quarrel. And he told them how he had seen that they were of different natures, that one would be tight and avaricious and the other prodigal and wasteful. Where there was such a contrast in them of mind and manner, he did not want an opposition and contradiction of wills to arise. Since they did not have the same opinion and desire in the matter of saving and spending, he provided against the possibility of anger arising between them, lest their firm friendship and love be ruined. This, then, was a man of good, praiseworthy concern. He did what it is a father's duty to do: he was curious and careful to watch every act of his children and used every sign to assess their will and temperament. Thus he observed what each would by nature be able and ready to do.

There are many ways a father can well observe the inclinations of any child. No man, however mature and experienced, no matter how full of malice, artifice, and cunning, is able always to hide his appetites, his desires, and the passions of his spirit. If you keep your mind and your eye on him for several days, watching his gestures, actions, and manner, you will be able to observe any vice he has, however well hidden. Plutarch mentions that a single glance Demosthenes threw at certain barbarian vases showed Arpallus all the avarice and greed that was in him. One sign, one act, one word will often reveal much to you and let you see deep into a man's spirit—this much more easily with children, of course, than with those who are older in years and in malice. Children do not know how to cover up nicely with lies or some kind of disguise.

It is my belief that it definitely shows a good mind if a child is rarely without occupation and is eager to do whatever he sees others doing. It definitely shows his good and easy temperament if he quickly quiets down and forgets an injury. Such a boy is not obstinate in his desires, but without resentment and without overcoming every will he encounters, he puts aside his wishes and gives in without obduracy. A great sign of a manly spirit in a boy is the way he responds to you quickly, showing that he is ready, eager, and ardent to appear among men. He is free of any strangeness in society or rustic shyness. For this it seems that practice and custom are very good. Thus it seems practical not to keep little boys, as some mothers do, always in a room or in a lap, but to accustom them to people and teach them there to behave with due reverence toward all. One should never leave them in solitude, to sit in feminine leisure, or let them withdraw to skulk among the girls. Plato used to reprimand his Dionysius for isolating himself too much. He said that solitude is the friend and spouse of self-will. Cato once saw a boy alone, doing nothing, and asked him what he was doing. The boy said he was talking to himself. "Watch out," Cato said, "you may find yourself talking to a bad fellow." A wise man, Cato was, who knew by experience in the wisdom of his age how the youthful mind is given to burning and corrupt desires of lust, anger, or some kind of malicious opinion or idea much more than to true and unclouded reason. He knew therefore that that young man, busily listening and responding to himself, would more easily consent to his own desires and wishes than to the demands of honor. He would easily disdain continence and the avoidance of sensuality in favor of the pleasures and delights on which his desires and expectations were fixed. By solitude and leisure combined, one becomes willful, vice-ridden, and strange. Young boys should, from the first day of life, be accustomed to life among men. There they can learn virtue rather than vice.

From early childhood they can be made virile by activities as noble and grand as are possible for their age. They should be segregated from all feminine activities and habits. The Lacedaemonians used to make their boys go out at night among the tombs in the dark, to accustom them to fearlessness and teach them not to believe the inventions and fables of old women. They knew what no man doubts, that experience is valuable at any age, but perhaps more than at any other time especially effective in early youth. A man who was raised from childhood to pursue manly and lofty goals will find any achievement that is not really too heavy for his age, if not easy, at least not difficult. Boys should be set from the beginning, therefore, to do arduous and laborious things and to win praise and great honor by their industry and exertion.

Body and mind should be exercised. Indeed it is not easy to give enough praise to the value and necessity of all sorts of exercise. The physicians, and those who have long observed and carefully studied what is good for the human body, say that exercise preserves life, kindles heat and natural vigor, skims off waste and bad elements, strengthens every muscle and sinew. Exercise is necessary to young men, useful to old ones. The only person who should not engage in exercise is one who does not wish to lead a happy, joyous, healthy life. Socrates, that father of philosophers, often used to dance and jump, both at home and in company, Xenophon tells us. In this way he kept fit, and so he even favored for exercise activities which certainly would otherwise have been lascivious and improper. Exercise is one of those natural medicines which anyone can without danger prescribe for himself. Such medicines include sleeping and waking, eating and fasting, heat and cold, a change of air, resting and taking more or less exercise according to need. At one time, indeed, the sick used to purge and strengthen themselves by the use of diet and exercise alone. To children who are still weak on account of their babyhood and can hardly hold themselves up, much rest and long periods of inactivity are proper. When they are kept up and made overtired, they only grow weaker. When little children have reached a somewhat stronger age, however, and ever after, inactivity is most detrimental. Inactivity fills the veins with phlegm, the blood becomes watery and pale, the stomach grows delicate, the sinews lazy and the whole body slow and sleepy. The mind by too much inactivity goes sour and murky. Every power of the spirit becomes weary and inert. Exercise, on the contrary, acts for the good. The whole constitution fills with vitality, the sinews grow inured to labor, every limb is strengthened, the blood thins out, the flesh gains solidity, the mind is quick and happy.

This is not the place to explain fully how useful exercise is and how needful at every age, but above all in youth. Look at boys raised in the country with plenty of physical labor and sunshine: how much stronger and more robust they are than our own children who grow up in leisure and, as Columella put it, in the shade. Death itself could not make them more hideous. They are pallid and dried out, have shadows under their eyes, and have runny noses. They need to be put to work, both to make them stronger and to save them, by training in every manly art, from sinking into lethargy and inertia. I admire men who accustom their sons to going bareheaded and having cold feet, to staying up well into the night and to getting up before dawn, yet give them such things as their personal dignity requires and as are needed for the strengthening and growth of the body. They get their children used to hardships and make them as manly as possible. These things when they do no harm do more good than things that do neither harm nor good.

Herodotus, the ancient Greek known as the father of history, wrote that after the victory of Cambyses, king of Persia, over the Egyptians, when they gathered up the bones of the many dead tumbled together, it proved easy to sort out the Persians from the Egyptians because the skulls of the Persians fell apart at the slightest shock while those of the Egyptians would hold up under sharp blows. The reason for this, he says, is that the Persians were delicate and always kept their heads covered, while the Egyptians accustomed themselves from childhood to go bareheaded in the heat of the sun, in the rain, at night, in wind and open air. One should certainly ponder the value of this custom, for it is also said that thanks to their habits hardly any of the Persians ever got bald. Lycurgus, that wisest king of the Lacedaemonians, wanted his citizens to habituate themselves from childhood, not to easy ways but to arduous exercises, not to loitering happily in the piazza but to spending their time in the fields in agriculture and in military pursuits. How well he knew that exercise is effective training. Aren't there, even among us, some who at first were weak and inept, but who became agile and strong? Haven't some men by vigorous practice turned into excellent runners, jumpers, throwers, javelin men, archers, though they were at first in these respects completely ignorant and useless? Did not Demosthenes, the Athenian orator, have by nature a slow and halting speech, but make it fluent and supple by exercising? He filled his mouth with pebbles and declaimed in a loud voice, standing by the seashore. This kind of practice improved him so much that eventually there was no smoother speaker than he, no one more precise and correct in his enunciation. Thus exercise is not only able to change the body, but in matters of mental skill it is also able to teach us as much as we, guided by reason and wisdom, decide to attempt.

Exercise certainly not only can turn a languid and drooping person into a fresh and vigorous one, but it can even more effectively make a bad and vice-ridden human being into an honorable and disciplined one. It can make a weak intellect powerful, and change a poor memory into a very precise and powerful one. No one can have been so spoiled and made so strange and hard that effective diligence and zeal cannot entirely transform and restore him in a matter of days. We hear of Stiphonte, a philosopher of Megara, that he was by nature inclined to drunkeness and lust, but devoting himself actively to learning and virtue he so successfully overcame almost his very nature that he became better than other men. Virgil, our divine poet, was a lover when he was young. Likewise many other great men had, as we know, some defect of character at one time. Later, however, by zealously engaging in honorable activities they reformed themselves. Metrodorus, an ancient philosopher who lived at the time of Diogenes the Cynic, achieved so much by the practice and training of his memory that he was not only able to link together things said by many different persons, but to cite their exact words in the original order and place. What about that Sidonian Antipar, who, by continual exercise and practice, was able at all times and on whatever subject was being discussed to provide hexameters, pentameters, lyrics, comedy, tragedy, and every sort of poetry, which he could quote straight away without even pondering for a moment! Thanks to the thorough exercise he had given his intellect, things were possible and even easy for him which learned men today, because they have less practice, find difficult even with time for preparation. Exercise in difficult skills did so much for these men, how can one really doubt its effectiveness in general? The Pythagoreans well understood this fact. They strengthened the memory by the use of exercise and by every evening committing to memory something they had done that day. Perhaps it would be good for children, similarly, to listen every evening to a recital of what they had learned during the day.

I recall that our own father often used to send us as messengers to various people on unnecessary errands, just to train our memory. He also often asked our opinion of different things in order to sharpen and awaken our intellect and mind. He would give high praise to the one who spoke best, and thus incite us all to contend for honor. It is good, in fact it is a duty, for a father to test his children's minds in many ways. He should be on the watch and note their every act and gesture. Then he can encourage the good and virile sort of boy and correct the lazy and self-indulgent ones by giving them exercise that suits the situation and the need. It is said that to exercise the body immediately after a meal is harmful. To move vigorously and sometimes to tire oneself out before food is not harmful, but it is not good to exhaust oneself. To exercise the powers of mind and spirit, however, is good at any hour, in any place, and in all things. Let fathers then take up this task not as a melancholy burden but rather as a pleasure. You go hunting in the forest, you tire yourself, sweat, stay all night exposed to wind and cold, all day exposed to sun and dust, in order to see an animal run and to catch it. Is it less pleasant to watch two or more minds racing to attain excellence? Is it less useful by your worthy and excellent efforts to dress and adorn your son with manners and a good education than to come home sweaty and exhausted, carrying some wild prey? Let the father gladly teach his sons to pursue excellence and fame. Let him encourage them to compete for honor, and celebrate the victor. Let him delight in having sons who are quick and eager to merit praise and love.

Adovardo: Certainly, Lionardo, I enjoy your abundance of ideas. I like each of your counsels, indeed I thoroughly approve of this principle of exercise. I agree that we can, by exercise, eliminate vices and strengthen character. But indeed, Lionardo, I don't know how to say or express very well what I feel in my own mind. This business of being a father includes cares and labors which are neither as rare nor as light, nor as welcome and pleasurable, as you perhaps think. How shall I put it? Children grow up, and the time comes, as you say, to shape their character. Fathers are not able to do it themselves, perhaps because of the pressure of greater concerns. Their mind and spirit are occupied elsewhere. They may not leave other public and private business in order to raise and educate their sons. Thus a tutor is needed. You often are forced to hear them protesting, to see them grow pale, to watch them being beaten. Often you yourself have to beat and punish them. This may seem nothing to you, I know, if you don't know the love and pity of a father, how tender and compassionate his feelings are. The children may still turn out gluttons, scoundrels, and liars, full of vice. I don't want to set forth all our sorrows here, nor could I without grief.

Lionardo: Perhaps so that I really may believe you don't mind the length of my remarks, here you immediately offer me another theme on which I might permit myself an even longer speech. I accept the opportunity, for at this moment I know no better way to make use of our leisure than to discuss useful things of this kind. It would please me to give you pleasure, if such is the case. If necessary, perhaps I may erase a wrong opinion from your mind.

Tell me, Adovardo, what do you think should matter most to a father, business, matters of state, trade, or the good and salvation of his children? The ancient and famous philosopher Crates used to say that he longed to climb up on the highest spot on earth and cry out to the whole world: "Oh foolish citizens, where are you rushing to—why, plunging to your ruin? You pursue your gathering of riches with so much effort, such anxious care, such a multitude of devices and infinite labor. Of those to whom you will give and leave them, do you have no care, no thought and concern?" Let concern for one's children come first. Concern for the things which we strive after because they may be useful and convenient to our children, let that come second. There is a kind of madness in doing nothing to make sure that those for whom you acquire property may deserve to possess it. It shows scant wisdom to want your children to have property to drag along and manage which they neither understand nor know how to manage. No one really thinks riches are anything but trouble and harm for one who does not know how to use and preserve them. I would hardly think well of one who gave a spirited and noble horse to a person who did not know how to ride.

Who could doubt that an army should and must carry machinery and weapons for making a siege, for walling in a host, for sustaining the attacks of the enemy, for throwing missiles, and for pursuing the fleeing enemy? But who is such a fool as not to know that an army loaded down with too many arms and too much machinery is useless? What wise person would not judge that all those things which are useful in moderation are harmful when they are present in excess? Arms in sufficiency are most useful in defending one's own safety and in attacking the enemy. If you have an excess of arms, certainly you must throw them away to win, or lose in order to keep them. Better, then, to arrive at victory without that perilous burden than, out of fear of losing, weigh yourself down. No ship, I think, is safe when overloaded with the things which help a ship to navigate safely, like oars, rigging, and sails. In all things it is true that too much is as dangerous as the right amount is useful.

It would be no small riches to leave our children if we might leave them deprived of no necessity. It certainly would be riches to leave our children so much of fortune's goods that they might never need to speak those bitter words, those words most hateful to a free man's mind: "I beg." But certainly still greater would be a heritage consisting in such a disposition of mind that our son would know how to suffer poverty rather than bring himself to beg or to enslave himself for riches. Great enough will be your heritage if it suffices not so much for all your necessities as for your will. I refer here only to an honorable will. Dishonorable desires always seem to me more like madness and vice than like true aims. That which you leave to your children in excess of their true aims becomes a burden. It is no work of paternal love to burden one's children, but rather to lighten their load. An excess load is hard to balance. What is not easily balanced may fall, and nothing proves more fragile than riches. I would not call it a gift from father to son, either, if it is a gift that will bring him pain and servitude when he tries to keep it. Troubles and heavy burdens we shall bestow rather on our enemies. To our friends we shall give joy and liberty. I won't admit that such riches as lead to servitude and suffering are true riches—yet that is what excessive riches certainly do. It will do our heirs less harm to have to work hard to support themselves than to end up losing the whole superfluous and clumsy load, including the useful and convenient part of it. This is what inevitably happens to those who do not know how to manage and use the goods of fortune. All that your children do not know how to handle and manage will be superfluous and disadvantageous to them. It is good, therefore, to teach your children character. Make them learn first of all how to govern themselves and moderate their own appetites and will. Give them an upbringing such that they may be able to win praise, grace, and favor far more than riches. Teach them to be wise in all civic matters, particularly in guarding their status and their claim on the general good will. Indeed if anyone knows in this way how to ornament his life with fame and dignity, he will certainly also be wise and well versed in the achievement and preservation of every other lesser thing.

If the father is not himself capable of teaching, or is too busy with more important tasks (if anything is more important than the care of one's children), let him find a person from whom the children may be able to learn to say and do honorable things in a good and wise way. Thus Peleus, they say, gave his boy, Achilles, into the care of Phoenix, who was very wise and very eloquent, so that his son might learn from him to be a good speaker in words and a good doer of things. Give him, in other words, to one who knows more than he does. Put him close to someone who can teach him good principles of action and instruct him well in knowledge and skills of general interest. Marcus Tullius Cicero, our prince of orators, was entrusted by his father to Quintus Mucius Scaevola, a lawyer, who never left his side. A wise father, he wanted his son to be close to someone who could, in a way which was perhaps beyond his own ability, make him learned and well read.

But if a man can himself endow his sons with character as well as with letters and science, as you, Adovardo, can, why should he not leave every other task in order to make them better educated, of finer conduct, more self-controlled, wiser, and more cultivated? Cato, that great figure of antiquity, thought it no shame and no burden to teach his son not only letters but how to swim, fence, and other useful skills both military and civilian. As a father he considered it his duty to teach his sons all that belong to a free man's dignity. He did not think a man should really be called free if he failed of any inner excellence. He wanted no one but himself to instruct his sons in these things. He did not wish to put anyone ahead of himself in them. He did not think he could find someone more interested in his own affairs than himself. He also did not believe that his sons would learn from others with as much love as they would from their own father. The faith, the zeal, and the concern of a father are more apt, than the greater knowledge of another very knowledgeable person, to make the children learn. Personally, I would like to follow Cato and the other good men of antiquity who acted as masters and teachers of their own sons. They taught whatever they themselves knew and wished, above all, themselves to correct every defect of character in their children and make them good. They also attached their children at the same time to wise and learned men, who by more of both practice and theoretical instruction made them become most knowledgeable and most graced with excellence.

Here is what I would do if I were a father. My first and foremost concern would always be to make my sons very well behaved and respectful, but if my child did slip into some misdeed, I would remember that some misbehavior is part of childhood. Children should be reprimanded in a moderate and reasonable way, and sometimes also with severity. One should not, however, fall upon them in a savage rage, as some wild and furious fathers do. I prefer punishment given without anger, without turbulence of spirit. I like what they say Architas the Tarentine did when he said, "If I were not angry, I would give you what you deserve." A wise speech. It seemed to him he could not punish another until he had first subdued his own anger. Anger does not go well with reason; and to reprimand someone without reason seems to me one of the most foolish things one can do. A person who cannot offer correction with a balanced judgment does not, I think, deserve to be either a father or a teacher. Let a father correct his children with a tranquil spirit free of all anger, but let him always prefer to see his sons weeping and chastened rather than laughing and licentious. They should be reprimanded and punished for all their deficiencies, I think.

Above all there are those vices which are most common in children, but also very harmful and dangerous and more worthy of care and concern than most fathers realize, namely the tendency to obstinacy and self-will. Any inclination a child may have to become a liar and deceiver must also be caught. The child who is obstinate and self-willed in saying and doing what suits his opinion never pays attention to the good counsel of others. He always has too much confidence in himself and believes more in his own opinion than in the prudence and reason of someone else who is very experienced and wise. You may see him standing proud, swollen, full of poison and of hateful, unbecoming words. Thus he lightly brings on himself the dislike of everyone. On this I like the saying of Gherardo Alberti, a great opponent of any sort of obduracy and himself liberal, affable, and humane. He would compare the head of an obstinate and stubborn fellow to glass, for just as no pointed instrument, however sharp and strong, can engrave on glass or penetrate it, so an obdurate man's opinions are fixed and rigid, and he never consents to any reason presented to him, however subtle and strong, or listens to any friend's advice or to anybody's plan, however sure and right, but persists always in his own unbending views. Like glass also, which shatters at a light blow, the hardened and willful man bursts into anger and pours himself out in mad and furious words which scatter and overflow. He is obliged to regret his hardness later and to suffer for it. Diligent, wise fathers and elders therefore must look ahead and early purge this greatest vice and every evil resembling it from the minds and habits of their offspring.

They must not allow any evil root to grow in the thought and behavior of their children. Old bad habits solidify as they strike roots that get big and tenacious. One who cuts down an old tree with strong roots later sees more and more branches and shoots growing from the the trunk. So it is with the vice that is well rooted in a man and confirmed by practice: once accustomed to extend itself and fill up space wherever the will urged it on, now bound in and cut back by the sharpness of the times and by necessity, the spirit still seems to branch out on all sides in other vices. A person who once, when he had a great and noble fortune, lived as a prodigal and indulged his lusts, later, impoverished by new adversities, still greedily pursues some old habitual luxury. To satisfy his appetites and gratify his willfulness he becomes a thief, a confidence man, an extortioner. He plunges into the ugliest practices and the most vile and infamous of occupations in order to restore by ugly deeds the riches which, by ugly deeds, he lost.

So it happens that a person who has long been accustomed not to tolerate anything that runs counter to his pleasure, and to pursue greedily whatever he enjoys, a man who has always bullied everyone in argument and action, will, if some chance blocks his way and interrupts the fulfillment of his wishes and plans, seem not even to care if he throws himself into abysses and amazing catastrophes. He does not respect possessions, honor, or friendship; everything praised and desired by mortal men he subordinates to the pursuit of his opinion. Simply in order to do what he is doing, he suffers the loss of his fortune, and even of his life. Such a one, caring little for his own welfare, cares still less for the tranquillity and welfare of his family. It is for this reason an important duty of the father to begin in early youth to dry up and to sap so great and so dangerous a vice in his children as this stubborness. It threatens anyone who is subject to it. It also promises pestilence and death to his whole family. In nothing, not even very minor matters, should the elders permit obstinate wishes or dishonorable plans to harden in their children. Any form of opposition should displease them the more, the more they see that its end is unworthy.

Likewise let them see to it that their children are extremely truthful in everything. Let them think, as is indeed the truth, that lying is a dangerous as well as ugly vice. One who accustoms himself to dissimulate and to deny the truth will often perjure himself trying to appear honest. One who often swears with a lying, deceitful heart accustoms himself from day to day to fear God less and to hold religion in contempt. One who does not fear God, who has extinguished religion in his spirit, him we may call thoroughly bad. Add to this that a liar is in his whole way of life disreputable, despised, and vile. He is a man whom others throw aside in counsel. Everyone scorns him as a joke. He knows no friendship and enjoys no authority of any kind. No virtue, great as it may be, will win respect or admiration for a liar, so disgusting and ugly is this vice. It stains and dishonors any other splendid honors he may have won. Since we have here touched on religion, one should fill the minds of children with the greatest reverence and fear of God, since loving and practicing holy ritual wonderfully restrains many vices.

If it grieves the father to have to correct and punish the children, let him do as Simonides, poet at the court of Hiero, says in Xenophon: "Let them do the enjoyable things for the children and leave the unpleasant ones to others: the acts that give rise to good feeling they should do themselves, the things that give rise to hatred, delegate." Let your children have a master whom they fear, one who, however, punishes them more by fear than by blows. And let this instructor be more concerned to prevent his pupils from making mistakes than to punish them. There are, however, many fathers who forgive their children everything, more from laziness than from compassion. They think it is enough just to say "don't do it again." Stupid daddies! If their son had hurt his foot, the doctor would be called at once, the whole house would be thrown into activity, everything else would be left standing. Yet when the child's spirit falls into some proud posture where he acts and speaks only on whim, when he ruins himself through a kind of greed and begins to sink deep into such an obstinate and self-willed way of working that no reason or argument of any kind can dig him out, why not want the doctor to quickly correct and cure his corrupted spirit? Why not try to quiet his discomposed mind and to bind up his appetites and animal will with reason, warnings, and reprimands? He may still be healed by a sense of honor and fear. The wound of open licence must be treated, that now makes him seem dissolute, disobedient, and subject to every wicked caprice of his spirit. What father is so foolish as to say that he does not want to hear his son weep, that his heart cannot bear to see him punished, and that he cannot attend to this, his primary duty. Would you consider your child's bad character the least of your troubles? I certainly don't think so. I would seem a great mistake, since you know full well that the vices and lusts of one who became wicked through your own negligence will eventually bring you not only shame but a heavy load of grief. In the end a bad son is the ultimate agony in a father's life.

To discipline his sons, therefore, to concern and exert himself to make them learned and good, this is a father's natural duty. He must be like the gardener in the field, who does not mind cutting some good and fruitbearing branches in order to sap the life of evil and harmful ones. The father likewise does not mind, when he is mending his son's ways, if he is a little more harsh than his natural tender feelings suggest. There are some, however, who not only do not guard their children from early youth against bad habits, but actually plant the seeds of a thousand vices. How much don't you suppose it harms a child to see that his own father is immoral, arrogant, and brutal in words and deeds? What if he raises his voice and talks arrogantly at every moment, swears, quarrels endlessly, blasphemes, and rages? The young think that they ought to behave or may behave as their elders do.

We have reached the point where those who raise the young are guilty of such irresponsibility and negligence that the gluttonous children demand chicken and partridge before they know the names of things. They ask for special delicacies before they are even able to chew them with all their teeth. Their father, then, being greedy and sensual himself and therefore sympathetic and amenable to the pleasures of his dear ones, grants them these things. Yet I could excuse such a father, dissolute as he is, if he did not also try to instill excellence and honor in his children by making them weep. He does that because he rightly fears that his children's conduct will someday make him weep. Some you will find who do not like to see in anyone else a vice which in themselves does not trouble them. They are gourmands but hate gluttons. They are perjurers but hate deception. They are obstinate fellows but condemn the quarrelsome. On this principle they are severe disciplinarians. They blame their children for the faults which they know mark their own conduct and disgrace. They slap and beat their sons, and pour out other angers and disgusts on them. How unjust not first to correct in themselves what they so strongly condemn in others! One could say to them: "You foolish, crazy fathers, how can you expect the little ones not to learn the object lesson of your venerable lusts?"

The father, then, should be zealous in all ways: teaching by his own example, instructing with words, and punishing with the rod. Thus let him expel the vices which still flourish in his children, then plant the seed of good qualities in them. His sons may be cultivated men and adorned with all the grace of fine conduct. Altogether, as he keeps them out of indulgence and the kitchen and holds them to the practice of honorable and great arts, he remembers that few things merit praise without hard work.

Adovardo: I am so glad that, however it happened, we entered on this discussion. It is both pleasant and useful, surely. I am delighted, Lionardo, with your presentation, which reminds me of something that sometimes happens at country weddings, when one dancer pulls two files of dancing persons along behind him. So you Lionardo, with a single flow of words, show me at the same time that fatherhood is a joyous and sweet condition, and teach me what makes a truly good father. Up to this point, if I have well understood you and followed your reasoning, you have desired that a father might be more conscientious than compassionate. I am pleased with this opinion of yours and find our discussion a very delightful one. One should not embark on discussions at all unless they be of worthwhile mature matters, as you are accustomed to do and as we have been doing. Let us, then, continue with this dance (to keep my metaphor) which you have begun.

I am going to be a little malicious with you, Lionardo, and act like those who want to be noticed and admired more than others in the circle, who cavil at every word that is not correct or fitting. Just now, Lionardo, you said that one should observe children to see what nature calls them to do. Then you said that it is good to turn them to other ways by means of exercise, and by practice to guide them toward more manly habits and as complete and as great fortitude of spirit as possible. Perhaps all these things seem easy to you. Because those philosophers could do so much with their own character, perhaps you think our labor and help will make the same thing not too difficult for our children, and that we fathers can do a great deal to shape our offspring. If those philosophers, being adults, could initiate and maintain such great changes in themselves, you may think now that it will not be very difficult and nearly impossible for us, first to observe the ambiguous and obscure inclinations of our children, and then to correct and twist them until they follow new paths contrary to those which they follow by the bent and pull of their nature. But even if, in fact, all were open for us to attack with our diligence and zeal, and it were not hard to look into obscure things and alter them with discretion and vigilance, do you think a father would have little trouble weighing two good potentials present in his son and choosing the better? Don't doubt that any father feels great grief at the known evils in his children's character. It is not as feasible as he would like for him to uproot and expel them. But one father mainly longs for them to be educated in letters, another is content if they know as much writing and arithmetic as is needed and necessary in civic life, another delights in seeing them robust, strong, and practiced in arms. I find that I know well enough what to do about this with my own children, but I often hear other fathers complain of the problem. They say that they do not know what to think and that they are afraid they may have made some bad choices.

Lionardo: Do this for me, Adovardo, listen and accept these poorly composed words of mine, but not as if we were disputing in the presence of many or in the public and celebrated schools, where they are accustomed to care about appearing subtle and acute as well as rich in style and erudition. Here between us a freer speech, less well weighed, not so finely polished as others might require, is permitted. This discussion between us has been a domestic and familiar one, not meant to teach you something which you are more informed and learned about than I. Nonetheless, since you draw me on, I shall unashamedly continue and follow your lead as far as you like. In this, as in all things, I shall be happy if I can please you.

The scholars, as you know, say that nature works as much as is necessary and fitting to make every being complete in its members and capacities. Nature tries to keep it free of any lack or defect, so that it may preserve itself in its time and be in many ways helpful to other procreated things. They further demonstrate that every animate being has from its beginning as much strength, reason, and virtue as it will require to seek its necessities and its rest. These will also be enough to give it the power either to flee or to repel whatever is contrary and harmful to it. Now it is true of man that as if guided by some innate power everyone who is not extremely stupid dislikes and condemns every sort of wickedness and dishonorable behavior in others. There is no one who does not see something wrong about a wicked man. Moreover, if we do not reject the opinion of those who argue, with more elaborate reasons, that everything by its first complete nature strives toward its own greatest possible perfection, it certainly seems to me we may say this much—all mortals are by nature sufficiently able to love and preserve some highly honorable excellence. Excellence, indeed, is nothing but nature itself, complete and well formed.

It seems reasonable to go on and say that wickedness in mortal minds and spirits arises through poor customs and corrupted reason. These stem from vain opinions and imbecility of mind. Perhaps I should also admit that nature itself does add some greater or lesser stimulus to the greed and appetites of men. I also remember that the sanguine temperament is more susceptible to love than the melancholy. The choleric is more subject to anger. Inactivity and laziness are characteristic of the phlegmatic. The melancholy person is more inclined to be fearful and suspicious than others, and therefore becomes avaricious and clinging. If in your children, therefore, there seems to be some natural disposition to excellence of mind, intellect, and memory, every effort should be made to encourage it. Following the indications of nature, let them pursue the highest sciences and studies, let them cultivate elegant and accurate thought. If you see that they are robust, high spirited, and eager, more suited to military arts than to the quiet life of letters, then follow nature by first accustoming them to riding, arms, shooting, and the other skills praised in men of arms. You should follow up every good inclination and teach the child as much as seems to take effect. Evil inclinations you must conquer with extreme care and attention. Wise men believe that wickedness feeds mainly on experience. Lascivious and intemperate habits do more harm than any natural appetite or inclination. This is proved every day by the effect of bad company and of frequent visits to licentious environments. There young men whose nature was tranquil, withdrawn, and modest change to become forward, wild, and rash. In other ways, too, some acquired habit may more effectively turn us toward evil ways than our natural appetites. An abundance of rich meals, for instance, makes a man lustful. Hence the ancient proverb: "Without Ceres and Bacchus, Venus would be cold."

Here then are the laws we shall take as established: bad habits corrupt and contaminate even a gifted and balanced nature; good ways of living eventually overcome and correct every appetite that runs counter to reason and every imperfection of the mind. It seems to me, therefore, if the child shows an inclination to sloth, to excessive anger, to avarice, and so forth, the father's business is to draw him up to better ways by having him pursue activities that are good and highly esteemed. If the boy is on the right road to virtue and praise himself, the father's job is to confirm him in this. He will need to sustain him by proofs and examples. For a man may be on the good and right way to the temple, yet he may stop at the theater to gaze and waste his time. Likewise, though the road to gaining fame and praise may lie open and accessible to the boy's nature, he can be led in many ways to tarry and lose his way. The father should be on the watch and quick to recognize the temperament and the will of his sons. He should aid them toward their praiseworthy goals, and draw them away from any loose ways and ugly indulgences. I cannot believe that it is very hard for an interested and mature father to find out to what extent his sons are naturally well disposed and eager to make themselves valued and praised. Nor do I think it too much work for him, if they are running astray in some way, to correct them. Nor do I believe it is a common occurrence for several useful possibilities to confront you with no clear disparity by which to prefer one to another. As to that, I am of those who would always choose honor first for their children—then, as far as it is compatible with honor, practical advantage.

Adovardo: I agree with you there, Lionardo. But I think one should perhaps consider it truly difficult to recognize and to correct the faults of youth. Youth pursues its desires with eagerness. The appetites of the young are vast and unstable. I think it may be almost impossible to establish any system really firmly in a youthful mind. Who, amid so much fluctuation of spirit, can say what is good and what is not good? Who, amid so much uncertainty, can hold to a certain order and system as he corrects and moderates the innumerable faults one seems to see in a young person as he changes from hour to hour?

Lionardo: And who can show a wise economy when talking with you, Adovardo? When I talk with you I find myself in the position of a person who receives a small but very precious gift, also perfectly suited to time and place. To equal it he must spread out an abundance of his household goods. That is how I felt things were going in our discussion just now. You, with a few brief words, give me much cause or provocation for an answer that may well be too prolific and ample. I see that you do like me to speak at length, though, since you listen with such attention and interest.

I say, then, that I would think a man was good enough if there were no manifest defect of any kind in his character. I will call perfect the man in whom much excellence is visible, and not the slightest fault. Those in whom there is excellence, but also some serious and obvious fault, I call less than half virtuous. Faults of character are perfectly clear. Their nature is according to the saying of the Emperor Vespasian: "The fox changes its fur, but not its color." Faults distinctly appear as faults to everyone at all times. They are always ready to reveal themselves and make themselves recognizable. One may note, too, that griefs or poverty or other troubles, though they stop the glutton and the lustful man from fulfilling his ugly desires, yet do not change the fact that when he is free to do so his desires will revive and he will at once return to his first state of mind.

That is why I have been praising the alert father who looks ahead and does not wait until vices have thoroughly taken root in his sons. One should follow the advice which they say Hannibal gave to Antioch of Syria, when he told him that the Romans could nowhere be more easily beaten than in Italy, with their own arms and in Latin lands. One must turn the river near the source if one wants to change its direction. One must not wait until it has grown larger in running over a long course. So should a father act. As soon as even a very small trickle of evil inclination springs up, he should staunch it by correction and seal it over by teaching better ways. He should not let it widen into a major stream, for once it has extended it will be much harder to turn in some other way. Then it will be no small reproach to the father that he was either too blind to see it or too lazy to take care of it.

If, unfortunately, a boy does already abound in wickedness, then the course of his youthful desires must be channeled elsewhere than through the field where excellence is developed. The manly exercises prescribed for his education must not be interrupted. Some place on the side must be found for his desires to run their course without undermining the work of cultivation. It is even possible to work effectively toward the conquest of a spirit already firmly rooted in vice by using wicked men themselves and turning their own arms against them. One may exhibit the life of other wicked men before him as a kind of mirror. There he may look at himself and recognize the ugliness and filth of his criminal ways. He may learn to loathe everything dishonorable and unpraiseworthy. I think it also greatly helps if you show and remind him how much men without excellence and honor are reviled. Show him how much they are hated by every good person and despised by any honest man. Remind him that the lustful are never received among people with pleasure, nor are they ever content or happy in themselves. They are never free of anxieties, always beset by cravings and worries. The spirit of a wicked man is always in disorder and always unstable. There is no mental suffering greater than that which is imposed upon itself by an undisciplined and unreasonable spirit.

I was reminded just now of something I heard Sir Cyprian Alberti say, something I have since thought over and have seen for myself in the world. The wicked man has no repose for his spirit and enjoys no peace of mind. What do you think it is that murderers, thieves, and extremely wicked men think about? Certainly I believe that, every hour, they realize and consider the infamy, the sin, into which they have fallen. Filled with shame, they dare not lift their eyes from the ground but, cowering, they fear the vengeance of God and are ashamed to be in the presence of men. They are always supposing that their evil deed is being discussed with horror by everyone. They constantly believe that other men hate them. They often desire death.

But let us consider other sorts of vice, perhaps less serious because more common. A gambler, a swindler, it seems, can never have any peace of mind either, for when he wins, you see him filled with anxiety and the thirst for further success, at least until he has enough to pay for his clothing, to buy him a horse, and to satisfy his creditors. The will to spend always outruns the money, and so, if he loses, he is consumed with grief and burns with the desire to make up for it. A glutton likewise never has a contented heart. Always some greedy thought is gnawing him. Not even amid wine and drunkenness does he feel content, for he is ashamed to be seen in his vile character. He is afraid that his lusts will be talked about. Then he suffers acute remorse for having ruined his own character. To a prostitute who asked him for ten thousand denari, Demosthenes the orator once replied: "I won't buy remorse for such a price." Thus it is with every vice and every lust. Everything foolishly and shamefully done or said fills the mind with remorse. As Architas the Tarentine philosopher said, no pestilence is as fatal as self-indulgence. This it is which brings treason to one's country, produces attempts to overthrow the republic, and leads men to plot with the enemy.

Ideas and reminders of this sort help to make young men hate wickedness. At the same time it is good to encourage young men to the pursuit of excellence. One should, in every discussion, praise good men to them. Show them how anyone well adorned with noble qualities deserves to be much loved by all men. Glorify good men in many ways. Act so that if our young men cannot attain the highest kind of excellence, at least they will desire to reach a high and outstanding level of praise and dignity. As they highly esteem excellence for themselves, they will also honor it in anyone else who possesses it. The ancients, at their rituals and feasts, used to rehearse in song the praises of their greatest men, those in whom extraordinary excellence had been manifested and had been wonderfully serviceable to many people. Such persons as Hercules, Aesculapius, Mercury, and Ceres were much celebrated and were called gods. This was done both to give due reward to these and to incite others to zeal for heroism and to a desire for similar praise and glory. What a prudent and useful custom! What a good example!

Fathers should not fail, in every discussion they have in the presence of children, to extol the virtues of other men. They should also clearly condemn the wickedness of such as are wicked. It seems to me that anyone not entirely cold and dull has by nature a strong desire for praise and glory. Young men who are more spirited and generous than others desire praise more intensely. It is very possible, therefore, to incite young men with words greatly to love things that are well esteemed and powerfully to loathe all dishonest and vile things. If there be faults in our sons, I would have the father condemn them with all modesty, showing his sympathy with the erring ones as being his own children. He must not berate them like an enemy or persecute them with very bitter words, for one who feels that he is being reviled becomes hardened with resentment and hate. Sometimes he truly abandons himself, loses faith, and falls into a servitude of spirit which makes him no longer care to straighten himself out. Likewise, if there be virtues in our sons, let the father praise them with restraint, because by excessive praise men often become proud and self-willed. I feel it is clear that no father, unless he be heavy and slow, can find this an ambiguous or uncertain system for training his sons well. These are simple and excellent means which allow him instantly to destroy the slightest fault he finds springing up in his sons, and he is able to fill them with a sense of honor and to adorn them in mind and spirit.

Adovardo: I won't deny, Lionardo, that a father as diligent as you would have him could, as you say, in large part improve the habits of his children. This labor could correct and guide them. For some reason that I don't know, however, something like excessive love veils and blinds the father's eyes. He rarely sees the faults of his children until they have already grown obvious and serious. You can imagine how hard it is then to uproot the vice that is already habitual and firm. Even with modest and well-behaved children it seems that fathers do not altogether know where to begin in order to steer them toward the desired fame and renown.

Lionardo: Who does not know that the first useful thing to teach children is their letters? This is so basic that a gentleman, no matter how well born, will never be thought anything but a country dunce if he cannot read. I would like to see the young noble with a book in his hand more often than a sword. I have never liked the common saying of some people, that if you know how to sign your name and can figure out your balance, you have enough education. I much prefer the old tradition of our own family. All our Albertis were educated people. Sir Benedetto was well known as a truly learned student of natural philosophy and mathematics. Sir Niccolaio made a great study of sacred letters, and all his children were not unlike their father. They were cultivated and humane in their conduct, and thoroughly familiar with various fields of letters and learning. Sir Antonio loved to savor the thought and style of an excellent writer. In his honorable leisure he always engaged in most noble arts. He has written the *Istoria illustrium virorum* and some love poetry as well, and he is, as you know, a famous astrologist. Ricciardo has always loved the humanities and the poets. Lorenzo surpassed all others in mathematics and music. You, Adovardo, pursued civil law for quite some time, so that you would always know what is required by law and by reason. I do not speak here of our extremely learned men of an older day, from whom our family originally took its name. I shall not expand on the excellence of Sir Alberto, the light of science and the splendor of our Alberti family. I think it better to keep silent since I could not praise him as greatly as he ought to be praised among us. I shall not speak of the others either, the very young fellows. Among them I hope there will be some useful examples to be passed on in our family. There is also myself—I have done my best not to be ignorant.

So a family, especially ours which has always been universally gifted and especially well versed in letters, demands that the young be trained to grow in knowledge and learning as they grow in years. This is not least essential because the family has many uses for educated persons, as well as because it preserves our fine and venerable tradition. In our family we want our children thoughtfully to follow the example set by their elders and to achieve great happiness through a general education in all sorts of remarkable and elegant knowledge. A father delights in making his offspring well read and learned. You, young men, should do just as you now are doing, you should work hard at the study of books. Be assiduous. Let it give you satisfaction to know past things worth remembering. Let it delight you to know past things that are good and useful. Savor the pleasure of storing your mind with charming aphorisms. Delight in ornamenting your spirit with most noble ways. Try to make your civil life shine by your splendid character. Seek to know human and divine things which, with good reason, are entrusted to writing. No conjunction of voice and song is so sweet and well matched as to equal the harmony of a verse of Homer, Virgil, or any other of the best poets. There is no recreation so wonderful and lovely that it can equal the entertainment and charm offered by an oration of Demosthenes, Tully, Livy, Xenophon, or other orators who like these are elegant and perfect in every way. There is no labor so rewarding, if we should call it labor at all rather than pleasure or recreation of mind and soul, as the reading and study of many substantial works. You come out of it filled with significant examples, abounding in aphorisms, rich in persuasive points, strong in arguments and reasons. Then you can make yourself listened to. You are eagerly heard among other citizens. They admire, praise, and love you.

I shall not, for it would take too long, expand on the usefulness and even the necessity of education for any person who must manage and govern things. I shall not elaborate on the way learning enhances the glory of the republic. Let them forget us, the Alberti family—such is the will of fortune in recent years—let them forget our ancient name. Once it was useful to the republic and known and loved by our fellow citizens. They made much use of us in public matters simply because of the great number of educated and wise men who flourished in our family more than in any other. If there is anything which combines handsomely with nobility or is a worthy adornment in human life or gives grace, authority, and reputation to a family, certainly it is the cultivation of letters. Without this no one can be considered truly noble. A man can rarely be said to have attained a happy life, and a family can hardly be thought of as entirely and solidly established without letters. I am glad, too, to be praising education before these young men here in your presence, Adovardo, since you have always loved the pursuit of letters. Certainly, Adovardo, I think that learning not only gives you pleasure, but is also an asset to your family. It is an advantage to everyone and a real necessity in anyone's life.

A father should make sure that his sons devote themselves seriously to their studies. He should teach his children to read and to write correctly. He should never consider his task as teacher finished until the boys are excellent writers and readers. This is a case, perhaps, where half-knowledge is hardly better than no knowledge. They must learn the abacus, and also, insofar as it may be useful, they should make the acquaintance of geometry. These two sciences are well suited to a boy's intellect, and enjoyable. They are also of no small advantage in my career and at my age. Then the children may go back and savor the poets, orators, and philosophers. Above all be sure they have responsible teachers, from whom good morals may be gained as well as a knowledge of literature. I would like my children boldly to attempt the good authors, to learn grammar from Priscian and Servius, and to become most familiar not with *cartule* and *gregismi* * but with Tully, Livy, and Sallust. In these

---

* *Cartule* refers to the *Cartula,* a much memorized medieval poem *De contemptu mundi* in "barbarous" scholastic Latin; *gregismi* refers to the *Graecismus,* a Latin grammar by Eberhardt of Bethune. Cf. C. Grayson in *Lingua Nostra* XIII (1952) and G. Billanovich in *Lingua Nostra* XV (1954).

extraordinary and splendid writers they may from the beginning encounter learning, a perfectly eloquent style, and elegant Latin. The intellect, they say, is like a drinking vessel; if you first fill it with bad stuff it always retains something of the taste. This is why one should avoid crude and rough writers. One should follow the finest and most polished, keep them ever at hand, never tire of rereading them, recite them aloud frequently, and commit them to memory. I do not say anything aginst the knowledge found in any erudite and abundant source, but I decidedly prefer the good writers to the poor ones, and as there are enough whose work is perfect, I am sorry when people select the others. The Latin language should be learned from those whose language is pure and correct. In the others we may find the other sorts of knowledge in which they are specialists.

A father should realize that education never does any harm, but is of great help in any activity whatsoever. Among all the learned men of whom there have been such a number of excellent ones in our family, none has ever been, by his education, made less than perfectly fit for other tasks. There is no need to explain here at length how much the knowledge of letters always helps achieve fame and success in whatever one undertakes.

Do not think, Adovardo, that I want the father to keep his sons always locked up with books, for I praise the practice of letting the young enjoy all the recreation they need. Their games should only be manly and honest, clear of any vice or any shady quality. They should enjoy the noble exercises practiced in antiquity by good men. I think hardly any game which is played sitting down is proper to a really virile man. Perhaps some such games should be allowed the old, chess and similar pleasures for the gouty, but no game that doesn't require exercise and effort seems to me permissible to young and robust boys. Young men should not be allowed to remain inactive. Let girls sit and grow lazy. Young men should naturally seek exercise, should move their persons and all their limbs—let them shoot, ride, and pursue other manly and noble sports. The ancients used the bow, and great lords were pleased to appear in public with bow and arrow, as well as honored for their skill in using them. We are told that the emperor Domitian was so skilled an archer that if a boy would hold his hand outspread for a target, he could shoot arrows through all the spaces between the fingers.

Our young men should also make use of the ball. It is an ancient sport and highly suited to produce the agility which is praised in a noble person. The greatest princes used to make much use of the ball. Gaius Caesar, for instance, used to enjoy this one noble sport particularly. They tell a little tale of him, how, having lost a hundred at ball with Lucius Cecilius, he gave him only fifty. To this Cecilius said, "What would you have given me if I had played with just one hand, when, after I played with both, you reward one only?" Likewise Publius Mutius, Octavian Caesar, and Dionysius, king of Syracuse, and many others whom it would take too long to list, but who were nobles and princes, used to exercise themselves with the ball. I would be far from sorry if the boys made riding their sport, and learned to carry arms, to run and turn and stop at will, in order to be useful to their country and against the enemy in time of need. The ancients, in order to accustom their youth to military exercises of this sort, used to play those Trojan games which Virgil beautifully describes in the Aeneid. There were some marvelous riders among the Roman princes. Caesar, they say, galloped a horse as fast as it could go, keeping his arms straight down with his hands loose. Pompey, at the age of sixty-two, could shoot darts as well as bare and sheathe his sword while his horse galloped as fast as it could. Thus would I like our young men to train themselves from childhood at these exercises and noble skills, which are no less useful than highly praised all through life. They should learn, along with letters, to ride, to fence, to swim, and all such things which it is often disadvantageous not to know in later life. If you think about it, you will find all these things are necessary to practical and civic life, and are, at the same time, such that little children learn them well and readily without much trouble. These are perhaps most of the skills traditionally cultivated by our ancestors.

Adovardo: Truly, Lionardo, I have been listening to you with joy and delight. Although it did occur to me now and then, I did not want to interrupt you because I so thoroughly appreciated all that your memory could find to offer us—but beware lest you give us fathers too much to do. All men do not have your intellect, Lionardo. There are few who would be willing to persist in their studies as you have. You may, indeed, never see another man as versatile as you, with all the skills and virtues which you would like to see in our young men. What father, my dear Lionardo, could manage to supervise so many activities? What son could ever be induced to learn all the things you have indicated to us?

Lionardo: I might believe you, Adovardo, and think that you enjoyed my various ideas, but I see now that you are but little pleased by all those too necessary things which I am calling on you fathers to do. You are revenging yourself on me by giving me new labors to perform. You are pretending not to know what human effort can accomplish in every domain.

Even a fellow working for money can successfully train an animal to do human things. He can teach a crow to speak, for instance, like the one at Rome. To Caesar it said "Chaere Caesare," and Caesar answered, "In my house there are many to greet me," whereupon the bird talked back and said "I spoke in vain." If we could teach so much to an animal, do you think we are less able to succeed with a human intellect, which seems to be fitted and sufficient to do even the most difficult feats? Yet I do not demand that your sons know more than what it is the business of free men to know.

Nor do I believe that there are many in our family who do not far surpass me in every accomplishment of mind and intellect. Among the many young men whom I see in our house not one seems to me less than handsome, less than capable, less than agile, less than altogether noble. The Alberti family has always had an ample store of fine minds and outstanding spirits. Even if the opposite were true, however, a father as hard working and diligent as you could by his labor do an infinite amount of good. Columella, if my memory does not deceive me, tells the story of a certain Papirius Veterense, who had given a third of his vineyard lands as a dowry for one of his three daughters. He worked so hard on the two remaining thirds that he drew the same crop from them as formerly from the whole field. When the time came, he married off his second daughter and dowered her with half of the field which remained to him after he gave the first dowry. But good God, what can't care and diligence do! What a difference it makes in anything, if a man truly applies himself. No labor is so hard and fatiguing that true zeal cannot accomplish it. This Papirius Veterense with his assiduous work and diligent care made the third of the land which remained to him after the second dowry yield in a little while as much as the whole field originally did.

It would be impossible to describe even half-adequately the great power of will and application in any field. Particularly is this true of the father's role. He lovingly and faithfully cares for his sons' honor and welfare. He feels that he in turn is loved and esteemed. He delights in the improvement of his offspring. He constantly hopes they will attain still greater honor. Indeed, if a father thus delights in doing well by his children, whatever he wishes to achieve he will be able to do. One who is lazy himself, however, and does not care to improve and correct himself, also seems to prove lazy in caring for others. He shows small concern if his children lack noble character. You, Adovardo, however, are as zealous a man as anyone can be. I have never seen you so busy outside your house but you also took an interest in your family, nor so much retired in your home but you were also concerned with matters outside of it. I see you writing letters all day long, sending messengers to Bruges and Barcelona, to London, Avignon, Rhodes, Geneva, and innumerable other places, receiving letters and answering innumerable correspondents all the time. You manage to be with your family and yet to be present in many other places and to feel and know what is being done everywhere. If you can do all this, Adovardo, and handle these distant matters, a father can surely sustain that lighter burden and pleasant duty of caring for the affairs which directly confront him—his children and his household.

Adovardo: I gladly let myself be convinced by you, Lionardo. You have brought me to the point where I am ashamed to keep saying all the time that sons are not a pleasure to their fathers. I see too well that your reasoning will lead to the conclusion that it is only the negligent fathers who have many causes of grief. I admit that the diligent fathers are the ones who turn out to be satisfied and proud of their sons. But tell me, Lionardo, suppose you had children yourself, and that they were getting fairly big. If they were as modest and obedient as you could wish, but you somewhat doubted, as does happen, that they were as capable and gifted as you had hoped they would be in the special arts and honorable activities which, as Lorenzo was saying, adorn a family's honor and make it fortunate, then what would be your thoughts? Not everyone can be Lionardo or Sir Antonio or Sir Benedetto. Who is there who can match your intellect and is equally adept and skillful in everything that brings a man admiration? Many things are easier said than done. Believe me, Lionardo, this is true of most of the work of a father. This may perhaps seem unimportant, but it is really no small cause of worry and grief to a father, who often wonders whether he is not perhaps accepting and following the wrong advice.

Lionardo: If I had children, you may be sure I should think about them, but my thoughts would be untroubled. My first consideration would only be to make my children grow up with good character and virtue. Whatever activities suited their taste would suit me. Any activity which is not dishonest is not displeasing to an honorable mind. The activities which lead to honor and praise belong to honorable and well-born men. Certainly I will admit that every son cannot achieve all that his father might wish. If he does something he is able to do, however, I like that better than to have him strike out in a direction where he cannot follow through. I also think it is more praiseworthy for a man, even if he does not altogether succeed, to do his best in some field rather than sit inactive, inert, and idle. There is an old saying which our ancestors often repeated: "Idleness is the mother of vice." It is an ugly and hateful thing to see a man keep himself forever useless, like that idle fellow who when they asked him why he spent all day as if condemned to sit or lie on public benches, answered "I am waiting to get fat." The man who heard him was disgusted, and asked him rather to try to fatten up a pig, since at least something useful might come of it. Thus quite correctly he showed him what an idle fellow amounts to, which is less than a pig.

I'll go further, Adovardo. However rich and noble a father may be, he should try to have his son learn, besides the noble skills, some occupation which is not degrading. By means of this occupation in case of misfortune he can live honestly by his own labor and the work of his hands. Are the vicissitudes of this world so little or so infrequent that we can ignore the possibility of adverse circumstances? Was not the son of Perseus, king of Macedonia, seen sweating and soiled in a Roman factory, employed in making his living with heavy and painful labor? If the instability of things could thus transport the son of a famous and powerful king to such depths of poverty and need, it is right for us private citizens as well as for men of higher station to provide against every misfortune. If none in our house ever had to devote himself to such laboring occupations, thank fortune for it, and let us make sure that none will have to in the future. A wise and foresightful pilot, to be able to survive in adverse storms, carries more rope, anchors, and sheets than he needs for good weather. So let the father see that his sons enjoy some praiseworthy and useful activity. In this matter let him consider first of all the honesty of the work, and then adapt his course to what he knows his son can actually accomplish, and finally try to choose a field in which, by applying himself, the young man can hope to earn a reputation.

Adovardo: This very thing, Lionardo, is often a worry to a father. He knows to what chances and dangers his young men and children will be exposed, and he would like to have the complete and best answer for every situation. But it often happens that children, contrary to all expectation, turn out stubborn and proud, so that no amount of fatherly diligence can help them. It often happens, also, that a blow of fortune, such as poverty, makes the father decide to take his children away from those good studies and sports by which they are developing in the direction of honor and fame. This deeply troubles the father, who fears either that the boy may refuse to return to the discipline of good learning when he will have reached more mature years and have become more willful and demanding, or that fortune may permanently interrupt the good course on which his children had begun to achieve honor and high standing. If a man is afflicted by so many anxieties, and always fears the instability of fortune and the inconstancy of character of the young, as is the father's case, how can we consider him happy or call him anything but unfortunate?

Lionardo: I do not see, Adovardo, how a diligent father can have sons who are stubborn and proud, unless you mean that he does not begin to be diligent until his son has been totally corrupted. If the father is really alert and provides against vices as they appear, if he is conscientious about uprooting them when he sees they have been started, if he is foresightful and careful not to wait lest a vice become so great and so thick that its infamy shadows and obscures the whole house, surely I think he will not have to fear any stubbornness or lack of obedience in his sons. It may even be that by his negligence and inaction some wickedness has grown and put out some of its branches. The father will never, by my advice, cut these off in such a way that they may in some manner strike his fortune or reputation. He will not separate his son from himself or send him out of the house as some uncontrolled and irate fathers do. Thus do young men already bursting with wickedness and filled with indulgence fall to doing vile things under pressure of necessity, committing dangerous deeds, and living in a way that disgraces themselves and their family. The father of the family will be careful and conscientious from the beginning about correcting every error in the appetites of any of his children. He will make an immediate effort to put out the sparks of any wicked greed. Then he need not later take on the heavy task of extinguishing with labor, grief, and tears a greater fire. As they say, at the crossing is the place to choose your road. The father should begin to note the path his son is choosing as soon as he reaches a certain age. He should never allow him to enter upon an ill-reputed or dangerous one. He must not allow his son to triumph over him in any contest, or to acquire vile and sensual ways.

A father must always act like a father, not odious but dignified, not overly familiar, but kind. Every father and elder should remember always that power sustained by force has always, inevitably, proved less stable than authority maintained by love. No fear can last very long: love lasts much longer. Fear diminishes in time: love grows always from day to day. Who would be so mad, then, as to think he must at all times appear severe and harsh? Severity without kindness produces more hate than obedience. Kindness, the more easy and free of any harshness it is, the more it wins love and acceptance. Nor do I call it diligence if a man, more like a tyrant than like a father, inquires too exactly into everything. This kind of severity and harshness usually makes young minds resentful and ill disposed to their elders rather than submissive. A noble mind by nature resents being treated like a slave instead of like a son.

Let the elders act rather as though they did not want to know some things, than as though they were not punishing something they obviously did know. It is less harmful to the son to think that his father is ignorant of something than to discover that he is negligent. The person who accustoms himself to deceive his father also will think less of breaking faith with some other person who is a stranger. Therefore let the father, present or absent, make every effort to be viewed as a father by his children. For this purpose the first requirement is diligence. It is diligence that will make him loved and revered.

If the father finds nonetheless that as a result of past negligence he has a grown son who is bad, let him rather incline not to wish to call him son than to watch his own boy being dishonest and wicked. Our excellent laws, the custom of our country, the judgment of all good men, permit a useful remedy in such a case. If your son does not want you for a father, you need not have him for a son. If he does not obey you as a father is obeyed, you may be considerably harsher with him than with an obedient son. You should prefer the punishment of a bad man to the disgrace of your house. Be less sorry to have one of your children in prison or in chains than to have an enemy free in your house or a public disgrace outside. A man who causes you sorrow and grief is a real enough enemy.

But certainly, Adovardo, if a man is diligent and cares in time for his children, as you do for yours, he will never encounter at any age anything but reverence and honor from his own offspring. He will always find in them contentment and joy. The character of the sons lies in the power of the elders and the father. Nor should anyone imagine that obedience and submissiveness toward their elders will diminish in children, unless laziness and sloth are on the increase in their elders.

Adovardo: If all fathers could listen to these admonitions of yours, Lionardo, what sons they might raise to their satisfaction! How much joy and wisdom they might gain! Fortune cannot take all from us, I do see, not all, I admit. She cannot give us certain things either—character, virtue, letters, or any skill. All these depend on our diligence, our interest. What of those things, however, which are said to be subject to fortune:

riches, power, and similar conveniences in life? They are almost necessities for the attainment of virtue and fame. Fortune has been ungenerous with us in these things. Fortune is unjust toward diligent fathers, as we have often seen. Most of the time she harms good men rather than less esteemed ones. Lionardo, what would be your grief if you were a father and not able to achieve the honorable goals you set yourself and toward which you had expected to strive. What if fortune did not permit you to do what you would and could do with her help, namely to guide your young sons toward the fame and honor you had expected for them and had already taught them to desire?

Lionardo: Are you asking me whether I would be ashamed to be poor, or whether I would be afraid that virtue might despise us and flee our poverty?

Adovardo: What, would poverty not cause you grief? Would it not weigh on your heart to be interrupted in every honorable course? Lionardo, what would you think then?

Lionardo: What do you think? I would be concerned to live as happily as I could. It would not grieve me much to suffer with a just mind, without annoyance, that which, as you say, often afflicts the good. Nor is being poor so ugly a thing, Adovardo, that I would be ashamed of it. Do you imagine that I think poverty would be so bad, so perfidious and unkind as to leave me no occasion for excellence, that it would give no reward of any kind to the efforts of a man who was hard-working and modest? Yet if you will look about you carefully, you will see more virtuous poor men than rich ones. Human life can content itself with little. Virtue is very well contented with itself. And the man who lives contentedly is rich enough.

Adovardo: Now, Lionardo, don't be such a Stoic about everything I mention. You can say what you will, I would never admit that poverty is not a very mischievous and miserable thing for everyone, and particularly for a father. I willingly agree with your opinion that diligent fathers receive true delight from their sons, but I shall like this still better if I see you supporting your view of all these things not only with most subtle arguments but also with the wisdom of experience. A way should be found, Lionardo, to provide you and the others with a mate and sons. You should take a wife, add to our Alberti family, and diligently raise many offspring. You should use your excellent education so that our house might multiply, as Lorenzo was saying before, in the number of its famous and immortal men. I don't doubt that, by following all the learned ideas which you have just been teaching me, our house may become more glorious from day to day and richer in fine young men.

Lionardo: In this discussion of ours my mind was fixed on nothing less than on teaching you how to be a father. Who is so mad as to take on himself the burden of making you more learned in anything, you who, in every particular field, are more knowledgeable than anyone. In this one, besides, you are taught by experience as well as by the ancient writers. What fool would try to be your teacher concerning the excellent thing which we call a liberal education, or try to contradict you in a discussion of it? But all the cunning was yours, for you spoke to me against having children, and led me to throw away and give up all my old excuses for not taking a wife. I am left with no excuse to avoid this nuisance. I am willing, Adovardo, since you have thus convinced me, that you should have the freedom and discretion to choose me a wife wherever you think wise. Do realize, however, that you owe me a labor in return for what I have done? If I have lifted from your mind the troubles you said beset a father, you likewise should arrange for me to be free of anxiety and continual strife. These, if I follow your advice and get married, I am afraid will not be easy to escape.

They smiled, and upon these words a servant came in saying that Ricciardo was outside. He had arrived by ship and was waiting for horses so he could come at once to see Lorenzo, his brother. Adovardo left to make the necessary arrangements. As Ricciardo was the father-in-law of Adovardo, he felt that he ought to ride out with those who were to meet him. He departed while we stayed behind in case Lorenzo might call for us.

BOOK TWO

De Re Uxoria

 hen Adovardo had left to pay his respects to Ric-
ciardo, who was arriving to see Lorenzo, our father,
my brother Carlo, and I remained with Lionardo.
We were silently reviewing in recollection the lofty
and excellent things which Adovardo and Lionardo
had been discussing at length, concerning the duties
of the elders of a family, the reverence which the
young owe them, and the education of children,
as I have related in the foregoing book. Lionardo,
after a little while, paced twice or three times the whole length of the
room, and then with much firmness, but with an expression of great
kindness, turned to us:

Well, now, boys, Battista, and you, Carlo, what are your thoughts,
what keeps you sitting so silent, self-contained, and inwardly preoccu-
pied?

Carlo did not say anything, but, I said:

I was considering in my mind how unpredictable and variable is the
course of a discussion. Who would ever have guessed, when you began
to talk about the kinds of love, that you would go on as you did to many
different philosophical topics relevant to the family, about which I
greatly appreciated hearing your excellent instructions? But I think we
might have profited more, and certainly our satisfaction would have been
still greater, if you had gone on speaking together about the matter of
friendships. This subject you began to amplify with a different order of
argument and an attractive way of thinking, different, it seemed to me,
from what we find in the ancient authors. I have no doubt that on this as
on those other subjects I might have become more knowledgeable, thanks
to you, and wiser.

Lionardo: As if, Battista, you had forgotten the saying of your Marcus
Cicero, whom you are always praising and whom you love so well, that

nothing in the world is so flexible and malleable as the spoken word. It yields and inclines in any direction you choose to move it. Our own discussion, which, as you see, is just a domestic talk among ourselves, certainly does not call for the kind of correction and emendation one would give to philosophers discoursing on obscure and difficult questions, debating and carefully pursuing every line of argument to its end, abandoning no topic until it is fully explained and cleared up. Discussion among ourselves does not aim to elicit praise of our intelligence or admiration for our eloquence. Rather it is and always has been my habit when talking with men of literary interests, particularly with Adovardo, whose ample learning and acute capacity for thought I well know, at times to ask questions and even, in order not to remain passive and silent among friends, to defend the opposite view from the one which others are expressing. I do not, however, wax obstinate and hard in defense of my chosen position, but yield to the judgment and authority of others as much as the logic of my side of the argument permits.

If I did not answer Adovardo as you may have expected me to do, Battista, I did not do so because I am aware that he is the most affectionate of all the men I know, not only toward his children but toward everyone in the family. I thought it would displease him if I did not admit the validity of love and charity toward one's children as he himself expresses it in practice as well as theory. While at other times I have been glad to contradict every statement he made, in this case I preferred to agree with him in order that he might reveal to me more fully his very affectionate and truly benevolent disposition toward his family. I did not wish to deny the argument he upheld more for emotional than for rational reasons.

Battista: Do you, then, Lionardo, not believe that Adovardo's view is really right? Do you think that children are less dear to their fathers and find less favor in their eyes than do other friends?

Lionardo: I don't doubt that not only Adovardo's sons but many members of his family have always been as dear to his heart and open to his favor as humanly possible. Yet I think it is hardly surprising if Adovardo, a learned man, as you know, but perhaps, on this point, too soft, makes the mistake of subordinating friendship to the other bonds of affection, such as those between fathers and sons, wives and husbands, brothers, or even lovers. Evil fortune has, in the last few days, taken his brothers from him. His ripe age and his reason and judgment, maturing from day to day, have, I suppose, taken away from him all amorous impulses. Our hard and bitter fortune, moreover, has deprived him and indeed all of us of the other delights and joys of friendship. The conditions of our time, the circumstances of our evil fate, keep the Alberti family separated and scattered. As you see them, some are in the East, others in London, Bruges, and Cologne; in Italy, a few are in Venice, Genoa, Bologna, and some in Rome; while quite a number are in France, in Avignon and Paris, or in the Spains, in Valencia and Barcelona. In all these places the Albertis have lived for some time now as merchants of integrity and honor. In Greece, too, as you know, some of our family are scattered, far from their relatives, so that we might well suffer that which people mean when they say "out of sight, out of mind," or "the friend who rarely sees you will not love you forever."

And so our true friendships have not followed us into exile, nor do those spirits who once wished us well wish now to share our misfortune and distress. Back in our country our former rights to favor are left behind, lost along with our real friendships. And many people here abroad who used to show us affection and be familiar with us now have long avoided us. Thus a man's condition, when he is fortunate, will draw many acquaintances to him, while in adversity every memory of his favors and kindness to others is erased. Adovardo does not now enjoy the joy of being among real friends. His sons mean more to him, since they are with him here and now, than his brothers and other relatives. It does not surprise me that he puts paternal love above any other kind. What do you think, Battista, if Adovardo had true friends near him here, and received as much reverence and attention from them as from his own children, what do you think he would think of friendship?

Battista: I think that Adovardo might perhaps differ greatly from your opinion, Lionardo, and from mine.

Lionardo: Among students of your age you constantly associate together in the process of learning and talking. Through this usual intimacy and familiarity you, Battista, are convinced, I am sure, that friendship is the most complete and reliable tie of benevolence there is. And if, as I hope, a noble character grows in you from day to day, you will come to see much more clearly in time how useful friendship is and how it is part of living well and rightly. You may become persuaded, as I am, that, after character, true friendship is the one thing in human life to be preferred and exalted, not only above all other kinds of love but above whatever is precious and highly prized.

Battista: It was always our wish, Lionardo, to become by every art, industry, and labor such men as acquire and maintain many friendships. Now, with your encouragement, we shall strive still more diligently and zealously, if we can, to gain for ourselves many well-wishers and much love. For many reasons will we do so, but most of all in order to follow, here as elsewhere, your example, which compells our admiration in every way. Now, you, Lionardo, in order not to be passive and mute, are accustomed to contradict what your companions have said, and it was your decision just now to consent to Adovardo's ideas in order clearly to bring out his great charity and love toward his own family. Would you consider it overbold if I, in order to learn from you, follow your own custom and defend some positions opposed to the one you have taken? If you permit me to learn from you, you must, with me no less than with Adovardo, show your kindness and good will as well as your excellent judgment. Examine me and see to what extent I may be suited to emulate you in these literary pursuits.

Lionardo: Nothing could delight me more. You, then, while you may, with any other person or in any other place, be anxious not to put yourself in a position to seem overbold or daring beyond what honor and modesty permit, with me have the license to dare whatever you will. I don't so much expect you to learn from me, for I suspect you are probably quite well educated already thanks to your own zealous studies, but I want you to exercise your wits. Wherever you strive to confute my opinions and to persuade me of yours, I shall think well of you for arguing. I shall be especially pleased when you exercise your memory in recalling statements, authorities, and examples and when you draw parallels or use arguments which you have found in good authors and which are pertinent to our subject. All this suits my habit and is what you want. So I shall be very pleased. So you shall see how glad I am to have you exercise your wits with me, both for your good and for mine. I, too, get a certain amount of mental exercise as I try to answer you and argue with you. I beg you, Battista, tell me of the kinds of love, how is your view somehow opposed to mine? And to make our argument clearer, I shall state here and now that true friendships engage a kind of love more durable and more powerful than any other. Now you should clearly oppose to me whatever may be your opinion. Do not hesitate. For the sake of argument, it is always permitted to defend any opinion at all, no matter how false. Do not be afraid, then, of seeming overbold. Fear, rather, to oppose me too timidly.

Battista: Well, then, since you offer me so much freedom, Lionardo, I shall be bold enough to oppose you. Yet I would not want you to judge me by my words, any more than you would by my conduct, as a man less chaste than modest.

Lionardo: I can guess from the way your face is getting somewhat red, and from the way you are stumbling about for words, how you wish to present your opposition. Go ahead. I shall not consider you anything but most chaste, seeing how moderate and honorable you are in discussion. Go ahead.

Battista: I dare then, Lionardo. And perhaps if I say something which you learned men find faulty, I shall be saying it not so much because I think it true as because I want to exercise my wits. If I seem to you to have fallen into the error which I might call the error of persons in love, I think I have enough excuses to offer you. I should quickly enough be able to rid myself by means of reason of whatever you might perhaps think reprehensible. I may be permitted to add, I think, that this love is a force and a law not altogether deserving contempt and blame. It is something imposed by divine nature on any living creature born to reproduce itself and to increase its kind. We see, to begin with, that even the brute animals feel the power of love in some ultimate and minimal way. They all pursue the fulfillment of this natural appetite, with great vigor and with such intensity that ignoring every other pleasure and necessity of their nature they suffer hunger and thirst, heat and cold, and any amount of exertion, just in order to fulfill the craving nature gives them for love. They forget their own lair. They quite forget all their other pleasures, natural pleasures, to which, nonetheless, as soon as they are released and free of love, they again seem entirely devoted. It is a most significant observation, too, that when they are kindled with love, they fight with absolute zeal and ferocity in order to be the first loved. Now, it is clearly apparent in every brute and insensate beast how deeply they are moved by a mere expectation of delight satisfying a low amatory desire. How much more vigorous and how much better armed is love to wound and to subjugate the human spirit. Young men especially lack the inner strength or power to restrain and stop themselves by thought and consideration. They have not enough maturity to resist their insistent and distracting natural appetites. I do not think we young men are able to oppose ourselves to love. We should not be blamed perhaps for yielding.

Alcibiades, a famous and celebrated figure among the ancients and even in our time, was a man wholly devoted to love. He bore to battle on his shield not the emblems common among his contemporaries, but a new sign, that of Cupid with his bow and arrow. Chrysippus, a learned philosopher, dedicated in Athens an image of Love. He set it up in a most sacred place, the special home of all philosophers, namely the Academy, where the good and sacred arts and the disciplines proper to good and honorable living were imbibed and cultivated. If love really deserved condemnation, this man, who was undeniably a very wise person, would not have put that statue in so sanctified a place to stand almost a tangible public witness and expression of his error. If it were an error, even, what man, however cold and insensible he might be, could help consenting to the many delights with which joyful and pleasant love allures him? What austere, altogether antisocial and bizarre creature would flee from love's consolations, from the music, songs, banquets, and many other marvelous things, aside from the ultimate pleasure of which I was just saying that it can effectively sway the most constant mind?

I have observed, in fact, that by its own or nature's law, or through some defect in man, love has always had the power to conquer and to govern mortal men. I do not think that among ancient historians there is any mention of someone, however virtuous he might have been and worthy of every sort of special praise, in whom love did not fully illustrate her power. It overcame not only young men, who are in every way least to blame if they do fall, but even old men, who might seem to have had their fill and to have outlived their capacity for amorous delights. It is written of Antiochus, king of Syria, a man of great age and a most grave and majestic king exalted by his enormous power, that in his old age he was occupied with love and lost control of himself for love of the virgin daughter of Neoptolemy. How audacious it was of love, in a being cold with age and heavy with authority, to kindle flames that you, who speak so severely of them, consider merely frivolous and lascivious. Ptolemy, king of Egypt, too, it is said, though he was as magnificent and proud as a king should be, was struck by love and enamored of Agathoclea, a vulgar prostitute.

Other men, too, and not a few of them, have been overcome in spite of lofty rank, high office, great dignity, and extensive reputation. They have surrendered to love's power great careers and high renown. Among the ancients, I recall Pompeius Maximus, the well-known citizen whose name was celebrated throughout Italy and all the provinces, the one who made the Pharsalian disaster take place and caused the terrible bloodshed of civil war. This man, all his life a zealous and diligent participant in public life, entirely withdrew when he became the slave of love, and took to living in the country among gardens and woods. All the gatherings and salutations of his hosts of noble friends, and all the power to administer public affairs of great importance, meant less to him than to live full of love in the sole company of his most dear Julia. It was certainly no small proof of the power of love, to keep in solitude the mighty soul of one who had unhesitatingly tested his strength in war in order to gain full political power. But it happens every day that we see men neglect their reputation and care less for fame and honor than for love. Infinite, moreover, is the number of those who prefer love to friendship.

We may consider the love of husband and wife greatest of all. If pleasure generates benevolence, marriage gives an abundance of all sorts of pleasure and delight: if intimacy increases good will, no one has so close and continued a familiarity with anyone as with his wife; if close bonds and a united will arise through the revelation and communication of your feelings and desires, there is no one to whom you have more opportunity to communicate fully and reveal your mind than to your own wife, your constant companion; if, finally, an honorable alliance leads to friendship, no relationship more entirely commands your reverence than the sacred tie of marriage. Add to all this that every moment brings further ties of pleasure and utility, confirming the benevolence filling our hearts. Children are born, and it would take a long time to expound the mutual and mighty bond which these provide. They surely ally their parents' minds in a union of will and thought. This is a union, indeed, which one may well call true friendship. I will not lengthen my discourse by describing all the advantages stemming from this conjugal friendship and solidarity. After all, it preserves the home, maintains the family, rules and governs the whole economy. It governs areas of life so vital to women that almost anyone would suppose nothing for them could be more sacred and constant than conjugal love. Yet somehow, I do not know why, it happens not infrequently that a woman prefers a lover to her own husband. There is even a story about a famous oriental queen, in the region of the river Ganges. If memory does not deceive me, her tale is told by Curtius in his description of the deeds of Alexander. She loved a lowly barber and, to raise her lover's status and estate, actually let her own first and true husband be killed.

Of the sacred duty of fathers, there is not much left to say, since you yourself just admitted to Adovardo that it was something deep rooted and firmly planted in the father's breast. Yet there is some greater force, what it is I know not, which sometimes drives this piety out of the paternal heart and, overcoming the defenses of nature, destroys it. In Sallust the historian one may read of Cataline, who for love of Aurelia Orestilla killed his own son that he might take her to wife. Surely love, then, would appear to be a force greater and more powerful than merely human strength. It is obvious that spirits pierced by the divine arrow, with which the poets say that Cupid strikes and wounds the human heart, are too completely subjugated and enslaved to be able to desire or to pursue anything other than what they think desired and loved by their beloved. It is truly astonishing to see how their labors, their words, their thoughts, their whole mind and soul, stand constantly ready and dedicated solely to obey the will of one to whom love has subjected them. Our very limbs are not more obedient and serviceable to us than the lover to the one to whom he has entirely dedicated himself. The beloved's wish he longs to fulfill at once, speedily and completely. From this I think wise Cato derived his saying, which, I believe, anyone would have to admit is very truth: a lover's soul dwells in another's bosom. This force is divine indeed, if love can fuse two spirits into a single will and enclose them in one breast.

What shall we say then, Lionardo? That love is vile? That there is little power granted to love? That love has only a weak hold on the human mind? You may say, perhaps, that love can only do as much and seize such power as we ourselves concede. I know you would like us young men to possess an old man's spirit full of philosophical wisdom, such as I admit belongs to you. But consider, is that reasonable? Are we indeed, as Cherea says in Terence, born full of years? * I am not sure that even your philosophers are able to escape the flame, the certainly heaven-sent power and divine fire.

Aristippus the philosopher, master of those philosophers called the Cyrenean, loved, you remember, a prostitute called Lais, but claimed that his love was not like that of others because, while he did have Lais, Lais had her other lovers. He wanted to convince us, I think, that he alone was a free man though a lover, love being a state which reduced all other men to bondage. Metrodorus, that other philosopher, . . . without excusing his love by any argument, openly loved the prostitute Leonzia. To her even

---

* The following passage is omitted in Grayson's edition but translated in the German version of Krauss: "Some things—it seems—are not permitted to those who are incapable of them, but are the duty, or at least the right, of those for whom they are the greatest pleasure and bring the fullest satisfaction."

Epicurus, that well-known philosopher, used to write love letters. Does not all this show love's awesome power? These were proud and sturdy spirits, whom things almost unbearably bitter to other men, like poverty, fear, and sorrow, could not bend. They proclaimed boldly that theirs was one generation of virtue's disciples. They claimed to despise riches, to conspire against grief, to fear nothing, neither the wrath of their enemies nor injuries nor death itself. Caring little for the gods, some of them, they wrote volumes in condemnation of any fear of things human and divine. All these they claimed are merely the products of that force which we meet and observe as mighty fortune. They despised any sort of indulgence in one's way of life. Even these austere thinkers, however, armed with reason and wisdom as they were, fell and fell low indeed when they were conquered by love. Soft and lascivious love shatters and saps the pride and the aloofness of human hearts! Mere error, delusive wish, contemptible love, whom spirits rich in wisdom, strong in constancy, beautiful and noble in every sort of treasure and ornament of the mind, obey!

Ah, Lionardo, I think of the majesty and fame of those great philosophers and plenty of others too, whom I have omitted for the sake of brevity. I contemplate the honorable and pious character of these men, yet see them descend to such depths for the sake of love. You can imagine, Lionardo, that it might not be hard to convince me not only of the view of these same philosophers, that love is a minister sent by the gods to cherish and to nourish our youth, but that it is indeed divine, far more divine than that. I have not seen friendship do what love can do, making the aged heart young again with fresh and amorous fire, restraining, despite the pride of empire, the royal will and royal appetite, raising an insignificant and meretricious creature to glorious dignity and high estate, or making us despise fame, forget all honor and noble deeds, and lightly tear even the closest bonds of kinship. I hesitate to continue in this vein, for I am much afraid that you may think I am pleading my own cause. Be quite sure, Lionardo, I am not in love. Though I do not experience this passion in myself, however, all the many things I remember having heard and read about it lead me to believe that, in the main, my arguments are sound. I may, of course, appear too extreme in my view and too indulgent toward love. Keep in mind what kind of person you have always known me to be, and whether, along with these views, you have known me to exhibit those habits by which love's cult and triumph are customarily apparent. Yet doubt not that I would put love not only above friendship but above whatever is glorious, whatever is most noble and divine.

Lionardo: I am pleased with your intellectual ability, nor do the examples you bring forward fail to satisfy me. They don't really bring strong evidence to bear, but they do show me that you are as serious a student as I had thought you. I am satisfied with you, Battista, for the way you have set out to try your strength against me. I must warn you, however, that perhaps it were better to admit you were in love and to think yourself in error than to be not in love, yet declare the man who is in love free of error. I would more zealously have refuted all your arguments in order to liberate you from the persuasion and servitude of love. Now, since I need not prove to you the evil of love's madness, which your own examples show in a sufficiently sinister light, I shall just follow up your argument with some notions that occur to me. To make our discussion more clear, that madness, that is, erotic love, I shall call infatuation, and anyone taken with it, I shall describe as enamored. The other love, free from all lasciviousness, which joins and unites our hearts in honorable affection, I shall call friendship. Those bound by such an honorable and benevolent affection may be called friends. The other kinds of love, among members of the same family, we shall call paternal or fraternal as the case may be.

Now let us return to our debate, where you, in order to show the strength, power, and near divinity of love, copiously exhibited the various follies of some infatuated persons. You almost seemed to be looking for all madmen and fools among the men of antiquity, as if no one young and in love might be found today who was just as totally mad as your ancients. But have it your way. Suppose all lovers are plunged into that madness which, even without Cato's admonition, we know is able to take weak and infirm minds to the point where a man finds himself out of control and dependent on the judgment and will of another. Thanks to his error and truly terrible limitless folly, the enamored person puts second all the values of human life, for even a partial attainment of which any reasonable person gladly pays in work, labor, sweat, blood, and life itself. All, however, mean less to the enamored man than his own single lascivious and brutish desire. He does not care for fame, for honor, or for any tie however sacred, if he may but fulfill his vile appetite. What shall we say, Battista, shall we really call this the power of love, or the vice of the weak mind encouraged by corrupt ideas? You, Antioch, and you, Ptolemy, who attracted your heart? Was it the charm of beauty, was it a lovely manner? Rather it was a shameful and immodest craving. You, Pompey, with your oriental queen, what power overcame you and laid you low amid lascivious luxury? Was it a strong affection; or rather a weak mind, a false philosophy, an error all too much your own? You, Cataline, how did you come to tolerate such cruelty in yourself? That was no divine fire and ardor, no indeed; it was your bestial and merciless lust. Love does not by nature bear hate as its fruit, but kindness; not injury, but good deeds; not madness, but lightness and laughter. Then do not attribute such tremendous power to love, since it was for our free will to choose it, for our reason to reject it, and to pursue it was towering folly.

Animals, driven by nature, can in no way restrain themselves. Then no more can men? Certainly not those who have no more reason and judgment than the animals, by which to distinguish dishonor and vice and flee from them. Certainly not those who never saw in man virtues so distinctly our own that nature never granted them to other earthly beings. What man could ever seem remarkable, indeed what man could one even separate from the other brute beasts in their vileness, if he lacked the power of mind, the light of reason? By means of this light he feels and distinguishes what things are honorable. By means of this he follows rationally after praiseworthy ends and seeks to avoid all cause of shame. In this spirit, as far as reason guides him, he loves virtue, detests vice, and urges himself on to gain fame and grace by his good works. By the force of reason, without which a man can hardly be called anything but stupid, he restrains himself from every sort of lust. Take from man the power and habit of reasoning, and nothing is left to distinguish him from the forest animals but a rather different and thoroughly useless set of limbs. The beasts, though without perfect speech, yet have this much at least of reason, that they obey their appetite only when nature demands it of them for procreation's sake. But man sometimes becomes entangled in this pleasure, not to satisfy nature but to satiate and finally disgust himself. He urges himself on in pursuit of an excessive and indeed bestial desire which, since it is subject to his will, is not natural. He keeps spurring his desire with a thousand provocations, little games, jests, songs, dances, and various delights.

Does such a creature not strike you as thoroughly contemptible, lower than any weak and insignificant beast, vile, and despicable? Can one be stupid and senseless enough not to see these dishonorable and wicked deeds as what they are: the betrayal of friendship, the abuse of kinship, the disregard of all morality? Who has ever been so completely lascivious that he did not often feel ashamed of many of his most ardent lusts and appetites? Everyone sometimes fears disgrace, holds back and turns to better things, more happily pursues good character than lustful longings, more gladly answers the call of friendship than that of love. Human nature would be too miserable, too idiotic, if we were always obliged to pursue our amorous lusts. We should be too unfortunate if when love took hold of us it were never possible for us to maintain our primary interest in what is honorable and to preserve the bond and sanctity of family and friendship.

That Pompey of yours, amorous as he was, did he not always put friendship first? Lovely Flora, you remember, was depicted in all her beauty in the temple of Castor and Pollux as a divine creature. Though Pompey was aflame with love of her, yet he allowed Geminius to enjoy her. Thus he preferred to satisfy his friend's desire rather than his own strong passion. Now that, Battista, was a sense of duty, an honorable thing. That was a noble deed of such friendship as always in wholesome minds outweighs the madness of sexual love. Such is the way of true and simple friendship, generous, as you see, and not willing to share and give only property to a friend, but to deprive oneself and yield to him in good will and faith even the object of one's personal and, as you say, divine affections and desires.

Enamored men, however, act not under the guidance of reason, but always in the spirit of madness. If such a man does wish you well, does somehow benefit you and make you more fortunate and prosperous, it is not for your sake he does so, but to fulfill his own notions and desires for the sake of his own satisfaction. True. In this respect, however, it is not only true friendship that surpasses infatuation, so does that other affection, the love of family. In this and in other ways, family has always seemed to me a far more honorable attachment than this foolish and insane passion you have been exalting. Even in old age, and all their lives before, fathers have worked in weariness and danger to earn a living which might maintain themselves and their families. Untiringly they have labored on in their last years, striving with every possible effort and care to leave their children better off after their death than they were themselves. Over and over again they have given themselves less reward in order to provide more abundantly for their children and make them happier. And now I remember the tale of the Roman mother who was waiting above one of the gates in the wall and saw her son returning after

she had thought him dead in the great disaster of the battle of Transi-
mene, whereupon, seeing him safe, she was so overjoyed her whole soul
breathed out of her for joy and she died. What a loving mother, what
passionate love, what marvelous affection, to which you perhaps will say
that it must rank below your divine infatuation! There only madness, here reason! There shame, here honor; there vice, here excellence;
there cruelty, here gentleness!

I do not think I should go further here in condemning that infatuation
you were praising. Nor is this the place to sing you the praises of
friendship, which is not something one can do in a cursory manner. Of
friendship I have always thought with Cato, the best of Latin Stoic
philosophers, who said that friendship is a more firm and lasting bond
than any tie of kinship. I might adduce for you the cases of Pylades and
Orestes, Laelius and Scipio, and a great number of other ancient friends.
United by love and affection, these men did not, like your enamored souls,
abandon public duties and gloriously disgrace themselves by going mad.
They did not kill their wives and children, but rather, with a lofty spirit
and great nobility, left high favor and long lasting memory of themselves
as they faced the danger of death itself in order to save the life and fame
of their friends. Who could recite the praises that friendship merits? This
much I do urge on you, my little brothers, let us flee this amatory
madness, nor seem to put it above friendship. Better, let us not even call it
one of the goods of this life. Love has always been burdened with deceit,
sorrow, suspicion, regret, and grief. Let us flee, then, from this kind of
love. Let us give it the ample detestation it deserves. Clearly do men see
and sadly do they experience that this is a source of all kinds of disgrace
and suffering.

Battista: Because of my age and my reverence for you, Lionardo, I dare
not resist your authority and your arguments. Indeed, were I not inclined
to think that perhaps you are as pleased to see me argue as fall silent, I
should hesitate not only to oppose you but even to defend any part of my
position, however just. I am sure you realize my view coincides with your
own in judging of friendship and infatuation. I too would never give
more glory and praise to the enamored than to the friend. Yet I wonder
whether you really want me to assent to the proposition that every
passionate love is mad and every friendship perfect. I would never dare to
deny your claim that true friendship is strong, but I think, perhaps, it is
less powerful as a force than passion. Who indeed, unless it be you with
your eloquence, could persuade me that today in our time there are

friendships like those of Pylades and Laelius? Passionate love, certainly, is just what it has always been, in rich and in poor, in lords and in serving men, in old and in young. It remains such that no age, no estate, no human heart is empty of that amorous flame. You call it madness. I do not know by what name I should rightly call it, for I have not now or in the past felt and known it in my own experience. I say of it no more than I have heard from yourself and read in the works of others.

Lionardo: Don't imagine, Battista, that the human mind can contain any fire of erotic love without an ample admixture of folly and madness. If that is your own view, it will be as generally acceptable to me as you hope. Let me remind you of what Sophocles, the ancient philosopher, said when he was asked how he got along with Venus: "Any other evil, dear God, sooner than not escape taking that ruffian and lunatic for one's master"—this, you'll agree, is no more than a just judgment of love. Truly she is a master to be fled and to be hated. While you say that in our days you find no perfect friendship, at least you will agree with Sophocles that all erotic love is mad and brutish.

But let us not insist on considering friendship only in the highest and most wholly perfect form. Let me grant you more freedom in argument than this. Let us accept as examples those six hundred friends of Diantunno who were in Gaul. Caesar in his *Commentaries* describes them as mercenaries who, by accepted custom, readily faced any danger for each other. Among so many men you certainly will not easily find that true friendship where you might insist on one will speaking for yea or nay where friend or honor is concerned, one spirit, as they say, ruling two persons. Yet you could not deny that these men showed a kind of true and perfect friendship. Whatever the degree of praise you would allot to this comradeship, it could never seem mere infatuation. Nor could you reasonably say it was a less powerful force than erotic passion or less potent in its practical effect. Suppose that one of these mercenaries did offer (as they customarily did for each other) to sacrifice labor, blood, and life to save someone's honor and fortune. Only an utter fool, I suppose, would think it less than the same offer from some enamored admirer, moved by a fit of generosity rarely found in love.

You can be sure, Battista, that you and any other young man will find more of such imperfect friends who will give you of what is theirs than loving girls who will not desire and ask you for what is yours. If for the sake of argument you should care to assert the opposite, I would ask you which seems more honorable, passionate love or friendship. I know that you believe good minds are sensitive to honor above any other sentiment, as they are in fact. I know that you would answer, therefore, that friendship certainly is more honorable, likewise more lasting and constant and therefore definitely both more useful and more pleasurable. To liberal minds with a good education, like your own, nothing dishonorable could appear other than ugly, useless, and wholly to be shunned. Be assured, Battista, and you, Carlo, that in the life of mortal men nothing except virtue itself is more useful than friendship—nothing more completely happy and adapted to every condition of life. Not by force of madness, but by reason and on the basis of a whole and consistent judgment, friendship serves the needs of the poor, delights the prosperous, pleases the rich, is necessary to families, to principalities, and to republics. It is a help to man at every age, in every sort of life, in every condition. This is a delight proper to human life. Seek to make many friends who will serve you and our family well. Continue with hard study and good reading and learning to flee all idleness, all sensuality, and lustful love, which is nothing but folly and a brutish thing. Love honor as I see you do now. I hope and pray you always will.

Battista: We shall never fail for lack of trying, Lionardo, or for lack of eagerness to be obedient to you. We long to model ourselves on you in this and every other question of moral wisdom. Since you further assure us that even ordinary friendships may serve not only our own welfare but that of the whole family, we promise you gladly, Carlo and I, to apply our energies and our minds to the family's honor and the family's good. You shall see the proof whenever some sort of work or danger tests our readiness and the firmness of our resolution.

Lionardo: For this I praise you, my little brothers. This is what I expect of you. May God and fortune be as kind and as propitious as I would have them to your studies. Always keep in mind that among the few things which are really vital to the family, and without which none can be fortunate and distinguished, friendship has always, under all circumstances, been the chief. Always remember what your father was just telling you. The first means to the love of others is avoidance of evil ways, and love of virtue. In this and in all that is important and valued in our family, I want you to do what you have promised me. For your effort and industry I know that you will be held very dear and cherished among your kinsmen as well as admired and honored by others.

Battista: Since this is your wish, Lionardo, and we mightily hope to satisfy you, now let it be your task to make us wiser in whatever may best serve our family. Having learned from you, we shall be more able to fulfill your will and our duty and also to satisfy the expectations of our kinsmen. Our studies and our will to learn seem acceptable to you, and you are at the moment perhaps more than usually free to help us. Thus by your efforts we may grow day by day in conduct and character. I pray you, please, relate to us what are the ways and the things that, as you were saying, are useful and vital to the family. We have enough time. Our father is resting now. You, I believe, are not at this moment obliged to attend to other duties. For us to learn from you here shall be great reward and high honor. Eventually we hope by our efforts to become as dear and as acceptable in the eyes of our kinsmen as is your wish. Therefore, Lionardo, if it please you now to be so kind, pray show us the humane and open manner which most effectively works every day to make us better men. Pray give your attention to our studies and our needs. Let us take advantage of this time to learn from you, and so someday, perhaps, we may arrive at glory. We may hope to bring advantage and high praise to our Alberti family. If you hope, Lionardo, that we shall never fail to follow your precepts, do not fail fully to guide and instruct us now.

Lionardo: All these things we have: time, and affection for you, and an interest in your education. Even if I were called to other occupations, I would always think this something that ought to come first—to satisfy your praiseworthy desires and wholly honorable ambition. You must realize, however, that these things are diffuse and more complicated than you may suppose. The answers are scattered and almost hidden among a great quantity of various and diverse authors. To order them all and set them forth in their proper places would be a heavy task even for a very learned man. I should need to have thought it all over first, to have made my selections, and to have polished up each part. Even then I could not set it forth and explain it all clearly without a better memory. But I know, little brothers, that all these things are hardly possible for me. If I should simply try to pour out here on the spot whatever I thought of, my listeners would feel like people taking a walk at the first whitening of dawn. Those who knew the country by experience and had seen all the places in the light of day would recognize them and could say what they were and who lived there. Even in that shadowy light they would still be able to see whether there were more or less things than usual there. But others, who had never seen the country in better light, would gaze hard and see little, some being pleased and others discontented.

That is what would happen to me soon enough unless I clarified my mind with much study and preliminary reading of various authors. This would be the result of not having distinguished and arranged my topics like a general who musters his troops and regiments in good order on the field. I would myself be excessively disturbed as I spoke. To yourselves I should be of small use, offering poorly prepared teaching. Nor could I, in the darkness and shadow of my unaided and poorly illuminated memory, be able to give you anything but perhaps the shadow of such learning as is perfectly presented elsewhere. Here it would be almost impenetrable to you and even less clear to me. I would incur the disdain of the learned and not even gain the admiration of the ignorant.

You would do better, in fact, to explore the realm of erudition for yourselves. Take better guides and higher authorities. Among the Greeks you have Plato, Aristotle, Xenophon, Plutarch, Theophrastus, Demosthenes, and Basil. Among the Latins you have Cicero, Varro, Cato, Columella, Pliny, and Seneca, and there are many others. With these guides you could more successfully reach the high ground where the fruits are rich and beautiful. Even if I were adept and familiar with so much material, Battista and my Carlo, too, would you not think it a little presumptuous of me to enter freely on such a great field? Would I be able to cut clear across it without making a fool of myself? Who do you think would listen to me? The learned I could tell nothing that they did not know well already. The ignorant, of course, would make poor judges. They would hardly know how to assess either me or my opinions. As for those with a smattering of learning, they would demand of me the most perfect and polished ancient eloquence. Then think whether it is not best for me now to preserve my silence. It is never any use, after all, talking where there is no one able really to listen.

Battista: If I did not know your generous ways, Lionardo, and that you have never been one who had to be begged for favors, I would almost suspect that perhaps you were denying me this great boon only because I had not pleaded hard enough. If you have no other reasons for remaining silent, you ought to be moved by my prayers to find some way of giving us what we ask and expect of you. Nor can I see why you should hold back at this time. No one will have any cause to do anything but praise you if you are willing to make yourself useful to your relatives and always try to help them reach worthy paths to fame and greatness. These are informal conversations. What sensible person would ask for more polish or more exquisite eloquence than necessary? I do not doubt that your

memory and your intellect are more than sufficient and that you are
equipped with every sort of knowledge to satisfy our needs. We in turn
are eager to learn—from anyone, of course, but most of all from you.
Gladly do we listen to others, as instructors. But to you we listen most
joyfully, as the best of teachers, a friend, and a brother. If you are really
falling away from your usual affability, if our studies are not close to your
heart, if you want to be more insistently begged, look then at Carlo here,
whose spirit and whose voice can always move your gentle nature to do
what he wants. Believe me, he is asking you now with a silence more
eloquent than any prayers he or I could offer. One who silently waits, as
he is doing, shows that he longs only to listen.

Lionardo: Would it please you then to hear me?

Battista: As greatly as you see it would.

Lionardo: Your desire is really great enough to hear me out?

Battista: Nothing could please us more.

Lionardo: Then I could not and would not fail to satisfy you. Don't
expect more of me, though, than just whatever comes to mind, bit by bit.
I shall tell you what it is best and most useful to know to keep a family
from falling into misfortune. I shall also tell you what is most suited and
likeliest to improve it and to raise it to highest prosperity and fame. How
shall we proceed? Have you something to ask me? I would then answer
you. Or does it seem better for me to continue my recital without
interrupting myself?

Battista: Whatever you think. The only question we have is what are
the things that make a family fortunate. Go on with what you have to say
and we shall listen.

Lionardo: All right. Let us proceed that way. You must hold me back
if I seem to be going too quickly. I shall try to cover this subject as briefly
as I can. Listen then. Often in these dreadful days, and particularly today,
I consider the way fortune seems to persecute us to our great undoing. She
never seems to tire of adding new sorrows to our lot from day to day,
miserable wretches that we are. Nor does she seem satisfied with having
scattered us through all the world and oppressed us with many disasters,
so that we go ever wandering in foreign lands far from our brothers, our
sisters, our fathers and friends and wives. Often when I think of all this, I
cannot hold back my tears, O cruel fate! I weep over our fall, and suffer
all the more, my brothers, now that I see your father, Lorenzo, thus
gravely ill. We are threatened with the loss of a man distinguished for his
intellect, for his dignity, for every noble quality of character, and one

most vital and necessary to defend and protect our Alberti family in these harsh and bitter times.

O fortune, how angry and how hardened against our family you are! In the midst of grief, however, I recall that excellent saying of Epicurus; I remember how fortunate we once were in our native land, how our family once numbered many men, possessed ample goods, flourished in fame and dignity, commanding favor, grace, and much good will. Then I compensate for present unhappiness with these happy memories, and I promise myself, even in the midst of this storm and all these evils, that someday our patience and fortitude will find a wholesome and quiet haven. To free my soul of all bitterness, I turn my thoughts elsewhere and consider that for a family which wished to be great no model could be more fitting than our Alberti family, our family, that is, as it was before. Thanks to the blows of fortune, it fell on adversity and stormy troubled days. I see and recognize this, that no family lacking the things we used to have in abundance, no family small in number of men, or poor, lowly, and friendless, let alone surrounded by enemies, no such family could ever be considered anything but wretched and unfortunate. So let us call that family fortunate which has a good supply of rich men, men who are highly esteemed and loved. Let us call the family unfortunate which has few men, and those obscure, poor, and disliked. While the first is feared, the second is inevitably injured and insulted. While the first is given honor and due dignity, the second is hated and treated with contempt. While the first is called and admitted to high and glorious enterprises, the second is excluded and shunned. Do you agree?

Battista: We agree.

Lionardo: In our discussion we may establish four general precepts as sound and firm foundation for all the other points to be developed or added. I shall name them. In the family the number of men must not diminish but augment; possessions must not grow less, but more; all forms of disgrace are to be shunned—a good name and fine reputation is precious and worth pursuing; hatreds, enmities, rancor must be carefully avoided, while good will, numerous acquaintances, and friendships are something to look for, augment, and cultivate.

We shall take up these four points of wisdom in order to see how men become rich, good, and well-beloved. First we must begin by seeing how a family becomes, as we may say, populous. We shall give some thought to the reasons for a decline in numbers. Then we shall turn to the second point. I am delighted to find that by some providential chance we happened to begin our talk with a kind of prelude to all this, in which I urged you to avoid all lust and lascivious greed. Did I not intend to be brief in this matter, as before so in what is to come? Perhaps I would show you more clearly how in all four things that remain to our consideration, sensual pleasure and lascivious love are the most destructive cause of total ruin. Another time and place for this discussion may arise, while you, I know, I need no persuasion to make you keep to your education, your noble pursuits, and your studies, and avoid idleness and less than honorable desires. So let us return to our subject. There we shall speak as lucidly and simply as we can, without any elegant and very polished rhetoric. I think among ourselves good thoughts are far more important than a pretty style. Listen to me.

Families increase in population no differently than do countries, regions, and the whole world. As anyone who uses his imagination will quickly realize, the number of mortal men has grown from a small number to the present almost infinite multitude through the procreation and rearing of children. And, for the procreation of children, no one can deny that man requires woman. Since a child comes into the world as a tender and delicate creature, he needs someone to whose care and devotion he comes as a cherished trust. This person must nourish him with diligence and love and must defend him from harm. Too much cold or too much sun, rain, and the wild blowing of a storm are harmful to children. Woman, therefore, did first find a roof under which to nourish and protect herself and her offspring. There she remained, busy in the shadow, nourishing and caring for her children. And since woman was busy guarding and taking care of the heir, she was not in a position to go out and find what she and her children required for the maintenance of their life. Man, however, was by nature more energetic and industrious, and he went out to find things and bring what seemed to him necessary. Sometimes the man remained away from home and did not return as soon as his family expected. Because of this, when he came back laden, the woman learned to save things up in order to make sure that if in the future her husband stayed away for a time, neither she nor her children would suffer. In this way it seems clear to me that nature and human reason taught mankind the necessity of having a spouse, both to increase and continue generations and to nourish and preserve those already born. It also became clear that careful gathering and diligent preserving were essential to the maintenance of human life in the married state.

Nature showed, further, that this relationship could not be permitted with more than one wife at a time, since man was by no means able to provide and bring home more than was needed for himself and one wife and children. Had he wished to find food and to gather goods for more wives and families, one or another of them would certainly sometimes have lacked some of the necessities. And the woman who found herself lacking what are or ought to be the necessities of life, would she not have had sufficient reason even to abandon her offspring in order to preserve her own life? Perhaps under pressure of such need she would even have had the right to seek out another companion. Marriage, therefore, was instituted by nature, our most excellent and divine teacher of all things, with the provision that there should be one constant life's companion for a man, and one only. With her he should dwell under one roof, her he should not forget or leave all alone, but to her return, bearing things with him and ordering matters so that his family might have all that was necessary and sufficient. The wife was to preserve in the house the things he brought to her. To satisfy nature, then, a man need only choose a woman with whom he can dwell in tranquillity under one roof all his life.

Young people, however, very often do not cherish the good of the family enough to do this. Marriage, perhaps, seems to them to take away their present liberty and freedom. It may be, as the comic poets like to tell us, that they are held back and dissuaded by some mistress. Sometimes, too, young men find it hard enough to manage one life, and fear as an excessive and undesirable burden the task of supporting a wife and children besides. They may doubt their capacity to maintain in honorable estate a family which grows in needs from day to day. Viewing the conjugal bed as a troublesome responsibility, they then avoid the legitimate and honorable path to the increase of a family.

If a family is not to fall for these reasons into what we have described as the most unfortunate condition of decline, but is to grow, instead, in fame and in the prosperous multitude of its youth, we must persuade our young men to take wives. We must use every argument for this purpose, offer incentive, promise reward, employ all our wit, persistence, and cunning. A most appropriate reason for taking a wife may be found in what we were saying before, about the evil of sensual indulgence, for the condemnation of such things may lead young men to desire honorable satisfactions. As other incentives, we may also speak to them of the delights of this primary and natural companionship of marriage. Children act as pledges and securities of marital love and kindness. At the same time they offer a focus for all a man's hopes and desires. Sad, indeed, is the man who has labored to get wealth and power and lands, and then has no true heir and perpetuator of his memory. No one can be more suited than a man's true and legitimate sons to gain advantages by virtue of his character, position, and authority, and to enjoy the fruits and rewards of his labor. If a man leaves such heirs, furthermore, he need not consider himself wholly dead and gone. His children keep his own position and his true image in the family. Dido, the Phoenician, when Aeneas left her, his mistress, cried out with tears, among her great sorrows no desire above this one: "Ah, had I but a small Aeneas now, to play beside me." As you were first poisoned, wretched and abandoned woman, by that man whose fatal and consuming love you did embrace, so another little Aeneas might by his similar face and gestures have offered you some consolation in your grief and anguish.

It will serve our purpose, also, to remind the young of the dignity conferred on the father in the ancient world. Fathers of families wore precious jewels and were given other tokens of dignity forbidden to any who had not added by his progeny to the population of the republic. It may also help to recall to young men how often profligates and hopeless prodigals have been restored to a better life by the presence of a wife in the house. Add to this what a great help sons can be as hands to get work done—how they give zealous and loyal aid and support when fortune is hard and men unkind—and how your sons more than anyone spring to your defense and are ready to avenge the injury and harm inflicted upon you by evil and outrageous men. Likewise, our children are our comfort and are apt at every age to make us happy and give us great joys and satisfactions. These things it is good to tell them. It also helps to point out how much children come to mean in old age, when we live under the pressure of various needs. As Messer Niccolaio Alberti in his wisdom and experience used to say, children are the natural and reliable crutch of the old. These and similar arguments, which it would take too long to detail here, will help to teach young men not to spurn an honorable mate. They will make them further the propagation, growth, and benefit of the family. It is no less useful, however, to offer them some reward: to give honor to fathers and to give first place in private and public life to the man who has the most children, while showing less reverence to those who are unmarried. If there are some who excuse themselves on account of their poverty, let that be the responsibility and the task of their elders, who, as Lorenzo was saying, are to care for all the family's needs. Let them seriously admonish the younger men, and encourage them to become fathers.

Let it be the responsibility of the whole house to see that once they have the desire they have also the ability honorably to establish a family. Let the entire family contribute, as if to purchase its own growth, and let them all join by gathering something from each member to put up a sufficient sum for a fund which will support those who shall be born. In this way an expense which would have been disastrously heavy for one alone shall be shared among many and become merely a light obligatory payment. It seems to me that in a family where good customs prevail, no one would be unwilling to pay any amount to ransom back from slavery a humble member, not even of his own family but of his country and language. No attempt should be made, therefore, to evade the light expense which might restore a greater number to one's own blood and to one's family. Year after year you give wages to strangers, to various outsiders. You feed and clothe both foreigners and slaves, not so much to enjoy the fruit of their labor as to have a large company in your household. To contribute to a single charity which would support your own kinsmen would cost you far less. The company of your own relatives will yield you more honor and more pleasure than that of strangers. Cherished and faithful kinsmen will do more useful work and suit your household better than the workers you have taken into your service, whose loyalty you have merely bought. One should show such kindness and charity toward one's family, then, so that a father may be sure his children need never want for the necessities of life.

Perhaps it will help to put our young people under some compulsion like this: fathers could say in their wills, "If you do not marry when you reach the appropriate age, you are no heir of mine." As to what is the appropriate time of life to take a wife, to relate all the ancient opinions on this matter would take a long time. Hesiod would have a man marry at thirty; Lycurgus wanted fatherhood to begin at thirty-seven; to our modern minds it seems to be practical for a man to marry at twenty-five. Everyone at least agrees that to give this kind of responsibility to the willful and ardent youth under twenty-five is dangerous. A man of that age spends his fire and force better in establishing and strengthening his own position than in procreating. The youthful seed, moreover, seems faulty and frail and less full of vigor than that which is ripened. Let men wait for solid maturity.

When, by the urging and counsel of their elders and of the whole family, young men have arrived at the point of marriage, their mothers and other female relatives and friends, who have known the virgins of the neighborhood from earliest childhood and know the way their upbringing has formed them, should select all the well-born and well-brought-up girls and present that list to the new groom-to-be. He can then choose the one who suits him best. The elders of the house and all of the family shall reject no daughter-in-law unless she is tainted with the breath of scandal or bad reputation. Aside from that, let the man who will have to satisfy her satisfy himself. He should act as do wise heads of families before they acquire some property—they like to look it over several times before they actually sign a contract. It is good in the case of any purchase and contract to inform oneself fully and to take counsel. One should consult a good number of persons and be very careful in order to avoid belated regrets. The man who has decided to marry must be still more cautious. I recommend that he examine and anticipate in every way, and consider for many days, what sort of person it is he is to live with for all his years as husband and companion. Let him be minded to marry for two purposes: first to perpetuate himself in his children, and second to have a steady and constant companion all his life. A woman is needed, therefore, who is likely to bear children and who is desirable as a perpetual mate.

They say that in choosing a wife one looks for beauty, parentage, and riches. The beauty of a man accustomed to arms, it seems to me, lies in his having a presence betokening pride, limbs full of strength, and the gestures of one who is skilled and adept in all forms of exercise. The beauty of an old man, I think, lies in his prudence, his amiability, and the reasoned judgment which permeates all his words and his counsel. Whatever else may be thought beautiful in an old man, certainly it differs sharply from what constitutes beauty in a young cavalier. I think that beauty in a woman, likewise, must be judged not only by the charm and refinement of her face, but still more by the grace of her person and her aptitude for bearing and giving birth to many fine children.

Among the most essential criteria of beauty in a woman is an honorable manner. Even a wild, prodigal, greasy, drunken woman may be beautiful of feature, but no one would call her a beautiful wife. A woman worthy of praise must show first of all in her conduct, modesty, and purity. Marius, the illustrious Roman, said in that first speech of his to the Roman people: "Of women we require purity, of men labor." And I certainly agree. There is nothing more disgusting than a coarse and dirty woman. Who is stupid enough not to see clearly that a woman who does not care for neatness and cleanliness in her appearance, not only in her dress and body but in all her behavior and language, is by no means well mannered? How can it be anything but obvious that a bad mannered woman is also rarely virtuous? We shall consider elsewhere the harm that comes to a family from women who lack virtue, for I myself do not know which is the worse fate for a family, total celibacy or a single dishonored woman. In a bride, therefore, a man must first seek beauty of mind, that is, good conduct and virtue.

In her body he must seek not only loveliness, grace, and charm but must also choose a woman who is well made for bearing children, with the kind of constitution that promises to make them strong and big. There's an old proverb, "When you pick your wife, you choose your children." All her virtues will in fact shine brighter still in beautiful children. It is a well-known saying among poets: "Beautiful character dwells in a beautiful body." The natural philosophers require that a woman be neither thin nor very fat. Those laden with fat are subject to coldness and constipation and slow to conceive. They say that a woman should have a joyful nature, fresh and lively in her blood and her whole being. They have no objections to a dark girl. They do reject girls with a frowning black visage, however. They have no liking for either the undersized or the overlarge and lean. They find that a woman is most suited to bear children if she is fairly big and has limbs of ample length. They always have a preference for youth, based on a number of arguments which I need not expound here, but particularly on the point that a young girl has a more adaptable mind. Young girls are pure by virtue of their age and have not developed any spitefulness. They are by nature modest and free of vice. They quickly learn to accept affectionately and unresistingly the habits and wishes of their husbands.

These things then are the logical outcome of our inquiry. They are the things it makes sense to keep in mind in order to find and select a well-suited, prolific wife. To all this I might add one more point, that it is an excellent sign if a girl has a great number of brothers and no sisters. It is reasonable to hope that she will, when she is yours, fare like her mother.

Now we have spoken of beauty. Let us next consider parentage, and what are the qualities to look for there. I think the first problem in choosing a family is to investigate closely the customs and habits of one's new relatives. Many marriages have ruined the family, as one may hear and read every day, because they involved union with a litigious, quarrelsome, arrogant, and malevolent set of men. For brevity's sake I cite no examples here. I think that no one is so great a fool that he would not rather remain unmarried than burden himself with terrible relatives. Sometimes the links of family have proved a trouble and disaster to the man, who has had to support both his own family and that of the girl he married. Not infrequently it happens that the new family, because they feel unable to manage their own affairs or because they really are so unfortunate, all settle down in the house of their new kinsman. As the new husband you cannot keep them without harm to yourself, nor can you send them away without incurring censure.

To sum up this whole subject in a few words, for I want above all to be brief on this point, let a man get himself new kinsmen of better than plebeian blood, of a fortune more than diminutive, of a decent occupation, and of modest and respectable habits. Let them not be too far above himself, lest their greatness overshadow his own honor and position. Too high a family may disturb his own and his family's peace and tranquillity, and also, if one of them falls, you cannot help to support him without collapsing or wearing yourself out as you stagger under a weight too great for your arms and your strength. I also do not want the new relatives to rank too low, for while the first error puts you in a position of servitude, the second causes expense. Let them be equals, then, and, to repeat, modest and respectable people.

The matter of dowry is next, which I would like to see middling in size, certain and prompt rather than large, vague, or promised for an indefinite future. I know not why everyone, as if corrupted by a common vice, takes advantage of delay to grow lazy in paying debts. Sometimes, in cases of marriage, people are further tempted because they hope to evade payment altogether. As your wife spends her first year in your house, it seems impossible not to reinforce the new bonds of kinship by frequent visiting and parties. But it will be thought rude if, in the middle of a gathering of kinsmen, you put yourself forward to insist and complain. If, as new husbands usually do, you don't want to lose their still precarious favor, you may ask your in-laws in restrained and casual words. Then you are forced to accept any little excuse they may offer. If you make a more forthright demand for what is your own, they will explain to you their many obligations, will complain of fortune, blame the conditions of the time, complain of other men, and say that they hope to be able to ask much of you in greater difficulties. As long as they can, in fact, they will promise you bounteous repayment at an ever-receding date. They will beg you, and overwhelm you, nor will it seem possible for you to spurn the prayers of people you have accepted as your own family. Finally, you will be put in a position where you must either suffer the loss in silence or enter upon expensive litigation and create enmity.

What is more, it will seem that you can never put an end to the pressure from your wife on this point. She will weep many tears, and the pleadings and insistent prayers of a new love that has just begun are apt to have a certain force. However hard and twisted your temperament you can hardly impose silence on someone who pleads with an outsider, thus softly and tearfully, for the sake of her own father and brothers. Then imagine how impossible for you to turn a deaf ear on your own wife doing so in your own house, in your own room. You are bound, in the end, to suffer either financial loss or loss of affection. This is why the dowry should be precisely set, promptly paid, and not too high. The larger the payments are to be and the longer they are to be carried, the more discussion you will be forced into, the more reluctantly you will be paid, and the more obliged you will feel to spend inordinate sums for all sorts of things. There will be indescribable bitterness and often totally ruinous results in setting dowries very high. We have said now how a wife is to be selected from outside and how she is to be received into the house. It remains to be seen how she is to be treated once she is within.

Battista: I would not interrupt your rapid exposition, if you had not yourself given me leave to do it. But it would help to stop a moment and let me turn my head to fix in my memory what you have traversed to this point, if I can remember it rightly. You have said, I gather, that one should select a virtuous woman of good parentage, one well dowered and suited to bear a fair number of sons. All these things are very difficult. Lionardo, do you think one could easily find them all combined in one woman, let alone in as many as a large family like ours requires? In various marriages I have noted that if a girl is well born she often comes without dowry. There is even a common saying, "If you desire gold, take her ugly or old." It is my impression that we regulate our lives rather like the ancient Thracians, among whom ugly virgins purchased their husbands at high prices, while, for the beautiful girls, sums to be paid were established by official assessors. Do you see what I mean, Lionardo?

Lionardo: I do see, and I am glad you listened so patiently to what we have been saying so far. I am glad, too, that you did not let me run on like this. For, yes, it is as you say: all marriages cannot be as I wish. Nor can all wives be like that Cornelia, the daughter of Metellus Scipio, who was married to Publius Crassus, a woman who was beautiful, well educated, skilled in music, geometry, and philosophy, and, most praiseworthy of all in a woman of such abilities and virtue, not at all haughty or aloof or demanding. But let us take the advice of the slave girl, Birria, in Terence: "If you can't do what you want, want what you can do." One marries the girl who seems to have less faults than the others. One does not give up beauty for parentage or parentage in order to get a dowry. Cato, who excelled as the father of a family, used to praise the girl who showed an old fashioned refinement of manners above the one who was loaded with money. Personally, I can well believe that both may be rather forward and self-willed, but that the one born and brought up not in the luxurious shade of wealth but under the bright influence of good character and habits will probably be a little more sensitive about bringing shame on herself and far more obedient. One takes a wife, in fact, mainly to have children by her. One then considers, further, that good kinsmen are a more reliable advantage than good fortune. They are worth more, in the judgment of good men, than wealth. Wealth is a fleeting and perishable thing, while kinsmen, if you think of them as such and treat them accordingly, remain kinsmen forever.

We shall speak more fully of this elsewhere—now let us go back to our point. But where were we? Certainly there's a problem—one needs time to work things out in advance, and then time to say what one has well deliberated. In this discussion of ours, not being well prepared, I rush on under my own momentum, like a person running down a slope, and I say what seems to be most natural at the moment. Please don't be shocked if I leave out more and more things which are actually important and vital and a shame to omit.

Battista: Is there anything else to be said? I thought there was no more to add.

Lionardo: So you think. When I realize that I have left out something so primary and altogether essential as this, how much more that is valuable and relevant may not now be fleeing away ahead of me or hiding unnoticed behind? But this one thing, which is highly significant and notable, I am glad has occurred to me in time. I say that when you have chosen your wife and decided on the girl you like best, when you have received the advice and permission of all your elders, and when she is highly pleasing to you and to your family for her ways and her beauty, then the first thing you ought to do is as Xenophon has the good husband say to Socrates: pray to God that he graciously grant that your bride will be fertile, and that you may always have peace and honor in your house. Address God with abundant piety, for these are the things essential to a wife and without which suffering abounds. With them, on the other hand, a man is happy and grateful for what are truly the gifts of God. Not every man who seeks finds a good wife. Not every man who would like a faithful wife has one, though some perhaps think they have. On the contrary, it has always been a rare and singular favor of God to settle a man with a wholly peaceable wife whose character is above reproach. One may consider oneself lucky if one's wife never gives rise to scandal or disgrace. Blessed is he who is not afflicted with grief through having a bad wife. Many should be the prayers addressed to God, therefore, that he may grant the young husband a wife who will prove good, peaceful, honorable, and, as we have said, prolific. This I repeat: one should never cease praying to God that he may keep one's wife faithful, tranquil, and loving.

Battista: If I had decided to take a wife, Lionardo, I don't know how much good it would have done me to hear all these reservations and doubts of yours about wives being not so virtuous in their conduct toward their husbands.

Lionardo: Quiet, Battista, don't do me an injustice; don't misinterpret my words to make it seem that I rail against feminine character and conduct. It's just that I believe in calling on the help of God in every undertaking, be it an easy or a difficult one. Nothing is so difficult that it is not perfectly easy for us with God's help. Nothing is so easy that is not occasionally, through a particular effect of nature or by force of circumstances, difficult. It is good to ask God, Battista, even to grant that what is easy for everyone else may not prove difficult to us.

But let us continue our original exposition. I have described the sort of woman suited to bear children. Now I think we should logically consider next in what manner it is best to conceive children, a topic which one might perhaps skip over on account of certain considerations. I shall, however, discuss this vital subject in so veiled and so compressed a manner that for anyone who does not like it it will be as if I had not spoken. If anyone expects us to deal with it here, they will find no omission.

Husbands, then, should be careful not to give themselves to their wives while their mental state is troubled by anger, fear, or some other kind of disturbing emotion. The passions that oppress the spirit slow up and weaken our vital strength. Those passions that inflame and excite the mind disturb and provoke to rebellion the masters whose task it is at that moment to form the human image. Hence it may often be found that a father who is ardent and strong and wise has begotten a son who is fearful, weak, and foolish. Sometimes from a moderate and reasonable man there springs a mad and bestial youth. Again, it is unwise to come together if body and limbs are not in good condition and health. The doctors say, and they give ample reasons, that if a father and mother are low and troubled because of drink or bad blood or weaknesses and defects of energy and pulse, it is reasonable to expect the children to manifest these troubles. Sometimes, in fact, they will be leprous, epileptic, deformed, or incomplete in their limbs and defective.

All these are things one certainly does not want to see happen to one's own children. The doctors have ordained, therefore, that intercourse be undertaken only when one is sober, strong, and as happy as possible. They say that that hour of the night is best which comes after the first digestion is over, when you are neither empty nor full of heavy food, but flourishing and lightened by sleep. They say that in this act it is good to make oneself intensely desired by the woman. They also have many other counsels, and instruct one that when it is excessively hot or when every seed and root is petrified by frost in the earth it is better to wait for more temperate weather. It would take too much time to set forth all their prescriptions. I should perhaps take more account of who my interlocutors are, too. You are only boys, after all. Perhaps this passage, which I can excuse as something I was accidentally driven to discuss by the course of my argument, would not be a part I could legitimately include *ex proposite*. Even if I am guilty and should here excuse myself, I am pleased the digression has brought you some enlightenment. For that reason I do not apologize too much for words that were if not actually unseemly perhaps a bit superfluous.

Battista: To us, Lionardo, you seemed to speak neither in unseemly nor superfluous words. If, as you said yourself and as I believe, the physicians find that one must be careful or leprosy, plague, and other extreme catastrophes may follow, should one not exercise great caution in this matter? What if, in fact, intemperance in the father can and does produce madness and insanity in the children? Then it is good to know the evil in order to avoid it. What wise person would not rather remain childless than have diseased and insane children? Go on, Lionardo, do not hold back, do not be afraid that some false condemnation may come from us. We would have more reason to find fault with you if you silently passed over such vital matters. It is most useful to observe the rules. Ignoring them can be most dangerous.

Lionardo: As you say, these are, in fact, useful prescriptions. Perhaps it may be that I would do better to appear less learned rather than to speak indecorously, as now I may seem to do. One thought gives food to the next and draws it on. I have spoken of intercourse, and it follows that now I ought to say how a woman is to be treated in pregnancy, then how in labor, and finally to give you some instruction concerning her period of recovery afterward. So, having set out to speak to you of the conduct of the family, I shall have given you precepts of medicine and taught you what the ancients used to call obstetrics. And then what? Shall we go on to imitate that Gaius Matius, the friend of Gaius Caesar, who described the art of cooking and of fishing? Shall we also teach you to make cereal and soup for babies? But since we have descended to these topics, it may be permissible to be very brief indeed and leave it to the doctors to explain the instructions which we succinctly set forth. The woman, then, who thinks she is pregnant should live discreetly, contentedly, and chastely —light nourishing foods, no hard, excessive labor, no sleepy or lazy days in idle solitude. She should give birth in her husband's house and not elsewhere. Once she is delivered, she must not go out in the cold and the wind until her health is fully restored and all her limbs have fully regained their strength. That's all I have to say.

Battista: How briefly you did say it!

Leonardo: Now, then, we have learned the way to increase the family. We shall consider next how it may be preserved. First of all let me point out two essentials in dealing with newborn infants which I have often seen fathers neglect. It is a delight to me to hear the names in our Alberti family, and especially those of Messer Niccolaio's children, which are very beautiful: Diamante, Altobianco, Calcedonio. And among other kinsmen we have Cherubino, Alessandro, Alesso. It seems to me a graceless name may well have the power to detract from the dignity and grandeur of a man, even if he is an excellent person. Some names, as we read, were extremely unlucky, like the virgins in Greece named Milesia who all killed themselves in a fit of madness, whether by hanging, leaping, poison, or the sword, and met death before their time. Beautiful and magnificent names, by the same token, seem to be propitious. They somehow add luster to our virtues and our dignity, and make them still more splendid and admirable. Alexander of Macedon, whose name was already famous throughout the nations, stopped once, as he was moving

his great armies to the conquest of a certain fort, and called to himself
one of his young Macedonians whose name happened also to be Alexander. "And you, Alexander," said he, wishing to teach the boy to seek high
honor, "it's up to you to have the character to match your name, which, I
notice, is not a vulgar one." I certainly think that to a man of some wit, a
handsome name is a challenge. It makes him eager to be worthy of the
name and of the qualities it implies.

Our ancestors, not unreasonably, used to reward and commemorate
anyone very strong and zealous in the service of his country by inscribing
him among the gods, which served as an incentive to other youths to
pursue the same honor. They gave to these heroes new names, as elegant
and shining as possible. Among our own Latins, for instance, there was
Romulus called Quirinus, and Leda Nemesis, and Juno Leucotea. We
have, however, spoken at too much length of this. Let us just conclude
that fathers ought not so much to respect the past names in their family
as to remember that the primary purpose of names is to be beautiful, and
that ugly names are repugnant and often harmful. Let the names in a
family be illustrious and glorious ones. They cost little and they often
help us and do a lot of good. For, to us Albertis, it has always come
naturally to seek with a kind of instinctive ardor to be, even more than
to appear, well skilled and well versed in everything men praise.

This was one of the two things I had in mind. The other is that as soon
as the child is born one should note in the family records and secret books
the hour, the day, the month, and the year as well as the place of birth.
These records should be kept with our dearest treasures. There are many
reasons for doing this, but, all else aside, it shows the conscientiousness of
a father. If it shows a kind of conscientiousness for a man to keep careful
note of the day and the agent from whom he bought an ass, is it less right
to make note on the day on which you became a father, when a brother to
your children was born? Occasions may arise when you will want this
information, and you might have to consult the memory of others. If you
could not find out from them, you might be sorry and perhaps some loss
would ensue. If you did find out from them, it would hardly make you
proud to realize that others were more interested and better informed of
your own affairs than you.

Now we have filled the house with people. We must soon take many
measures to be sure that this crowd does not find itself in need. I think we
should first consider, however, the reasons why some families decline in
numbers. When we know the reasons, we may find means to guard

against them. This point may first be made perfectly clear: families diminish when men die without heirs. Would that men might live on immortally! That cannot be. Let us take all those who are living, may they live among us as long as possible. Besides other advantages, the longer they live the longer they are useful to the family. If they do not help by their wealth, then by their fame; if not by their fame, by their prudent counsel; if not by their counsel, at least by providing new offspring.

How shall we keep men alive a long time? I think we had better follow the example of the wise shepherd as he preserves his flocks. What is his method? He sees that goats are content on steep and infertile ground, that buffalo like watery terrain, and other cattle other places. He places and pastures each kind where it will receive the most of what its nature requires. Fathers of families should do the same. If the air of Florence is too thin for a certain one, let him be sent to Rome; if that is too hot a climate, send him to Venice; if it is too damp there, he shall move on—always put health before any other consideration. If there is a place where he is free of his infirmities, there let him stay. The unhealthy person cannot help being a burden, and even if he should make himself useful, it will be for a brief period. Even if it could be for a long time, I still would think health should come before utility. The father should prefer, therefore, to keep his children far away but healthy and strong, rather than by his side but ill and weak.

Is it enough for this purpose just to place one's children in climates suited to their constitution? No, of course not. What else must be done? Remember that poor food, a disorderly life, and serious hardships cause them to fall ill and die. It is important, therefore, to see that none of these things brings them harm. Every care also must be taken in case of infirmity or illness to keep them in and to nurse them back to health. No pains should be spared, for to be careful and frugal in providing this sort of necessity would be not prudence but avarice. Frugality is praiseworthy precisely because it enables one to provide and supply what is needed in these and other moments of need. To be incapable of liberality and even prodigality when these are required were shame and ruin. It would seem to me only enormous and extreme avarice could fail to value the life and health of a man above money—terrible cruelty, I think, to abandon a sick man and not to care if one loses a certain kinsman as long as one can save one's money and put it in something else.

And since we have started on this subject of not abandoning a kinsman in time of illness, I feel I should not pass in silence over my next point, though it is a matter more important to the family's survival than pleasing to the tenderhearted. Kindness and humane feeling have always been among the prime virtues of a noble mind, and it has always seemed the duty of a good person, the obligation of a just man, the aspiration of a generous one, to visit, help, and support one's kinsmen in every misfortune and need. Reason demands this much, and charity, humanity, and every habit of good men. But, it seems to me, it is hardly prudent not to avoid contact with persons to whom, because of a contagious and most dangerous disease, you can show kindness and be helpful only at the risk of your own health and your life. The laws permit, even in cases of nonfatal contagion, that a man abandon the dearest thing and disengage himself from the first and best natural union of matrimony. If even the husband is allowed to leave a leprous wife, shall we assert that to leave a man with the plague is not legitimate?

What actions are we praising then as kind ones—offering one's hand and one's support to lift up and rebuild the state of those who, whether through the hardness of fortune or the harshness and iniquity of men, or in some other way, are fallen in body or mind or deeply oppressed by trouble and illness? Certainly gentleness and mercy require that we attend as much as we can to these and make ourselves helpful and useful. But it would be reckless and cruel to expose oneself to the ultimate danger of death where slight or even no reward of honor and fame is to be expected. Let us put the principle this way: not without great reasons should our hearts be moved not to avoid dangers and not to value our own lives. To harm oneself without doing any good to others does not, it seems to me, show any sort of humanity. We shall praise the justice and fortitude which is able, in every adversity and against every evil, to defend fame, fortune, family, and life itself. But how can it be just to do oneself harm unless it be to defend another? What man ever gained a glorious name for fortitude in harming himself? Liberality and prudence are admired in magnificent and highly useful deeds; but who except a thorough fool would think it anything but entirely reprehensible to put oneself in extreme danger, not to save, but merely to comfort, a single person? It certainly seems most foolish wisdom not to prefer the certain survival of many healthy persons to the dubious recovery of a single one. If these things are so, who can doubt the kindness, justice, and prudence of providing in such cases for the patient's recovery, but at the same time wisely and rationally providing also for the prevention of illness among the healthy?

If a man wishes for the relief of another man's illness, he wishes him health. Let him cherish in himself, then, what he wishes for another. If we want our prudence and our kindness praised, let us make every effort to assure the sick man of all he can use and all he may need, without peril to our own life. Let us obtain doctors, call druggists, provide plenty of attendants. But we shall also take care of our own health, by means of which we shall prove more helpful to the sick man and to our family than we would by running risks. By persisting in exposing himself to such danger, a man would be of small use to the patient, and he would endanger all his family, since, if he is infected, he can easily infect another, and that one another, until in this way a whole family may be brought low by illness and wiped out.

How many lands have we not seen go from a small beginning of contagious illness to a terrible conflagration of plague. Almost the whole of the youth has been broken and destroyed in a matter of days. There is no need to cite examples or to describe cases. No one doubts the fact that this poison expands and spreads, great and terrible, till it reaches the very extent of the power of death. At Genoa not many years ago, on the occasion of a public celebration of religion, some people in the crowd climbed up to a certain place where someone had previously lain ill and died of the plague. A few days later the persons who had sat in that place at the time of the spectacle—ah miserable fate—they all died, and so did everyone who had given them shelter, and everyone who had visited them, so that the whole country felt the destruction and the scourge of that plaguey poisonous rage. O most destructive poison, O most horrible illness, O most justifiably feared!

I do not know whether I can fairly be called hard and merciless in my views, but since this is our subject we cannot reasonably ignore the welfare of the family. I shall merely repeat what learned physicians command, what the judgment of every prudent person confirms, what any man who is not entirely mad can ascertain from his own experience. The father should flee, the son should flee, the brother should flee, all should flee, because there is no help against this great poison, this great curse, except flight. Let them flee, since other arms or arts avail nothing against this evil. We cannot repel, we cannot hold off the fatal and hideous delirium. Wise men, therefore, will rather save themselves by flight than remain, not to help others but to bring destruction on their own heads. To merciful men their own safety is not less important than a vain reputation for goodness. Who would deny the moral and legal right of man to kill an enemy in self-defense? If that is justified, who would stubbornly deny what I say, that a man has even more right to forgiveness if he abandons one who constantly places him in jeopardy of death? What man of judgment, who cares about the welfare and safety of his family, would actually consider himself abandoned when he was given plenty of all the things which might help him in his need—doctors, servants, and medicines? In this way he may recover, while if his dear ones were near him he would not have a better chance of recovery, but he could quickly kill them. I do not want to be long in setting forth this argument. I pray God it may never happen in our family that I shall be forced to act on it for the sake of the family's survival and welfare. Let us go back to our original discussion. As we have said, men should flee all places and circumstances which bring sickness to the family.

Another way to the decline of the family exists, I have found, and that is the path of division. It has sometimes happened in certain Italian families, a single family, populous and great, has become two that are neither populous nor great. I shall not seek now to establish the causes of this. I do know that it seems to me fair to say that if a father wishes to see his family divided and small, and therefore weaker, simply to assure himself of a greater and firmer position in it, he is most unjust and condemnable. In the judgment of all prudent men the welfare and honor of the whole family ought to come before one's own, as we shall fully prove when we come to it. The man who commits such an injustice cannot call himself prudent. If his thought and soul are fixed on being a greater head than the members of his family require, he has actually made a terrible mistake. Weak members cannot support an overweighty head: they falter under too great pressure, and the head, unsupported by all the members, falls and is broken. The wise man, therefore, who by thinking is able to learn what others have had to find out by painful experience, will recognize that when a beam is sawed, neither one part nor the other is able to support what it could hold before. Nor can the wood be as firmly and solidly refastened as ever. We shall speak of this matter more fully in due time, when we come to the friendship, concord, and union required by the family. For the moment let it suffice us to say that, through division, the family not only decreases in size and in the number of its youth, but its authority shrinks and its importance and dignity diminish to such an extent that a good part of all the fame and honor acquired over the years is lost. Many will love, fear, and honor a united family but will not respect either of two families that quarreled and separated.

We have now explained how the house may be made and kept numerous, and how, to make it numerous, a wife is chosen, children are procreated, and how, to conserve it, efforts are made to keep the young living a long time in health and harmony. All these are things which we can do by application and effort for the welfare and good of the family. It sometimes happens, however, that inspite of all human precautions the numbers in a family diminish, perhaps because wives are sterile or because death takes the children who were born. It therefore seems necessary here to consider how we may even then legitimately keep up the family's numbers. Among the ancients, who attended to all the wants and convenience of the family with the utmost prudence and ingenuity, it was a permitted and accepted custom to divorce one's spouse, divide the property and end the union of marriage, separating from one's wife. This they did when they saw that the marriage would not produce fruit, and recognized by experience that they could not in this union be useful in the way of married men by being fathers. This was a custom and a freedom which did not arise in Rome until two hundred and thirty years after the rape of the Sabine women, so much did Romulus wish to secure the stability and restraint to be found in marriage. Yet Spurius Corvinius, or more correctly Corpilius, the first to repudiate his wife on the grounds of infertility and sterility, did not do so without excellent reason. It seemed to him no disgrace to leave her, since he desired to have children with another. But the civil law today and the religious authorities as well declare that marriage is not so much a mating of bodies as a union of will and of mind, and for this reason consider marriage a sacrament and a religious tie. They forbid persons thus joined by a divine sacrament, therefore, ever to separate by an act of human will. For this reason the ancient custom of leaving the sterile woman for one with whom one could obtain offspring, which was useful to the family, does not have the power today to loosen the sacred marriage tie. The breaking of the physical union is permitted only where it is dangerous to health and life. This separation serves not to augment the family but to preserve it.

There remains another very ancient custom which used often to be put into practice by the strongest citizens, who had sometimes spent their lives under arms, serving with the armies in remote provinces in order to uphold their country's glory and authority. When these retired to their own family and in their last years ceased to engage in public activity and took up the honorable leisure of citizens, they were ambitious to be prized and loved by their fellow citizens, no longer for their hard work and exertions but for their prudence and good counsel. They knew how excellent in this state of leisure is the dear and beloved companionship of a wife, which was something denied them when they were in the army. Not doubting, then, the usefulness to the republic and to the private family of the procreation of children, and being anxious not to depart this life without knowing who would be the disciple and successor to take over their name and fortune, they did as some do today and as, among many others in those days, the son of the elder Africanus did, who adopted a boy born to Paolo Emilio. This, it seems to me, is a most practical and legitimate custom, to adopt children born to others when you cannot have any of your own. I could give many arguments for it; but for brevity's sake I shall give only one: to avoid leaving a barren solitude, to prevent the decline of the family into emptiness and sadness one should legitimately adopt a son. One may also consider that even when we have children we do not know with any certainty in the beginning how strong and healthy of body and mind they will be when grown; but concerning those who are already partially raised there can be no doubt what sort of men they can become with our help and our care, since their character already shows itself and can be largely understood from their habits and temperament and appearance, so that you can form a fairly clear expectation. But let us return to our brief style of speech, and let us agree that adoption is a well-established procedure, right in itself, and most beneficial to the family.

Since adoption is almost the same as adding a new cousin to your relatives and a new member to your household, you should make your choice such that the family will readily accept him. It is wise to consult everyone, so that no one can afterward find fault with the person whom they themselves have liked and consented to accept; one should be careful to find one born of good blood and good character, a person of noble appearance and in other ways one whom the house will never with good reason regret. Then the elders of the family must do their best, first to give advice and concern themselves, then to watch over and care for the education and upbringing of the boy and the preservation of his good character. The one who adopts should realize that if he does not love the boy like a son, the other members of the house will not view him as a member of the family. Then he will not only be a stranger in the house but will suffer as an object of envy and perhaps of insult and injury. Yet everyone knows how vital it is to the family to be free of conflict. So one should adopt children born to excel, and love them and improve them, so that the whole family may rejoice and be happy to have such a person in their midst. I think I have now said all there is to say on the subject of making a family numerous, unless there is something else you can think of.

Battista: I don't know what I admire more in you, Lionardo, your kindness in thus telling us what we asked you, or the brilliance with which you have made distinctions and ordered topics in an area where I would never have thought it could be done. Especially, Lionardo, with such a quantity of excellent precepts as you have been giving us, your wonderful compact mode of procedure delights me. For all the brevity of it, your style of speaking seems to me elegant, smooth, and clear. I should never have believed that there was nearly so much to be said on these subjects. We do thank you. Whatever happens, it will certainly help us to have received from you these beautiful and useful lessons concerning the family. So we await the rest that is still to come. If I recall rightly, it still remains to be said how the family may grow wealthy, esteemed, and famous. Go on.

Lionardo: So be it. But first I think we should do one thing. It seems to me your duty is always with your whole heart and every attention to see whether you can help, please, or somehow be of use to your father. Go now, therefore, and see first whether Lorenzo needs anything. Let us not put anything before the claims of filial piety. Go, Battista. You can find me here again.

Battista: Oh most happy day! I go. Carlo, you stay with Lionardo, so that he may not be left alone.

This I did. I went, and I saw that our father needed nothing. I asked his permission, therefore, if it pleased him, that I might return to Lionardo, who was waiting to continue what he had begun in teaching us many useful lessons. Our father, Lorenzo, then said:

From Lionardo you can learn nothing but good. I am glad. Go, don't waste any time; here I need nothing from you for now, and if I needed it, I should still be happier to have you where you might become more learned. Go Battista, and, my son, consider all time wasted in which you are not engaged in good works. There is nothing you can do that will please me more than to become a good man. Leave behind any occupation you may have in order to pursue excellence and honor. Go, don't delay. Go, my boy.

So did Lorenzo speak, and so did I do. I returned to Lionardo and told him the reply I had received.

Lionardo said, then:

How fortunate the father who has no greater wish for his sons than to see them become good men, and who works to make them desire excellence in the noble arts and the grace of being men of the highest conduct and generally admired. Go on, my little brothers, Battista and you, too, Carlo, fulfilling the desire and hope of your father to the best of your ability since there is nothing he desires of you but this and nothing open to you which is more admirable for any man to do. Work on as you are doing to become, day by day, more learned and more recognized for it. And now what shall we do? Shall we continue with what remains of our discourse? But it seems rather late to me now. It will not be long now before Ricciardo and Adovardo join us; therefore, I am afraid we have not enough time, and our discussion will be interrupted. Perhaps, then, we had better leave it for tomorrow, when we may speak more deliberately and with more thoroughness, for I now feel that I am in suspense to see Ricciardo, that finest and kindest of friends, who has always been a father to me, both in his benevolence toward me and in my reverence for him. I don't know why, but every time I hear someone pass, I think it is Ricciardo already, so eagerly and tensely am I waiting to see Lorenzo pleased by seeing him, for he awaits him with still more acute longing than I.

To this I replied:

Lionardo, let us do as our father just told us, let us consider as wasted any time not spent in some worthy pursuit. I think we have nothing else to do now. Set to work, then, to make us better. Up to now, it seems to me, you have said as much as can be said of these things, in a manner not lacking in structure, and with an eloquence no less compact than clear and elegant. I don't doubt you will go on to do likewise with the remainder. Ricciardo, I think, will not arrive so soon, nor were you ever inclined to turn your mind less to our needs than to your love for him. We have always accounted you a brother for your kindness and goodness to us, and for your willingness to impart to us your knowledge of the highest arts. We see in you not only a teacher, but even a father. We think your teaching of how to stand in life so as to attain praise and honor is no less great than our father's gift to us of being and life. Therefore, Lionardo, please go on. There will be so much the less left for tomorrow. Go on. We are eager to attend you.

Lionardo: All right, then, I am willing. I shall, nonetheless, since our time is limited, be as brief as the material permits. Listen. We have, as I said, made the house numerous and full of young people. It is essential to give them something to do now, and not let them grow lazy. Idleness is not only useless and generally despised in young men, but a positive burden and danger to the family. I do not need to teach you to shun idleness, when I know you are hard workers and active. I do encourage you to continue as you are doing in every sort of activity and hard discipline that you may attain excellence and deserve fame. Only think this matter over and consider whether any man, even if he is not necessarily ambitious of gaining glory but merely a little shy of falling into disgrace, can ever be, in actuality or even if we merely try to imagine him, a man not heartily opposed to idleness and to mere sitting. Who has ever dreamed he might reach any grace or dignity without hard work in the noblest arts, without assiduous efforts, without plenty of sweat poured out in manly and strenuous exertions? Certainly a man who would wish for the favor of praise and fame must avoid and resist idleness and inertia just as he would do major and hateful enemies. There is nothing that leads more quickly to dishonor and disgrace than idleness. The lap of the idler has always been the nest and lair of vice. Nothing is so harmful and pestilent in public and private life as the lazy and passive citizen. From idleness springs lasciviousness; from lasciviousness comes a contempt for the law; from disobedience to law comes ruin and the destruction of the country itself. To the extent that men tolerate the first resistance of men's will to the customs and ways of the country, their spirits soon turn to arrogance, pride, and the harmful power of avarice and greed. Thieves, murderers, adulterers, and all sorts of criminals and evil men run wild.

Idleness, therefore, the cause of so much harm, ought to be greatly hated by the good. And even if idleness were not, as everyone knows it is, pernicious and damaging to good ways, source and mother of every vice, what man, however poorly endowed, would want to pass through life without making use of his mind, his body, and all his capacities? To me a man who does not feel the distinction between honor and shame and does not control the movement of his mind and of his body with thought and discretion seems hardly alive at all. I truly think the man who lies buried in idleness and laziness and who avoids all good works and hard labors is not alive at all. Moreover, a man who does not much care to make all his feelings and all life be excellent and honorable does not seem to me to deserve to live. That same idle creature as he grows older in passivity and inertia, not giving any sort of active support to his people and his country, will certainly seem to men who are manly less estimable than a mere stump. We clearly see that whatever is endowed with life is also able by nature to move and feel. Unless it has these gifts, nothing can be considered truly alive. Now, just as you have eyes but if you keep them closed and do not use them for the purpose they were meant to serve, you get no more use from them than if you did not have them, so the creature which does not use the functions that are the distinguishing features of life itself can be considered in this sense not alive at all. Grass, plants, and bushes are seen to labor at growing and at offering themselves to your pleasure or your need. Other living things, such animals as fish and birds and the four-footed beasts, exert themselves unceasingly in work and productive activity; they never appear idle but ever prove their usefulness either to themselves or to other living things. Some build nests for their young, some range abroad seeking food for their offspring. All behave as if nature herself had taught them to shun idleness. All by some good work cast aside empty repose. It seems to me that man, too, is not born to stagnate at rest, but to be up and doing.

Intelligence, intellect, judgment, memory, appetite, anger, reason, and discretion—who would unreasonably deny that these divine forces, by which man outdoes all other animals in strength, in speed, and in ferocity, were capacities given to us to be amply used. I must object, therefore, to the saying of Epicurus the philosopher, who teaches that the highest happiness of God consists in doing nothing. It may be permissible to God. It seems bad for men, however, to wish to imitate doing nothing. I believe that there is probably nothing more inherently displeasing to God and less permissible to man, wicked deeds aside, than simply aimless being. It is easier for me to believe Anaxagoras the philosopher, who, when he was asked why God had created man, replied: "He was made to contemplate the heavens, the stars, and the sun, and all the marvelous works of God." This is a most plausible idea, especially when we observe that there is no animal but is bent and bowed with its head close to pasture and earth. Man alone stands erect with brow and countenance raised up, as though made by nature herself to gaze upon and know the paths and bodies in the heavens. The Stoics taught that man was by nature constituted the observer and the manager of things. Chrysippus thought everything on earth was born only to serve man, while man was meant to preserve the friendship and society of men. Protagoras, another ancient philosopher, seems to some interpreters to have said essentially the same when he declared that man is the mean and measure of all things. Plato, in a letter to Archytas of Tarentum, declared that men were born to serve their fellow men, and that we owe a part of ourselves to our country, a part to our kinsmen, and a part to our friends. But it would take long to tell all the teachings of the ancient philosophers on this question, and far longer still if we were to add the many opinions given by our later theologians. These have occurred to me for now, and, as you see, all of them think that man should live not in idleness and repose but in works and deeds.

You will find this common and true teaching confirmed if you stop to think how man, from his very childhood on through every age, is inclined to be busier than any other creature. He is so much inclined that way that even those who have no honorable and manly occupation whatsoever amuse themselves in their idle hours by doing something. The more I hear a man praise the state of leisure and claim not to prefer the exercise of body, mind, and thought, the more I think he is mistaken. Indeed he seems more mistaken than if he agreed with the sentiments of that father who, in his lamentations over the death of his daughter, cried out for his own consolation that he believed mortal men were born only to suffer punishment in life for their dreadful crimes and sins. More and more do I find myself appreciating the teaching of Aristotle, who found that whenever man thinks and acts with reason and with virtue, he, in his felicity, is like a mortal god.

Most of all I praise the true and wise teachers who tell us that man was created for the pleasure of God, to recognize the primary and original source of things amid all the variety, dissimilarity, beauty, and multiplicity of animal life, amid all the forms, structures, coverings, and colors that characterize the animals. He was made to praise God together with universal nature, seeing in every living thing such great and perfectly matched harmonies of variegated voice and verse and music combined in concord and loveliness. He was meant to thank God for the wide use that he can make of things and find in things produced for human needs, whether to counter illness or to protect our health. He was created, finally, to fear and honor God by hearing, seeing, and knowing the ways of the sun, the stars, and the course of all the heavenly patterns, the sound and shape of which man must perforce confess do manifest an order established, created, and given to us only by God himself.

To this I might add that man ought to give some reward to God, to satisfy him with good works in return for the wonderful gifts which He gave to the spirit of man exalting and magnifying it beyond that of all other earthly beings. Nature, that is, God, made man a composite of two parts, one celestial and divine, the other most beautiful and noble among mortal things. He provided him with a form and a body suited to every sort of movement, so as to enable him to perceive and to flee from that which threatened to harm and oppose him. He gave him speech and judgment so that he would be able to seek after and to find what he needed and could use. He gave him movement and sentiment, desire and the power of excitement, so that he might clearly appreciate and pursue useful things and shun those harmful and dangerous to him. He gave him intelligence, teachability, memory and reason, qualities divine in themselves and which enable man to investigate, to distinguish, to know what to avoid and what to desire in order best to preserve himself. To these great gifts, admirable beyond measure, God added still another power of the spirit and mind of man, namely moderation. As a curb on greed and on excessive lusts, he gave him modesty and the desire for honor. Further, God established in the human mind a strong tie to bind together human beings in society, namely justice, equity, liberality, and love. These are the means by which a man can gain the favor and praise of other men, as well as the mercy and grace of the creator. Beyond this, God filled the manly breast with powers that make man able to bear fatigue, adversity, and the hard blows of fortune. He is able to undertake what is difficult, to overcome sorrow, not even to fear death—such are his qualities of strength, of endurance and fortitude, such can be his contempt for transitory things. These are qualities which enable us to honor and serve God as fully as we should, with piety, with moderation, and with every other perfect and honorable deed. Let us agree, then, that man was not born to languish in idleness but to labor and create magnificent and great works, first for the pleasure and glory of God, and second for his own enjoyment of that life of perfect virtue and its fruit, which is happiness.

You may wonder, perhaps, whether I have not digressed far from my subject. In fact these things were all necessary to prove what I hope I have successfully conveyed to you. We shall not argue now about which of these opinions is most correct and best to hold. For our purposes let us merely say that man is given life in order to make use of the world, to be good, and to become happy. The man one might call happy must be good to other men, and he who is good to other men certainly gains also the love of God. Poor use of the world is harmful to men and angers God. If a man angers God it is folly to call him happy. We may come to this conclusion then: man is by nature suited and able to make good use of the world, and he is born to be happy.

Not all men know happiness, however. Rather, it is differently understood by different men. Some think it happiness to lack for nothing, and these seek after riches, power, and expansion. Others think that happiness consists in not feeling the weight of any burden or discontent, and these give themselves over to pleasure and enjoyment. Others put happiness on a height which is steeper and harder to scale, but more honorable also and further above lascivious desires. These think it consists in being honored and admired by other men. They undertake labors and attempt great deeds, they submit to vigils and plunge into manly exertions. Perhaps everyone of these is able to attain something not far removed from happiness by acting with virtuous resolve and by making a rational and moderate use of the world.

Dealing with the world and with oneself in a reckless and disorderly fashion, on the other hand, leads to grave error. One who provokes trouble by his vices and impiety is led to transgress further and fall deeper into error the more he deserves evil from oneself and from God's gifts. This is the way things go when a man full of vice seeks from particular activities more or less reward than can be had by the dictates or with the consent of reason and honor. Being avaricious, he would grow rich by ugly cunning. Being full of vice, he longs nonetheless to be honored by men. He wishes to live in lascivious ease and to bear no responsibility. This, it seems to me, means that a man is prepared to make a poor use of the world, to harm men, and to anger God. He will finally make himself unhappy and miserable, a fate heartily feared by any man not quite out of his senses, and especially by a man who wishes to make his family happy.

Let men seek their own happiness first, and they will obtain the happiness of their family also. As I have said, happiness cannot be gained without good works and just and righteous deeds. Works are just and good which not only do no harm to anyone, but which benefit many. Works are righteous if they are without a trace of the dishonorable or any element of dishonesty. The best works are those which benefit many people. Those are most virtuous, perhaps, which cannot be pursued without strength and nobility. We must give ourselves to manly effort, then, and follow the noblest pursuits.

It seems to me, before we dedicate ourselves to any particular activity, it would be wise to think over and examine the question of what is our easiest way to reach or come near to happiness. Not every man easily attains happiness. Nature did not make all men of the same humor, or of the same intelligence or will, or equally endowed with skill and power. Rather nature planned that where I might be weak, you would make good the deficiency, and in some other way you would lack the virtue found in another. Why this? So that I should have need of you, and you of him, he of another, and some other of me. In this way one man's need for another serves as the cause and means to keep us all united in general friendship and alliance. This may, indeed, have been the source and beginning of republics. Laws may have begun thus rather than as I was saying before; fire and water alone may not have been the cause of so great a union among men as society gives them. Society is a union sustained by laws, by reason, and by custom.

Let us not disgress. To decide which is the most suitable career for himself, a man must take two things into account: the first is his own intelligence, his mind and his body, everything about himself; and the second, the question requiring close consideration, is that of outside supports, the help and resources which are necessary or useful and to which he must have early access, welcome, and free right of use if he is to enter the field for which he seems more suited than for any other. Take an example: if a man wished to perform great feats of arms while he knew he was himself but a weak fellow, not very robust, incapable of bearing up through dust and storm and sun, this would not be the right profession for him to pursue. If I, being poor, longed to devote my life to letters, though I had not the money to pay the considerable expenses attached to such a career, again this would be a poor choice of career. If you are equipped with numerous relatives, plenty of friends, abundant wealth, and if you possess within yourself intelligence, eloquence, and such tact as to keep you out of any rough or awkward situations, and you decide to dedicate yourself to civic affairs, you might do extremely well.

It is best, then, to weigh inwardly first, as I said, the qualities which nature gave to you and to your body, and second what fortune has been generous enough to grant you and not take away. Problems may still arise, should your situation, your fortune, the times, or other circumstances change. Then you must do as Thales the philosopher once said "Bow to the times." After all, if you were going out to your country house and there were a small road you could very well use, would you still prefer to travel by the royal military highroad when it was full of holes, wound along precipices and was hard and dangerous? No indeed, I think. Not being a fool, you would rather go by one of the other paths, finer in itself and easier for you. Such is the way of human wisdom in choosing our road in life. If the rivers and tides of events, the winds and floods of fortune, make our road impassable, if the loss of resources we had counted on stands in our way and cuts us off from our goal, then we must find another pursuit to convey us as best may be toward the happiness we seek.

As to the nature of happiness, I think it can only be this, to live contentedly, free of any want, and with honor. If you find that you are suited for more than one career, steer first for the one that has more honor attached to it and that is more useful to yourself and your family. Whatever the work you devote yourself to, always remember that you were born to labor for your own happiness. Hold fast to the idea that there is nothing more sure to help you attain that end than to make it your purpose entirely to be in actuality that which you would like to appear to others to be.

If a man would be accounted liberal, Battista, it is his duty to give freely to many persons on various occasions, to be truly generous. If a man would be accounted just and good, he must harm no one at any time and reward people according to their merit. He must struggle against opposition not with violence but with kindness and humanity. A man who succumbs to sorrow and fears adversity, a man much attached to fortune and to transitory goods, will never deserve to be credited by others with spiritual strength, with a magnanimous soul. One whose memory, whose knowledge, whose wise, firm, and comprehensive thinking has been tried and tested by his fellow citizens, such a man is the only one who can call himself a man of judgment and consider himself one. Whatever the career a man pursues, let him apply his mind, let him make every effort, to be that which he would appear.

There is no one, I think, who wishes to appear wicked or malevolent. Everyone would, I think, be glad to be generally thought modest, humane, temperate, kind, amicable, helpful, active, and hardworking. Our duty is not merely to admire and aspire to these virtues but to apply all our energy, our intellect and our will to put them into practice, and once we have them, others will also see them in us. Nothing is so hard to keep hidden as human excellence. This has always been the brightest and most glorious jewel in any man's treasure. That is why you must bend all your efforts, and labor with hands and feet, with every nerve and sinew, to become the wisest and the most skilled among all the wise and clever persons in your field of work. If you persevere, if you labor to master whatever lies before you and to make yourself by far the best, you will not, I think, find it hard to take all the prizes of honor and fame. What a man wants to do, they say, that he can do. If, as I said, you apply all your strength and all your cunning, I have no doubt you will attain in some profession the very height and acme of perfection.

If a man chooses a field which is not entirely suited to his capacities, his efforts are still not to be despised. If he gives all his energy and zeal to the work which nature and fortune put before him, he ought to be praised and truly esteemed even if it does not turn out profitably. Yet one may reproach a man for choosing an unsuitable profession. It is not always admirable to oppose oneself to fortune. There is much to be said for knowing how to swim with the tide in the direction of a life which is good, peaceful, and calm. It is best to find a course of action such that if things turn out badly one has no cause for self-reproach, but fortune alone is to blame. The man who does choose a suitable and appropriate field of work, however, and cleaves to his path has only himself to blame if he does not attain high honor.

In talking of these matters a simple analogy comes to mind. Let us suppose a great regatta were being organized in the harbor of Venice, a display of many ships with a multitude of participants. Suppose you were the captain of one of the ships which was to race on a long course like the one Virgil describes in the games of Aeneas near Sicily. In this case, however, there would be a choice of sails or oars according to the pilot's own view of what was the faster way to victory. You would strive mightily to reach the goal, where the garlands and trophies of victory were stored and where the prizes and honors were given out to the winning contestants. You would want your ship to share with no more than two others in the first three prizes. Perhaps a fourth place might also give you if not a supreme prize at least some reputation and remembrance. This would be true especially if in the talk after the race its being only fourth place were excused by some accident or mistake, and you were nonetheless honored and praised.

The other participants in the race, however, would remain unknown. No one would speak of them. These contestants might perhaps have been better off if they had remained on land, taking no active part. They might have been judging, laughing, criticizing the slowness and tardiness of others as much as they liked instead of having, so to speak, shown only languorous enthusiasm in the race. As it is, they find themselves far from admired, indeed they are generally mocked. In the race of human life and the general contest for honor and glory, likewise, I think the first step is to choose an appropriate, manageable vessel for your powers and talents, then to strive hard for first place. For spirits which are neither lazy nor mean, it is best to hope and desire and fight wholeheartedly for a place among the first, if not for first place. One must surpass entirely that obscure and forgotten crowd behind. One must struggle with all the force and cunning at his disposal for a certain fame and a measure of glory.

To gain glory a man must have excellence. To gain excellence he need only will to be, and not merely to seem, all that he wishes others might think him. For this reason they say there are few prerequisites to excellence. As you see, only a firm, whole, and unfeigned will, will do. What is false will in a man? Is it to show the desire to pursue something one does not actually care for? We shall not here undertake to prove at length how easy it is to attain excellence. That will be better told in another place. We shall merely state here the fact that a man who strives for first place may with honor sit in the second. No one comes in among the last, however, without incurring obscurity and ignominy. No one takes last place with honor.

We should also consider at this point how much reward and profit, how much honor and fame, you can gain from any work or achievement you undertake to perform. The only condition is that you surpass everyone else in the field. In every craft the most skilled master, as you know, gains most riches and has the best position and the greatest stature among his companions. Think how even in so humble a profession as shoemaking men search out the best among the cobblers. If it is true of the humblest occupations that the most skilled practitioners are ever most in demand and so become most famous, consider whether in the highest professions the opposite suddenly holds true. In fact you will find it still more to the point to be the best in these, or at least one of the best. If you succeed in these fields, you know that you have been given a greater portion of happiness than other men. If you are learned, you realize the misfortune of the ignorant. You know, in addition, that the unhappiest lot falls to those who, being ignorant, desire still to appear learned.

Here let me draw a facetious but very exact parallel. It may make the point quite clear. If there were some fellow who wanted to appear to know how to swim, while in fact he could not swim, and he stood safely on shore moving just like the swimmers, extending his palms, throwing his arms about, breathing to this side and to that, even lying on the earth as the others lay in the river while swimming, could you, with God's help, keep from laughing at the sight? I somehow think someone in the crowd would want to go at him for it, one way or another. What do you think? Wouldn't he seem crazy? He would certainly not appear wise. But if this fool were really so eager to seem a competent swimmer that he threw himself right into the flood and the river's currents, would that not be enough to prove he really was mad? I think so, certainly. What if that reckless fool began drowning, who had been so eager to prove he was what he was not and so presumptuous as to try to show he understood what he did not understand? And what if there were some other man there, one who had just been standing quietly by with his clothes on, not thinking of attracting attention or being noticed as a good swimmer. Now suppose this man quickly undressed and threw himself into the water and rescued the madman? What would you say? Would he deserve gratitude and high praise? Now you see how much better it is to be, than merely to seem to be, someone of worth.

Consider in your own mind what a boon to know more than others and to put the knowledge to good use at the right time and place. If you think it over, I am sure you will realize that in every field a man who would appear to be valuable must be valuable in fact. Now we have stated this much: that youth should not be wasted but should be directed to some honorable kind of work, that a man should do his utmost in that work, and that he should choose the field which will be most helpful to his family and bring him most fame. A career should suit our own nature and the state of our fortunes, and should be pursued in such a way that we may never, by our own fault at least, fall short of the first rank.

Riches, however, are for nearly everyone the primary reason for working at all. They are also most useful in making it possible to persevere in our undertakings until we win approval and attain public favor, position, and fame. This is the time, therefore, to explain how wealth is acquired and how it is kept. It was also one of the four things which we said were necessary to bring about and to preserve contentment in a family. Now, then, let us begin to accumulate wealth. Perhaps the present moment, as the evening grows dark, is just right for this subject, for no occupation seems less attractive to a man of large and liberal spirit than the kind of labor by which wealth is in fact gathered. If you will count over in your imagination the actual careers that bring great profits, you will see that all basically concern themselves with buying and selling or with lending and collecting the returns. Having neither petty nor vulgar minds, I imagine you probably find these activities, which are solely directed to making a profit, somewhat below you. They seem entirely to lack honor and distinction.

Selling is, in truth, solely mercenary. You serve the needs of the buyer, and he pays you for your labor. You gain your reward by demanding more of others than you paid for the things they buy. Essentially, then, you sell not the commodity but your labor. For the commodity you receive the equivalent in money, and for your work you receive the profit. Lending, on the other hand, would be noble generosity if you asked no reward for it, but then it would not count as a kind of work by which men gain wealth. Some people, moreover, think that these professions, which we shall call mercenary, are never quite clean, never untainted by considerable fraud. They say that ugly intrigues and false contracts are frequently involved. They urge that men of liberal mind spurn them altogether.

Those who thus dismiss all mercenary activities are wrong, I believe. If the pursuit of wealth is not as glorious as are other great pursuits, yet a man is not contemptible if, being unsuited by nature to achieve anything much in other finer fields of work, he devotes himself to this kind of activity. Here, it may be, he knows he is not inadequately equipped to do well. Here everyone admits he is very useful to the republic and still more to his own family. Wealth, if it is used to help the needy, can gain a man esteem and praise. With wealth, if it is used to do great and noble things and to show a fine magnanimity and splendor, fame and dignity can be attained. In emergencies and times of need we see every day how useful is the wealth of private citizens to the country itself. From public funds alone it is not always possible to pay the wages of those whose arms and blood defend the country's liberty and dignity. Nor can republics increase their glory and their might without enormous expenditure.

Indeed, as Master Ciprian of our Alberti clan used to say, empires are bought from fortune with gold and blood. If the words of this most prudent man be true, and I think they are true indeed, the wealth of private citizens who come to the aid of their country ought to be esteemed at its real value. Messer Benedetto of our Alberti clan used to say this, too: a great treasury does not depend on a great number of men who are forced to pay. It is one that commands the loyalty of those who are not poor. It is a treasury to which all rich citizens faithfully and conscientiously contribute. I do not believe, therefore, that we should listen to those who consider all mercenary activity vile.

Our Alberti clan, in fact, has for long been able to conduct itself with highest honor in mercenary as in all other activities. It has preserved such an honorable name and reputation for integrity in the East and in diverse regions of the world that we have gained, no less than merited, repute and authority among all peoples. No man who ever played a role in our affairs—this is a fact of our history—has permitted any kind of dishonest dealing. In every contract our agents have acted with justice, with perfect simplicity, and with purest honesty. Thus have we gained our fame as great merchants, a fame we enjoy inside and outside Italy, in Spain, in the East, in Syria, in Greece, and in all the ports. The Albertis, too, have always come most effectively to the aid of our country. Of every thirty-two pounds of gold spent in the days of the Albertis by our government, the records show that more than one represented the contribution of our family alone. This means a great sum of money, but still greater was the good will, the love, the readiness to serve which we showed at all times. Thus did we acquire great reputation, fame, and high esteem among all men. Yet we gained greater love and loyalty among foreign peoples than among our own fellow citizens. But there will be some other occasion to talk about our evil fortunes.

Let us rather remember and exalt with pride the glory which truly belongs to our family. To you, Battista and Carlo, I am glad to speak of this, for the memory and fame of our family and of our greatest and finest members may inspire you eagerly to pursue, as you do, the dignity, authority, fame, and glory of our house. You will do your best to maintain and, when possible, to increase those virtues which we would be ashamed not to perpetuate in ourselves. One can glory in our family, I say, for over two hundred years not so poor as to be below the richest families in Florence. Neither the memory of our old men nor our family records would fail to confirm that the Alberti family has never lacked for great and famous, sincere, good, and trustworthy men of business.

Even to this day you can find no family in our country which has so long and so honorably preserved its wealth. Indeed in our country no family but that of the Albertis has ever managed to transmit great wealth to its descendants. All have been quickly exhausted, and their treasure has, as people say, gone up in smoke, leaving sometimes only poverty, misery, and disgrace. I do not wish to go on here and to give specific examples, or look into the reason or the misfortune that has destroyed great wealth among our fellow citizens. There would be too much to say and innumerable cases which it would be true but malicious to describe. Let me name some families with all respect and reverence, grieving over their misfortune, not blaming anyone: Cerchi, Peruzzi, Scali, Spini, Ricci, and innumerable other great families in our country did once abound in measureless wealth but suddenly, through fortune's cruelty, fell before our very eyes. Though still eminent for their character and high nobility, they have suffered hard times and even, in some cases, dire need. The members of our own family, though persecuted by fortune in every other way, at least have never had to complain of unfair treatment or unkindness from the family itself. No member of our family ever broke faith in his business dealings or failed to pay his honest debts. Those honorable principles which have always been observed by our family show that we have never been greedy for gain, unjust, or careless of our duties. Indeed the honorable success of our family may be due less to our prudence and wisdom than, as I believe, to God's rewarding us with his favor. May God continue thus to favor them, delighting in their honesty and justice. May they long enjoy prosperity.

Why have I gone on at length on these topics? Only to show you that, among occupations, there are quite a few, both honorable and highly esteemed, by means of which wealth in no small measure may be gained. One of these occupations, as you know, is that of merchant. You can easily call to mind other similar careers which are both honorable and highly profitable. You want to know, then, what they are. Let us run through them. We shall spread out all the occupations before us and choose the best among them, then we shall try to define how they make us wealthy and prosperous. Occupations that do not bring profit and gain will never make you rich. Those that bring frequent and large profits are the ones that make you rich. The only system for becoming rich, by our own industry and by the means that luck, friends, or anyone's favor can give us, is to make profits. And how do men grow poor? Ill fortune certainly plays a part, this I admit, but excluding fortune, let us speak here of industry. If riches come through profits, and these through labor, diligence, and hard work, then poverty, which is the reverse of profit, will follow from the reverse of these virtues, namely from neglect, laziness, and sloth. These are the fault neither of fortune nor of others, but of oneself. One grows poor, also, by spending too much. Prodigality dissipates wealth and throws it away. The opposite of prodigality, the opposite of neglect, are carefulness and conscientiousness, in short, good management. Good management is the means to preserve wealth. Thus we have found out that to become rich one must make profits, keep what one has gained, and exercise rational good management.

Let us first discuss the general characteristics of profitmaking, then you will hear about good management. Profits come in part through our own efforts, in part through force of circumstances outside ourselves. The qualities in ourselves most conducive to profit are industry, intelligence, and the like. To be a navigator, an architect, a physician, for instance, or a member of other professions like these, one must have good judgment and high intellectual powers. The powers of the body also are suited to bring us profit, for in all mechanical and mercantile labor it is essential to walk, to work with the hands, and to be physically active in various ways. The best profits come to the worker who exerts himself and sweats. There are other activities in which powers of body and mind function together to bring profit. Such are the occupations of painters, sculptors, musicians, and others like them. All these ways of making a living, since they depend mainly on our own personal powers, are what men call arts. They remain with us and do not go down in shipwrecks but swim away with our naked selves. They keep us company all our lives and feed and maintain our name and fame.

There are also things outside themselves which may bring profit. These lie under the scepter of fortune, for instance, finding hidden treasure, coming into an inheritance, receiving gifts—these things are the hope of many men. Many persons make it their chief occupation to seek the patronage of great lords, to become the intimate friends of rich citizens, only hoping to obtain some part of their wealth. Of these persons we may speak at more length in due time. This sort of occupation depends on fortune, and in these activities industry avails nothing. Luck and circumstance alone can satisfy such hopes and desires. No work and no wisdom can gain any profit here unless fortune is in a liberal and smiling mood. There are other sorts of profit which depend on outside circumstances, particularly on material things. These include the results of usury and the fruitfulness of flocks, of horses, of woods, or, as in Tuscany sometimes, of heaths. These things bear fruit of themselves without much effort from us.

Now the general types of occupation we have set out here have an almost infinite number of subdivisions in which are mobilized one or more of the sources of profit I have mentioned—mind, body, fortune, and natural resources. It would be lengthy and perhaps superfluous to enumerate them all here. Anyone running over the occupations of men can easily recognize the types for himself. Since our principles have now enabled us to assess the character of any occupation, let us distinguish those most suited to a great and noble family like our own.

The most praiseworthy activities, some will say, are the ones over which fortune holds no sway, and in which the mind rather than the body is employed. This seems to me a fine and manly view to take. If fortune can not disrupt your activities, they will remain at your disposal, always ready, and cannot fail to offer you utility and pleasure. I agree particularly with those who commend the arts for the liberty they give us. Thus implicitly they exclude usury, avarice, and all mercenary and greedy labors. As you know, a spirit subject to avarice cannot be called free, and no mercenary labor can really be considered worthy of a free and noble mind.

Yet if you entirely exclude the domain of fortune in choosing one's career, I am not sure how far I could agree. I don't know whether I am right to say this. I don't want to make a mistake, but I do almost believe that probably no highly esteemed sort of work actually is free from some basic dependence on fortune. In military matters, I believe, they say victory is the daughter of fortune. Literary endeavors also depend on a thousand chances. Sometimes a man has no father, his relatives are envious, hard, and inhumane, and poverty strikes him down or he suffers some accident. Surely over your studies, as over human affairs in general, fortune has great power. You cannot persevere unless you have certain things which lie under fortune's scepter. In the pursuit of every most noble and glorious enterprise, then, you must not omit fortune from your considerations but must moderate its influence by the use of discretion and judgment.

You may object that profitmaking alone, where industry and wisdom together with zeal and industry seem to count for practically everything, is not like this. Good enough, yet I shall not retract my argument on this point, for it seems to me largely answered thus: if profits in business come by our zeal, our efforts, still they will never be great if our zeal and our efforts are applied within a narrow field. From small business affairs no great profits come, however vigorously the enterprise is carried through. Profits can grow only as the affairs themselves expand, and with them our industry and labor. Great affairs bring great profits, but in these, as no one doubts, fortune is often vitally involved. In such business as our Alberti firms have traditionally done, for instance, enough wool was brought from faraway Flanders to fill all the baskets in Florence itself and in most of Tuscany. We shall not trouble here to relate how many other goods were brought at great expense, by steep and difficult mountain passes, to Florence through the efforts of our house. Did so many bales of wool by any chance travel outside the reach of fortune's hand?

How many risks they ran, how many rivers and barriers they traversed, before they rested in security! Thieves, tyrants, wars, negligence, cheating on the part of middlemen, all these things did not fail to threaten them.

Such is the way, I think, with all great business enterprises, all merchant and trading ventures worthy of a noble and honorable family. Hence merchants ought always to be what our great ancestors were and what, no doubt, the Albertis are and always will be—leaders in great enterprise, men of the highest usefulness to their country, bringers of honor and fame to the family, men who grow from day to day, not in money and goods only but likewise in dignity and in the eyes of men. Then we, like them, can say that in our labors the spirit is never enslaved but always free. Our body is subjected to no dishonorable or vile burden but adorned always by modesty and temperance. Insofar as fortune controls the outcome of our undertakings, I shall not claim we never, but generally we do not, let it upset our minds through the turbulence of our feelings.

Now we have distinguished which are the very best professions. The second best are those which come closest to the best. After these come others far below those which least enslave us and which least depend on fortune. We have them all sorted out now. And what are the ones we shall personally choose among them? Certainly those, as we have said above, which are most appropriate to our situation. And how shall we practice them? Here perhaps we need a more precise reply to the question. For the sake of brevity, however, I shall just sum up some general principles. You, by application of these, cannot fail of the right path whatever your particular profession.

Here is what I say to you: where the spirit is concerned, act by this rule —the spirit must be free. The spirit is unfree when it becomes greedy, avaricious, miserly, timid, envious, or suspicious. These vices subjugate the spirit and oppress the mind, and keep us from aspiring freely and with soaring heart to win noble praise and fame. As the diseases of the body keep it lying prone and deprive the sick man of the liberty of bodily movement, so do avarice, timidity, suspiciousness, thirst for gain, and similar complaints sap the strength of the intellect and keep the intelligence in subjection. Thought and reason, then, are prohibited from the adequate performance of their functions in the spirit. Just as freedom from pain, vitality of blood, and healthy muscles are essential to bodily health, so to the mind, peace, tranquility, and truth are requisite.

Now, the body keeps its health by moderate and clean living. The mind keeps its health by this means, and also by the exercise of reason and virtue. This virtue, which is a necessity for the spirit, encounters opposition from vice. Vice weighs down the mind, the reason, and all the operations of the spirit to make them unfree. The spirit must, therefore, shun vice as it would shun slavery: it must ennoble itself by excellence and so be free. The spirit must not be subject to any error or tolerate any despicable ways for the sake of gold. It must shun all unworthy ways lest it lose fame: virtue may not be sacrificed for the sake of treasure since, as Plato, the most noble prince of philosophers, used to say, "all the gold hidden in the earth, all the gold stored up above ground, all the possessions on earth do not compare with virtue." Virtue maintained with constancy and strength far outshines all that is subject to fortune's sway, all that is transitory and destructible. Fame and a good name rooted in excellence surpass in worth all the profits the world can offer. It is greater profit, truly, to gain favor and praise, since it is for favor and praise that men seek abounding wealth. The spirit, therefore, must resist enslavement for the sake of riches. The body must not be formed in idleness and indulgence; our only use for wealth must be to make us free.

It is, perhaps, a kind of slavery to be forced to plead and beg from other men in order to satisfy our necessity. That is why we do not scorn riches, but learn to govern ourselves and to subdue our desires while we live free and happy in the midst of affluence and abundance. Although some would describe practically any kind of physical labor as a sort of servitude, I think we shall count only labor performed at the command of others as servitude. The command of others means nothing less, I think, than that others reap the fruit of one's labor. The minimum of enslavement, then, is work performed for love, and not for payment. One would rather work for one's own family than for others, rather for friends than for strangers, rather for good men than for such as are not good. One's own country, of course, has more right to command one than any other person.

Fear none of the things that fortune can inflict. And do not desire what fortune can give. If fortune brings you riches, use them to serve the fame and honor of your own name and that of your family, help your friends, and spend your wealth in honorable and splendid ways. If fortune be mean and miserly, do not let it make you anxious or discontented, or weigh down your mind with hopes and expectations of more than you have been given. Despise fortune; it should be easy enough to despise what you don't have. If fortune takes away from you the wealth you once enjoyed and which you used with wisdom, what can you do but bear it in quiet fortitude? To live filled with sad longing, to yearn with heavy heart for the return and repossession of that which is barred off from you, this would be servitude of a kind. It is unhappiness, certainly. As to profits depending on external things, finally, we should be neither so lazy nor so busy that we cannot freely engage in more praiseworthy works.

To round off these instructions, let me say what has always seemed to me the most important thing in anyone's life. It is one thing without which no enterprise deserves praise or has real value. No authority or dignity can be maintained without it. It is the ultimate source of all the splendor our work may have, the most beautiful and shining part of our life now and our life hereafter, the most lasting and eternal part—I speak of honor. In every thought and action, in every deed and habit, work and occupation, in word, hope, longing, in our entire will and desire, in absolutely everything that concerns us, let us always take the counsel of honor. Honor remains ever the best teacher of virtue, the loyal companion of our good name, the kind sister of right conduct, and the most pious mother of calm and blessed peace.

Here is an analogy quite proper to the case: consider this holy and sacred source of honor as our very shadow, always beside us, always comprehending, weighing and judging whatever we do and the manner and purpose of all our actions. This sense of honor sees, distinguishes, examines everything. It concentrates full attention on whatever concerns us. It praises you affectionately for the good you do, thanks you abundantly, gives you confidence and abundant strength. For evil it reprimands you angrily, casts harsh blame, laughs in a troubled way at you, tells the world your vice and disgrace. Be sure you consult your honor and that it behaves like this. Follow its dictates with reverence and care, for it will give you faultless and precious counsel, sincerely and with certainty. Your honor will never let you be enslaved, it will shield you against all the blows of fortune, and, if you scrupulously follow and obey its commands and counsels, marvelous and incredible though it sounds, you will never have to regret anything you have said or done. Satisfying the standards of honor, we shall grow rich and well praised, admired, and esteemed among men. The man who scorns to hear or to obey that sense of honor which seeks to advise and to command him grows full of vice and will never be contented even if he is rich. Men will neither admire nor love him. Being unhappy, he often feels he would sooner live in poverty than in a splendor accompanied by bitter regrets: bitter regrets feed on the heart of the dishonest man. Remember always that poverty does us less injury than dishonor. Fame and men's favor help us more than all the riches in the world. This we shall take up elsewhere.

We who are here, indeed, will make our decisions in life by consulting at every step not utility or pleasure but virtue. We shall ever give ground to honor. It will stand to us like a public accountant, just, practical, and prudent in measuring, weighing, considering, evaluating, and assessing everything we do, achieve, think, and desire. With the help of our honor we shall grow if not wealthy in goods at least abundantly rich in fame, in public esteem, grace, favor, and repute. All these things are to be preferred over any degree of wealth. Thus let us act. Let the sense of honor be always in our hearts, let us fear and love it.

I think these general principles to guide us in the avoidance of poverty may suffice for now. We shall look for no others. Riches are wanted to escape need, and the man who is free of need is rich enough. I should say, if a man labors in his occupation as we have been telling him to, certainly he will suffer no need; rather he will abound in everything a man should have. We have now seen, also, what sort of work is most useful and best to choose, as well as how to conduct our performance of it. I imagine that you would now like me to explain further and to define the actual fields of work that exist, noting the military, agriculture, the arts and sciences, business. After my account of these occupations, you would also want to hear about good management. Of this I have said that it constitutes half the art of being wealthy.

Battista: But listen, Carlo, I think I hear something.

Lionardo: So do I. I told you, Battista, and now you see it's true, no sooner are we well launched in our discussion . . .

Carlo: It is Ricciardo.

Battista: Yes?

Carlo: Yes.

Lionardo: Let's go and greet him, then tomorrow, early, we can meet here again.

Battista: Fine. Go, I follow you.

Prologue of Book III to
Francesco d'Altobianco Alberti

Francesco, your uncle, Messer Antonio Alberti, a most learned man, used often to walk in those lovely gardens of yours with his learned friends and discuss, as our father, Lorenzo Alberti, told us, which was the greater loss, the fall of our ancient, most extensive empire, or the dying out of our ancient, most beautiful Latin tongue. Our father himself never doubted but that the loss to our Italian people of the general respect and obedience once given us as a natural tribute to our excellence was a far lighter misfortune than the fact of finding ourselves shorn of a flourishing language in which so many great writers had recorded their lofty knowledge of the good and blessed way to live. In our ancient empire there certainly was some wondrous grace and majesty, for it gave sound justice and perfect equity to all peoples; yet a prince probably derived, from the eminence of that position which he held by fortune's favor, no more power and authority than from his knowledge of the Latin language and familiarity with Latin letters. We might add that perhaps it was no great wonder if the nations, with their natural love of liberty, in time withdrew their submission to us and stubbornly fought against and overthrew our dictates and our laws. But by whose fault but our own could anyone explain this other calamity, the loss of something which no one took from us and no one stole? It even seems to me that our imperial splendor was not wholly extinguished until the light and the far-reaching influence of Latin and of Latin letters faded away. Strange indeed that a thing preserved by use came to be corrupted and diminished while still, in those days, certainly current among all men.

It may perhaps be thought a consequence of the other catastrophes that then befell us. Italy was repeatedly occupied and subjected to various nations: the Gauls, the Goths, the Vandals, the Lombards, and other like harsh and barbarous peoples. As necessity or the wish to communicate prompted them, therefore, people learned one foreign language or another, partly just to be understood and partly to please in their manner of speaking persons whom they had to obey. The foreigners, meanwhile, being newly arrived, also adapted their ways to ours, with considerable admixture, I believe, of barbarisms and corruptions. This mixing, then, made our originally refined and polished language grow from day to day more rustic and degenerate.

I do not think we should accept the idea of some people, however, who find this loss so astonishing that they claim there was in Italy, even in those times and earlier, only the language that we employ today. They cannot believe that the women in those days knew things which are obscure and difficult even for the most learned scholars today. They therefore conclude that the language in which men of education wrote was only an academic and artificial invention, understood but not truly used by many people. Were this the place to debate the question, I would ask these people who among the ancients ever wrote, not of scholarly and learned matters but of everyday, domestic things to his wife or children or servants in any language but Latin? Who, I would also ask, ever used in private or public communication any but this form of speech in which, because it was common to all, they in fact wrote all they had to say, whether to the general public or to friends. I would ask them, further, whether they think foreigners today find our present language less difficult to use with precision and clarity than we the ancient tongue? Don't we see with what difficulty our slaves learn to employ our own idioms comprehensibly simply because, in their unfamiliarity with our variations of case and tense, they do not know how to make words agree as required? How many women in those days were highly praised for their good Latin; indeed, the speech of almost all women was praised above that of men for being less contaminated by contact with foreigners! How many orators there were, too, who were entirely unversed in anything academic and totally illiterate! Why, moreover, would the ancient writers, when they were taking such pains to be of use to their fellow citizens, have written in a language known only to a few? This hardly seems to be the place, however, to discuss this subject at length; perhaps we may argue it more fully elsewhere. Yet no true scholar will deny the only sound hypothesis, I think, namely that all the ancient writers, when they wrote as they did, wished to be understood by all their contemporaries.

If that is how it was, my learned friend Francesco, and you agree with me, what need have we to fear the criticism of a few ignorant readers? Who, on the other hand, will dare to say that I should not have written in a language which permits the ignorant to read me? The wise, indeed, are more likely to praise my zeal if, by writing so that all could understand, I have made an effort rather to educate many than to please a few, for you know how few these days are the educated. How pleased I would be, indeed, if my vociferous critics were capable of earning praise as well as of condemning others. I fully admit that the ancient Latin language was rich and beautiful, but I see no reason why our present-day Tuscan is so contemptible that anything written in it, however excellent, should fail to satisfy us. I think it will do for me if I can say approximately what I want to say and speak in a manner that may be understood. These critics' own knowledge of the ancient tongue, meanwhile, extends only to keeping silent in it, and of the modern to maligning those who do not keep silent. Here is my view: if someone else be more learned than I, or be what many would like to be thought to be, he will find our common tongue no less beautiful than the one they so much prefer and wish to force on everyone. I cannot approve of the contempt so many people show for what they themselves speak, while they praise what they neither understand nor cultivate by reading. It is not honorable to demand of others what you refuse to do yourself. As to the great authority among all nations which my critics attribute to the ancient language, this authority exists simply because many learned men have written in it. Our own tongue will have no less power as soon as learned men decide to refine and polish it by zealous and arduous labors.

I do not try to hide from the comprehension and, with it, the criticism of all our fellow citizens. Let my adversaries either quell their envious spirit or take more valuable matter and prove their own eloquence in it. Anyone should prefer to apply his energies to something better than maligning those who do not stagnate in idleness. I do not hope to be praised for more than my good will in attempting, as far as my intelligence, industry, and zeal permit, to make some useful contribution to our Alberti family. I think it is more valuable to work as I do, by writing, than by silence to escape the criticism of those who cry me down.

Therefore, Francesco, as you know, I have already written two books, in the first of which you learned how, in the well-conducted family, elders exercise care and discretion in the training of the young, and the young, in turn, behave as they are obliged and duty-bound to do toward their elders. There you saw what diligence is required of fathers and mothers in the bringing up of their offspring to good behavior and high character. My second book set forth what are the chief considerations in marrying, and discussed the proper occupations for young men. So far, then, we have made the family large and set it on the road to success; now, since good management is reputed to be extremely important if wealth is to be well enjoyed, here is this third book. Here you will find a description of a proper *pater familias*. I think you will not find it tedious. You will notice the bare simplicity of the style, and in this you will recognize that I have done my best to imitate the charming and delightful Greek writer Xenophon. You, Francesco, since you have always held me dear and liked my works, will read this good *pater familias* and learn from him how to rule and preserve your own person, first of all, and then whatever you possess.

You will understand, of course, that I am not attempting by the gift of this book—a pledge and symbol of our friendship—to repay all that your goodness has been to me. As you can imagine, I shall consider myself more than ever in your debt if you will take the trouble to read and correct this work. With your help there will be so much the less for our adversaries to use against us. Read me, my dear Francesco, and love me as ever.

BOOK THREE

Liber Tertius Familie: Economicus

ionardo had already answered our questions on a number of points where Carlo and I, on thinking over the discussion of the previous evening as reported above, had found ourselves doubtful or puzzled as to what he had said. He had begun to praise warmly the diligence of our efforts, for Carlo and I had made notes during the night of the discussion we had heard. Now Giannozzo Alberti arrived on the scene. Here was a man whose humane and noble conduct made everyone call him a good man, as in truth he was. He came to see Ricciardo. He greeted us and asked how Lorenzo was feeling and how he had responded to the consolation of seeing his brother. Lionardo gave him reverent welcome, and said,

I would have been happy, Giannozzo, had you been with us last night, when Ricciardo arrived.

Giannozzo: I, too, would have been glad to be here, but I did not know of it in time.

Lionardo: Your heart, I assure you, would have been touched. Lorenzo's condition was serious indeed, to tell the truth, and he was very weak, Giannozzo. This illness of his grows heaviest toward evening and burdens him then more gravely than in the daytime. Lorenzo heard and recognized his brother's voice, and he tried, in the manner of a most weary man, to raise himself up. He lifted both his eyes, and one hand he raised enough to uncover the whole arm. He held it up for a moment and let it fall, sighed, turned his gaze toward his brother, looked upon him with great fervor, and weak as he was, did what he could to show his brother an honorable welcome. He gave him his hand; Ricciardo drew closer, and they embraced and held each other close for quite some time. Each seemed to want to speak to the other and to say various things, but they could not say anything. They wept.

Giannozzo: Ah, for pity's sake.

Lionardo: Then they let each other go. Ricciardo did all he could to hide his weeping. Lorenzo, after a little while, spoke to him, and these were his first words, "My brother, Battista here and Carlo will be your children from now on." No one among us could restrain his tears any longer.

Giannozzo: The pity of it. And Ricciardo?

Lionardo: You can imagine.

Giannozzo: Cruel fortune. But how is Ricciardo now?

Lionardo: Fine, as far as I saw.

Giannozzo: I came to see him.

Lionardo: I think at this moment he is resting.

Giannozzo: How unlike the old Ricciardo to be idly sleeping. I think I never knew a man livelier or more devoted to work than Ricciardo.

Lionardo: Don't be surprised, Giannozzo, if Ricciardo lies in bed late today. He went to bed very late last night, exhausted by travel and his mind, too, probably much burdened with many troubled thoughts.

Giannozzo: It's true we old fellows find the slightest exertion a painful strain. I feel it myself even now. This morning at dawn I went up to the Palazzo to plead for the honor and property of a friend. It was not yet time for the business I wanted to do, so I came down here quickly. If, during this interlude, I might greet Ricciardo, I would go back to the temple to see the sacrifice and worship God, then return to do what my friend needs to have done. Yet I am already exhausted, I am weary through and through. The truth is that the winter season treats us very differently from the trees, for winter lightens the trees, unclothing and stripping them of leaves, but to us old men winter brings heavy burdens and clothes us in shadow and in pain. Thus it is, my children, that the longer one lives, the more one weeps in this world. That friend of mine, he, too, feels the weight of the years and of poverty, and if I did not undertake to carry a part of his burden, God knows in what dire state he would be.

Lionardo: I have heard our kinsmen, and others as well, call you a good man, Giannozzo. Now I see they have good reasons, and that you particularly merit the name for your unwearying interest in helping your friends, supporting the needy, coming to the aid of those in trouble. But sit, Giannozzo. You are tired, and it befits your age to be seated. Sit down.

Giannozzo: Yes, so I shall. But you should understand, Lionardo, it is only in the last few years that I have come to this. I just can't do as much as I used to.

Lionardo: And how many things didn't you do in your youth which you would no longer want to do now? Other things give you pleasure now, perhaps, which did not appeal to you then.

Giannozzo: Many, my dear Lionardo. I vividly remember how in my youth, in those days when our country was in a prosperous state, jousting or public games were frequent. There always used to be sharp disagreements between my elders and myself because I wanted, above all things, to go along with the others into the midst of it all and prove my worth. The men from our house always came home with high praises and honor. I enjoyed their triumph myself, it is true, yet I also grieved because I was not among those whose noble exertions won the honors. Oh, the Alberti family more than any other great family of florence sent young men into the field. I used to watch them, joyful, spirited, full of strength as they performed feats of arms. The whole people seemed to care only for the Alberti men; they did not know how to applaud a man who was not an Alberti; everyone felt that if anyone else was praised, anyone who was not a member of our clan, it was honor stolen from us. You can imagine how I delighted in the great acclaim thus enjoyed, and justly, by our men. Imagine, on the other hand, Lionardo, how a youth with a lively and manly spirit such as I then possessed would suffer at being prevented from taking his own place among his kinsmen as he longed to do, and making everyone praise and admire him. Thus did I suffer.

I hated everyone who kept me away from the joust, and every word my elders spoke seemed a stone smiting my ears, Lionardo. I could not listen to what they said when they all warned me that jousting was dangerous, useless, expensive, more apt to produce envy than love, more likely to bring a man shame than fame, that too many accidents happened, that quarrels arose there, and that they held me more dear than I thought or, indeed, deserved. And I—silent, sullen. Then they would tell me many a tale of men who came out of those maneuvers dead or broken, useless for the rest of their lives. You would laugh if I told you how many devices I hit on to gain their permission, for I still would not have done this, or anything else, without the permission of my elders. I would get kinsmen, friends, and friends of friends to intercede with them for me. I said that I had promised, and produced persons who confirmed my having sworn it to my companions. Nothing helped. Thus there were times when I did not love them as I usually did. I well knew that they did all this because I was all too dear to them, and because they, in their love, feared lest some disaster befall either my person or my honor, as often happens to a strong and courageous boy. Yet did they seem hateful to me when they opposed me and stood firm against my too obstinate, though manly will. I was angrier still whenever I thought they acted as they did from motives of economy, for they were, as you know, excellent and careful managers, as I, myself, have since learned to become. In those days I was young, I spent and gave away my money.

Lionardo: And now?

Giannozzo: Now, my dear Lionardo, I have become wise. I know that it is madness to throw away what you possess. The man who has never experienced the sorrow and frustration of going to ask others for help in his need has no idea of the usefulness of money. If a man has no experience to tell him how painfully money is acquired, moreover, he spends it with ease. If a man spends without measure, he is usually quickly impoverished. And if a man lives in poverty, my children, he will suffer want and many deprivations, such is this world, and perhaps he would be better off dying than living in need and misery. Therefore, dear Lionardo, believe me, as one who knows by experience and could not have more certain knowledge, the proverb of our peasants is most true: "He who finds no money in his own purse will find still less in another's." It is most desirable my dear children to be thrifty. One should guard against too great spending as if it were a mortal foe.

Lionardo: Yet I think, Giannozzo, that with all your desire to avoid expense, you would still wish neither to be nor to appear avaricious.

Giannozzo: God forbid. Let our worst enemies be avaricious. There is nothing like avarice to destroy a man's reputation and public standing. What virtue is so bright and noble but that, under the cloak of avarice, it is wholly obscured and passes unrecognized. A hateful anxiety perpetually troubles the spirit of a man who is too tightfisted and avaricious. Whether he be worriedly gathering or reluctantly spending his wealth, he has always a great gnawing and heavy burden. He lives in constant torment. I never see such men happy. They never enjoy any part of their possessions.

Lionardo: To avoid appearing avaricious, people think they must spend lavishly.

Giannozzo: And to avoid appearing mad, they must be thrifty. But why, with God's help, should one not prefer to be thrifty rather than lavish? Believe me, who have some knowledge and experience of the matter, those great expenditures which are not particularly necessary are not admired by prudent men. I have never seen, or think that you will see, any expenditure so great and lavish or so magnificent but that a multitude of men found in it a multitude of shortcomings. There was always too much of the one thing or too little of the other. You know how it is. If a man plans a dinner, though a dinner is a most proper and civilized kind of expense, almost a sort of tax or tribute to preserve good will and to confirm relationships of friendship, yet, aside from the confusion, worries, and anxieties—this is wanted, that is needed, this other thing also—upheaval and annoyance overwhelm you until you are tired before you have even begun your preparations. Aside from all this there is the throwing away of things, the washing and sweeping all over the house; nothing stays locked, this is lost, this other thing demanded—you seek here, you borrow there, you buy, you spend, you spend some more, you waste. To this just add the regrets, the second thoughts which trouble your mind during the proceedings and afterward as well, an infinite variety of anxieties and troubles that beset you, serious ones, too. And nonetheless, when the smoke is out of the kitchen, the favor you have won by the whole thing is already consumed, all the favor, Lionardo, and you will hardly be noticed for all you have done. If the affair has received some approbation, a few will praise it for some part of its splendor, and many will blame you for the smallness of your largesse. The many, moreover, are right. Any expenditure that is not particularly necessary, it seems to me, can only come from madness. And if a man goes mad in any respect, he ought to go wholly mad in that respect, for to try to be only moderately mad has always been mere double madness and utter folly.

But let all these things go, for they are minor compared with the matters I shall speak of now. These expenditures for the entertainment and due honoring of your friends can only come once or twice a year, and they bear an excellent medicine in themselves for anyone who has tried them once: if he is not wholly out of his mind, I think he will avoid the repetition of them. Lionardo, come to my aid yourself, and think this over a bit. Consider whether there is anything more apt to cause the ruin not only of a family but of a village or a whole community than those—what do they call them in those books of yours, those persons who spend money without reason?

Lionardo: Prodigals.

Giannozzo: Call them what you like. If I had to give them a name, what could I find to call them but "damned pestilence"? Thoroughly off the road themselves, they lead others astray too. Other young men see these prodigals of yours abounding in every sort of entertainment, and since it is the vice of the young to prefer places of delight to the workshop and to seek out spendthrift young companions rather than thrifty old ones, they quickly join them in the consumption of luxuries and delicacies. They live a life of idleness, avoid the kinds of activity men praise, and put their pride and happiness in their power to waste their own resources, neither caring as much for their honor as they ought nor valuing moderation of any kind. True enough, who among them could even hope to become a good man, living in the midst of so many greedy, lying flatterers and besieged by vile and dishonest men, musicians, players, dancers, buffoons, pimps, rubbish dressed in livery and frills? Perhaps this whole crowd does not connive to sit on the doorstep of anyone who is a prodigal, as if at a school and factory of vice, whence the young men used to this kind of life are unable to get out? Oh Lord, what crimes do they not commit, merely to continue in it? They rob their fathers, their relatives, and their friends, they pawn and they sell. Who could tell half the hideous tale? Every day they cause new complaints, every hour brings some fresh infamy; they constantly collect more hate and ill will and enmity and disgrace. Finally, my dear Lionardo, these prodigals are left poor and full of years, without honor and with few, or rather no, friends. Those joyful leeches whom they took for friends in their great days of spending, those lying flatterers who praised their overspending that was their very self-impoverishment and called it a virtue, who, glass in hand, swore and promised to lay down their life— you have seen the water swarming with fish while the bait's afloat; when the bait is gone, all is deserted and empty. I do not want to go on at length on this subject, or give you examples and tell you of all the men I have seen with these very eyes go from great wealth to want through lack of thrift. That, Lionardo, would be a long story—the whole day would not suffice us.

So, to be brief, I shall say only this: as prodigality is evil, so in the same measure is thrift good, valuable, and praiseworthy. Thrift does no one any harm and is good for the family. I tell you, moreover, that I know thrift alone is able to keep you so that you will never suffer need. Thrift is a holy thing, and how many lascivious desires, how many vile longings does it not put from us? Do not doubt it, Lionardo, prodigal and pleasure-seeking youth has ever been inclined to cause the ruin of the family. The old, who are thrifty and modest, are the family's salvation. It is good to be thrifty if only because, in your own mind, you gain the wonderful comfort of knowing that you live very well with what fortune has granted you. The man who lives contentedly with what he possesses does not, in my opinion, merit a name for avarice. It is the spendthrifts, on the contrary, who are truly avaricious, because, since they never tire of spending, they are never content with their gains but seek rapaciously at all times to obtain more money from this source and from that. Yet do not think that I delight in any excessive closefistedness. I say only this much, that the father of a family seems to me unworthy of honor if he is a spendthrift and merely enjoys himself.

Lionardo: If spendthrifts irritate you, Giannozzo, you ought to like those who do not spend. But avarice, which, according to the wise writers, consists in too great a desire for wealth, also consists in not spending.

Giannozzo: What you say is true enough.

Lionardo: Yet you don't like avarice.

Giannozzo: Indeed not.

Lionardo: This thrift you are talking about, then, what sort of thing is it?

Giannozzo: You know, Lionardo, I am not an educated man. I have tried all my life to know things by experience, and not to count much on what others have said. I know what I know more from the actual truth of it than from anyone's persuading me. If one of those people who spend all day reading says to me, "this is how it is," I believe him only if I see a reason for believing it. I like a reason which amounts to a clear demonstration rather than an argument which forces me to admit a point. If another, an uneducated person, gives me the same reason for the same thing, I will believe him without his citing authorities, just as much as I would the man who gives me evidence from a book. I assume the writer of a book was only a man like myself. So, now, perhaps, I shall not be able to answer you in the well-ordered way you would do, since you always spend the day with a book in your hand.

But see here, Lionardo, those spendthrifts of whom I was talking just now I dislike because they spend without reason. The avaricious also irritate me, because they do not make use of their possessions when needed, and because they want wealth too much. You know the sort of man I like? The sort who uses his possessions as the need arises and spends enough, but not more than enough. What is left over he saves, and this is the sort of man I call thrifty.

Lionardo: I see what you mean: those who maintain the mean between too little and too much.

Giannozzo: Yes, yes.

Lionardo: But how do we know what is too much and what is too little?

Giannozzo: Easily, by the ruler in our hand.

Lionardo: I am waiting and hoping to see this ruler.

Giannozzo: This is a simple matter, Lionardo. It can be briefly stated and is most useful to know. With every expenditure one must only be sure that the cost is no greater or heavier or larger than is needed, yet no less than honor requires.

Lionardo: Oh, Giannozzo, how much more help in the things of this world is a man of your wisdom and experience than a scholar without experience.

Giannozzo: What do you mean? Don't you have these things in your books? Yet they say you can find anything in books.

Lionardo: That may be, but I don't remember having seen it anywhere. And if you knew, Giannozzo, how helpful and exactly to our purpose you are proving yourself today, you would be amazed.

Giannozzo: Is that so? I am glad if I can be of any service to you.

Lionardo: The greatest possible service, for these young people here, Battista and Carlo, were hoping to hear some thoughts on the subject of good management, and I was hoping for the same myself. Now from whom could we hear more valuable and more comprehensive ideas on this subject than from you? You are well known among our kinsmen as a man neither so eager to spend as not to be absolutely thrifty nor so thrifty that anyone could ever accuse you of being less than liberal. I want to beg you, therefore, since thrift is such a very useful thing, do not deny us the advantage of learning about it from you. We will listen more faithfully to you than to another, who might teach us avarice rather than thrift. Go on, Giannozzo, and tell us what you think of this holy virtue of thrift. I hope to hear, on what remains of the subject, as on the matters you have already considered, some very distinguished thoughts.

Giannozzo: I would not know how to deny you, Lionardo, for it is you who ask me. It is also my duty to do the things which may give satisfaction to my kinsmen. I tell you more willingly what I know through my own experience of this matter of good management, because you do desire to know and because having listened to me will prove most helpful to you. Your desire to hear me, indeed, is no greater than mine to make you thrifty. I tell you this, thrift has done much for me. If I have any good fortune at all (as at present, thanks be to God, I have middling good fortune), I can say that I have achieved it more by thrift than by any degree of diligence in acquisition. True enough, but sit down. Sit down, Lionardo. These young boys will stand.

Lionardo: I am all right standing.

Giannozzo: Sit down.

Lionardo: You sit. You know the custom of our house, that none of us would ever sit in the presence of his elders.

Giannozzo: Certainly not in public. But these are private talks we have here, and for our own benefit. Sit. It is better to yield in obedience than to insist willfully on what seems to look like better conduct. Sit. Now, what were we saying about thrift? That it was helpful. I don't know your books and what they say about it but I shall tell you what sort of thrift I believe in myself, applied to what things and practiced in what ways. No one, I suppose, has any doubt that thrift is helpful, necessary, honorable, and praiseworthy. What do your books say about it?

Lionardo: What do you suppose, Giannozzo, since as you said those ancient writers were only men like yourself?

Giannozzo: Yes, but more learned ones. And if it were not so, their works would not have lived through so many ages.

Lionardo: I admit that, but it seems to me on these things they say nothing different from what any diligent father of a family observes for himself. What more could they say than you can on things you have seen with your own eyes and know by experience? They say over and over again that if there were no one able to preserve things, it would be folly to bring home what one had earned, and if nothing were being brought in, it would be no less absurd to try to preserve anything.

Giannozzo: Yes. How well they speak! What is the use of earning if there is no thrift? A man exerts himself in the process of acquiring goods in order to have what he needs when he needs it. He provides for sickness in health, as the ant provides for winter in summer. At need, therefore, one must consume; when things are not needed, they should be preserved. And so you have it: all of thrift consists not so much in preserving things as in using them at need. Do you see?

Lionardo: I do indeed, since to fail to use at need would be mere avarice and dishonorable.

Giannozzo: Yes, and poor economy, too.

Lionardo: Poor economy?

Giannozzo: Very poor. Did you ever notice the little old widows? They gather apples and other fruit. They keep them locked up and save them, until the fruit spoils before it is eaten. Then they are always eating the most rotten. In the end all are maggoty and spoiled. Consider: you'll find that all they had to do was throw three or four out of the window, and you could have said they were preserving them by throwing them away. Wouldn't it have been better, foolish old lady, to have thrown those first few away, and to have taken the good ones for your table or to have given some away? This is not preserving, but wasting.

Lionardo: How much better—they might have had some use of them, or at least received some thanks for them.

Giannozzo: Take another example: a drop of rain comes through the roof. The miser waits until tomorrow, and again until the day after tomorrow. It rains again, the miser does not want to spend his money. Again, it rains; the water. And what would have cost a *soldo* costs ten. True?

Lionardo: Often true.

Giannozzo: So you see it is poor economy not to spend money and use things at need. But since thrift consists in using and in preserving things, let us see what things there are to use and to preserve. Now, first of all, I think that to want to use and to preserve the things which belong to someone else would be either presumption or robbery or fraud. Am I right about that?

Lionardo: Very.

Giannozzo: So it is right that the things of which we are truly and carefully thrifty had better be really our own. Now what things are those?

Lionardo: I dare say my wife, my children, my house—those, maybe?

Giannozzo: Oh, those things are not ours, Lionardo. If I can take something from you anytime I like, shall we say that it belongs to you or to me? To you?

Lionardo: I would say it is more yours.

Giannozzo: But fortune can always, at her whim, take your wife, your children, your property, and such?

Lionardo: Certainly she can, yes.

Giannozzo: Then those things belong rather to her than to us. And what do you say of things that cannot be taken from you in any way? Whose are they?

Lionardo: Mine.

Giannozzo: Can the power to love, to desire, to wish, to disdain, and so forth according to your will, can this be taken from you?

Lionardo: Certainly not.

Giannozzo: These things, then, are truly yours.

Lionardo: You speak truly.

Giannozzo: But, to put it in brief, there are three things which a man can truly call his own. They are such that nature gave them to you the day you saw the light, with the freedom to use them well or badly just as it pleased and suited you. These are things nature ordained should always remain with you and never leave you till your last day. One of these things, as you realize, is that moving spirit within us by which we feel desire and anger. Whatever fortune's wish, this remains with us. Another such thing, as you realize, is your body. Nature has made it a vehicle, a kind of cart for moving the spirit about, and nature has commanded that it should never obey any spirit but its own. Thus any animal caged and subjected to others never ceases to try to be free and again to make use of its own self, its wings or feet or other parts, not at another's will but with liberty, at its own behest. Nature hates to have the body escape the guardianship of its spirit, and man, above all, naturally loves liberty. He loves to live at his own command, loves to belong to himself. And this seems to be the general appetite shared by all mortal beings. So these two things are our own, the spirit and the body.

Lionardo: And what is the third?

Giannozzo: Ha! A most precious thing. My very hands and eyes are not so much my own.

Lionardo: Amazing! But what thing is this?

Giannozzo: It cannot be bound, it cannot be diminished. In no way can it be made other than your own, provided you *want* it to be yours.

Lionardo: And at my will it can belong to another?

Giannozzo: And if you wish it can be not yours. Time, my dear Lionardo, time, my children.

Lionardo: No doubt you are right, yet it would not occur to me to call something my own if I could not give it away. Thus it seems to me that I can put all the operations of my spirit at the service of others, so that they would be no longer my own: I could love and hate and be moved at the persuasion of others, desire and not desire, laugh and weep, at the will of another.

Giannozzo: If you were in a boat and floating along with the current in the midst of our river Arno, and if, as sometimes happens to fishermen, you had dirty hands and your face all daubed with mud, would all that water not be yours, if you used it to wash and purify yourself? Right? And, likewise, if you did not use it?

Lionardo: Certainly then it would be not mine.

Giannozzo: That is exactly how it is with time. If a man uses it to wash off the dirt and mud—the ignorance and low desires and vile appetites—that cling to our mind and impure understanding, and if he makes use of time to learn, to think, and to do admirable deeds, he makes time his own. But a man who lets one hour after the other glide by in idleness, never engaging in any worthwhile occupation, certainly loses time. Thus time spent unused is lost, and time well used belongs to him who knows how to use it. Now, my children, you have the actions of the spirit, the body, and time, three things which truly belong to you by nature; and you know how valuable and precious these are. To heal and to care for the body every precious thing is willingly given, and to make the spirit noble, tranquil, and happy, all the desires and longings of the body are suppressed. As to time and how vital it is to the good of the body and the happiness of the spirit, you can consider the matter for yourself and realize that time is a most precious thing. It is of these things that a man ought to be wise and sparing, for they are more our own possessions than any others.

Lionardo: Keep these thoughts in your memory, Battista, and you, too, Carlo. These are not sayings of the philosophers but, like the oracles of Apollo, perfect and holy wisdom such as you will not find in all our books. We are deeply indebted to you, Giannozzo. Proceed.

Giannozzo: I have said that thrift consists in using and in preserving things. It seems to me we must consider these three goods—body, spirit, and time—and see how they may be preserved and also how they may be used. But I intend to be most brief. Listen, then. First, of the spirit, here is how to take proper care of it, Lionardo. I apply it to things that vitally concern myself and my family, and seek to keep it in a state pleasing to God.

Lionardo: What are the things that vitally concern yourself and your family?

Giannozzo: Virtue, kindness, helpfulness. I was not devoted to study when I was young, and that was mainly through my own laziness rather than through lack of talent. My kinsmen, therefore, put me to other work, such as seemed necessary to them in those days. Perhaps they sought profit rather than glory from my gifts. The occupations I then took up I neither knew how nor felt able to abandon. Personally, however, I have always occupied myself in such ways as might win me people's good will, using every means that intelligence and skill could find. Above all, I have always wished to be and to appear good, just, and tranquil, a man who would never irritate or harm others. Neither by my words nor by my deeds did I do anyone any injury, either in his presence or in his absence. These, in truth, are the best activities of the spirit. What I am now doing nearly equals them, teaching what one knows of good, warning those who go astray, offering with all faith and charity to correct them like a father, to counsel with care, in truth and love. Thus I employ my intelligence, energy, and spirit in the service of my own honor and that of my family. There are further activities of the spirit, which I have mentioned above—to love, to hate, to disdain, to hope, to desire, and so on. Again, one must know how to use and how to restrain these—to love the good, to hate the wicked, to disdain the envious, to hope for worthy ends, to desire what is best and noblest.

Lionardo: Devoutly. See Battista and Carlo, how full of pith and marrow are the words Giannozzo speaks. But go on, Giannozzo. Then what is your way of keeping the soul pleasing in the sight of God?

Giannozzo: I have two ways. One is to try and do all I can to keep my spirit joyful. I try never to let my mind be troubled with anger or greed or any other excessive passion. This I have always believed to be an excellent way. The pure and simple spirit, I believe, is the one that pleases God the most. The other way I have of pleasing God, it seems to me, consists in doing nothing of which I am doubtful whether it be good or bad.

Lionardo: Is this enough, do you think?

Giannozo: Yes, I think it is enough, according to what I remember having learned. Eh, my children, do you know why I say never do something about which you are doubtful? Because things that are true and good are luminous and clear in themselves. They are attractive. They appear desirable to us. They are things we want to do. But things that are not good always lie in the shadow of some vile and dirty pleasure, or of some wicked inclination, whatever it may be. They are not things that we truly want to do, but things we ought to flee from. We can follow the light and avoid all shadows. The light of our deeds consists in truth, and spreads by praise and fame. There is nothing in a man's life more shadowy than error and disgrace.

Lionardo: No thrift can ever be more perfect than this thrift which you practice. We are learning today not only true thrift but the way to live well and in a civilized manner. Here is the way to become noble, to live with excellence, to be happy, and to do the things concerning which we are free of any doubt. But, Giannozzo, if it be permitted to ask, did you yourself invent these remarkable and holy precepts or did you, as I thought you said before, learn from others?

Giannozzo: You really like them, do you, my children? Keep them in mind then.

Lionardo: So we shall, for nothing could be more delightful to us or more worthy of being forever remembered.

Giannozzo: When was it now? The year after forty-eight, is that right? No, it was the year after that, in the house of Sir Niccolaio and of Nerozzo, your great uncle, father of your uncle Bernardo, who is both your uncle, Lionardo, and the father of Sir Benedetto and of Francesco, uncle of Bivigliano. These were brothers fathered by Alberto, the brother of Lapo and Neri. Those three were sons of Jacopo the lawyer, who was a son of Sir Benci, another lawyer. The same Lapo was the uncle of Sir Iacopo the knight, and that Sir Iacopo was the brother of our own father, Tomaso. That Jacopo was himself the father of Bishop Paolo, our cousin and the cousin of Sir Cipriano, whose grandson, Sir Alberto, is still alive today. Also that Neri I mentioned, the brother of Lapo and Alberto, was the father of Sir Agnolo. Yes, that's it.

Lionardo: And all that multitude of ancestors of ours whom you just called Sir, were they all really knights, or were they so called only by virtue of age and position?

Giannozzo: They were knights, and very eminent ones, almost all knighted for some particular merit. That Sir Niccolaio of ours, a man of noblest mind and conduct, was one of those who sat as a judge holding the highest place in the administration of justice among the few who ruled the whole republic. He gave to the captain of our troops the standard and banner as he set out against our Pisan foe. This Niccolaio was knighted on the steps of the Signoria, the seat and fort of our government. All our fellow citizens celebrated the occasion and worthily honored all our family. From this foundation and beginning our Alberti family has preserved and increased its dignity and majesty, and has gladly contributed all the labor and expense we could muster. As you know, the first foundations of our public palace were built when Alberto, the son of Sir Iacopo, the lawyer, was a prior in the administration of the republic. Often do I think to myself that from the earliest times to the present there has never been anyone born in our house of Alberti who was not father or son or uncle or grandson of some knighted person of our blood.

Let us pass over this matter of genealogy, however. It is irrelevant to both the subject of thrift, in which we are interested, and the question you raised as to my having developed my own precepts or learned them from others. I wanted to say that in the house of Sir Niccolaio, where Sir Benedetto used to visit, it was ever the custom to talk not about trivial matters but about important questions. These men would discuss in their home what was best for the whole family as well as for the honor and well-being of each member. These were men who constantly read the books of which you are so fond, who were always active in the Palazzo giving counsel to their country, and who talked wherever they might find themselves with men of worth. In discussion they showed their own excellence and improved those who listened to them—that was always their way. For this reason I myself and other young members of our family used to try, as far as our other duties permitted, to remain nearby. We wanted to learn, as well as to show our reverence.

Sometimes at the house of Sir Niccolaio, and sometimes at the homes of the others, there would be a certain old priest, who was white haired, blessed with a pervasive air of modesty and gentleness, had a full, very dignified beard, and expressed in his countenance much goodness and reverence. This man of many excellent thoughts once began to speak of these things there, not of thrift exactly, but of the gifts God gave to us mortals. And he went on to say how much gratitude man owes to God for these great blessings, and how ungrateful a man would prove himself if he failed to take note of, and to make good use of, the grace he had received from God. He declared, however, that nothing properly belongs to us except a certain power of will and force of reason. If anything further could be said to belong to us, it could only be the same three things I spoke of earlier—the spirit, the body, and time. Though the body is subject to many ills, to accidents and to pain, yet, as he explained to us, it does belong to us. When we suffer and overcome our illnesses and troubles with manliness and patience, we achieve no less than when we use our bodies in ways that are happy and joyful.

I would not be able to explain these matters, however, in the wonderful systematic way he could. He expounded at length the question which of these aforesaid three things was truly most entirely the possession of a mortal man. If I remember rightly, he made a great issue of the decision between spirit and time. So we all listened, and he said many things which Messer Benedetto and Messer Niccolaio admitted they had never heard before. I myself liked this old man so much that I gave him my rapt and fixed attention while he spoke for several hours, and I never grew weary. I have never forgotten his weighty thoughts. The noble quality of his manner, too, has remained with me forever. Even now I seem to see him before me, modest, gracious, calm, and unruffled in discussion. Then, as you see, I appropriated for myself certain ideas of his which I remembered, and I made them part of my philosophy of life.

Lionardo: May God reward that old man and bless you for having so well passed on his teaching to us. Now, however, since this is the order of your argument, having spoken of the spirit, would you tell us something of the management of the body?

Giannozzo: It is noble and valuable work, and similar to the management of the spirit. I keep my body active in honorable ways. I engage in as noble and useful activities as I can find. I have tried to keep my body healthy, strong, and beautiful for a long time. I keep myself neat, clean, and well groomed. I take care above all to use my hands, my tongue, and every member as I do my intelligence and all that is mine in the service of the honor and fame of my country, my family, and myself. At all times I strive toward ends both practical and honorable.

Lionardo: You have certainly earned our thanks and our admiration, for, with these words, you remind us to model ourselves on your own example. But what, Giannozzo, have you found most helpful in the preservation of health? I shall believe your answer, for I have never seen, I think, an old man as fresh, as straight, and altogether as handsome as you. Your voice, your vision, and all your sinews are pure and whole and unencumbered. This is an all too marvelous and rare thing at your age.

Giannozzo: Heh, thank God I do feel quite well and healthy, though less vigorous than I used to be. But it isn't vigor a man needs at my age so much as prudence and discretion. I do wish I could at least walk as I used to do. No doubt about it, just on account of this lack of vigor, I often leave undone things which it would be well for myself and for my friends to get done. I cannot be as zealous in caring for my friends' concerns as I would be for my own. But, though I thank God, still I also feel it is partly by my own merit that at my age I am freer from ailments and less hampered by infirmity than many younger men. Health in an old man is generally a sign of continence in youth. It is important to take care of one's health at every age by exercising some caution, and more care is required to guard the more advanced years. We ought to be extremely watchful in the management of so precious a commodity as health.

Lionardo: This I admit is the way to manage health wisely. But what do you find are the most practical means to health?

Giannozzo: Exercise in moderate and pleasant form.

Lionardo: And what else?

Giannozzo: Exercise in pleasant form.

Lionardo: And after that?

Giannozzo: Exercise, my dear Lionardo, exercise, my dear children— this was ever the watchman and the doctor of health.

Lionardo: And what if one does not get much exercise?

Giannozzo: It is rarely indeed that I find I cannot manage to take some form of exercise, but when it does happen that other occupations cause me to exercise less than I usually do, I find that a well-controlled diet is good. Don't eat when not hungry, don't drink when not thirsty. For my own purposes this is what I have discovered: hard as some foods may be to digest, and old as I am, there is usually nothing that I cannot digest within twenty-four hours. This is the best rule for you, my children, and it is brief as well as correct: find out by careful attention what is bad for you, and avoid it; learn what is good for you, and be sure to obtain it.

Lionardo: All right. Cleanliness, then exercise, diet, and the avoidance of their opposites keep up our health.

Giannozzo: And our youth and beauty, too. The difference between old and young, after all, I think consists in this: the one is weak, the other strong, the one fresh, the other flaccid and shriveled. If a man preserves his health, therefore, he also preserves his strength and youth and good looks. Good looks, in my opinion, are largely a question of good color and a fresh complexion, and nothing is so salutary for the blood or keeps one's color up like a combination of exercise and temperance.

Lionardo: Now you have told us of the management of both spirit and body. There remains the matter of time. And how, Giannozzo, do you economize with time? Time unceasingly escapes us, and there is no way of preserving it.

Giannozzo: Did I not say that thrift consists as much in making good use of things as in preserving them? My plan, therefore, is to make as good use as possible of time, and never to waste any. I use time as much as possible on praiseworthy pursuits. I do not spend my time on base concerns. I spend no more time on anything than is needed to do it well.

And to waste no part of such a precious thing, I have a rule that I always follow: never remain idle. I avoid sleep, and I do not lie down unless overcome by weariness, for it seems disgraceful to me to fall without fighting or to lie beaten—in short, like so many people, to take an attitude of defeat sooner than enter the battle. This then is what I do: I avoid sleep and idleness, and I am always doing something. To be sure that one pursuit does not crowd out another, and that I don't find I have started several things but completed none, or perhaps have done only the less important and left the best undone, do you know, my children, what I do? First thing in the morning, when I arise, I think to myself, "What are the things I have to do today?" There are a certain number of things, and I run through them, consider, and assign to each some part of my time: this for the morning, this later today, and that this evening. In this way I find every task gets done in an orderly way, almost without effort.

Messer Niccolaio Alberti, who was himself a most active and energetic individual, used to remark that he never saw a diligent man walk along at any but a leisurely pace. It may seem paradoxical, but in my own case he spoke the truth. The man who neglects things finds that his time escapes him. Then necessity or at least desire brings him to action. Having, by then, almost let the season go by, he must act in a mad rush. With strenuous effort he accomplishes the same thing that earlier and at the proper time would have been easy. Remember, my children, that there is never such an abundance of anything, or such ease in obtaining it, but that it becomes difficult to find out of season. For seeds and plants and grafting, for flowers, fruits, and everything else, there is a season: out of season the same thing can be arranged only with a great deal of trouble. One must, therefore, keep an eye on time, and plan to suit the season; one must labor steadily, and not lose a single hour. I could tell you how precious a thing is time, but it will have to be said elsewhere, with more polished style, more brilliance, and greater learning than mine. Just remember not to waste time.

Do as I do. In the morning I plan my whole day, during the day I follow my plan, and in the evening, before I retire, I think over again what I have done during the day. Then, if I was careless in performing some task, and can repair the damage immediately, I do so; for I would sooner lose sleep than lose time, that is, than let the right moment for doing something slip by. Sleep, food, and things of that sort I can catch up on tomorrow, and take care of my needs, but the moment for doing something that must be done, no. Though it happens rarely to me—if I have arranged my tasks well with a time assigned for each, have planned a good order, and have not been negligent in carrying it out—it rarely or almost never happens to me that I must give up or postpone some necessity. If it does happen, however, and it is too late to change the situation, I view this as a lesson so that I shall not let time get away from me like that again.

So I manage these three things as you have been hearing. I employ the spirit and the body and time in ways only that are good. I try to preserve them adequately, and I take care not to waste them at all. In this I expend much care and I try to be as watchful and as effective as I can, for it seems to me these are the most precious things there are, and much more truly mine than any others. Riches, power, government—these are the possessions not of men, no, but of fortune—yes. To men they belong only insofar as fortune grants them their use.

Lionardo: But what of these things which you enjoy by fortune's favor, do you try to manage them with thrift?

Giannozzo: Dear Lionardo, it would be negligence and folly not to try to manage anything which, by our use of it, becomes our own. For fortune's gifts are ours only with her favor and, second, only insofar as we know how to use them. Though the truth is that in these terrible days fortune so cruelly opposes us Albertis—she does not give us kindly or generously of what is hers, but rather tries wickedly and spitefully to trouble even those things that are ours—that we hardly find occasion to practice wise management. We have always hoped, in this exile of ours, to return again to our own country, to come together again in our own house, and to rest among our kinsmen. This hope and longing have grown more fervent, indeed, as we continually suffer and decline while unable to settle our spirits or to root our lives in some kind of stable order. Had I been able from the beginning to imagine—I shall not say to know—what misfortunes, how much misery, and for how long our Alberti family would suffer, if I could have believed, when I was a young man, that I should someday be what I now am, an old man grown gray far from his home, perhaps, my children, I would have done things differently.

Lionardo: Yet, says Battista here, remember the teaching of that Terentian character, Demiphus. Every man finds it hard in prosperity to envisage how in time of need he will sustain the cruel tyranny of fortune and the dangers, injury, and exile that may come. When you return from a journey, therefore, think of some misdeed that children or wife may have committed or of some accident that may have befallen them, for these things happen every day—thus your spirit will never be overwhelmed by some unexpected calamity. The sword a man has seen ahead of time usually strikes less deep. Also, if you find things safe and better than you had imagined, you will count all that as gain. If this is a good rule to follow in prosperity, how much more so when things are on the decline and falling apart.

Giannozzo: Ah, my dear Lionardo, how could I have supposed that others would be more vengeful in our time of troubles than I myself? How, my children, should I have thought that those who, for some reason, had dishonorably or for slight cause gravely offended our family would persist more obstinately in their rancor and hate than we, who daily suffer the effects of their attacks and depredations? Yet I am one of those who for years now has canceled out the name and record in his heart of the ones who caused us so much unjust grief lasting even to the present. Never, it seems to me, did any man so harden his heart as these monstrous and cruel persons, who expelled us unjustly and persecute us unmercifully. Nor are they content to keep us living in miserable circumstances. They still reward anyone who increases our sufferings in any way. But let God be our judge in this quarrel, a judge more merciful than severe toward the sinner. My children, I still say it would have been a good thing for me had I taken a different view of our lot many years ago.

Lionardo: What would you have done then? How would you have planned for a life of thrift and temperance?

Giannozzo: Very well—my life might have been a tranquil one, free of any serious worries. I would have considered as follows: "Come now, Giannozzo, tell me, what has fortune granted you?" And I would have realized that she gave me a family and certain possessions within my house, true? Anything else? Yes. What? Honor and friendship outside my house.

Lionardo: Do you, by any chance, use the word honor [*onore*] as some of our fellow citizens do, to signify holding public office and being in the government?

Giannozzo: Far from it, my dear Lionardo, far from it, my dear children. There is nothing I think which a man should consider further from enhancing his honor than his participation in all these governments. And do you know why, my children? Partly because we Albertis are excluded from those murky waters now, and partly because I never thought well of them anyway. I always have thought any other way of life preferable to that of all these public men, as we might call them. Who can help being repelled by such a life? A life of worries, anxieties, and burdens, a life of servitude.

What is there to distinguish those who work in governments from mere public servants? You construct here, appeal there, bow before one man, quarrel with another, insult a third; many suspicions and a thousand grudges, innumerable enmities, no true friendships, but plenty of promises and abundant offers, all full of pretense, vanity, and lies. And the greater your need, the less likely you are to find anyone who will keep his promises or prove faithful. Thus it is that all your labors and all your hopes can break down at one stroke, with suffering and grief for you and the ruin of your estate. Should you succeed, however, by infinite prayers, in obtaining some good fortune, what have you gained? There you are, seated in office. What does your advantage there consist of but this: you can now steal and use violence with some degree of liberty.

You hear constant complaints, innumerable accusations, great disturbances, and you are personally beset by litigants, avaricious creatures, and men of the grossest injustice who fill your ears with suspicions, your soul with greed, your mind with fear and trouble. You are obliged to ignore your own concerns in order to untangle the folly of other men. Now you must organize taxes, now expenditures, now provide for wars, now clarify and revise laws; there are always so many connections between various tasks and activities of government that neither you alone nor you with the help of supporters can ever accomplish as much as you want. Everyone considers his own aims honorable and his own judgment admirable, his own opinion better than any. Whether you follow popular thought in its errors or rely on the arrogance of a leader, you are disgraced as though the mistake were your own; even if you labor to serve others, when you please one you displease a hundred. What a madness, though unrecognized, what an affliction, though men do not shun it, an evil which, inspite of its consequences, is not generally detested—and this, I suppose, only because this one form of servitude is somehow thought to bestow a kind of glory. The madness of men—who think so much of going heralded by trumpets and with staff in hand—is that they abandon domestic tranquillity and true peace of mind.

Madness, vanity, pride, and tyranny—what excuses are made here for wickedness! If you cannot bear to have men who, though less rich than you, are perhaps of more ancient lineage considered as your equals, which they are, you seek power. You cannot live without oppressing the weak, and so you seek power. And to have power, what do you, in your folly, do? Maniacs, you rush into every danger, you risk death. Brutes, you call it honor to be encircled by vice-ridden men and not to know how to live with good ones; it suits you to serve and to be allied with all the thieves, with men whose condition is so vile that they care little if they risk their lives in the service of your cause. You call it honor to be among robbers, honor to appease, to feed, and to serve men of servile state—brutes.

You deserve to be hated if you enjoy the perversion of moral life and endless travail which overwhelms those who fill public offices and administrative functions. What can be the inward delight of a man whose ears are assailed by complaints, grief, the weeping of orphans and widows and of victims of disaster and destitution—what delight, if he be not, in fact, a fierce and brutish creature? What sort of man is content to confront all day long and to live always among a thousand bands of scoundrels, embezzlers, spies, scandalmongers, robbers, and criminals practicing every sort of fraud and immorality? What sort of recreation is it, as a butcher and render of the human body, to go every evening and twist a man's arms and legs, hear him cry with anguished voice for mercy, and still resort to further horrible tortures. A disgusting thing even to contemplate, a thing to avoid at all costs. Yet, cruel creatures, you desire to govern?

Certainly you will say yes, for I think it is a noble deed to suffer such burdens in order to punish the wicked and to raise and reward the good. So to punish wicked men you must first become worse? I think no man is good if he cannot live contented with his own. The man who covets and seeks the goods of others, I think, is worse. And worst is he who thirsts after and usurps the public wealth. I don't blame you if, after you display great excellence and enjoy great fame, your country calls on you and imposes a part of its burdens on you. I call it an honor to be thus entreated by your fellow citizens. But that I should do as many do, cast myself at the feet of this or that important person, make up the tail of some man's procession, seek by serving to become a commander of others, that, indeed, I should lend my hand to doing harm and disservice to someone in order to suit someone else whose favor I need in order to climb to power, that I should wish, as almost all of them do, to inscribe my name in the rolls of state almost as a way of making money, as if it were my store, treating the state as if it were to be the dowry of my daughters, that I should in any way make private what is public and use for gain what my country grants me as an honor, making my country my prey—no, my dear Lionardo, no, my dear children, no.

A man wants to live for himself, not for the community. He is willing to be asked for help by his friends, true, where this does not mean that you neglect your own concerns and where it does not lead to serious losses for you. A man is no friend of mine if he does not avoid doing what would lead to my injury or shame. One is willing to leave part of one's own affairs for the sake of friends, if you then receive in return, not necessarily a reward, but good feeling and gratitude. That is how, you know, men have always been happiest, following the middle of the road.

You who have read many histories could give more examples than I to show that this is so. The histories will all confirm that no one ever fell to ruin who had not first climbed too high. As for me, let it suffice me to be and to appear good and just. As long as that is my state I can never be truly disgraced. That honor [*onoranza*] alone is mine even in exile, and it will remain with me as long as I do not abandon it. Let others enjoy pomp, and let the winds blow wide their sails while fortune wills. They delight in their power, but they sorrow when they do not have it. They weep when they fear they must lose it; they grieve having lost it. To us who are content with what is ours and never desire what belongs to others, meanwhile, it will never be a source of regret not to possess what is public or to lose what we have never prized. Who, in any case, could value those obligations, labors, and innumerable pangs of spirit? My children, let us stand on the plain, trying only to be good and just householders. Let us delight in our excellent family. Let us delight in those goods fortune bestows on us, sharing them with our friends. A man is highly enough honored when he lives untainted by vice and untouched by shame.

Lionardo: If I understand you rightly, Giannozzo, yours is that magnificent and noble spirited will which has always seemed to me greater and more worthy of a manly temper than any other aspiration or desire of mortal man. I see that your first aim is self-sufficiency, a worthy resolve and proper to a princely spirit, to live with no need of anyone else, to be contented with what fortune grants us. There are some, whom I feel you justly reproach, who think it greatness and breadth of spirit to undertake everything hard and difficult, every sort of toilsome and painful labor in order to gain more power than other citizens. There are quite a few such men in our own country as well as in other states. Having been raised in the most ancient liberty of our city and being filled with bitterest hate against any kind of tyrant, they are not satisfied with the common liberty of all, but want more liberty and license than anyone else. Certainly, Giannozzo, if a man takes it into his head to want a place among the magistrates who guide public affairs, not because he wishes and hopes to merit the praises and the gratitude of good men but because he longs with a single, immoderate appetite to rule and be obeyed, I agree such a man is much to be condemned. He will, as you say, prove himself anything but a good citizen.

Like you, I would say that a good citizen loves tranquillity, but not so much his own tranquillity as that of other good men. He rejoices in his private leisure, but does not care less about that of his fellow citizens than about his own. He desires the unity, calm, peace, and tranquillity of his own house, but much more those of the country and of the republic. These good things, moreover, cannot be preserved if men of wealth or wisdom or nobility among the citizens seek more power than the other citizens, who are also free but less fortunate. Yet neither can these same republics be preserved if all the good men are solely content with their private leisure. Wise men say that good citizens should undertake to care for the republic and to toil at the tasks of their country, not shaken by the follies of men, in order to further the public peace and preserve the general good. Thus they also avoid giving a place of power to the wicked, who through the indifference of the good and through their own dishonest wish soon pervert every plan and undermine both public and private well-being.

So you see, Giannozzo, that the admirable resolve which would make private honor one's sole rule in life, though noble and generous in itself, may still be not the proper guide for spirits eager to seek glory. Fame is born not in the midst of private peace but in public action. Glory springs up in public squares; reputation is nourished by the voice and judgment of many persons of honor, and in the midst of the people. Fame flees from every solitary and private spot to dwell gladly in the arena, where crowds are gathered and celebrity is found; there the name is bright and luminous of one who with hard sweat and assiduous toil for noble ends has projected himself up out of silence and darkness, ignorance, and vice. For these reasons I have never felt that one should object to a man's seeking by means of praiseworthy works and studies, but no less by a devout and careful adherence to good conduct, to gain the favor of some honorable and well-established citizen. I would not call it servitude to do my duty; there is no doubt, however, that it has always been the duty of young men to respect their elders and eagerly to seek among them for the same fame and dignity by which the elders themselves enjoy love and reverence. Nor would I call it power lust if a man shows much care and interest in doing hard and generous things, for these are the way to honor and glory. It may be because there is now in our country no public official but seems to you distempered of mind and servile of spirit that you thus severely condemn anyone who would want to be inscribed in that number, among not good but rather the vilest citizens.

Yet this is my own longing, Giannozzo, so much so that if I might earn fame and favor and reputation, and stand honored, loved, adorned with dignity and the respect of my fellow citizens in my own country, I would never shun this, Giannozzo, nor be afraid of the enmity I might incur from some citizen who was baneful and wicked. Even where it was necessary to deal with men, sometimes with fatal severity, I would esteem this a pious act, to root out and destroy thieves and all scoundrels and to extinguish every last flame of lawless greed, even among my own relatives. As this is not open to us, for the present, however, let us cease to pursue it; I do not say with you that it is worthless, for I continue to esteem honor and fame above any other of the blessings of fortune. Let us not pursue with our longings, however, what the force of circumstances makes inaccessible to our exertions. Let us go by your teaching and await the season when, perhaps, our patience and moderation will receive some recompense. Then the injustice and spite of ill-willed, intemperate enemies who still exceed all bounds in their insults and cruelties toward us will perhaps, by God's justice, be rewarded with some fair and well-earned vengeance. In our present situation, Battista and Carlo, let us merely attempt to earn some praise and fame by our excellence, zeal, and skill, and so prepare ourselves to be of service to the republic, to our country. When the time comes, then, we may prove ourselves such men that Giannozzo and other most wise and moderate elders may not deem us unworthy to receive the honor of a high place in public life.

Giannozzo: Thus would I have you do, my children. Thus do I hope and expect you will do, and thus shall you gain and maintain a name of some distinction. But let me impress upon you once more that one must never—I do not say for honor's sake, for indeed honor may lead one to give up many things, but for the sake of ruling others—never cease to bear rule over oneself. Do not abandon your private concerns to guide public affairs. I remind you of this, for if a man finds he has less than he needs in his home, he will find still less outside; nor will the public power he has redeem his private necessity. Public honors will not feed the family. Be as careful and diligent in fulfilling your domestic charges as you must be, but to public matters give, not whatever ambition and pride might suggest but what your conscience and the gratitude of your fellow citizens dictate.

Lionardo: You give us a clear idea, Giannozzo, of what we ought to do. And so we shall. Tell us, however, you have named four private and domestic needs: family and wealth within the house, honor and friendship outside it—now which of these is dearest to your heart?

Giannozzo: By nature, love and piety make the family dearest of all to me. And to govern the family you must have possessions; and to preserve the family and your possessions, friends are necessary. With them you may take counsel when you must avoid or else successfully endure adversity. And to enjoy possessions, family, and friendship with your friends, it is necessary to hold some position and to exercise honorable authority.

Lionardo: What do you mean by family?

Giannozzo: Children, wife, and other members of the household, both relatives and servants.

Lionardo: I understand.

Giannozzo: And do you know how to apply our system of good management to them? No differently than to ourselves: we shall employ them in honorable ways, put them to virtuous and valuable tasks, keep them healthy and contented, and see that no one wastes his time. And do you know how to be sure no one is wasting his time?

Lionardo: Be sure each of them is busy?

Giannozzo: Not good enough. Rather, be sure each of them is doing what it is his business to do. See that the lady is watching over the children, seeing to the provisions, supervising the household, that the children are at work on their studies, that the others are trying diligently and well to do what their superiors tell them. And do you know, on the other hand, how they would be merely wasting time?

Lionardo: Doing nothing, I suppose.

Giannozzo: Certainly, and also if what one could do is occupying two or more; or if, where two or more are needed, one is toiling and sweating all alone; or if one or more are given tasks for which they are useless or ill suited. Where too many are employed, some are wasted. Where there are fewer than needed or where the workers are not sufficiently skilled for the job, it is worse than if they did nothing, since they labor in vain and largely upset or spoil the thing they are set to do.

Lionardo: Well said.

Giannozzo: Certainly they should not be allowed to waste their time like this. Each should be ordered to do what he knows how to do and can do. To be sure, moreover, that each one can and will act with diligence and love in the position assigned to him, let them follow the same system I do in performing my own task. My job is to make just demands on my family, to teach them diligent and good work, and to give to each what is needed and proper for the task. Do you know how I go about my job to do it better? First, I think for a long, long while about what I could use and what is best, then I go about obtaining it, and endure hardship in order to have it, then I preserve it with care, and finally I teach my household to take care in keeping it for its proper use and then in using it.

Lionardo: Do you take just so much of things as you think you will need and no more?

Giannozzo: Always somewhat more, so that if some is spilled or spoiled or lost, there will not be less than needed.

Lionardo: And if something is left over?

Giannozzo: I decide which is better, to offer it to a friend who can use it or, after all, to keep it for the family's use, for there should not be the least insufficiency of anything required in the family. I have always wished to have in my house all the things that my family found useful or necessary.

Lionardo: And what do you, Giannozzo, think that a family requires?

Giannozzo: Many things, my dear Lionardo, good fortune and much that men cannot control.

Lionardo: But the things men can control, what are they?

Giannozzo: Those are, to provide a house where all your flock can gather, to provide food for them, and to give them clothes to wear.

Lionardo: And to make them good and well brought up?

Giannozzo: Indeed, nothing is more vital to the family, in my opinion, than to educate the youth to be well behaved and to have excellent character. But it is not part of our present discussion of the household to consider the raising of children.

Lionardo: And those other matters, how do you manage them?

Giannozzo: I have told you already that in these calamitous days, I am not in a position to be a truly thrifty householder.

Lionardo: So you did say, yet I know you have a big family and you want them all to be honorable and temperate as you are yourself, and so you live in a companionable and fine way together in your house. That is why I ask you how you order these matters.

Giannozzo: As well as I can, given the times and the adverse circumstances.

Lionardo: But, that we may hear your full teaching, suppose that you were of my age, had a wife and children, were also prudent and as experienced as you are, and altogether determined to maintain a well-run household. How would you arrange things?

Giannozzo: Oh, my son, if I were your age, I could do many things which, at present, I cannot and therefore do not do. My first concern would be to select my house where I could remain as long as I wished, living in comfort and having no need to move. It is unbelievable, my dear Lionardo, and, not having the experience, you may not altogether believe me, how much trouble and expense, how much discomfort and irritation accompanies a move from place to place. Things are lost, misplaced, and broken. In addition there are the anxieties with which your mind is afflicted when spirit and thought are distracted and disrupted, and it is a long time before you are once again well settled. As to the expenses that grow out of settling yourself in a new house, I shall say nothing. This is why it is essential to find, from the start, a place as convenient and suitable as I was saying.

Lionardo: Alas, dear Giannozzo, we who are still young and who were either born in exile or raised in the lands of others are no longer ignorant of the troubles and toil involved in moving. Our cruel fortune casts us hither and thither from day to day and never gives us peace. We are her victims, and she is ever on our trail, ever wounding, even overwhelming us with new calamities more terrible than the old. But let us thank God, who thus provides us with the opportunity to gain no little honor by our infinite patience in the face of evil and by our rare, marvelous, indeed incredible faithfulness amid adversity. Back to our subject, now, however. I ask you, Giannozzo, what would you do to find a place of lasting repose, and that in the lands of others?

Giannozzo: I would look for the sort of land best suited to give me just such repose, from which I would not have to move and where I might live without inconvenience and with honor.

Lionardo: But what criteria would you apply to find the country suitable for your purposes? Wouldn't it be difficult not only to know what it should be like but also to find it?

Giannozzo: Not at all. It would certainly not be very hard for me, my dear Lionardo, and you shall see why. First, I would find out how good, how healthy life was in that spot. I would look mainly at the young people and the children—if they were fresh and handsome I would assume the air was good and healthy, for childhood is very susceptible and sensitive to the kind of air and to things harmful to health. And if there were also many old people there in a thriving, upright, vigorous state, I would suppose that I, too, might grow old there. Then, next, I would look at the neighboring lands and the neighbors to see whether this were an area open or protected in case of foreign invasions, and I would note whether the place were fertile in itself or whether it depended on many resources brought from outside. I would also discover by what means these outside things came in and whether, in case of sudden need, the emergency could be quickly and easily met. I would investigate to learn whether the neighbors were helpful or harmful, and I would ask about other troubles, such as plague and pestilence, and consider whether, in case of need, I could withdraw to that place without great expense.

Above all, I would look closely and diligently into the matter of the character of the people who lived there, whether they were rich and honorable persons, and learn whether the region had a good and stable government, just laws, and moderate leaders. For, my children, if a land is justly ordered and governed with wisdom, it will never suffer the attacks of enemies or evil fortune or the wrath of God. It will have neighbors who are well disposed, peaceful conditions, and a stable government. If the citizens are honorable and wealthy, they will have no desire to rob others, rather they will help the industrious and honor the good.

Lionardo: But where could one ever find such a country, one so entirely praiseworthy in its ways? I certainly think it would be hard to find unless, indeed, you who love to live in Venice think that that one land is less corrupt than any other in all these respects.

Giannozzo: And yet I would look for it. I should not like to have to regret my failure to try. And I would settle down in the country I found did have the most and the most important of these qualities.

Lionardo: Which are most important?

Giannozzo: Listen, my dear Lionardo, it seems to me a matter of no slight difficulty to try to find the most important among them, but though I do not know for certain, I shall say freely what occurs to me just as it comes to mind. Among all the conditions, health seems to me primary; therefore I would particularly search for a place where the air and other features of the country were good for the health. A healthy man, as you know, my children, is going to earn his living somehow anywhere, and if he is just and good, everyone will respect him.

Lionardo: And give him honor?

Giannozzo: My dear Lionardo, a man who is good and who knows how to make it apparent to others that he is good will be honored and esteemed anywhere.

Lionardo: I am satisfied. But first, what conditions do you find most conducive to health?

Giannozzo: The most important condition is the thing you must use just as you find it, like it or not: the air.

Lionardo: And after that?

Giannozzo: Other good things required for our food and nourishment, and particularly good wine. You are laughing, Lionardo.

Lionardo: And where would you settle, then?

Giannozzo: Where I could stay in tranquillity and was looked upon with favor.

Lionardo: What would you do, buy your house or rent one?

Giannozzo: Definitely not rent, for in the course of time a man finds he has bought his house several times over and still does not own it. I would, furthermore, buy a house that was airy, spacious, and suited to hold my family and if a good friend should come by to offer him good lodging too. And for this purpose I would try to spend a minimum.

Lionardo: Would you perhaps choose an out of the way house, where they sold cheap or, as they say, at bargain prices?

Giannozzo: Don't call that a bargain. No price is good when you pay it for something that does not suit you. I would try to spend money on a house that would do for me, and not pay more than it was worth. I would not be impetuous about it or show myself an eager buyer. I would choose a house in a good neighborhood and in a well-known street, where honorable citizens lived with whom I could safely make friends, and with whose wives my wife could enjoy honorable and wholly blameless companionship. I would also inquire carefully about who had lived there in previous times, and ask how healthy and fortunate they had been. There are certain houses in which no one ever seems to have been able to live happily.

Lionardo: Yes, indeed, how true. I recall one beautiful and magnificent room of which I have observed the story. Some grew poor there, another was left all alone, another was expelled in disgrace, all reached such straits as to suffer grief. Your thought is truly excellent, to take a suitable house in a good and honorable neighborhood, in a justly governed, wealthy, and peaceful healthy country where good things abound. And then, Giannozzo, when you have fulfilled these conditions, how do you manage the rest of your household economy?

Giannozzo: I would want all my family to live under one roof, to warm themselves at one hearth, and to seat themselves at one table.

Lionardo: For your greater comfort, I suppose; not to live in solitude, to be the father in their midst, surrounded every evening, loved, revered, the guardian and teacher of all the youth, a state which is generally the greatest satisfaction in the life of older people.

Giannozzo: A very great satisfaction. And also, my dear Lionardo, it is more economical, my dear children, to live thus enclosed behind a single door.

Lionardo: Is that so?

Giannozzo: Yes, and I shall convince you of it. Tell me, Lionardo, if it were night right now and dark and there burned a torch here in the middle of this place, you and I and these others would all be able to see enough to read, write, and do what we liked, is that not right? And if we were to separate, you over there, I upstairs, the boys elsewhere, and all wanted as much light as before to see by, do you think the pieces of this same torch which we might have shared out among ourselves would burn as long a time as the whole torch in one piece would have?

Lionardo: Certainly less long. Who could deny that? After all, the wood burned before from one spot, now from three.

Giannozzo: And now suppose it were very cold and we had many logs burning here. If you wanted your share of them elsewhere, and these boys took their part to still another spot, do you think you would keep warm better or less well?

Lionardo: Less well.

Giannozzo: Thus it is with the family. Many things are sufficient when unbroken that are insufficient when taken to pieces and widely separated. A different warmth will a man feel from one of his own fellow citizens than among strangers, and a different light of prestige and authority will emanate from one who is accompanied by his own people, whom there are many reasons to trust and many reasons to fear, than from one who walks with a few strangers or without company. The father of a family followed by many of his kinsmen will be more eminent than one who is alone and seems abandoned. Now let me talk to you like the practical rather than literary man that I am, and give you the kind of reasons and examples that are in my mind. I understand this, that at two tables, two tablecloths are spread, two hearths consume two piles of logs, two households need two servants, while one can do with one. But I don't know how to explain well to you what I think; yet I feel I am telling you the truth. To make two families out of one requires double expense, and many things happen that it is easier to judge of by experience than by talk, easier to feel than to explain. Indeed, I am not pleased with this dividing of families, this going in and out of separate entrances, nor has my spirit ever suffered Antonio, my brother, to live under a different roof than my own.

Lionardo: That is admirable.

Giannozzo: Yes, my dear Lionardo, families are to be gathered under a single roof, and if, when the family has grown, a single room no longer holds them, at least let them all repose in the shadow of a single will.

Lionardo: Words worthy of the great authority you enjoy. I take note of this and shall keep it forever in memory. Let families remain united in will. And then, Giannozzo, when everyone is in the house, would they all ask to dine?

Giannozzo: True enough. Then let lunch and dinner be served them, my dear Lionardo, at the right times and of good kind.

Lionardo: Good dining? Shall I take that to mean eating good things?

Giannozzo: Good, yes, my dear Lionardo, and abundant too. Not pheasant and capon and partridge or other delicacies such as are prepared for the sick, but let there be a proper table for good citizens, so that no well-disposed member of your family would want to eat elsewhere in hopes of assuaging hunger better than at home. Let your table be a good domestic spread, with no lack of wine and plenty of bread. Let the wine be pure and the bread, too, good enough, and let there be fine and sufficient condiments for the bread.

Lionardo: Good. And would you buy these things, Giannozzo, from day to day?

Giannozzo: No, I would not buy them; that would not be thrifty.

When a man sells things do you think he will let out of the house what is best or rather what is worst?

Lionardo: The worst, and what they think they cannot well preserve. But things that are good and useful are also sold, because of the need for money.

Giannozzo: This I admit. But if a man be wise, he will first sell the worser sort. And when he does sell the better, does he not attempt to sell higher than it came to him? Does he not try with every trick to make it seem better than it is?

Lionardo: Often.

Giannozzo: So you see, the buyer spends that surplus, and he runs the risk of finding he has been duped, drawing something of poor durability or low quality. Right? And even aside from other reasons, to me it means better value to possess all that I need ready at hand and to have tried out my crops over the years so that I know their seasons of perfection, rather than to go looking for things elsewhere.

Lionardo: Would you perhaps wish to have in your house all that you will need in your domestic stores for the whole year?

Giannozzo: Yes, I would like to have in the house whatever can be kept there without danger or great effort and whatever can be well preserved. And what I cannot keep well except by taking great trouble and using too much space in the house, that I would choose to sell and then reprovide for myself in due time, for I would rather suit myself to the season and leave the labor, trouble, and danger to others.

Lionardo: Would you sell what you had first bought?

Giannozzo: As fast as I could if keeping it caused me loss. But if possible I would prefer not to have to sell or to buy now this and now that. These are tasks for merchants and are low preoccupations. It is better thrift really to avoid such concerns—better to spend a bit extra on something and give your attention to matters of more moment. But the best thrift of all, I think, is altogether to provide for things on time. And I tell you this further thing, I would like not to have to remove some money every year from my supply of cash.

Lionardo: I don't see how that can be.

Giannozzo: I shall tell you how. I would make every effort to have estates from which my house could be kept furnished with grain, wine, wood, and straw—all much more cheaply than by purchase in the market. I would there raise flocks, pigeons, chickens, and fish as well.

Lionardo: I agree entirely with your view, Giannozzo, but I have doubts on one point: can it be true economy to establish these undertakings on the land of others; for your farm is useful to the family and apt to win the favor of the landlord, yet I fear you will always find the owner recalling it in order to enjoy it himself and exploit the great improvements which you have added at your own expense and by your own labor. And if you do not make such expenditures, the farm will not, I think, be such as you want to raise food for your family. Truly wise husbandmen can hardly praise, I think, your paying workers anew day by day and giving them a salary and lending them the necessary tools, and then, when you value their work and services and want them again, losing them through a change of lands.

Giannozzo: For this very reason, and for others too, I would buy my land with my own money, so that it might belong to me and to my children and then to my grandchildren, so that I would see to its management and cultivation with more love and so that my own people, remaining there through the passage of time, would gain the fruit of the plants and the work I had put into it.

Lionardo: Would you want fields which were all together in one place to yield the different crops and fruits you have mentioned: grain, wine, olives, straw, and wood?

Giannozzo: I would if I could.

Lionardo: But tell me something, Giannozzo. To grow good wine one needs steep slopes and sunshine; for good grain you need the open plain with light and loamy ground; good wood is found on well-watered mountain ridges; hay where it is moist and swampy. How would you obtain such diverse conditions in a single place? Tell me Giannozzo, do you think that there are many places to be found equally suited for grapes and grain and woods and pasture? And if you found them, do you think you could have them for less than a staggering price?

Giannozzo: Certainly they exist—and how many! My dear Lionardo, I remember in Florence how many such places there were aside from the estates we had, the place of Messer Benedetto, and those of Messer Niccolaio and those of Messer Cipriano and those of Messer Antonio and of our other Albertis—estates which left nothing to be desired, situated in purest air, in lovely country, with a beautiful view in every direction, hardly ever a cloud, no bad winds, good water, everything healthy and clean. But let us not speak of those, which were more mansions of great lords, rather taking the form of castles than of villas. Let us not recall now the glories of the Alberti family, let us forget those proud structures with heavy ornamentation where many now pass and sigh, seeing their new inhabitants and longing for the older style of countenance and manner characteristic of our Albertis. I do say I would try to purchase a property such as my uncle Caroccio, the grandson of Messer Iacobo, knight, whose son was the second Caroccio Alberti, used to describe as ideal: a place to which one could bring a quarter peck of salt and it would be enough to feed the family all year.

This is what I would do, then. I would see that the estate was, first of all, suited to yield all that might be needed to feed the family, and if not all, at least the most necessary commodities, namely bread and wine, should both be there. As for the road to go to the estate or close to it, I would use the meadows, so that as I passed to and from the place I could look it over and see what was wanted. I could always make use of a path through it to check over the fields and the whole estate. I would also very much prefer to have the whole place united or to have the parts close together, so that I could often pass through all of it without going too much out of my way.

Lionardo: A good idea, for when you watch over workers in one place, those in another are often apt to be neglecting their work even more.

Giannozzo: This also reduces the number of peasant families one has to deal with; it is hard to believe how much wickedness there is among the plowmen raised up among the clods. Their one purpose is to cheat you, and they never let anyone deceive them in anything. All the errors are in their favor; they try constantly and by every means to get and obtain what is part of your property. First the peasant wants you to buy him an ox, goats, a sow, a mare also, and then sheep, too. Next he asks you for loans to satisfy his creditors, to clothe his wife, to dower his daughter. Finally he asks you to reinforce his hut, to rebuild various structures and improve various parts of the housing, and still he never stops complaining. Even though he be richer than his master, he is always wailing about how poor he is. He forever needs something, and he never speaks to you but to bring you some expense or burden. If the crop is abundant, he keeps the better two thirds for himself. If through bad weather or for some other reason the land was sterile in a certain year, the peasant gives you only the damage and the loss. So does he always take for himself the most or the best of what is useful, while he throws the uncomfortable and burdensome aspects of farming entirely on his teammate.

Lionardo: Perhaps, then, it would be better to spend a little more on the market in order to supply the house rather than have to deal with such ill-disposed people.

Giannozzo: On the contrary, my dear Lionardo. It is better, far better to bear the weight of such villainous ingenuities which teach you the better to tolerate your fellow citizens who may have similar inconsiderate ways—and to teach the peasants to exercise some degree of diligence. Besides, if you don't have too great a number of peasants to deal with, their malice will not be insufferable, and if you are careful they will not be able to cheat you much. You will even take much secret delight in their little tricks and laugh heartily at them.

Lionardo: I truly admire your wisdom, Giannozzo. You know how to get some edification and pleasure even out of malicious people.

Giannozzo: But of course, my children, that's what I would do. But I would try to locate this property in a place where neither a river nor heavy rains could ruin it for me by flooding, where there were no robber bands, and where the air was very pure. I hear there are farms which are otherwise fruitful and fertile where the air is full of tiny and invisible insects; they are not felt but they pass through and fly into the lungs, where they feed by gnawing at the interior, killing animals and also many people.

Lionardo: I remember reading about that in the ancient writers.

Giannozzo: So I would try to have good air as well as good land. In good air, if the fruits do not grow in great quantity, as they certainly may, still those that do grow will be much more flavorful and much better than those grown elsewhere. Add to this that good air contributes to your health whenever you visit your estate and gives you inestimable pleasure. Also, my dear Lionardo, I would strive to have an estate in such a location that the fruits and crops could reach my house without too much difficulty, and I would be particularly delighted if the estate could be near the city, for then I could go there often, often send for things, and walk every morning among fruits and fields and fig trees. While I took walks there for my own exercise, I should also oversee the workers, and they, seeing me, would rarely behave badly and would have greater sentiments of love and reverence for myself and would work the more diligently. I think, too, that there are quite a few such places situated in good air, far from floods, close to the city, fertile in bread and wine. As to the woods, I would soon have that resource also, for I would always be planting trees on my boundaries, shading thereby my neighbor's field rather than my own.

I would try to raise every delicious and rare fruit. In this I should emulate Messer Niccolaio Alberti, a man altogether devoted to refinement of every kind, who wanted his farms to contain every fine fruit that exists in any country. And what discrimination that man had! He sent to Sicily for pines the offspring of which bear fruit before they reach their seventh year. He also wanted certain pines in his gardens which bear a split pineseed, its shell broken on one side. Also, from Apulia he imported those pines which have pine nuts with such a delicate shell that you can break it with your finger, and of these he planted a whole wood. It would be a long tale to recount all the exotic and diverse fruits that man's discrimination established in his gardens. All were arranged in rows by his own hand, so that one could see and admire them with ease.

So should I do, too: I would plant many, many trees in good order and in rows, for they are more beautiful to look at if so planted, they shade the seedlings less, they litter the field less, and the workers have less difficulty in picking the fruit. And it would give me keen pleasure to plant them, to introduce and add various sorts of fruit in one place, and to tell my friends afterward how, when, and from where I had obtained such and such fruit trees. You know, Lionardo, having my trees that I planted bear good fruit would be most useful, but even if they did not bear good fruit they would be useful, since I would cut them for firewood, prune out the older ones and the least fruitful every year, and replace them with better plants. To my mind, this would be the keenest pleasure.

Lionardo: What kind of person could fail to take pleasure in his farm? The farm is of great, honorable, and reliable value. Any other occupation is fraught with a thousand risks, carries with it a mass of suspicions and of trouble, and brings numerous losses and regrets. There is trouble in purchasing, fear in transporting, anxiety in selling, apprehension in giving credit, weariness in collecting what is due you, deceit in exchange. So in all other occupations you are beset by a multitude of worries and suffer constant anxiety. The farm alone seems reliable, generous, trustworthy and truthful. Managed with diligence and love, it never wearies of repaying you. Reward follows reward. In spring the farm gives you a multitude of delights, greenery, flowers, aromas, songs. It tries to please you, it smiles and promises you a magnificent harvest, it fills you with good hopes as well as sufficient joy in the present. Then in summer how courteously it attends on you! First one sort of fruit, then another, comes to your house—your house is never empty of some gift. Then there is autumn: now the farm gives liberal reward for your labors, shows great gratitude for your merit—gladly, copiously, and faithfully serves you! Twelvefold reward is yours—for a little sweat, many casks of wine.

Your farm replaces what is old and stale in your house with what is new and fresh and clean and good, everything with generous interest. It brings you currants and other grapes to hang and dry. To this add nuts to fill your house in winter, and fragrant and beautiful apples and pears. The farm never stops sending you periodic gifts of its later fruits. Even in winter it does not fail to be generous. It sends you wood and oil and juniper and laurel, so that when you enter your house out of snow and wind you can make a joyful and aromatic fire. And if you deign to lend it your company, the farm invites you into splendid sunlight, offers hares and bucks and deer for you to chase, lets you enjoy the sport and shake off the cold and harshness of the weather.

I shall say nothing of the chickens, kids, fresh cheeses, and other delicacies produced on the farm and preserved for you in year-round supply. It amounts to this: the farm labors that you may lack for nothing in your house, that your spirit may be free of all melancholy, that you may be nourished with what is pleasant and good. If the farm also demands some work from you, this work at least is unlike other occupations that depress and worry you. It does not exhaust your energies and make you weary but fills you with joy. It tends to the benefit of your own health as well as of the farm.

Giannozzo: What need to say it all, Lionardo? You cannot praise the farm half as much as it ought to be praised. It is excellent for our health, helps maintain us, benefits the family. Good men and prudent householders are always interested in the farm, as everyone knows, and indeed the farm is, first of all, profitable and, second, a source of both pleasure and honor. There is no need, as with other occupations, to fear deceit and fraud from debtors or suppliers. Nothing goes on under cover; it is all visible and publicly understood. You will not be cheated, nor need you call in notaries and witnesses, undertake lawsuits, or engage in other irritating and depressing intrigues most of which are not worth the convulsions of spirit involved in carrying them through to a successful conclusion.

Consider, too, that you can retire to your farm and live there at peace, nurturing your little family, dealing by yourself with your own affairs, and on a holiday talking pleasantly in the shade about oxen and wool or about vines and seeds. You can live undisturbed by rumors and tales and by the wild strife that breaks out periodically in the city. You can be free of the suspicions, fears, slanders, injuries, feuds, and other miseries which are too ugly to talk about and horrible even to remember. Among all the subjects discussed on the farm there is none which can fail to delight you. All are pleasant to talk of and are heard by willing ears. Everyone tells what he knows that is useful to agriculture. Everyone teaches and corrects you where you erred in some of your planting or in your manner of sowing. The cultivation and management of fields does not give rise to envy, hate, and malevolence.

Lionardo: In addition, you enjoy on the farm clear and happy days of clean, open air. You have a lovely view when you look at those leafy hills and verdant plains. Clear springs and streams go leaping through and losing themselves in the waving grass.

Giannozzo: Yes, by God, a true paradise. And, what is more, you can in the enjoyment of your estate escape the violence, the riots, the storm of the city, the marketplace, and the townhall. On the farm you can hide yourself and avoid seeing all the stealing and crime, the vast numbers of depraved men who are always flitting past your eyes in the city. There they never cease to chirp in your ears, to scream and bellow in the streets hour after hour, like a dangerous and disgusting kind of beast. What a blessing to live on the farm, what an unheard of happiness.

Lionardo: Do you think one should, in fact, live in the country rather than in the midst of town?

Giannozzo: As for me, seeing that it is freer of vice, involves less cares and less expense, offers more health and more enjoyment of life, yes, indeed, my children. I do praise the country estate.

Lionardo: Are you sufficiently convinced of this to raise your children there?

Giannozzo: If my children could expect to spend their whole lives never talking to any but good persons, I would certainly want to have them grow up in the country. But the number of men who are not of the very worst sort is so small that we fathers, to protect ourselves from the wicked and their many devices, must make sure that our children know them. A man cannot distinguish who is wicked if he knows nothing of wickedness. If you have never heard the sound of the bagpipe, you cannot judge the quality of the instrument. Let us imitate those who wish to become skilled shieldsmen: first we must learn to wound so that then we may know how nimbly to avoid the pointed lance and how to protect our flank from the blade. If vices dwell among men, as they do, I can see the wisdom of raising the young where vices abound no less than men, in the city.

Lionardo: Also, Giannozzo, it is in the city one learns to be a citizen. There people acquire valuable knowledge, see many models to teach them the avoidance of evils. As they look around them they notice how handsome is honor, how lovely is fame, how divine a thing is glory. There they taste the sweets of praise, of being named and esteemed and admired. By these wondrous joys the young are awakened to the pursuit of excellence and come to devote themselves to attempting difficult things worthy of immortality. Such high advantages may not, perhaps, be found in the country amid logs and clods.

Giannozzo: I have some doubts, for all that, Lionardo, as to which is better, to bring up one's children in the country or the city. But let us assess it thus: every situation has its own natural advantages. In the city are the workshops of great dreams, for such are governments, constitutions, fame. In the country we find peace, contentment, a free way of pursuing life and health. For myself I think if I had such a farm as I was describing I should wish to stay there a good part of the year and enjoy myself while cultivating the means to feed my family abundantly and well.

Lionardo: Now would you tell us also how to dress the family, another necessary expenditure you mentioned?

Giannozzo: Among first considerations, my very first would be and always has been to keep my household well dressed, each member in accordance with his station. If I neglected to do this, my flock would give me but poor loyalty, indeed my own household would hate me. I should be generally despised, those outside my family would blame me, and I should be reputed miserly. It would be no true thrift, therefore, to dress them less than well.

Lionardo: How would you have your family dress?

Giannozzo: Well, that's the point: good clothing for civic life must be clean, suitable, and well made—that's the main thing. Joyous colors are proper to wear, whatever bright colors suit the wearer best, and good cloth is imperative. The slashed garments and laces one sees on some people have never seemed attractive to me except for clowns and buglers. On great holidays a new garment, on other days clothing that has been worn. Very old clothing is only to be worn inside the house. Your clothes should bring you respect, right, my dear Lionardo? You, too, then, should give some respect to your clothes. I have given some thought to the matter, and I think people do not generally consider it as much as they should. To generous and easy spenders it may seem unimportant if you belt your robe; but in fact belting a robe is doubly wasteful. Without a belt your dress appears fuller and more dignified; in addition, the belt, of course, makes the cloth shiny and rubs off all the nap. Soon, while your robe may still be new, the waist will already be worn out and old. Beautiful clothes, therefore, should not be belted. We want to have beautiful clothes. Since they do us honor, we too should have some consideration for them.

Lionardo: Would you dress your whole household in beautiful garments?

Giannozzo: According to what was appropriate for each one, yes.

Lionardo: And would you give clothes to those who work for you in the house as a kind of bonus?

Giannozzo: I would be generous with them, indeed, if I saw they were loyal and hard working in my service and in the service of my family.

Lionardo: And I suppose you would reward them in this way.

Giannozzo: Yes, it would be a reward, and an incentive to others as well, to try to merit as much as those good servants had received from me. There is nothing like honoring and rewarding the good members effectively and surely if you want to make the whole household temperate, well conducted, and conscientious. What is praised will soon be valued by the good, and as for the not-so-good, rewards and praises given to the good kindle in them a desire to earn the same things by similar behavior and a similar character.

Lionardo: I like what you are saying. You speak most beautifully, too. I confess that this is how things are. But how would you go about getting clothes for your family? Would you sell the fruits of your farm?

Giannozzo: If there were a sufficient surplus, why not turn it into money and spend it on whatever is needed? That's always been a good thing for the whole family, if the father sells rather than buys. As you know, however, all year the family runs into small expenses for household furnishings and all sorts of things that must be made; there are also certain major expenses, of which almost the chief is for clothing. Young people grow, there are weddings to prepare, payments on dowries to be made, and if one tried to pay for it all from one's farm surplus, I think that income would prove insufficient.

I would, therefore, exercise some civic occupation as well, something suited to myself and beneficial both to me and to my relatives. In this occupation I would be able to earn money constantly and to provide for all necessities. The surplus I would keep for times of major expenditure, perhaps to aid my country, to help my friends, to give to my kinsmen, or other things like that. These are necessities that can arise at any moment, and they are not easy to cope with. Nor are they avoidable, since duty is involved, and also since one's feelings of sympathy are aroused. These, moreover, are the very deeds that gain a man friendship, reputation, and honor. I, for one, am glad to have an occupation which keeps me busy and lets me be sure my sons are not growing up lazy or idle.

Lionardo: What occupation would you choose?

Giannozzo: As honorable an occupation as possible and, if possible, one useful to many people.

Lionardo: Would it be trade, perhaps?

Giannozzo: Yes, yet to increase my tranquillity, I would like to have something secure, something I could see improving under my hands from day to day. Perhaps I would have men working wool or silk or something similar. This kind of business is less trouble and much less nerve-racking than trade. I would gladly take on an enterprise like that, which requires many hands, for the money goes to a large number of persons. It helps many poor people.

Lionardo: An act of noblest piety, it would be, to help many people.

Giannozzo: Who would deny that? Particularly if it were carried out as I would like to see it—for I would employ workers and would not use my own labor except to oversee and regulate everyone's performance of his task. Here is what I would say to all of them: be honest, fair, and friendly with everyone who comes in, with strangers no less than with friends. Be truthful and precise at all times. Beware that no one ever, through your roughness or malice, leaves your shop feeling cheated or discontented. For, my children, it is less profit than loss, I think, to gain cash and lose good will. A seller who is well liked always has plenty of customers. A good name and the affection of one's fellow citizens are worth more than the greatest amount of money. I should command them also to sell nothing at an extra high price. Whether confronted by a creditor or a debtor, they would be told always to remember to be fair and square with everyone. They must not be proud or spiteful or negligent or quarrelsome, and above all they must be most diligent in keeping records. Thus I should hope that God would grant me prosperity, that plenty of clients would fill my shop, and that my name would be widely known. These are not things to be viewed lightly, for the favor of God and the good will of men bring ever increasing profits.

Lionardo: Yet agents, Giannozzo, are often far from zealous in their work. They rarely seek to represent your interests first and their own second.

Giannozzo: For that reason I would select with care and have good and honest employees. I would keep a close check on things, too, and go over even minor transactions. Even though I already knew the answers, I should ask questions just to appear watchful. I would not do this in such a way as to seem oversuspicious and distrustful but in a way that might influence my agents to avoid becoming careless. If it is clear to my agent that nothing remains hidden from me, he thinks it essential to be both careful and truthful. Even if he wished to be just the opposite, he could not be. My checking things over carefully would mean that errors could not escape me for long. A mistake not caught today would still come out tomorrow and be corrected in good time. If something were maliciously hidden, however, believe me, a bit of cheating soon reveals itself to a master who is always turning things over and looking through them. Messer Benedetto Alberti used to say, and he was a prudent man not in public affairs only but also in every aspect of private civic life, that it was a good sign if a merchant had ink-stained fingers.

Lionardo: I am not sure I understand.

Giannozzo: He considered it essential for a merchant or anyone who does business with a large number of persons always to write everything down, to note all transactions, and to keep a record of every item brought in or taken out. As he watches over the enterprise, he should almost always have his pen in his hand. I, for one, think this an excellent precept. If you put things off from today to tomorrow, they elude you or are forgotten, and the agent finds excuses and occasions either for dishonesty or for carelessness like his master's. Don't ever suppose that others work harder for you than you for yourself—you will only lose money in the end, or lose the agent. No question about it, my dear Lionardo, it is worse to have a bad agent than to have none. A diligent master can even improve an inferior agent, but when the man who ought to be chiefly concerned is himself negligent, even a good employee tends to deteriorate.

Lionardo: How true! Even if you are a careful master, a villainous agent may rob and cheat you with clever tricks, but if he discovers that you yourself neglect your affairs, he will do you far more damage. This, too, is something we have learned in our family by all too frequent experience. We have often had employees whose villainy did us far more harm than our own negligence. But it is hard even to dissociate oneself from a dishonest man without suffering some damage.

Giannozzo: I think of all the losses and damage I have known merchants to suffer, and I think that five out of six times the catastrophe was due to the incompetence of the man who was supposed to be responsible for management. I feel I may assert with certainty that there is nothing so apt to make employees loyal as having a hard-working master, and nothing makes them worse than the master's negligence. Laziness, negligence, not watching carefully over one's business, these are the things that injure our condition, my children, and bring us down. A man who cannot report on his own affairs except by the mouth of another is a fool. He is blind who can see only with another's eyes. One must be careful, alert, and diligent. One must check everything, and at frequent intervals. Things cannot easily go astray then, and if they do they are soon found.

Neglected tasks pile up till they cannot be finished in a day. You cannot give them, then, the attention they deserve. What you might at one time have done well and with pleasure now, under the pressure created by delay, must be done hastily. You cannot now do each of the various portions of the task as well as before, in their proper time, you certainly could have. I should, therefore, work hard at every task. In the business that mattered most to me, I should, first, exercise extreme care in choosing my agent and, second, zealously investigate all things and know the business so intimately that the agent would not grow careless. To give my employees incentive to improve, I should respect them, treat them generously, and try to make them feel an attachment both to myself and to my affairs.

Lionardo: I certainly agree that one must very carefully choose good agents, and no less carefully prevent them from turning into bad ones. One must as you say, watch them diligently so that they remain, as time goes by, still loyal and zealous in your service.

Giannozzo: This is essential, and do you know how to do it? It is necessary, first, to make wide inquiries about your future agent, to inform yourself of his background, to appraise his past conduct and carefully consider his habits and character.

Lionardo: Which do you prefer as agents, outsiders or members of the family? I have often noticed quite some controversy on this point among merchants. Some say it is easier to punish a stranger and to get your full value out of him than to manage a member of your own family. Others think that outsiders are more obedient, more submissive than relatives. Others find it undesirable that their kinsmen should do so well as to arrive in time at a high place, take authority, and eventually replace the man now in command. Thus do their opinions run.

Giannozzo: As for me, my dear Lionardo, I would not even call a man my agent, but rather my enemy, if I expected to punish him, and then I would not want him among my servants. Nor do I fully understand why I should expect strangers to give me more reverence, although it is true that from my own kinsmen I would feel it more honorable to accept good will and love than obedience and servitude. I do not think, however, that to have the loyalty and zeal of men who love me is less valuable in my business than to have the obedience of such as fear me. I also would not consider a man worthy of good fortune or deserving of authority or in any sense a man to be respected if he found it painful to see his own kinsmen enjoying honor and happiness. A man would seem an utter fool to me, indeed, if he thought he could maintain his dignity and preserve his fortunate position without the favor and aid of his family. Believe me, my children, I know a great many examples to show this, but for brevity's sake, I won't recount them now. Believe me, no one can keep good fortune for any length of time unless other men put hand and shoulder to the wheel. If a man is in disgrace with his own family, he is a fool to think he could win the favor of strangers. But to look at your question more closely, Lionardo, do you assume that your relatives are good or bad people?

Lionardo: Good ones.

Giannozzo: Well, if they are good ones, I am very sure that they will be better in my service than strangers. It seems reasonable to me, first, to assume that my own people will be more loyal and affectionate than outsiders and, second, to prefer to do them a favor rather than to help others.

Lionardo: But what if they are bad?

Giannozzo: How bad, Lionardo? If they are incompetent, Lionardo, would I not be under a greater obligation to instruct my own relatives than to do the same for strangers?

Lionardo: Yes, certainly, but what if, as sometimes does happen, they cheated?

Giannozzo: Tell me, Lionardo, would you find it more distasteful to discover that one of your own kinsmen had acquired goods of yours or that a stranger had stolen them?

Lionardo: It would trouble me less if my wealth were useful to one of my kinsmen, but I would be more indignant at the betrayal by one whom I had trusted more.

Giannozzo: Erase that false opinion from your mind, Lionardo. Don't believe that a kinsman would ever cheat you if you treated him like a kinsman. What relative of yours would not rather deal with you than with a stranger? A stranger, indeed, only joins you to gain what he can for himself.

Remember this—I keep repeating it because it is something you should always keep in mind—there is more honor and value in helping your own family than outsiders. The little or much that the stranger takes away with him will never come back into the possession of your family, nor will it be useful in any way to your grandchildren. If a stranger grows rich with you, he will have small gratitude toward you, because, as he thinks, he has earned it. Your own kinsman, benefiting by association with you, will admit his obligation and will retain a memory that makes him eager to help your own children in a similar way. Even should he fail to be grateful and to recognize your benificence, if you are good and just you would sooner see your own kinsman enjoy prosperity than any outsider whatsoever. This is something you need never fear anyway, as you should realize, if only you are diligent in making a careful choice of agent and watchful to keep him from slipping.

Tell me something else, however—when you are choosing an agent, in which case will you find it more difficult to learn what his true character is, if you take him from your own family, who grew up under your eyes and with whom you have conversed every day, or if you draw him from among strangers, whom you know much less well and have far less experience of? I believe, Lionardo, that it is far more difficult to know the mind of a stranger than to know one of your own relatives. If so, and if to make a good choice we need to know and to investigate character, who would ever think it easier to accomplish that task with a stranger? Who could prefer a stranger whom he did not know well to one of his own family whom he did know well?

When our relatives are good and talented, we should help them, and when they are not already endowed with these qualities, we should apply all our efforts and give them all our help, to make them gradually improve. It is a sign of meager charity if a man disdains his own people to benefit others. It is a sign of grave disloyalty to distrust one's own kin while trusting other men. But perhaps I go on too long on this point. What do you think about it Lionardo?

Lionardo: Your opinion seems to me charitable, just, and true. It is my own belief, too, and perhaps, if everyone held it as tenaciously as I, our family would not now have so much cause to complain of injuries sometimes received from strangers. Certainly I admit the wisdom of your view; I might put it this way—the man who does not love his family does not know how to love.

Giannozzo: How true that is. If you can have the service of your kinsmen, never, never call on others. And it is a good thing if you solicit their service, take pleasure in teaching them, enjoy being accounted a father to them. You can give yourself the happiness of having a great number of young people who, thanks to your kindness, stand to you as children. In aspiration and action, they will always live in harmony with you. The stranger does not do all this. Instead, as soon as he has begun to know a little something or to gather a little property, he wants to be a partner. Soon he tells you he wants to leave, creates difficulties in order to force you to improve his condition. He cares little whether you suffer harm or disgrace as long as he profits. But let that go.

I could bring forward an infinite number of arguments to show that a stranger abides with you as an enemy, while a kinsman is always your friend. Relatives seek your welfare and your good name. They want to avoid any harm befalling you or any disgrace coming to you, for every honor that you gain brings them honor also, and part of the dishonor attached to any disgrace of yours falls on them. A crowd of further reasons rushes to mind by which I might clearly show you that it is better form, more honorable, more practical, more noble, and safer to draw your help from your family, not from outside. Even if you should think the opposite, I counsel you always to show greater charity toward your own kin than toward strangers. I would remind you how great is our debt toward the young, how much it is our duty to teach them excellence and to guide them toward honor. To us, fathers of families, surely it is a terrible disgrace if we hold back available honor and benefit from our own family, as if we disdained and despised them.

Lionardo: I don't need to hear any more reasons. I consider it a real disgrace if a man will not answer the needs of his own relatives. I also admit that one who cannot live on good terms with his own kind will be still less able to live happily with outsiders.

These young people and I are deeply obliged to you for your remarks, for they are of the most extraordinary value for good household management. It would be a still greater gift and paternal kindness if you would let us hear the rest also. We do know that more should follow. You have spoken of the house, of the farm, and of the occupation which good management requires. Teach us now how to deal with the further expenditures which arise every day, besides those for clothing, food, and the liberal entertainment of friends. There are times when we ought to undertake some expense for the honor and fame of our house. On a number of occasions our family has embarked on such expenditures, among them the construction added by our fathers to the temple of the Agnoli, and to many other places within and outside our city. They built at San Miniato, at Paradiso, at Santa Caterina, and added to various other public and private edifices like these. Now what rule or method would you say applied to this kind of spending? I know that for this, as for the other sort, you can probably give us some excellent principles.

Giannozzo: None better than some I know.

Lionardo: And what are they?

Giannozzo: Listen. I have certain ideas about this—now you think, too, and see if I am right. It seems to me, you see, that all expenses are either necessary or unnecessary. I call those expenses necessary without which the family cannot be honorably maintained. The man who fails to spend for these purposes harms his own honor and the comfort of his family. The greater the harm it does not to make a certain purchase, the more necessary is that purchase. The number of such expenses is so great it would be hard to count them all, but they may be summed up in the fact that together they comprise the whole acquisition and maintenance of the house, the farm, and the shop. These in turn are the three sources of all that is useful and valuable and needed by the family. Unnecessary expenses, on the other hand, are those which give pleasure if undertaken wisely, but which it does no harm to omit. Among these are works like the frescoes for the loggia, the silver, embellishments that add pomp to one's way of life, like fine clothing and largesse. Likewise unnecessary but not unreasonable are the expenses which one undertakes in pursuit of pleasure and civilized distraction, expenditures without which you could still live honorably and well.

Lionardo: I understand: like buying beautiful books, handsome steeds, and other things that attract a proud and liberal spirit.

Giannozzo: Exactly.

Lionardo: These might be called voluntary expenditures, then, since they satisfy our will rather than our necessity.

Giannozzo: All right. Beyond these there are also insane expenditures, the ones that bring disgrace on the man who plunges into them. Such would be the cost of keeping serpents in one's house, or other still more terrible, cruel, and poisonous beasts than these.

Lionardo: Tigers maybe?

Giannozzo: Worse than tigers, my dear Lionardo, nurturing wicked and depraved persons. Wicked men are worse than tigers or any beasts however dangerous. A single member of the family thus devoted to evil can ruin them all. There is no worse poison, nothing as unhealthy as the words of a wicked tongue. No madness compares with the madness driving the spiteful talker. And if a man supports such criminals as these, he certainly engages in expenses that are mad and bestial, and earns justified contempt. One should avoid acquaintance or intimacy with evil speakers like the plague. These talkers and scoundrels come between a family and its friends and acquaintances. One should never cultivate the friendship of men who willingly consort with such scoundrels. If a man loves dissipated men, he loves dissipation; and if he loves dissipation he is not good; and good men have never cared to befriend the wicked. It is neither useful nor easy, in any case, to gain the friendship of men whose doors and ears are not securely locked against malicious tongues.

Lionardo: Giannozzo, you are surely telling us the truth. These expenses are not only mad, but dangerous. Malicious people with their spitefulness usually, by means of gossip and false accusations, even manage to make you feel suspicion and hate of your own family. You will then not even believe those who truly love you and try to warn you of the wicked spite that animates those persons.

Giannozzo: Let us never take on these mad expenses, or anything of the kind. These are ways to be shunned. If anyone invites or even counsels you to act this way, he is not a man to heed or trust.

Lionardo: And by what method, Giannozzo, are we to manage the other two kinds of expenses, the necessary and the voluntary?

Giannozzo: What do you think? Do you know what my system is with necessary expenditures? I get them out of the way as fast as I can.

Lionardo: Don't you deliberate first about the best way of handling them?

Giannozzo: Yes, certainly. Don't imagine that I ever rush madly into anything if I can help it. I try to do these things with deliberate speed.

Lionardo: Why?

Giannozzo: Because if something must be done I like to get it done quickly, if only to have it off my mind. I pay what I must pay immediately. Voluntary expenses I handle quite differently, for a good reason.

Lionardo: What is your way?

Giannozzo: It's the best and most sensible method. I'll tell you I go slow, Lionardo, I delay again and again. I go as slow as I can.

Lionardo: And why?

Giannozzo: For a very good reason.

Lionardo: I want to know what good reason moves you, for I know you do nothing without the best of reasons.

Giannozzo: I'll tell you, to see if this particular desire will leave me along the way. If not, then to give myself time to think how I may fulfill it with a minimum of expense and with most satisfaction.

Lionardo: I thank you, Giannozzo. You have now taught me the way to avoid many expenses which I, like other young men, have hardly been able to avoid.

Giannozzo: That is the reason why reverence toward us elders is a duty. Thus you young men profit by asking your elders about your problems and hearing their advice. Many things in this world are better understood by experience than by speculation and theory. We who are not schooled in books become erudite through practice and time. We have considered the whole art of living and sorted out what it is best to do. We undoubtedly know, by virtue of experience, more than you with all your learning and subtleties and wily schemes. I'll tell you this, too, the shortest way to what you call good philosophy, as I've always thought, is to frequent and treasure the conversation of your elders. Ask them questions, listen to them, and obey their injunctions. Time, the best teacher of all things, has instructed the old and taught them to do those things that help us mortals get along in life and reach at last the haven of a quiet, tranquil, and respected old age.

Lionardo: We certainly expected to learn many valuable things from you, but with this, as with many of your other remarkable and precious remarks, you have far surpassed our expectations. You have taught us more than I ever thought was connected with the good management of the household. But I wonder if I am right about something. It is my impression, Giannozzo, that to undertake to be the father of a family as you have defined him to us would be a heavy task: managing one's own possessions, ruling and moderating the affections of the spirit, curbing and restraining the appetites of the body, adapting oneself and making good use of time, watching over and governing the family, preserving one's property, maintaining the house, cultivating the farm, managing the shop—all these are things which it would not be easy to do really well even if one undertook only one or another of them. To combine them all and, difficult as they are, to give each no less attention than it requires would be well nigh impossible.

Giannozzo: Don't take that attitude—these things are not what they may seem to you now, my dear Lionardo, they are not as difficult as you think now. They are all so closely connected and intertwined that, if a man tries to be a good father to his family and takes good care of one of his duties, the others follow by themselves. If a man knows how to keep from wasting time, he knows almost everything. If he knows how to make good use of time, he can be lord of anything he pleases. Even if these were hard duties, however, they offer so much practical advantage and pleasure to those who are devoted, and lay so heavy a burden of disgrace on anyone who is negligent that your interest should never cool or weary. To any good person not subject to laziness and apathy, they should be a delight. It should give us pleasure to concern ourselves with these things. Nothing is so pleasant as to satisfy ourselves, nothing gives so much satisfaction as doing what we like. We should view it as a point of honor, also, to take proper care of our own affairs, since we know by experience that neglecting them brings no less disgrace than disadvantage.

Should you still be anxious to lighten your burden, then undertake to do only part of all your work yourself, the part which best suits your mind, age, temperament, and position. Always keep your authority over all of it, however, so that your concerns are as honorably handled as they should be. You must not submit them completely to the hands and judgment of others, but only let others, as your servants, act according to your own will and plan. You must, therefore, take the responsibility for the good of all your people. Keep your agents distributed over your various affairs, one on the farm, one in the city, others where needed, and everyone doing the job that best suits his abilities.

You, men of letters, when you discuss practical wisdom and life in general, often draw a parallel with the life of ants, and say that we should learn from them to be providential and to think of the future. Messer Benedetto Alberti, I remember, often followed that literary example. He was a man who studied and who zealously applied himself to books while at home. Outside his home, he was a gregarious person. He was always discussing with attentive fellow citizens and friends matters both honorable and beautiful, both pleasant and useful, applying a characteristic mixture of wit and gravity. On the same principle, you often draw an illustration from the bees, who unite in obedience to a single leader and are all busy for the sake of the general good. They work with manly vigor and passionate zeal, some reaping precious pollen from the flowers, others bearing the burden home, some distributing it among the workers, others building the house. All together defend the riches and delights they have accumulated. You have many such analogies by means of which to make your point and to delight your hearers. Let me now also draw an analogy, if not so perfectly appropriate as yours, still not wholly misplaced. I may thus be able to set what I think more perfectly and more clearly before you. I shall almost paint it for you, placing before your very eyes the idea of what a father should do. Allow me, therefore, now to follow you in this respected and noble custom.

You know the spider and how he constructs his web. All the threads spread out in rays, each of which, however long, has its source, its roots or birthplace, as we might say, at the center. From there each filament starts and moves outward. The most industrious creature himself then sits at that spot and has his residence there. He remains in that place once his work is spun and arranged, but keeps so alert and watchful that if there is a touch on the finest and most distant thread he feels it instantly, instantly appears, and instantly takes care of the situation. Let the father of a family do likewise. Let him arrange his affairs and place them so that all look up to him alone as head, so that all are directed by him and by him attached to secure foundations. The father of the family should reside, then, in the midst of all, alert and quick to feel and to see everything, ready, wherever there is need of intervention, to provide it immediately. I don't know, Lionardo, how little this analogy of mine may suit you.

Lionardo: How could I find fault with anything you say? I swear to you, Giannozzo, I have never seen so apt or so useful an analogy. I certainly understand; it is indeed as you say. The system and diligence of the master makes even the heaviest and most difficult tasks easy and manageable. For some reason, however, I don't know why, it still does seem that public affairs get in the way of private ones, while private needs often conflict with our attention to public affairs. I am led to doubt, therefore, that all our devotion, given to all things at once, will prove sufficient.

Giannozzo: Don't take that view when there is a quick and excellent remedy at hand.

Lionardo: What remedy?

Giannozzo: Let the father of the family follow my example. Since I find it no easy matter to deal with the needs of the household when I must often be engaged outside with other men in arranging matters of wider consequence, I have found it wise to set aside a certain amount for outside use, for investments and purchases. The rest, which takes care of all the smaller household affairs, I leave to my wife's care. I have done it this way, for, to tell the truth, it would hardly win us respect if our wife busied herself among the men in the marketplace, out in the public eye. It also seems somewhat demeaning to me to remain shut up in the house among women when I have manly things to do among men, fellow citizens and worthy and distinguished foreigners.

I don't know whether you will approve of my solution. I know some people are always checking on their own household and rummaging around in every nook and cranny lest something remain hidden from them. Nothing is so obscure that they do not look into it and poke their fingers in. They say that it is no shame or harm to a man to attend carefully to his own affairs and to lay down the law and custom in his own house. They point out that Niccolo Alberti, who was a very diligent person, said diligence and universal vigilance was the mother of wealth. I too admire and like this saying, for diligence always helps; but I cannot convince myself that men who are engaged in other concerns really ought to be or to seem so very interested in every little household trifle. I don't know, perhaps I am wrong about this. What do you say, Lionardo, what do you think?

Lionardo: I agree, for you are, indeed, precisely of the opinion of the ancients. They used to say that men are by nature of a more elevated mind than women. They are more suited to struggle with arms and with cunning against the misfortunes which afflict country, religion, and one's own children. The character of men is stronger than that of women and can bear the attacks of enemies better, can stand strain longer, is more constant under stress. Therefore men have the freedom to travel with honor in foreign lands, acquiring and gathering the goods of fortune. Women, on the other hand, are almost all timid by nature, soft, slow, and therefore more useful when they sit still and watch over our things. It is as though nature thus provided for our well-being, arranging for men to bring things home and for women to guard them. The woman, as she remains locked up at home, should watch over things by staying at her post, by diligent care and watchfulness. The man should guard the woman, the house, and his family and country, but not by sitting still. He should exercise his spirit and his hands in brave enterprise, even at the cost of sweat and blood. No doubt of it, therefore, Giannozzo, those idle creatures who stay all day among the little females or who keep their minds occupied with little feminine trifles certainly lack a masculine and glorious spirit. They are contemptible in their apparent inclination to play the part of women rather than that of men. A man demonstrates his love of high achievements by the pride he takes in his own. But if he does not shun trifling occupations, clearly he does not mind being regarded as effeminate. It seems to me, then, that you are entirely right to leave the care of minor matters to your wife and to take upon yourself, as I have always seen you do, all manly and honorable concerns.

Giannozzo: Yes, you see that's my long-standing conviction. I believe that a man who is the father of a family not only should do all that is proper to a man, but that he must abstain from such activities as properly pertain to women. The details of housekeeping he should commit entirely into their hands. I always do.

Lionardo: You, however, can congratulate yourself on having a wife who probably surpasses other women. I don't know how many women one could find as vigorous and as wise in their rule of the household as your wife.

Giannozzo: My wife certainly did turn into a perfect mother for my household. Partly this was the result of her particular nature and temperament, but mainly it was due to my instruction.

Lionardo: Then you taught her?

Giannozzo: Many things.

Lionardo: And how did you do it?

Giannozzo: Well, I'll tell you. After my wife had been settled in my house a few days, and after her first pangs of longing for her mother and family had begun to fade, I took her by the hand and showed her around the whole house. I explained that the loft was the place for grain and that the stores of wine and wood were kept in the cellar. I showed her where things needed for the table were kept, and so on, through the whole house. At the end there were no household goods of which my wife had not learned both the place and the purpose. Then we returned to my room, and, having locked the door, I showed her my treasures, silver, tapestry, garments, jewels, and where each thing had its place.

Lionardo: All those valuables, then, were assigned some place in your room, I suppose because they were safer there, better secluded and more securely locked up.

Giannozzo: Yes, but primarily so that I could look them over whenever I liked without witnesses. You may be sure, children, that it is imprudent to live so openly that the whole household knows everything. It is less difficult to guard a thing from a few persons than from all. If something is known only to a few, it is easier to keep safe. If it does get lost, it is easier to get it back from a few than from many. For this and for many other reasons, I have always thought it a good precaution to keep every precious thing I had well hidden if possible, and locked up out of the reach of most hands and eyes. These treasures, I always felt, should be kept where they are safe from fire and other disaster, and where I can frequently, whether for my pleasure or to check them over, shut myself up alone or with whomever I choose while giving no cause for undue curiosity to those outside. No place seemed more suited for this purpose than the room where I slept. There, as I was saying, I wanted none of my precious things to be hidden from my wife. I opened to her all my household treasures, unfolded them, and showed them to her.

Only my books and records and those of my ancestors did I determine to keep well sealed both then and thereafter. These my wife not only could not read, she could not even lay hands on them. I kept my records at all times not in the sleeves of my dress, but locked up and arranged in order in my study, almost like sacred and religious objects. I never gave my wife permission to enter that place, with me or alone. I also ordered her, if she ever came across any writing of mine, to give it over to my keeping at once. To take away any taste she might have for looking at my notes or prying into my private affairs, I often used to express my disapproval of bold and forward females who try too hard to know about things outside the house and about the concerns of their husband and of men in general. I used to remind her of a truth which Messer Cipriano Alberti once voiced to me. A most honest and wise man, Messer Cipriano once saw that the wife of a good friend of his was overeager to ask and inquire into the place where her husband had stayed the night and the company he had kept. He was anxious to warn her as best he could and to show her the respect he perhaps felt he owed to his friend. Finally he said to her, "I counsel you, friend, for your own good—be far more eager to learn what goes on in your own house than to find out about what lies outside it. Let me remind you as I would a sister that wise men say a woman who spies too much on men may be suspected of having men too much on her mind, being perhaps secretly anxious whether others are learning about her own character when she appears too interested in them. Think for yourself whether either of these passions is becoming to a lady of unblemished honor." Thus Messer Cipriano, and thus I too, spoke to my wife.

I always tried to make sure, first that she could not, and second that she did not wish, to know more of my secrets than I cared to impart. One should never, in fact, tell a secret, even a trivial one, to one's wife or any woman. I am greatly displeased with those husbands who take counsel with their wives and don't know how to confine any kind of secret to their own breast. They are madmen if they think true prudence or good counsel lies in the female brain, and still more clearly mad if they suppose that a wife will be more constant in silence concerning her husband's business than he himself has proved. Stupid husbands to blab to their wives and forget that women themselves can do anything sooner than keep quiet! For this very reason I have always tried carefully not to let any secret of mine be known to a woman. I did not doubt that my wife was most loving, and more discreet and modest in her ways than any, but I still considered it safer to have her unable, and not merely unwilling, to harm me.

Lionardo: An excellent lesson. You have been no less wise than fortunate if your wife has never dragged any secret out of you.

Giannozzo: Never, my dear Lionardo, and I'll tell you why. First, she was very modest and never cared to know more than was her business. Furthermore, I made it a rule never to speak with her of anything but household matters or questions of conduct, or of the children. Of these matters I spoke a good deal to her. From what I said, and by answering me and discussing with me, she learned the principles she required and how to apply them. I did this, also, my dear Lionardo, in order to make it impossible for her to enter into discussions with me concerning my more important and private affairs. This was my practice: I always kept my secrets and my notes carefully hidden; everything else of a domestic nature, I thought then and later, could properly be delegated to her. I did not, however, leave things so much in her hands as to be uninterested or not examine the details and be sure all was well managed.

When my wife had seen and understood the place of everything in the house, I said to her, "My dear wife, those things are to be as useful and precious to you as to me. The loss of them would injure and grieve you, therefore should you guard them no less zealously than I do. You have seen our treasures now, and thanks be to God they are such that we ought to be contented with them. If we know how to preserve them, these things will serve you and me and our children. It is up to you, therefore, my dear wife, to keep no less careful watch over them than I."

Lionardo: And what did your wife say to that?

Giannozzo: She replied by saying that her father and mother had taught her to obey them and had ordered her always to obey me, and so she was prepared to do anything I told her to. "My dear wife," said I, "a girl who knows how to obey her father and mother soon learns to please her husband. But do you know how we shall try to be? We shall imitate those who stand guard on the walls of the city; if one of them, by chance, falls asleep, he does not take it amiss for his companion to wake him up that he may do his duty for his country. Likewise, my dear wife, if you ever see any fault in me, I shall be very grateful to you for letting me know. In that way I shall know that our honor and our welfare and the good of our children are dear to your heart. Likewise be not displeased if I awaken you where there is need. Where I am lacking, you shall make it good, and so together we shall try to surpass each other in love and in zeal.

This property, this family, and the children to be born to us will belong to us both, to you as much as to me, to me as much as to you. It behooves us, therefore, not to think how much each of us has brought into our marriage, but how we can best maintain all that belongs to both of us. I shall try to obtain outside what you need inside the house; you must see that none of it is wasted.

Lionardo: How did she seem to take all this? Was she pleased?

Giannozzo: Very much so. She said she would be happy to do conscientiously whatever she knew how to do and had the skill to do, hoping it might please me. To this I said, "Dear wife, listen to me. I shall be most pleased if you do just three things: first, my wife, see that you never want another man to share this bed but me. You understand." She blushed and cast down her eyes. Still I repeated that she should never receive anyone into that room but myself. That was the first point. The second, I said, was that she should take care of the household, preside over it with modesty, serenity, tranquillity, and peace. That was the second point. The third thing, I said, was that she should see that nothing went wrong in the house.

Lionardo: Did you show her how to do what you commanded, or did she already have an expert knowledge of these things?

Giannozzo: Do not imagine, my dear Lionardo, that a young girl can ever be very well versed in these matters. Nor is such cleverness and cunning required from a young girl as it is from the mother of a family. Her modesty and virtue, on the other hand, must be much greater. And these very qualities my wife had in abundance. In these virtues she surpassed all other women. I could not describe to you how reverently she replied to me. She said her mother had taught her only how to spin and sew, and how to be virtuous and obedient. Now she would gladly learn from me how to rule the family and whatever I might wish to teach her.

Lionardo: And you, Giannozzo, how did you manage to teach her these things?

Giannozzo: What things? How to sleep with no other man but myself, perhaps?

Lionardo: You are wonderful, Giannozzo. Even in giving us these holy and austere lessons, you know how to joke and make us laugh.

Giannozzo: It certainly would be funny if I had tried to teach her how to sleep alone. I don't know if those ancient authors you like to read were able to teach that.

Lionardo: Everything but that. They do say, however, how they instructed their wives never, in bearing and behavior, to let themselves appear less virtuous than they really were. It is also described how they tried to persuade women, for this very reason, never to paint their faces with white powder, brazilnut dye, or other make-up.

Giannozzo: I myself, I assure you, did not omit this.

Lionardo: I would like to hear how you handled it. When I have a wife of my own I should like to know how to do something which, it seems, few husbands can manage. For everyone hates to see make-up on his wife, yet no one seems able to prevent it.

Giannozzo: In dealing with this problem, I exercised great discretion. You'll not be sorry to hear my fine method for making her detest the stuff. So, since it will be most useful to you to have heard me, listen carefully now. When I had given the house over to my wife's keeping, I brought her back to our own locked room, as I was saying. Then she and I knelt down and prayed to God to give us the power to make good use of those possessions which he, in his mercy and kindness, had allowed us to enjoy. We also prayed with most devoted mind that he might grant us the grace to live together in peace and harmony for many happy years, and with many male children, and that he might grant to me riches, friendship, and honor, and to her, integrity, purity, and the character of a perfect mistress of the household. Then, when we had stood up, I said to her:

"My dear wife, to have prayed God for these things is not enough. Let us also be very diligent and conscientious and do our best to obtain what we have prayed for. I, my dear wife, shall seek with all my powers to gain what we have asked of God. You, too, must set your whole will, all your mind, and all your modesty to work to make yourself a person whom God has heard and to whom he has granted what you prayed for. You should realize that in this regard nothing is so important for yourself, so acceptable to God, so pleasing to me, and precious in the sight of your children as your chastity. The woman's character is the jewel of her family; the mother's purity has always been a part of the dowry she passes on to her daughters; her purity has always far outweighed her beauty. A beautiful face is praised, but unchaste eyes make it ugly through men's scorn, and too often flushed with shame or pale with sorrow and melancholy. A handsome person is pleasing to see, but a shameless gesture or an act of incontinence in an instant renders her appearance vile. Unchastity angers God, and you know that God punishes nothing so severely in women as he does this lack. All their lives he makes them notorious and miserable. The shameless woman is hated by her whose love is true and good. She soon discovers that, in fact, her dishonored condition pleases only her enemies. Only one who wishes us to suffer and be troubled can rejoice when he sees you fall from honor.

"Shun every sort of dishonor, my dear wife. Use every means to appear to all people as a highly respectable woman. To seem less would be to offend God, me, our children, and yourself. To seem so, indeed, brings praise and love and favor from all. Then you can hope that God will give some aid to your prayers and vows.

"To be praised for your chastity, you must shun every deed that lacks true nobility, eschew any sort of improper speech, avoid giving any sign that your spirit lacks perfect balance and chastity. You will disdain, first of all, those vanities which some females imagine will please men. All made up and plastered and painted and dressed in lascivious and improper clothing, they suppose they are more attractive to men than when adorned with pure simplicity and true virtue. Vain and foolish women are these who imagine that when they appear in make-up and look far from virtuous they will be praised by those who see them. They do not realize that they are provoking disapproval and harming themselves. Nor do they realize, in their petty vanity, that their immodest appearance excites numerous lustful men. Such men all besiege and attack such a girl, some with suddenness, some with persistence, some with trickery, until at last the unfortunate wretch falls into real disgrace. From such a fall she cannot rise again without the stain of great and lasting infamy upon her."

Thus I spoke to my wife. To convince her still more fully of the danger, as well as of the shame, in a woman's covering her face with the powders and poisons which the silly creatures call make-up, see, dear Lionardo, what a nice lesson I gave her. There was a saint in the room, a very lovely statue of silver, whose head and hands alone were of purest ivory. It was set, polished and shining, in the center of the altar, as usual. "My dear wife," I said to her, "suppose you besmirched the face of this image in the morning with chalk and calcium and other ointments. It might well gain in color and whiteness. In the course of the day the wind would carry dust to it and make it dirty, but in the evening you would wash it, and then, the next day, cover it again with ointments, and then wash it again. Tell me, after many days of this, if you wanted to sell it, all polished and painted, how much money do you think you would get for it? More than if you had never begun painting it?

"Much less," she replied.

"That's right," said I, "for the buyer of the image does not buy it for a coating of paint which can be put on or off but because he appreciates the excellence of the statue and the skill of the artist. You would have lost your labor, then, as well as the cost of those ointments. Tell me, though, if you went on for months or years washing and redaubing it, would you make it more beautiful?"

"I think not," she said.

"On the contrary, you would spoil it and wear it out. You would scrape off the finish of the ivory. It would become rough and end up colorless, yellowed, softened by those powders. Certainly. But if those poultices could have that effect on ivory, which is hard stuff by nature and able to last forever if left alone, you can be sure, my dear wife, that they can do your own brow and cheeks still greater harm. For your skin is tender and delicate if you don't smear anything on it, and if you do it will soon grow rough and flabby. Don't deny that those things are poison. You know that all those make-up materials do contain poison. They do you much more harm than they would to ivory. You know, even the least bit of dust or a drop of sweat makes a smear on your face. No, you will not be more beautiful with that stuff, only dirty, and in the long run you will ruin your skin."

Lionardo: Did she seem to agree and to realize you were telling the truth?

Giannozzo: What sort of silly girl would fail to realize this was the truth? Besides, to make sure she did believe me, I asked her about a neighbor of mine, a woman who had few teeth left in her mouth, and those appeared tarnished with rust. Her eyes were sunken and always inflamed, the rest of her face whithered and ashen. All her flesh looked decomposed and disgusting. Her silvery hair was the only thing about her that one might regard without displeasure. So I asked my wife whether she wished she were blond and looked like her?

"Heavens, no," said she.

"And why not? Does she seem so old to you? How old do you think she is?"

To that she replied most modestly that she was no judge of these matters, but to her the woman seemed about the age of her mother's wetnurse. Then I assured her of the truth, namely that that neighbor of mine was born less than two years before me and had certainly not yet attained her thirty-second year. Thanks to make-up, however, she had been left in this diseased condition and seemed old before her time.

When I saw she was really amazed at this, I reminded her of all the Alberti girls, of my cousins and others in the family. "You see, my dear wife," I said, "how fresh and lively our girls all are, for the simple reason that they never anoint themselves with anything but river water. And so shall you do, my wife," said I. "You'll not poison yourself or whiten your face to make yourself seem more beautiful for me. You are white and bright enough complexioned for me as you are. Rather, like the Alberti girls, you will just wash and keep clean with water alone. My dear wife, there is no one but me for you to think of pleasing in this matter. Me, however, you cannot please by deception. Remember that. You cannot deceive me, anyway, because I see you at all hours and know very well how you look without make-up. As for outsiders, if you love me, think how could any of them matter more to you than your own husband. Remember, my dear wife, that a girl who tries harder to please outsiders than the one she should be pleasing shows that she loves her husband less than she does strangers."

Lionardo: Wise words. But did she obey you?

Giannozzo: It is true that at weddings, sometimes, whether because she was embarrassed at being among so many people or heated with dancing, she sometimes appeared to have more than her normal color. In the house, however, there was only one time, when friends and their wives were invited to dinner at Easter. My wife, on this occasion, had covered her face with pumice, in God's name, and she talked all too animatedly with each guest on his arrival or departure. She was showing off and being merry with everyone, as I observed.

Lionardo: Did you get angry with her?

Giannozzo: Ah, Lionardo, I never got angry with my wife.

Lionardo: Never?

Giannozzo: Why should we let quarrels arise between ourselves? Neither of us ever desired from the other anything that was not wholly right.

Lionardo: Yet I imagine you must have been troubled if in this matter your wife failed to obey you as she should have.

Giannozzo: Yes, yes, true enough. But I did not, for all that, show her that I was troubled.

Lionardo: Didn't you scold her?

Giannozzo: Ha, ha, yes, in the right way. To me it has always seemed obvious, dear children, that the way to correct someone is to begin gently, put out the evil quickly, and kindle good will. This you can learn from me—it is much better to reprimand a woman temperately and gently than with any sort of harsh severity. A slave can bear threats and blows and perhaps not grow indignant if you shout at him. A wife, however, will obey you better from love than from fear. Any free spirit will sooner set out to please you than to submit to you. It is best, therefore, to do as I did and correct your wife's failing kindly but in time.

Lionardo: How did you reprimand her?

Giannozzo: I waited till we were alone. Then I smiled at her and said, "Oh dear, how did your face get dirty? Did you by any chance bump into a pan? Go wash yourself, quick, before these people begin to make fun of you. The lady and mother of a household must always be neat and clean if she wants the rest of the family to learn good conduct and modest demeanor."

She understood me and at once began to cry. I let her go wash off both tears and make-up. After that I never had to tell her again.

Lionardo: What a perfect wife. I can well believe that such a woman, so obedient to your word and so modest by her own nature, could elicit respect and good behavior in the rest of the household.

Giannozzo: All wives are thus obedient, if their husbands know how to be husbands. But some I see quite unwisely suppose that they can win obedience and respect from a wife to whom they openly and abjectly subject themselves. If they show by word and gesture that their spirit is all too deeply lascivious and feminine, they certainly make their wives no less unfaithful than rebellious. Never, at any moment, did I choose to show in word or action even the least bit of self-surrender in front of my wife. I did not imagine for a moment that I could hope to win obedience from one to whom I had confessed myself a slave. Always, therefore, I showed myself virile and a real man. Always I encouraged her to love virtue. Always I reminded her to be most disciplined. I kept her always conscious of all that I, myself, knew was right for a perfect mother of a family and wanted her to know also.

"My dear wife," I often told her, "if we want to live in peace and harmony, all our household must be well behaved and modest in their ways. You must gladly take on yourself the task of making them obedient and respectful toward yourself. Unless you yourself are very modest and self-restrained, however, you may be sure that what you cannot do for yourself you can still less produce in others. To be regarded as a very modest and restrained woman, you must be such that all vileness offends you. This will help to discipline the household, for all its members will take care not to displease you. Unless they have the highest example of chastity and decorum in you, however, do not expect them to show obedience, let alone reverence, toward yourself. Respect is something one must earn. Only character gives a man dignity, and one who wears dignity can gain respect; one who can gain respect can win obedience. One who does not live up to his own standards soon loses all dignity and all respect. Therefore, dear wife, make it your concern to be and to appear in every gesture, word, and deed most modest and most virtuous.

"A great part of modesty, remember, consists in tempering all one's gestures with gravity and a mature manner. One must temper one's mind and every word of one's speech, even within the household and among one's own family, all the more outside among strangers. I shall be truly glad if I see that you disdain the frivolous mannerisms, the habit of tossing the hands about, the chattering that some little girls do all day, in the house, at the door, and wherever they go. They talk now with this friend, now with that one; they ask a lot of questions and say a lot of things that they don't know as well as a lot that they do. All that is the way to get yourself the reputation of an irresponsible featherbrain. Silence is as it always has been, the peak of dignity and the source of respect for a woman. Talking too much has been ever the habit and sign of a silly fool. So be glad to listen quietly and to talk less than you listen. If you do talk, never on any account tell our secrets to others or be too eager to know their affairs. A woman who spends all day chattering and agitating about things that do not concern the welfare of her household, while neglecting the things that do, indulges an ugly habit and brings contempt on herself. But if you govern the family with proper diligence, you will preserve and put to good use all the resources of the household."

Lionardo: And I imagine you taught her the management of the household as you taught her other things?

Giannozzo: Don't you doubt it. Of course I did my best to make her in every way an excellent mother of the household. "Dear wife," I told her, "you should view it as your job to give the house such an orderly routine that no one is ever idle. Give everyone some suitable job to do. And where you see reliable loyalty and hard work, give all the responsibility that may properly be given. At the same time, keep your eye on what everyone is doing. Make sure that those who are busy with things that are useful and beneficial for the family are aware that you will witness their merit. If someone works more diligently and lovingly at his task than the others, be sure, dear wife, that you do not forget to praise him in their presence. Thus in the future he will long to be still more helpful every day, knowing he can count on your appreciation. The others will want to please you, too, as much as those you have praised most. Together, let us reward everyone according to his merit. In that way we shall make all our servants loyal and devoted to us and our affairs."

Lionardo: But, Giannozzo, we all know that servants and even other members of the household are apt to be persons of small intelligence. Generally if they had more capacity for work and finer feelings, they would not stay with us but would learn some other trade. Did you teach your wife how to handle rough and uncouth persons, therefore, and how to make them obey her?

Giannozzo: The fact is that servants are as obedient as masters are skilled in commanding. Some people as I have observed myself, want their servants to obey them in matters where they themselves can give no direction. Others never know how to be the real master or to convince others that that's what they are. Remember, my children, no servant will listen and obey unless you know how to command. Nor will any resist and rebel if you know how to rule in a spirit of moderation and wisdom.

It is good to know not only how to make your servants obey but how to make them love and revere you. I find that the best way to make the impression of a real master is to do what I told my wife to do, talk as little as possible with her maid and even less with other servants. Too much familiarity kills respect. I also told her to give her orders in detail and at frequent intervals. She should not act like some people, who call everyone together and announce, "one of you do this," and then, when no one does it, all are equally at fault and no one is personally responsible.

I also said that she should order maids and all her servants never to leave the house without permission. They should all be on call and ready to help. She was never to give permission to all to go out at once, for there should be someone in the house on guard at any time. If anything happened, someone should always be there. I have always preferred to organize my house so that at any hour of the day or night, one person in the house was in charge in case something came up. There should also always be geese and dogs in a house, animals that are watchful and, as you know, both suspicious and affectionate. One wakes the other and calls out the whole crowd, and so the household is always safe—that is my way. To return to our subject, however, I told my wife not only never to give them all leave to go out at the same time, but also, if they came in late, to insist firmly, gently, and with deliberation on knowing the reason for it.

Besides this I said: "Since it does often happen that among servants, however obedient and reverent, occasional disagreements and conflicts arise, I charge you, dear wife, never to interfere in any such quarrel. Don't ever give any member of your household cause to feel that, in act or word, he can overstep what ought to be his bounds. Don't listen, dear wife, or show favor when one of them reports evil of another or brings an argument to you. The household full of quarrels can never abide in constancy of plan and purpose and, therefore, can never serve you well. If someone thinks that he has been injured through another's report to you and through your listening to it, he will carry a fire in his bosom and always be watching for a chance to revenge himself. In many ways he will try to make you condemn that person. He will be delighted to find that the other has committed some grave offense against the service of our house, for which he may be sent away. Should this wish of his be fulfilled, he will also feel free to contrive a similar disgrace for anyone else he dislikes. But if anyone can at his whim cause someone else to be discharged from our household, don't you see, dear wife, that he is no longer our servant, but our master? Even if he cannot quite gain his ends, he can keep our household in a state of agitation. He will be constantly thinking how, since he may have lost your good will, he can manage best for himself. He does not care at all if his profit be our loss. Even after he has left your service, such a man will keep trying to lay the blame on us and thus excuse his own past conduct. As you see, there is danger in a servant who speaks ill of the other servants and quarrels with them, whether you keep him or send him away. In either case he brings public disgrace. If you keep him, besides, you must always be changing your household staff, for people who don't want to serve our servant will always seek new masters. For this they will excuse themselves and cast the blame on you. Their words will get you a reputation for being either proud and aloof or avaricious and petty."

The truth is, my children, that when there are quarrels in the household, the masters inevitably suffer part of the harm done. But if the masters are not unwise, the house will not be quarrelsome. It is the poor judgment of the master that makes some families shameless and undisciplined and, as a result, always turbulent, poorly served, loaded with practical difficulties and public ignominy. The father of a family must detest talebearers, who are the source and cause of every quarrel, conflict, and intrigue. He should discharge them instantly. To see his household free of argument, peaceful, and harmonious should make him happy. This excellent state is one he can make sure of if he so desires. He must only do as I instructed my wife—never lend his ear or his mind to any sort of complaints or quarrels.

I further said to my wife that if a member of the household failed to obey her or to be as amenable and devoted as the peace and quiet of the family required, she should never be provoked into fighting with him or screaming at him. "It is an ugly thing," I said, "if women like you, dear wife, who are honorable and worthy of all respect, are seen with wild-eyed contorted expressions, screaming, threatening, and throwing their arms about. All the neighbors would reprove and mock you, and you would give everyone something to talk about. A woman of authority, such as I hope you, dear wife, will gradually come to be, maintains a constant modesty and dignity of manner. She would be grievously mistaken, not only if she raised her voice in reprimanding members of the household but if in commanding and discussing things she used a very loud voice. Some women talk in the house as if the whole family were deaf, or as if they wanted the whole neighborhood to hear every word. This is a sign of arrogance, a peasant habit. It suits the mountain girls who are used to calling to each other from slope to slope. You, dear wife, should admonish people with gentleness of gesture and of words, not with an air of indulgence and laxness but with calm and temperance. You must give orders in so reasonable and moderate a way that you will not only be obeyed but, because you show kindness and all the modesty compatible with your dignity, obeyed with love and devotion."

Lionardo: Where can you find such good advice for the edification of a perfect wife and mother as in these instructions of Giannozzo's? First he shows her the necessity of seeming and being most honorable and chaste; then he teaches her how to make herself duly obeyed, feared, loved, and respected. We ourselves shall be fortunate husbands if when we are married we have the wisdom to make use of your remarks, Giannozzo, and to teach our own wives to be like yours—shining examples of so many virtues!

But when you had showed her, as you say, how to maintain the modesty and discipline essential if she would rule the family, did you also show her how to preserve things and put them to good use?

Giannozzo: Indeed, on this point, what I shall tell you will make you laugh.

Lionardo: Why, Giannozzo?

Giannozzo: Dear Lionardo, my wife, being of the purest simplicity and free of any shade of cunning, thought that after listening attentively to me she was all ready to be a wise mother. I mentioned to her, then, that a good wife and mother must not only have the best of intentions, but must know how to carry out her tasks. I asked her if she had all the knowledge needed for this. Since she had always observed her mother's household functioning smoothly, she answered in all simplicity that she thought she was quite well instructed in these matters.

"Good, dear wife," said I, "I am glad to hear how competent you are. I do think it is your intention to make yourself in every way a perfect wife and mother. May God help your good will and preserve your fine character. Tell me, though, dear wife, how would you go about things generally?"

Lionardo: What did she say to that?

Giannozzo: She answered very eagerly, yet with a little blush of shyness in her cheeks. "I would do well, wouldn't I," she said, "to keep everything locked up properly?"

"No, indeed," said I. And you know, dear Lionardo, the illustration that then occurred to me I think will please you. Said I to her. "Dear wife, if you put into your marriage chest not only your silken gowns and gold and valuable jewelry, but also the flax to be spun and the little pot of oil, too, and finally the little chicks, and then locked the whole thing securely with your key, tell me would you think you had taken good care of everything because everything was locked up?"

At this she lowered her eyes to the ground and seemed silently to regret her haste in answering before. I was no little pleased inwardly, seeing that becoming air of repentence on her face. I could see that she was indeed aware of having been too quick to answer me and that she would, in time, become more and more careful of her words, more mature, more deliberate. After a little while, with humble and modest slowness, she lifted up her eyes to me and, without speaking, smiled.

Said I, "Do you think the neighbors' wives would admire you if, when they came to call on you at home, they found you had locked up the house to the very threshold? I'm sure you realize, too, dear wife, that to lock up the chicks with the flax would mean trouble, to put the oil in with the clothes would be risky, and to lock up things that are used every day in the house would be small wisdom. It is best, therefore, not, as you say, to lock everything up properly, but to be sure everything is in its place as it should be, and not just in its place, but so arranged as to do no harm to something else. Everything should be set where it is absolutely safe, yet accessible and ready to hand, while encumbering the house as little as possible.

"You have now seen, dear wife, where everything belongs. If you think something would be better placed elsewhere, more convenient and more securely locked, think it over carefully and then arrange things better. And so that nothing gets lost, just be sure that when something has been used it is immediately put back in its place, where it can be found again. If something has been mislaid or lent to a friend, you'll be able to see that its place is empty. You can set about getting it back at once, so that nothing will be lost through negligence. When you receive it back again, you must put it back in its place. If it should be locked up, lock it up and be sure the key is in your keeping, for you, my wife, will have to keep in your custody and to preserve whatever is in the house.

"To do this well, however, you must not spend all day sitting idly with your elbows on the window sill, like some lazy wives who always hold their sewing in their hands for an excuse, but their sewing never gets done. You, instead, should take up the pleasant task of inspecting the house from top to bottom more than once a day. You should check whether things are in their places, and see how everyone is working. Praise the ones who perform their tasks the best, and if someone is doing something one way which could be done better in another, show him the better way. Altogether avoid idleness, always keep busy. Being busy will make you a better housekeeper and will help you greatly in every way. You will eat with a heartier appetite. You will be healthier, better complexioned, fresh and lovely. Your household, too, will be better run, and your people will not be able to let things go to waste."

Lionardo: You are certainly right. When the servants are not afraid they will be seen and no one watches them, they throw more away than they ever wear out.

Giannozzo: There are dangers beyond this, too. They become greedy and lascivious. From the master's neglect they take encouragement to indulge in idleness and in greater vices. I told my wife to be as diligent as she could be, making sure things were arranged reasonably and properly in the house. She must not, I told her, permit anything in the house to be used that was not needed. She must save the surplus of things, and keep it safe. If some object is of no use to the household, let her put it aside to sell, and always be more pleased to sell than to buy. With the money let her buy only what the family needed.

Lionardo: Did you teach her how to decide whether something was really superfluous?

Giannozzo: I did. I said to her, "Dear wife, anything without which we could honorably supply our needs is a luxury. It should not be left to lie about the house and get into everybody's hands, but should be put away. Our silverware which is not used every day you put in its place until the occasion arises of our entertaining honored guests; then you display it on the table. Likewise things used only in winter should not be left lying about in summer. What is only used in summer should be put away in winter. You should consider anything you are able to save without depriving the household as a luxury in this sense. You should save it, put it away, preserve it.

Lionardo: And didn't you give your wife a system for saving things?

Giannozzo: Yes, I did. "First," I said, "if you want to save things, you should see that they don't spoil just by lying around. Second, you should see that they are not eaten or destroyed by others. Therefore, it is necessary to put things away where they will keep well—grain in a cool place, open to the north, wine in a spot that is neither too warm nor too cold and where no draft or bad odor can damage it. Things must be watched so that if part has begun to spoil, it can be immediately made good or used before it becomes altogether useless or treated so that it will not deteriorate all together. It is also essential to store such things well away in a place where everyone cannot use or destroy them." This I told her, and in this case, I said, I would not blame her for using lock and key to keep things from falling into the hands of the whole company. I would insist, too, that those keys should remain always in the custody of the mistress of the house, who would see that not too many hands touched them but that they stayed with her. Only keys used every day, like the pantry keys and those to the storeroom, should she put into the keeping of one of the best servants, the most loyal and honest, the most trained and scrupulous and conscientious about our property.

Lionardo: And would you give those keys to whoever had to go up and down getting things as they were needed?

Giannozzo: I would, if only because it would be annoying for the lady of the house to be forever handing out the keys and demanding them back. But I also said, "Dear wife, see that the keys are always in the house. When they are needed, we do not want delays looking for them.

"Also see that the man you put in charge of the other servants gives all of them enough so that they are spared hunger and thirst. If they lack necessities, they will serve us poorly and not give zealous care to our concerns. To healthy servants you will see that good things are given, so that none of them grows ill; for those who are not healthy you must arrange a proper diet and take good care to restore them to health. It is mere thrift to cure them quickly, for while they lie ill you can get no service from them and all you have is the cost of maintenance. When they are healthy and free, they will serve you all the more faithfully and devotedly. Thus, my dear wife, you should see that everyone in the house has what he needs."

Beyond this, I added another point. "Dear wife, be sure that the supplies you need for this and other household needs do not run short. Do just as I do with things outside the house. Think well ahead and consider what you are going to need, how much of each thing is already in the house, how much you usually need, how long the supply will last, and how much more is wanted for our use. Then you will easily know when the supplies need replenishing and will tell me at once, long before anything actually runs out. That way I can set to work to find it outside at the lowest cost and the highest quality. Things bought in haste are often bought out of season, unclean, about to spoil, and expensive. Then in the end more is thrown away than ever gets used."

Lionardo: And did your wife act to make provision and to keep you informed, as you taught her?

Giannozzo: Yes. As a result I have always had time to obtain the best of supplies.

Lionardo: Is it thrifty always to buy the best?

Giannozzo: Yes, indeed, it is the height of thrift. If you get wine that's too strong or rotten vegetables or anything else that is not good for the provision of the household, no one, I think, is going to be careful with it. The stuff is thrown out, spilled, no one cares, everyone dislikes it, and they serve you less well for this reason and consider it a sign of avarice, for which they call you mean. All you get is damage and disgrace, and people learn neither to love nor to respect you, since they dislike your miserable provisions. But if you have good wine, better bread, other things that are adequate, the household will be contented and happy to serve you. If the provisions are good, the steward is careful when he is doling them out, but with poor supplies he is as discontented as everyone else. Your household will cherish good things, and outsiders will honor you. Good things also always last longest.

Look at this gown I am wearing now. I have spent a good many years in it, for I had it made at the time of my first daughter's marriage, and I was honorably attired in it on all holiday occasions for a number of years. Now, as you see, it is still not too bad for everyday use. If I had not then chosen the best cloth in Florence, I might have had two for the price, but I would not have been as well dressed in them as I was in this one.

Lionardo: They do say good things cost less than shoddy ones.

Giannozzo: No doubt about it. The better things are, the longer they last, and they do you more honor, and make you happier, and are viewed by others with more respect. We want good things in our household, and an adequate supply of them. The saying "better scarce in the market than too much in the house," which some hold true, has always seemed to me adapted only to a poorly run family and one that lacks all discipline. If one knows how to rule oneself and one's family in an orderly way, one should have the house provided for in full and abundant supply. It would be hard to convey the degree of harm which mere disorder does or, on the other hand, to explain the real value of discipline. I don't know which is more damaging to families, the neglect of the father or the lack of discipline within the house.

Lionardo: Did you tell your wife how important it is to preserve this kind of order?

Giannozzo: I omitted nothing on that score. I found innumerable ways of praising good order and of casting disapproval on disorder of any kind.

To describe all that would take a long time. I showed her the necessity of good order, how things are happily and well done where there is good discipline. Finally, after many explanations, I gave her this parable to think about. "Well, dear wife," I said, "suppose it were a solemn holiday and you went out in public with your maids and servants walking in front of you. And suppose, as you walked very straight and elegant behind them, you wore a brocade gown, and had your head tied up for going to bed, and bore a sword at your belt, and carried a distaff in your hand. How do you think people would look at you? Do you think you would be generally respected?"

Lionardo: Notice the vivid image, Battista and Carlo. What an excellent figure of speech. But how did she reply, Giannozzo?

Giannozzo: "Surely," she said, "I'd be thought mad, poor me, if I dressed like that."

"Therefore, dear wife," said I, "we should have order and system in all that we do. It does not befit a woman like you to carry a sword, nor to do other manly things that men do. Nor is it always and in all places fitting for a woman to do everything that is proper to woman, for instance holding a distaff, wearing gold brocade, having one's head tied up in a kerchief. These things are all proper in their place and time. Your duty, dear lady, shall be to stand first in the household, not to be aloof and proud but with great gentleness to keep the whole house in order and in harmony through your conscientious supervision. You shall see that things are done in their proper time. What is needed in autumn is not to be consumed in May. What should be enough for a month is not to be used up in a day."

Lionardo: Did your wife seem amenable to your directions?

Giannozzo: She stood quite lost in thought for some time. Then I said to her, "My dear wife, these things I have been telling you will all, if you are well disposed to do them, prove easy for you. It should not seem hard to you to do what will win you praise. Rather it should weigh heavy on you to omit anything which you will be blamed for omitting.

"Up to this point I think you have understood all that I have said without any trouble and I am well pleased. As it was easy for you to follow these lessons, it will also be pleasant for you, I assure you, to put them into practice. Loving me and wishing to do the best for us both, you will put your mind to doing a good and orderly job of applying my teaching. And, dear wife, if you do something willingly, though it be difficult, you will do it well. Always when we are doing something we don't really want to do, though it be easy, we do it less than well.

"I don't want you to do everything, however. There are many tasks which you should not properly take on yourself. There are others to do them. Even in minor matters, however, it is up to you to give the orders. You must always, I tell you again and again, always be aware what everyone is doing."

Lionardo: What a fine and most pious lesson you gave your wife: to wish to be as well as to appear a woman of honor, to command the household and to make herself respected, to care for the welfare of the family and to preserve the things that are in the house. How proud she must have been to be the wife of such a man!

Giannozzo: You may be sure she knew I was telling her the truth. She knew I was speaking out of concern for her own well-being, and she knew too that I was wiser than she. She did, therefore, always have the greatest love and reverence for me.

Lionardo: What a great help, what a wonderful thing, to be able to teach one's family! Do you think she felt much gratitude for this, too?

Giannozzo: The deepest gratitude. She often used to say, in fact, that all her wealth and fortune lay in me. To other women she always said that I was her one adornment. I used to say, "Dear wife, your real adornment and your real beauty are found in your modesty and virtue. Your wealth is rooted in your diligence. For diligence is a more praiseworthy quality in a woman than beauty. Your beauty never made the house prosperous, but by our diligence it grows rich indeed. Thus, my dear wife, even more than beautiful, you should be and appear diligent, modest, and discreet. Thus let all your good fortune depend only on yourself."

Lionardo: These words must have kindled such feelings in her heart that all her thoughts and her whole mind never ceased striving to please you in every way. She must have sought constantly and labored strenuously to do everything right, never resting from her diligent care for the household, in order to show you that her zeal and love were all they should be.

Giannozzo: In fact she was at first somewhat timid about giving orders, for she had been used to obeying her mother. I also saw her inclined to remain inactive and to be somewhat melancholy of mood.

Lionardo: Did you do anything to remedy this?

Giannozzo: Oh, I remedied it. When I came home I always greeted her with a cheerful face, so that, seeing me happy, she too grew happier. She found no cause in my sadness to become sad herself. I also told her about a friend of mine, a very wise man, who used to know at once when he came home whether his wife, a rather difficult woman, had quarreled with anyone, for if she had she was sure to be less happy than usual. In this connection I voiced my hearty disapproval of all contention in a house. I also said that wives should always be contented in their household, both in order not to seem bizarre, like the bitter and quarrelsome ones, and in order to delight their husbands. A happy wife will always be more beautiful than a frowning one. "Remember, dear wife," I said, "that when I sometimes come home in a rather sour mood, as happens to us men after we've spent the day talking and contending with malevolent, scheming persons and with enemies, it always makes you sad as well, and really unhappy. So you must imagine it is the same with me, only more so, since I know your spirits can only be drooping through the unfortunate results of your own mistakes. You need do nothing but live happily, make sure the household obeys you, and keep the family well. I am doubly grieved when I see you sad, for I know that by your very unhappiness you are confessing some fault."

I repeated this notion and similar ideas to her several times. I encouraged her wholly to avoid melancholy of any kind. She should show a face of guiltless joy, affection, and affability to my kinsmen and friends.

Lionardo: I am sure she had no trouble recognizing her kinsmen, but I wonder if such a young girl would easily know who was a friend. We find that there is really nothing more difficult in the world than to distinguish true friends amid the obscurity of so many lies, the darkness of people's motives, and the shadowy errors and vices that lie about us on all sides. I should be glad to learn, therefore, how you taught your wife to distinguish a friend from a foe.

Giannozzo: No, I did not try to teach her to distinguish my true friends. This kind of knowledge, as you say, is all too fallible. We can hardly tell who is our true friend in spirit. But I did teach her to know for certain which were our enemies and whom she might consider as friends. "Never, dear wife," I told her, "think of someone as our friend if you see his energies directed against our benefit. If anyone wants to reduce our honorable condition in any way, count him for an enemy. For dignity ought to mean more than property, and honor more that comfort. The man who steals some of our possessions injures us less than the one who brings us disgrace. Now, there are only two ways of dealing with enemies, my dear. One is to defeat them in open fight; the other is flight, if one is weak. Men ought if possible to fight and win, but women have no alternative but flight for their safety. Flee, therefore, and do not let your eye rest on any enemy of ours. Call only him a friend whom I honor when he is present and praise when he is absent."

Thus did I speak to her, and thus did she act thereafter. She was most chaste and most content. She ruled the family wisely and took good care of the household. Her only failing was that sometimes, showing a mistaken zeal, she tried to do things that were below her. I, however, would instantly forbid this and tell her to let others do it. I insisted that she make herself the object of firm respect among her domestics by always behaving as the lady and mistress of all. Outside the house, too, she had to maintain a certain dignity. On a few occasions, in order to teach her a certain air of authority and to have her appear as she should in public, I made her open our own door and go outside practicing self-restraint and grave demeanor. This led our neighbors to observe her air of discretion and to praise her, which increased the respect of our own servants.

Lionardo: It seems only reasonable to me that the lady of the house should command respect.

Giannozzo: It has always been not merely reasonable but essential. If the lady of the house cannot command proper reverence and respect, the household does not obey her. Everyone does what he likes, and the family lives in turmoil and squalor. If the wife is vigorous and discreet, however, in carrying out her tasks, everyone will obey her. If her conduct is exemplary, all her house will revere her.

At this point in our conversation, Adovardo came among us. Giannozzo and Lionardo rose to meet him. Carlo and I immediately went upstairs to see if we could do anything for our father or if we might visit him. We found servants standing at the door to his room, with orders to let no one in. We were amazed and came down again to hear Adovardo explaining to Giannozzo that Ricciardo had spent the whole morning going over secret records and documents and that he was now alone with Lorenzo, who appeared to be doing much better.

Had I realized Ricciardo would be so busy today, *Giannozzo replied,* I would not have stayed on here like this, but would have gone in the middle of the morning to praise God and to adore the sacrifice, as I have done every morning for many years.

Adovardo: An excellent habit. A man who would emulate you in winning the love and favor of his fellow men should always seek first the favor of God.

Giannozzo: To me it seems proper also to render thanks to God for the gifts which he in his mercy has given me. I also pray for tranquillity and enlightenment of heart and mind, as well as for our long continued enjoyment of health, life, prosperity, a fine family, an honorable estate, and good name and renown.

Adovardo: Are these the prayers you address to God?

Giannozzo: They are. Thus do I usually pray, every morning. This morning, however, they have kept me here. The time flew so as we talked that we did not notice how it went.

Lionardo: Remember, Giannozzo, that this was an act of parental piety which you performed here, and no less pleasing to God than your presence at the sacrifice would be. What you have been teaching us also is good and is sacred.

Adovardo: What have you been talking about?

Lionardo: The noblest of subjects, Adovardo, and at the same time the most practical. How delighted you would have been, too, to hear his many and most excellent ideas.

Adovardo: I know that where you are only the most worthy topics are discussed. I know too that all the ideas of Giannozzo are well worth listening to.

Lionardo: Giannozzo is worth listening to on all subjects, but on this one you would have found his remarks particularly interesting and wonderful. Concerning the management of the household, his remarks were elegant, wise, rich, and original.

Adovardo: Would I had been there!

Lionardo: You would have found it profitable. You would have learned that thrift consists no less in making good use of things than in being careful not to waste them, and how important it is to be most thrifty with those things which truly belong to us. You would have heard how possessions, family, honor, and friendship are not altogether our belongings, and how we ought to apply prudence in their management. This, you would have said to yourself, is a lucky day in my life.

Adovardo: I am sorry I was otherwise occupied. For truly, Giannozzo, nothing would have given me more pleasure than to have sat beside this disciple of yours here and learned something which directly concerns me today, namely the prudent management of the household. It seems to me, as we become fathers, we ought to grow in our wise management of things as our family grows in numbers.

Giannozzo: Don't be too easily persuaded, Adovardo, of what is not even true. Lionardo here has always been partial to me, and perhaps I gave him pleasure in talking about the household because he, who has no real experience of these things as yet, found it a novel subject. Now if I delighted him more in our talk than my words themselves deserved or than I even tried to do, you must give the credit not to me but to Lionardo's affection for me, which makes all my words seem golden.

How can I, by my words, win the approbation of educated persons like yourselves, who read and converse every day with divine intellects? You transcribe noble thoughts and fine, wise sayings among those ancient writers of yours such as are altogether beyond my scope. Certainly I tried to say something worth saying, but I lacked the knowledge and the skill to adorn my thoughts with eloquence, to organize well, to weave in examples and cite authorities and use fine words; for, as you know, I am ignorant of Latin.* What I might say on some other subject, with which I have less direct familiarity would be unworthy of attention, nor could I speak even of the management of the household on any basis but my long years of experience and the useful lessons they have taught me. So Adovardo, my dear, don't worry about what you have been missing. You have a wife and children; you experience and learn from day to day just what I have learned myself. As you are both more intelligent and more educated than I, moreover, you can comprehend more quickly and more deeply than I could what are the demands, the method, the system and all that belongs to good management.

Adovardo: Lionardo thinks no better of you than you deserve, and you, in discussing the subject of the household, could not help being most helpful. I would have been glad to listen to you, both for other reasons and in order to find out whether your judgment confirms my own opinions.

Giannozzo: Could I attain to a judgment on anything that was not entirely obvious and commonplace? On what question, Adovardo, would my opinion not be entirely outweighed by your thought and your education? I have always been satisfied to learn no more than I needed to know; it suffices me to understand the things I see and feel in my hands. You educated people want to know what happened a hundred years ago

---

* Literally, "illiterate."

and what will happen sixty years from now. On every subject you demand intelligence, skill, knowledge, and eloquence to equal your own. Who could satisfy you? Certainly I can't. I am not one of these people. And to tell you the truth, perhaps I am happier, Adovardo, that you were not present. Not that I respect the judgment of Lionardo less than your own, but I would then have had two of you educated folk to please— which might have disconcerted me into trying to seem what I am not. Then I might have said something foolish, and I would have been very ashamed realizing that I could not please you.

Lionardo: Rest assured, Giannozzo, as long as you were talking about the management of the family, educated people who were not peevish souls would gladly listen. I cannot imagine anyone wanting you to have a different style or material or manner of arranging your ideas.

Adovardo: I certainly would not have wanted you to deal with different material, and to tell the truth, Lionardo, I never would have believed that the subject of household management had so many divisions as you tell me Giannozzo found to distinguish.

Lionardo: And I didn't tell you half of it.

Adovardo: What?

Lionardo: There were many more points: that a family should have a house, a farm, and a place of business, so that they can all gather together and feed and clothe their children, and how one may take care of all these needs most thriftily.

Adovardo: And what about money? Did you say how one should manage money?

Giannozzo: Why speak of that? Is it not like everything else? Things must be used to supply the necessities, the surplus must be put aside in case of need, and help should be given to one's friends, kinsmen, and country.

Adovardo: You see, Giannozzo, here is a difference from what I myself had thought, and perhaps I did not arrive at my opinion without a good reason. It was my belief that a man need only know how to exercise proper thrift in regard to money in order to be an excellent householder. I came to this conclusion seeing how money appears to be the root of all things, or the hook to get them with, or the nourishment of them. Money, as no one denies, is the sinews of any kind of work. If a man has plenty of it he can easily fill all needs and satisfy a great many desires. With money you can have both house and farm and all the labor of men. All the crafts work like slaves for anyone with money. A man who lacks money wants for almost everything. One needs it for all things: the farm, the house, the workshop, all require servants, workers, tools, cattle, and so forth. And all these things are not owned or obtained without the expenditure of money. If money supplies our needs, however, why trouble our minds with the management of other things?

Consider, furthermore, Giannozzo, in these days of bitter misfortune and unjust exile for our family, consider how much less suffering has afflicted those of the Albertis who possessed money rather than lands. Consider how much less our family possesses now that they are here, because it was always their way to spend so much on buildings and land. Judge for yourself how much greater our property would be if we had been able to walk off carrying our houses and fields as we could our money. Do you doubt in the slightest that we would be better off if the value of those great properties there were paid to us here in cash?

Giannozzo: You educated people, as I have noticed before, are argumentative to a fault. There is nothing so certain, obvious, and clear but you with your arguments plunge it into doubt, uncertainty, and obscurity. Now, whether you are trying to debate with me according to the custom of such people or are merely interested in seeing what I think, I know it is my duty to give you a satisfactory answer, Adovardo, and not just to talk to uphold my position. I do not want to deny, Adovardo, that money is of some value as a means to supply our needs and satisfy our desires. I shall not admit on account of this, however, that you are right. Even if I had cash, many, many things would still be essentials which are either not always available on the market or not of good quality or too expensive. Even if goods were being sold cheap, I would still much prefer to perform the pleasant task of watching over my own estates, to plan for my own needs, to keep in mind whatever should be required, rather than spend my energy searching for things from day to day and give much more for them than if I had them coming in season to the house. If it were not for our time of misfortune, which makes you wish rather to have money here than land elsewhere, I think you would agree with me. If you had enough of an estate to fill your needs and wishes and those of your family, you would not be much interested in money. For myself, I have never seen the use of money if not to serve our needs and wishes.

If you really think money more precious than land, I must oppose your argument. Do you imagine, merely because you know that you yourself have lost less money than lands, that money is generally easier to preserve than more stable things? Do you imagine that the fruit of money is more useful than that of land? What is there that's more likely to go astray, more troublesome to get back, more easily dissipated, spent, and consumed in smoke? What is there more likely to disappear in all sorts of ways than money? There is nothing less stable, less solid. It is incredible what a lot of work it takes to hold on to money, and this is a kind of work more fraught with suspicion of other people, likelihood of trouble, risk of accident, than any other. There is no way to safeguard money, for if you keep it under lock and key, well hidden, then it does not serve you or your family. Nothing can be said to be useful if you cannot actually use it.

I could tell you more of the great perils money is exposed to: poor handling, deceit, poor advice, poor luck. Innumerable other catastrophes can swallow up all sorts of money at one gulp. Every bit goes down, and you will never even see ruins or ashes. Do you think I am mistaken about this, Lionardo, and you, Adovardo?

Lionardo: As for me, I agree with you.

Adovardo: Who did you say, Giannozzo, was so good at arguing that they turn every sure truth around with words? We educated persons? I would not want to deny my love of books, myself, but if educated persons are the ones who, as you say, can turn everything around and prove its opposite, then I must surely be considered an illiterate, so utterly do I now lack all means to confound your arguments. I shall not surrender too quickly, however, for you know, Giannozzo, there has always been more honor given to the man who wins against someone who defends himself than to one who defeats someone who gives up at once. Just for the sake of a more manly defeat, then, I shall assert that your argument does not entirely satisfy me. I cannot give any other reason but that it seems to me the movement and onslaught of fortune takes estates as well as money away, and perhaps sometimes money can be hidden somewhere, while lands and buildings stand open, exposed to war and enemies, and are destroyed entirely by fire and sword.

Giannozzo: I am glad to see you are like the wise old veteran fighters who use no less cunning than they do force, and who pretend to flee, sometimes, only to lead the enemy into some trap. Thus do you do, but you fortify your position with more cunning than strength. You shall be the judge of that, however. I will not be afraid of your snares, in any case, though perhaps I ought to be.

Consider, Adovardo, that neither the hands of thieves nor looting nor fire nor sword nor mortal treachery nor, I dare say, arrows, thunder, or

God's anger can rob you of your land. If the year brings heavy storms, floods, or much ice, if winds or heat and drought should rot or burn the seed, still another year will come to bring you better fortune, or if not to you, then to your children and grandchildren. How many wards, citizens of all kinds, have gained more returns from their lands than from money? You can find innumerable examples of this everywhere. And how many bankrupts, pirates, and such have used up the money of the Albertis? Inestimable wealth, enormous sums, riches such that one can hardly imagine them, have gone to enrich other men through our loss. Would to God these sums had been spent on meadows, woods, or some other anchorage which we might still call ours and which we might still hope to have back again in times of better fortune. Do not think money, therefore, more useful than estates; consider land precious and essential to the family. I don't know what use money was invented for if not to be spent and used in getting goods. If you have goods, however, what need have you of money? And goods have the further advantage, which money does not have, that they supply your needs.

Let us not entangle ourselves in this argument, however. Let us, like practical householders, leave debate aside. My conclusion is simply this: the good father knows all his wealth and does not like to see all in one place or all invested in one thing. If enemies attack or adverse fortune presses you on one side it is good to be strong and have resources on the other. If things are risky here, you save them there. If fortune does not smile on you in one enterprise, it will not strike you in the other too. I am not in favor, therefore, of having only lands or only money. Better have some of this and some of that, some stowed far away and located at a variety of places. The returns of all, moreover, should be used for your needs, and the surplus saved for the future.

Lionardo: Why do you look amazed, Adovardo, and almost dumb-struck by Giannozzo's words? Had you heard his earlier remarks, you would have seen that all he says of the management of the household is like a divine oracle. Every point was vital to the proper rule of the family inside and outside the house. Nothing was lacking, everything was uttered in a coherent way, all clear and lucid. You would have been full of praise.

Adovardo: If this be Lionardo's counsel, I shall willingly assent, Gian-nozzo, and I too shall judge that the good householder ought not to limit himself to money alone or to lands alone but should divide his fortune among various enterprises in various places. I shall be willing, then, to have him undergo toil and trouble in order to maintain and preserve things other than money, which is merely one thing among many. I had thought, however, that money was enough.

Lionardo: Would you think you could go wrong, Adovardo, in agreeing with Giannozzo's views on matters of good management?

Adovardo: No, indeed, it would be a grave error to think the judgment and the beliefs of Giannozzo imperfect. On some points, however, Lionardo, even if he is right, it seems to me no fault in a man to have some doubts. Good God, you have talked money down so much that, by your account, there is nothing lower—money merely serves as a means to buy goods. It seems to me you were trying to make money sound less valuable than it is. You put it in such a poor light, made it appear so much beset with dangers, that if men were ever to believe you, they would not even try to manage it with thrift. They might merely wish never to set eyes on it at all. Now though I see that in many ways you are right, yet I have a notion that money is a commodity which actually contains every other commodity. It seems to me you are forgetting here how, in one small purse, money enables you to carry about with you bread, wine, all victuals, clothes, horses, and every useful item. And who would deny the added usefulness of having money to lend to friends, as you say, and to do business with?

Giannozzo: Didn't I say you would be setting some snares for us, Adovardo? But the ways of you educated folk are too much for me. Nothing can be so carefully said but that you find fault with it. I lack the skill to strive with you in wit.

Adovardo: I certainly asked you what I did with no other purpose than to learn how you, in your wisdom, would answer this question. You have been dealing with questions related to it.

Lionardo: I shall answer, then, according to what I gathered from Giannozzo. I shall tell you how to deal with money. Every purchase and every sale should be transacted with simplicity, truth, good faith, and integrity. Whether you deal with stranger or with friend, all should be clean and straight.

Adovardo: Excellent. But what about lending money, Giannozzo? What if some noble lord asks you for a loan, as happens every day?

Giannozzo: I would sooner give him twenty as a gift than a hundred on loan. I would gladly avoid him altogether so as to have to do neither.

Adovardo: What do you think, Lionardo?

Lionardo: I feel the same way. I would rather lose twenty to gain a little favor than risk a hundred without assurance of getting any gratitude for it.

Giannozzo: Hush, don't say that—no one should ever hope for gratitude or favor from a noble lord. A great lord loves and esteems you just exactly as long as you are useful to him. He does not appreciate you for any good quality you may have, nor is it possible for a great lord to recognize goodness. Wicked, ostentatious flatterers and vicious gossips are always more common in the household of such lords than good men are. If you will stop and consider, you will realize that probably the majority of courtiers live in idleness and waste their time. They have no occupation by which to earn an honest living. They live on the bread of others and shun all work requiring industry and honorable effort. If there are good men among them, they live modestly and hope to get more favor by their virtues than by ostentation—these would rather be loved for their merits than for the harm they inflict on others. But virtue is not recognized unless it is put to some kind of work, and when that happens, and when it is recognized at all, the lord thinks it sufficient to give praise—rarely is virtue well rewarded.

If you are an honest man, you cannot hold converse with the scoundrels you find there, for they will take offense at your continence, your austerity, and your piety. Among wicked men you can find no use for your good powers. It cannot serve your honor to compete with wicked men for a prize: better let them win and seize the thing you wanted. If you persevere in such a contest, you will suffer more evil done you by those bold scoundrels than you will gain praise from other good men. Those bold and careless beings will overcome you. With one bad report the flatterers can do you more harm than much testimony in your favor can repair. I think, therefore, that a man should shun those great lords.

It is good to ask for and to receive things from them, believe me, but never to give nor lend to them. Whatever you give them is thrown away. They have plenty of people to give them things, both purchasers of their favor and persons who seek to repair some offense. If you offer them a trifle, you will be despised for it and lose the gift besides. If you offer them much, they will give you no payment for it. If you offer excessive bounty, still you will not satisfy their immense greed. They want enough not only for themselves but for all their kin besides. If you give to one, you create the necessity of satisfying all the others, and the more you give, the more trouble you draw down on your head. The more they hope for, the more they think they have a right to receive. The more you lend, the more you will have lost. With noble lords, your promises are obligations, your loans are gifts, and your gifts are thrown away. A man can consider himself fortunate if his acquaintance with great lords does not result in some grievous price to pay.

Messer Antonio Alberti had this to say on the subject: lords should be greeted with gilded words. You will find that noble lords who are in debt to you will grow displeased with you in order not to have to pay. They will quarrel with you and try to provoke some remark or some answer which they can use as an excuse to do you harm. They will constantly try most viciously to bring you to an unfortunate end. If there are many ways they can harm you, they will choose the worst.

Adovardo: Then I shall be prudent and, in accordance with your advice, shall avoid all dealings with great lords. Should I find myself nonetheless engaged in some commerce with them, I shall always ask for cash. If, in spite of all, a demand is made of me, I shall give a minimum.

Giannozzo: That is the way to act, my sons. By all means, avoid any sort of courtier's role and attendance on a tyrant. This will prove your best course.

Adovardo: And what of friends?

Giannozzo: Why ask? You know that with a friend one should always try to be generous.

Lionardo: Lend and give to them?

Giannozzo: You know well enough. Where there is no need, why should you give? Not to make them love you, for these are friends already. Not to show them your generosity, at least not when there is no need. No gift seems an act of generosity to me unless need calls for it. I am one of those who would rather have friends of noble character than rich ones, yet I am happier with friends who are prosperous than with unfortunate and poor ones.

Lionardo: But if my friend asks me for help, can I deny him anything?

Giannozzo: Don't you know the answer to that? You can deny him all that he asks that is not honorable.

Adovardo: But I think there is no dishonor in asking something from a friend when there is need.

Giannozzo: If to do what my friend asked were to impose too heavy a burden on me, why should I put his welfare before my own? I certainly want you to lend to your friend, when no excessive burden is put on you by it. Do it in such a way, however, that, when you want your own back, you will not have to sue him for it, and he will not become your enemy.

Lionardo: I don't know how much approval I shall win from you wise managers of these affairs, but I myself would give a lot of latitude to a friend in any situation, would trust him, lend to him, give to him: nothing should stand between him and me.

Giannozzo: And what if he did not do the same toward you?

Lionardo: If he were my friend he would. He would communicate all things, all wishes, all thoughts to me. All our wealth would be held in common, no more his than mine.

Giannozzo: Could you tell me of one you have found who gave you more than words and empty chatter? Show me one whom you can trust with even the least of your secrets. The world is full of deceit. Take it from me, the person who tries by some sort of art or cunning subterfuge to take from you what is yours, that person is no friend. He asks you for gifts or loans or he wants to gain these things by threats or come at them by flattery—I say he tries to steal from you and he is not your friend.

Adovardo: That is true. People who greet you, who praise and flatter you, are common enough, but not friends—as many acquaintances as you like, but very few persons you can trust. How, then, shall we act toward them?

Giannozzo: Do you know what a friend of mine does? In other ways his character is most upright and disciplined, but perhaps on matters of finance he is a little close. He has a technique for dealing with irresponsible people who come with their importunate demands under color of friendship, kinship, and old acquaintance. The greetings of such a fellow he returns with an infinite number of greetings. If he smiles, my friend returns a warmer smile. If he praises him, my friend praises him still more than he has been praised. The man is confronted by generosity in all these things, where he finds himself surpassed in liberality and kindness. To all his words and all his whining, my friend lends a willing ear, but when he comes to the story of his needs, my friend immediately invents some of his own to tell, and as the man comes to the point of actually asking him, in conclusion, for a loan or at least to stand surety for one—suddenly he is deaf. He misunderstands and gives a reply to something else, and quickly changes the subject. Those who are masters of the art of finagling, however, then respond to him with some little joke and, after that bid of laughter, return to the question. He then repeats his maneuver. When at last by continued persistence they make their request, if it is a small sum they are asking, he lends it to them to get rid of the nuisance and because he can find no excuse, but he lends as small an amount as he can. If the sum demanded seems large to him, my friend— but what a bad teacher I am! What am I doing? When I should be urging you to be courteous and liberal, I am showing you how to deceive and hold back more than you should. No more. I don't want you to call me a master of slyness. Toward friends one should have a liberal spirit.

Adovardo: No, Giannozzo, rather think it a virtue to overcome slyness with slyness.

Lionardo: Indeed, I often think some shrewdness is required in dealing with shrewd people.

Giannozzo: Then you would like me to give you a method of eluding such petitioners. If my teachings help you to fight artifice with artifice, I am well pleased. If instead they do you harm by helping you to be niggardly and narrow rather than liberal and generous, I am still pleased that at least you will have a way of seeming merely clever when what you really are is avaricious. If you take my advice, however, you will prefer the honor gained by seeming generous to the appearance of cleverness. Generosity combined with reason has always won praise, while cleverness is often censured. I do not admire good management so much, moreover, as to condemn occasional generosity, nor do I view generosity as the prerogative of friends alone—sometimes I think it is wise to show generosity toward strangers, whether to make it evident that you are not niggardly or to acquire new friends.

Adovardo: It seems to us, Giannozzo, that now you are employing your friend's technique with us, for in order not to tell us what we wish to hear, you have turned your discourse to another subject, namely liberality. We want to hear and learn about that friend of yours, so that we, too, may defend ourselves against petitioners such as annoy us every day.

Giannozzo: So you insist! I shall tell you, then. My friend used to tell these tricksters, first, that he did feel it was his duty to do all things for his friends, and yet that it was not now possible for him to do what he would like to or as much as was his custom and their right. Then, with an abundance of words, he would explain that it was not best for them nor necessary at the moment to spend that sum. He told them it was not useful to them, it was to their advantage to wait or to take some alternative course. He was thus generous and even prodigal with advice. Finally he would suggest to them that they ask someone else, and promise to do all he could to talk with friends of theirs about getting them money.

And if they continued to try to persuade him by repetitions of their request, he would finally say in exhaustion: "I shall think it over and find some good solution. Let's talk about it tomorrow." Then he would not be at home, or be too busy, and so the man would finally grow tired and prefer to look elsewhere.

Lionardo: But perhaps it would be best to say no in a forthright and manly way.

Giannozzo: At first that was my opinion, and I often used to reproach my friend. He would answer, however, that it was he who was right, for these devious fellows think they have found a way of petitioning us that we cannot deny. At the same time we must satisfy them without its costing us anything. "If I openly said no right away," my friend used to explain, "I would show that I was indifferent to them, and I would make myself an object of their hate. This way they feel they may be able to fool me, and I also show that I have some regard for them, and so, when in the end they see I have outdone them in shrewdness, they think the more of me. It is no small pleasure, either, thus to loosen the hold of men who hoped they had me."

Adovardo: I like this man well who, being asked for deeds, gives words —and instead of money advice.

Lionardo: But if someone of your own family asked you, as happens every day, how would you treat him?

Giannozzo: If I could do it without great loss to myself, and if it would help my kinsman, I would lend him all the money and property he wanted, all I could possibly lend. It is my duty to help my relatives with property, with sweat, with blood, with everything even to the sacrifice of my life, for the honor of my house and my kinsmen.

Adovardo: Oh, Giannozzo!

Lionardo: Noble, good, wise father. Thus should all good kinsmen be.

Giannozzo: Property and money are to be spent and made right use of. Those who don't know how to spend money except on food and clothes, who don't know how to benefit their kinsmen and the honor of their house, certainly do not know how to make good use of riches.

Adovardo: I must ask you another question now, Giannozzo. Pretty soon I shall see my boys beginning to grow up. Some fathers in Florence are accustomed to give their children a certain allowance for small expenses, and they believe the boys are less apt to go astray if they have a way of satisfying their youthful desires. They say it is keeping children on a tight leash with regard to money that drives them into many vices and wicked ways. What do you say to this, Giannozzo? Do you think one should be so openhanded?

Giannozzo: Tell me, Adovardo, if you saw one of your children playing with a sharp and dangerous thing, such as a well-sharpened razor, what would you do?

Adovardo: I would take the razor out of his hand. I would be afraid he might hurt himself.

Giannozzo: And you would be angry, I know you would, with whoever had let him have it. Right? But is it more proper to a child to handle razors or to deal with money? What do you think?

Adovardo: Neither one seems naturally his concern.

Giannozzo: And do you think a little boy can handle money without danger? Even I, at my advanced age, still find the use of money not without peril. That is the nature of money. Do you suppose it is not very dangerous to inexperienced youth? Let us leave aside the fact that greedy and insidious persons will take it all away from them, for young people find it very hard to defend themselves against such persons. What use do you suppose a young man has for money; what are the needs of a boy? His father feeds him at his own table. If he is wise he does not allow him to eat elsewhere. If the boy wants clothes, he can ask his father for them. His father, being kind and wise, will satisfy his desire, yet not permit him to dress in a licentious or frivolous manner. What needs or desires can a boy have unless it be to plunge into luxury, folly, and gluttony? I would rather urge fathers to teach their sons, my dear Adovardo, that they should not wallow in lascivious and dishonorable indulgence. If the boy does not wish to spend money, he does not need it. If your son's longings are honorable ones, he will be glad to inform you of them, and you will be kind and generous in gratifying him.

Lionardo: Yet, Giannozzo, prudent citizens do uphold this practice, and they would hardly do so if they did not see some good in it.

Giannozzo: If I thought that the will and the course of youth could be restrained at all, I would vehemently condemn the father who does not at least attempt to turn his sons away from their appetites before he decides to help them toward their satisfaction. The more I think about it, the less do I know which is more harmful to young people, needing money too badly or being too well supplied.

Lionardo: I gather that Giannozzo wants fathers first to try to turn the young people away from their appetites as much as possible. Then, however, I am sure, he does not want them made even worse by lack of money.

Giannozzo: Exactly.

Adovardo: Oh, Lionardo, Giannozzo is really helping me today.

Lionardo: He was an even more valuable teacher before when he set forth all that can be said of thrift, and how to manage property wisely, and how to rule the family. It seems to me Giannozzo in fact taught us how to apply thrift to all things, to everything one needs in life.

Adovardo: Don't you think, Giannozzo, that friendship, fame, and honor are useful in life?

Giannozzo: Most useful.

Adovardo: And did you teach the application of thrift to them?

Lionardo: That, no.

Adovardo: Perhaps you did not think that these were matters about which one could give instructions?

Giannozzo: On the contrary.

Adovardo: Then what do you say about them?

Giannozzo: For myself, what do I know about friendship? Perhaps I might say that a rich man will have more friends than he wants.

Adovardo: Yet I see the rich much envied by others. They say all the poor are the enemies of the rich, and perhaps what they say is true. Do you want to know why?

Giannozzo: I do. Go on.

Adovardo: Because every poor man wants to get rich.

Giannozzo: True.

Adovardo: The poor are almost innumerable.

Giannozzo: True, much more numerous than the rich.

Adovardo: And all of them struggle to increase their property, each with his art. They use deceit, fraud, and robbery no less than labor.

Giannozzo: True.

Adovardo: If riches, then, are surrounded by so many itchy fingers, can they be called a thing that brings friends or enemies?

Giannozzo: And still I am one of those who would prefer the self-sufficiency of wealth. I would be glad never to have to ask a friend for help. It will hurt me less to refuse those who ask for a loan than to lend to everyone.

Adovardo: Perhaps it is possible in time of peaceful prosperity to live without friends to sustain you. Don't you need them, however, to defend you against injustice and to assist you in adversity?

Giannozzo: I don't deny that friends are exceedingly useful in human life. But I am a man who asks for help as rarely as possible. Not unless an urgent necessity pressed me would I impose a burden on a friend.

Adovardo: If you had a bow, Giannozzo, don't you agree that you would string it and shoot an arrow or two in time of peace, to see how it would do in time of war?

Giannozzo: Yes.

Adovardo: And if you had a fine gown, wouldn't you want to try it on in the house sometimes, to see how it ennobled your appearance for feast days and public occasions?

Giannozzo: Yes.

Adovardo: And if you had a horse, wouldn't you want to make it run and jump to see how well it would bear you over difficult roads or carry you to safety?

Giannozzo: Yes, but what do you mean by all this?

Adovardo: I wish to point out that the same applies to friends. They, too, should be tested in easy and peaceful situations to see what they would do in time of trouble. In a private and minor way, they may show in a domestic situation what they would be worth in public and weighty affairs, how much they will do for your benefit and honor, how much they are likely to endure for you, to sacrifice for you in ill fortune, and in order to save you from trouble.

Giannozzo: I don't think these ideas of yours are without value. It is better to have tested friends than to be forced to rely on the hope that they will prove good. But to judge by my own experience, I have never injured anyone, always taken care of my own affairs, minded my own business, and gained by this a good many acquaintances. I do not need to ask for anything or to wear out my friends. I make my living honorably and do not, thank God, stand low among men. Let me encourage you, therefore, to go on as you do: live in honor and take no pleasure in doing anyone harm by word or deed. If you do not covet what belongs to others, if you know how to manage your own affairs wisely, you will but rarely have to test your friends, and then but little.

I would be glad to stay here with you as long as you like, but I see my friend for whom I must do something at the palazzo. It was arranged early this morning, and now it is almost time to go there. I don't want to forsake him. I always like helping others better than asking them for things. I would rather have others obligated to me than find myself under obligation to them. I like this work of piety, supporting and helping a man with deeds and words as best I can. I like it not so much because I know he is devoted to me as because I know he is a good and just man. Good men should all consider themselves friends. Even if you do not know them personally, you should always love and help good and virtuous men.

You will stay here, then, and we shall soon be together again. There is one thing I do not want you to forget. Keep this in mind, my children: let your expenses never exceed your income. If you can keep three horses, prefer to keep two that are nice, fat, and well groomed, not four that are hungry and poorly caparisoned. As you educated men say, the eye of the master fattens the steed. As I understand it, that means the household is nourished no less by your diligent care than by your expenditures. Isn't that how you would interpret this ancient saying?

Adovardo: It seems right.

Giannozzo: If you think so, then which of you, wise as you are, would not rather have two public witnesses doing credit to your diligence than four proclaiming your negligence to all the world? Right? Therefore do this: make your expenditures equal to your income or less.

Be in all things—in words, in thoughts, and in actions—just, truthful, and wise. Thus will you be fortunate and well loved and honored.

BOOK FOUR

De Amicitia

t was almost time to take out the plates and to place on the table the last dish of the evening meal when Buto, an old servant of the Alberti family, arrived at the house. He had heard that several of the elders of the family, Giannozzo, Ricciardo, Piero, and others he had known well from the time of his own childhood, had come to see our father. He, as we have explained in the foregoing books, lay ill in critical condition. Buto, then, had come to see these persons. He presented them with the gift of some fruit, not a great many pieces but a few selected ones, out of season, and superlative in flavor and fragrance. This led to some remarks about friendship. After the first greetings had been exchanged, everyone praised the faithfulness and constancy of Buto, who had preserved toward our house a kind of absolute devotion that had first sprung up and been cultivated in the time of his grandfather. It was generally agreed that a true friend is one whose affection no change of fortune can change or diminish. All thought that a man like Buto deserves the highest praise for not ceasing in times of adversity to manifest his love and his complete alliance with the family in continued, daily, open, and gracious expressions of affection and practical kindnesses. The discussion went on until it was declared that in fact there is almost nothing to be found in the life of man as well worth cherishing and keeping as is friendship.

Buto was a man of gay temperament, and perhaps also one who had learned, through constant poverty and the resultant necessity of living submissively and cheerfully in the houses of various people who supported him, to act the clown and to be a fine jester. Said he, Now why do you so warmly sing the praises of friendship? Why do you view it as proof of high wisdom to give and preserve toward oneself constant benevolence and much favor? There is no one in the world who can honestly imagine he could ever find a man actually able to call himself well loved.

I have often heard Messer Benedetto, Messer Niccolaio, and Messer Cipriano, all knights of the Alberti family and men whom everybody called well learned, arguing loud and long among themselves on this subject. I was glad enough to be the ignorant fellow I am, seeing that those who are educated must always be bickering and shouting at each other. It seems they could not make each other understand without throwing their arms and hands about, raising their brows and making faces, shaking their heads and jumping around—so inadequate to these educated people were mere tongue and loud voice once they got quarreling. They said many beautiful and well-sounding things about friendship, but everything they said was such that, if you test the proposition, you will find it untrue.

They said, for one thing, that good friendship requires the union of two persons so that they become one. For that you need more salt * than I can tell. I assure you I loved my wife a lot better when she was still a virgin than later, when I had married her and made her mine. It was an evil hour when we were joined in matrimony, for as long as she was with me in this life, I never enjoyed a half hour of sitting near her without a barrage of shouting and attacks of scolding. Perhaps the wise men who wrote those pretty things about friendship cared little about making friends with women, or perhaps they thought everyone knew you could never have a true friendship with a woman. As for me, I have grown wiser by now and don't blame women anymore for the annoyance they certainly do give when, lord in heaven what a pain, they won't ever be quiet. A heap of salt would not do the trick, so help me God. It would take twenty mountains, and that wouldn't be enough either. I know this, the more salt my wife ate, the stupider she got all around. So here's my advice to you, don't put too much faith in the words of your friends who speak beautifully but to no useful end. Believe me, you'll find it's the truth: nothing is such a block to your power to win men's love as happening to be poor. Make yourself seem rich and you will soon have more friends than you want.

Ricciardo, Adovardo, and Lionardo, who were all well-educated men, thoroughly enjoyed these and other absurdities which Buto uttered amusingly and with appropriate gestures. He made them all laugh.

* Salt stands for wit, as in the expression "dolce di sale"—lacking salt—which can be applied to a person, meaning dimwitted.

This reminds me, *said Lionardo,* of those philosophical banquets described by Plato, Xenophon, and Plutarch, abounding in gaiety and laughter, yet not empty of prudence and wisdom, and graced with much charm and dignity.

How pleased I am with Buto's wit, *said Piero Alberti,* and I can confirm his saying by my own experience, as true indeed. Poverty does block our way in acquiring friends. It causes a host of difficulties and undermines every beginning we make. As you know, all my earnings and private fortune, when we still lived in our own country, came from lands and houses almost exclusively. In this heavy exile of ours, then, to protect myself from the hatred and the enmities which had first robbed us of our public dignities and which still severely persecuted us, I found it expedient to join the court of some prince. There I might have more standing than I could as a mere exile, be less anxious about my safety than I must be as a man naked of defense, and enjoy more security. I followed this plan, and I acquired, with much diligence and care, the favor of three princes who were, as you know, among the best of Italy and famous throughout all nations. These were Gian Galeazzo, duke of Milan, Ladislas, king of Naples, and Giovanni, the pope. Everything I attempted in this direction proved to me clearly what a hindrance and obstacle it was to me to be no richer than I was.

Here Lionardo spoke up. I think, Piero, that riches indeed help make a man more popular with other men, especially with princes. Whether by nature or custom, they almost all seem to appreciate only those who can at some time further their own wishes or needs. Princes, moreover (because they are unencumbered by any sort of honest work if they like and soon, in their leisure, become devoted to the pursuit of pleasure and surrounded not by friends but by deceivers and flatterers), rarely experience desires that are not self-indulgent and shameful. Often they need to make use of their citizens' wealth and of that of every propertied and rich person whom they count as a friend. Further, the signs of riches are more easily discerned at first than those of virtue, especially by princes who find it harder to recognize virtue than fortune since it is in much shorter supply around them. The rich are thus at first perhaps more readily welcomed by them than the good. Because they also suspect that a man who is good will but little encourage them in the pursuit of their ignoble desires and appetites, they tend to prefer the immoral men they happen to meet. They search out the friendship of those who will astutely and maliciously encourage them on their ill-chosen path. Yet, Piero, though people have always seen your virtue, they have appreciated its worth and have always universally noticed, appreciated, and loved your excellence. Your virtue and integrity have always more than offset in your favor the lack of riches and of the good fortune you deserved.

What? *said Adovardo.* Would you make me confess that, if a man wants to win the esteem of princes, virtue is not a far better foundation than wealth? Is it possible that virtue has fallen so low that a man on the pinnacle of fortune hardly sees it at all or does not even recognize it? Virtue, on the contrary, seems only the more marvelous to princes because they see so many more rich men than good ones. Virtue has always by its very nature attracted men, it has seemed worthy of love, however poor the good man. Perhaps you could even find a fair number of rich men who, for lack of the adornment of virtue and honesty, are but little loved—more of these, perhaps, than poor men of virtue and honor who are generally rejected and unappreciated. So great is the power of honor over any soul that has not been entirely brutalized and lost that it makes a prince, however intemperate and lacking in shame, never quite use all his license in pursuit of his desires. The sacred name of honor imposes some restraint and limits on his conduct. It sometimes seems a miracle to me that a man who can do anything he wants to do conquers and restrains himself nonetheless in order not to be thought and spoken of as evil. This clearly shows that almost everyone shares by nature the sense that it is a vile thing to be and to seem a man without virtue. Almost all men try to avoid being thought ill of for their vices. They also admire in others the virtue they prize in themselves.

Perhaps, moreover, those signs of friendship and approbation with which princes nourish and blandish their rich and fortunate followers are solely aimed at making use of them. Look at what Suetonius writes about the emperor Vespasian, who, as I gather, put in office over his ports and customhouses and such not friends but rapacious men zealous for gain, men of the sort born only to make money. Then, when they were well steeped and filled up like sponges, heavy with loot, he could show anger with them, listen to more and more of the accusations and grievances expressed by their victims, and finally squeeze them hard, to leave them dry and poor. He took away their inheritance as well as what they had accumulated, and for this reason Vespasian called them his sponges. In the end, left dry of all possessions and of the juice of property, rich only in hate and ill will, they discovered that they were not his friends.

I think that Piero, likewise, found that, in practice, virtue was of more use to him than any other thing which fortune might have bestowed upon him and added to his estate. This might, I think, be his opinion of the matter: that there is nothing so helpful and useful in winning favor as virtue.

Piero: I am not sure whether I should declare to you that it is virtue that makes a man well loved, or wealth. You learned men will be better able to decide than I, accustomed as you are, by subtle disputation, to find and expound the certainty that lies hidden at the heart of difficult and obscure problems. To me, being no richer and no more fortunate was certainly a disadvantage. I could not undertake the expenditures and offer the liberal gifts that appeared necessary. I won't deny that my industry and diligence helped me greatly to gain from princes the favor and good will that I sought. I do think, however, that if my fortune had been more abundant, I should have needed to apply far less art and labor.

Ricciardo: I am certain that anyone is mistaken who asserts that he can arrive at favor and obtain good repute without the shining adornment of virtue and in the absence of simple courtesy and good character, or that the gifts of fortune alone are enough to make a man well loved. It is rare that men full of vice are not hated. It is also true that when fortune does not help a man it is not easy for him to acquire name and fame for all his virtue. Poverty, as anyone knows by experience, I won't say wholly hinders a man, but keeps his virtue in the shade and often leaves it hidden away in obscure squalor, resembling some cloth which people say is good stuff under the dirt and grime. It is necessary that the goods of fortune should be added to virtue, therefore. Virtue ought to be dressed in those seemly ornaments which it is hard to acquire without affluence and an abundance of the things which some men call transient and illusory and others describe as practical and useful supplements to virtue. Don't you agree, though, that perhaps the first thing necessary is not so much either virtue or riches, but a certain something for which I cannot find a name, which attracts men and makes them love one person more than another. It is something that resides I don't know where, in the face, the eyes, the manner, and the presence of a man, giving him a certain grace and charm full of modesty. I cannot express it in words at all, yet you know if you are faced with two men of equal virtue, equally zealous, equal in every other aspect of fortune, noble and rich, you are likely to see one of them happy and well loved, while the other is held back and almost despised.

Perhaps after all the thinker who claimed that friendships have hidden, almost divine origins and roots was a man to be listened to. In the things nature produces there are marvelous secret forces which make for hate and love, concerning which, so far, I know of no cause or clear reason. Columella writes that there is so much natural enmity between the olive tree and the oak that, even if the oak is cut down, as long as the roots remain in the ground, they will kill off any olive tree planted nearby. Pomponius Mela tells us that at the borders of Egypt, near the people called the Aesphogi, a great number of birds called ibises gather together, driven as if by some innate and natural hatred, to fight the many serpents that live there. The horse, according to Herodotus, has some inborn enmity to the camel and fears him so much that he not only runs at the sight of him, but is troubled by the mere smell. The same thing working in the contrary direction appears in Pliny, who tells us that rue is most likely to thrive if planted under a fig tree. Cicero also said that there are animals which are special friends, as in the case of the so-called spiny oyster, who is big and who opens his shell like two walls until a huge number of little fish gather inside—then the shrimp, a very small creature, causes him to close the prey within, which the two animals consume. The crocodile, too, well known as a most ferocious animal, lies quiet and tractable after he has fed, holding his jaws open while certain birds which gather around him take care of his teeth by cleaning out the particles left clinging to them.

There is something else. I don't know, perhaps it has also happened to you, but I shall tell you since I don't remember mentioning it to you before and I have often observed it: if a man strikes me at first sight as disagreeable and disquieting, I have almost always found that eventually he does me some slight or harm which justifies my first dislike. It is as if nature, by first making his face offensive to me, warned me and indicated ahead of time some natural enmity was as if fated between us. Other persons, blessed with a heavenly and divine gift, immediately make a good impression and suggest a felicitous grace to anyone who looks at them.

Piero: Perhaps it is virtue one needs, or perhaps wealth, or perhaps one must have primarily that divine gift of which you speak, Ricciardo. Certainly if ever in our time anyone had it, it was Messer Benedetto Alberti, your father, who possessed it in marvelous and singular degree— no one could see him and not love him. One was inspired by him to immediate good will and a longing to see fortune favor him, such was his great modesty, kindness, and courtesy combined. I could not say what other subtle thing shone in him that made you aware of a gentle dignity and unlimited wisdom and of a most manly, utterly civilized spirit. Indeed study and a well-ordered sort of life may well be of assistance if you apply yourself to them, as valuable as any other asset in winning you benevolence.

Lionardo: And did you find study and a well-ordered way of life were useful, Piero, in making you an intimate and accepted friend of great princes? Did you find them truly valuable in practice?

Piero: To answer this I should have to tell you the story of my life. It would involve almost the whole progress of my activities and education. That would be a long business and perhaps not altogether relevant, either, to these matters you are discussing. Perhaps it would serve, however, to instruct these young boys, Battista and Carlo, by providing a useful model. It might help them to find their way as I did into the secret and private chambers of princes, and to remain there, as they may need or wish to do, thanks to the prince's benevolence and friendship, with no danger of being rejected.

Giannozzo: All of us, and especially I myself, would certainly be happy if you would here and now take this burden on yourself, Piero, and do as I did this morning. It would surely be a worthy and worthwhile act if, just as I told them about household management, you set forth all your thoughts and ideas to make the rest of us learn, as these days we are all eagerly trying to do, how to make ourselves well loved. We would, by this means, do our family much good and obtain for it as much support and favor as possible. It will be most useful, certainly, and most relevant to our discussion to hear all that you did and to learn to imitate both your prudence and your zeal.

Piero: You certainly are persuading me that I must not go counter to my duty and my wish to obey you. I clearly see that you really want to hear what I have to say. I shall tell you, therefore, first, of what means I made use in order to become an intimate and follower of Gian Galeazzo, the duke of Milan; then I shall tell you how I went about winning the good will of Ladislas, king of Naples; finally I shall recount to you what sort of conduct enabled me to preserve the favor and good will of Pope Giovanni. I think, too, that you will be pleased to learn of my various and different devices, my devious and seldom-used means, which have rarely been described. These are most useful ways to deal with men in civic life; therefore listen well to me.

In order to arrive at the friendship of the duke, I saw that it would be necessary to make use of one of his old friends and present intimates.

Such a man would be the path and the means for presenting myself to him at an appropriate time and in a suitable way whenever an occasion offered of the duke's being less busy than usual with the grave public affairs that normally engaged him. You know, of course, what a great host and power he commanded, with which he attacked whatever stood in his way and by his triumphs won immortal glory. Our own Florentine Republic was one of those that felt the power of his arms to create dominion. He was much occupied in administering his lands with perfect justice, also, and in maintaining internal peace. He strove to make public treaties and arrange friendship with all his neighbors; he was never reluctant to make alliances with any worthy and noble republic or prince in Italy or outside it. From day to day, in short, he worked with cunning and with zeal to make his name and his greatness celebrated. Another quality, which I would not put last among his virtues, was his eagerness to have excellent men about him. He loved good men and was a father to the nobility. Among all those about him, then, I chose one who seemed to me intimate with the prince and of whom I also heard from others that he had more influence than anyone on his secret and private affairs. This was a man whose acquaintance I could cultivate freely without giving offense, a man of a helpful nature, and one to whom the name of our Alberti family was not unwelcome. He was so placed in fortune, more-over, that he would not, in order to hold on to what he had or in hopes of making some later use of me, be slow and backward in mediating for me and in making available to me the valuable generosity of his patron. For you know that some men are so stingy with the presence and the very words of the prince they have some power over that they will hardly give you a chance to see him without forcing you to make heavy payment. Sometimes, too, they avoid making any use of the favor they have with him except for themselves alone.

This man, Francesco Barbavara, therefore, a man of intelligence and of noble manners, an intimate servitor of the prince, kind, liberal, and in no way reluctant to grant me his friendship, was the man I assiduously cultivated with my visits and greetings. Since he loved the poets, I used on occasion to recite to him as much as I had memorized of various poets, and especially of our Messer Antonio Alberti. His poems, which are full of sweet ripeness and adorned with touches of much delicacy and grace, delighted this learned man, for Antonio is, like the other Tuscan poets we have, well worthy of being read and praised. From day to day, then, I gradually became Barbavara's close friend, so that he wanted to help me and to find some way of augmenting my standing and my fortune. Then I opened my heart and mind to him and obtained by his request a welcome, warm reception and frequent access to the prince.

When the duke heard my family name and my country, he said many things to me, speaking with great gravity and princely modesty. What he said, though spoken with more words, was essentially as follows: His spirit was not so hardened against the Florentines but that he would much prefer their friendship to their enmity. It seemed to him, on the other hand, that the combat in which he was engaged was not less honorable than manly, for he was contending with them in warlike glory and force of arms, which are the proper concerns of princes. He was merely seeking not to be forced to accept a lower standing and dignity than those he had always wished to equal. He regretted that due to the actions of others than himself, the fate of the well-known excellence of our citizens was being practically exposed to the power of pure chance— for, he said, it often happened, through lack of zeal and through the foolish temerity of persons little experienced in arms, that men who were superior and stronger in other ways might fall defeated in a war of fist and sword. In war no amount of diligence and prudence could make certain of safety and victory, for in war these virtues could never out- weigh the power of mere fortune. Therefore, he said, since he wanted the world to admire him rather for his virtue than for his fortune, he was much inclined to do all he could to make those now opposed to the path of his glory choose rather to have him as a valued friend than as a fearful enemy. And he added, too, that he wished our family might have been better dealt with by our fellow citizens. Thus the duke.

I said what came to me and seemed right at the time: that our people, being less reckless and foolish than other free states, were naturally more interested in peace than in war. I also said that one can only call it justice if men who love liberty defend it, and one can hardly call it heroism to oppress and disturb that liberty. I went on to express the opinion that if, thanks to his virtue, our citizens obtained a firm and honorable peace from the duke, I was quite certain everybody would praise their good service to their country. But if fortune were more hardened against us than men who rightly cherish liberty deserve, nobody would blame us for our stand.

I added that, like other citizens, I owed it to my country to give advice in good faith, with devotion and zeal, whenever the government was willing to hear me, but it was not up to me, nor up to any private citizen, to judge for myself the justice or injustice of the actions taken by the republic. It was any citizen's duty not to be forward in exhibition of his own discretion but to obey and bow to the laws with due submission and to make sure that his character and praiseworthy conduct in no way fell below that of his fellow citizens. If the disaster that had struck us Albertis had come about through the imprudence, or perhaps even through the wickedness, of the men in charge of public affairs, I should rather regret their error and the harm done to the republic through their maladministration than try, or even think of trying, to express my enmity to a few by doing something harmful and detrimental to my country. Indeed, they say that to attack one's country is as deep a sacrilege as to do violence to one's own father.

My reply pleased the duke, and it seemed to him to live up the repute and renown of our family, who always had been known as men to put the safety and welfare of their country above any private wishes of their own. When I left him I had gained such favor that from that day on he made sure I lacked for nothing needful to an honorable life and proper dress. He often welcomed me at like gatherings, which were always worthy of a great prince. From these I came home with ever more of his affection and with higher standing than before. I also kept the esteem of his followers for my character. I saw that I could act as intermediary for my kin, other Albertis who were there, and so I did. They too enjoyed the liberality and munificence of the duke. It is our duty, as you certainly know, to serve each other whenever we can and to supplement each other's honor and fortune. The friendship of princes is particularly valuable if we can make use of it to increasse the name and repute, the dignity and standing of our kinsmen, and to exalt the family.

Lionardo: Your counsel is wise, Piero, and worthy of praise. Wise men say that if you would seal together and unite two persons in a firm compact, you must have a third who acts as intermediary. You used as a kind of interpreter, then, and as the middleman of the friendship, the man you described as an assiduous servitor of the duke's, yet not too busy to give you honorable attention, one who was also kind, liberal, and inclined to cherish you. Now if this man had not proved such a friend as you hoped, I think you would have acted with similar zeal, by means of like art and method, to gain the intimacy of some other.

Piero: It would not have delighted me, however, to have been forced to spend a great deal of time testing each person to see the exact value of his good will toward me. In fact, perhaps, rather than trying inconsistently to pursue this occasion and that, I should have been very persevering, as indeed I was, in trying to win the favor of one person chosen as the most suited to my purpose. I do think that any reasonable enterprise which we undertake will almost always yield to our will and turn out well if prosecuted with firmness and reason. Inconstancy and lack of perseverance were ever the enemies of success.

Even with Barbavara, this friend of ours, as well as with that prince, the duke of Milan, I had to exercise great patience and to exert an almost incredible firmness of purpose. Not infrequently, I assure you, I spent a whole day without food, pretending to have other concerns, merely waiting to encounter and greet these persons. I absolutely refused to lose by lack of diligence any occasion that seemed useful to win me more welcome in their eyes and suited to make me more familiar to them by daily acquaintance. To make sure, moreover, that I never left them with a feeling of surfeit, I never departed their company without giving some promise of good things to come; I made sure I was always a happy sight, one who would give some new service, while I also made myself likable by my modesty and reverence toward them.

By my own request, the Albertis in England, Flanders, Spain, France, Catalonia, Rhodes, Syria, Barbary, and in all those places where they still today take care of the direction of commerce kept me ever well informed of the revolts, mobilization of ships and men, fires, shipwrecks, or whatever was going on in those regions worth knowing. At that time the learned astronomers were anxiously expecting some sort of great trouble, for the sky showed them clear indications of upheaval, particularly of the overthrow of republics, governments, and persons in high command. It was their almost unanimous opinion that the comet which shone brightly in the middle of the sky and was for months visible even in the daytime would not be shining so long if it did not portend, as comets usually do, the end and death of some famous, powerful prince, like the duke himself. Someone had also told the duke of this common idea, and they say he gave a splendid reply, one worthy of a prince. The duke said he was not sorry to meet his mortal end in a manner which clearly showed him an object of divine solicitude; he thought it a glorious thing to die thus, and to have eternal fame live after him. The heavenly intelligences' concern to give him a rare and marvelous omen and sign, he said, surely proved to the world that the divine and immortal spirits in the skies were interested in his life and death.

Yet I do think that he actually felt, as a result of the predictions, some considerable inward anxiety which was hardly visible to others. Fortunately I myself was able to allay this fear, for it happened that our people in Rhodes informed me on the instant of the death of Timur Lenk,* a great conqueror who had led over three hundred thousand troops and was ruler of the magnificent city of Samarkand. The duke, as I could see, easily drew the conclusion that the warnings of heaven had now been satisfied through the disaster befalling so great a prince. With all such precious news, it was almost always I who brought the best as well as the first account to the prince, something which increased my welcome and preserved his benevolence toward me.

Upon the death of the duke, then, I transferred my attendance to the court of Ladislas, the king of Naples. He was a man by nature considerably more open than the duke in his style, habits, and way of speaking, and one more suited to command armies than to sit in council and carry on weighty deliberations. I joined him without having an acquaintance or friend to present me, and so I had to manage it alone. I had given this some quiet thought, and at last the time and place were granted me that most answered my hopes. Ladislas had gone out to hunt, and I came upon him dismounted, boldly pursuing wild beasts alone. He was in a place where flight was difficult, and he was trying to fight a great bear whom he had provoked to violent anger, yet he could not sustain the beast's attack without great danger. Then suddenly he faced the onrush and stood stupefied, armed only with two Sardinian daggers; he had hardly a moment in which to hesitate, to think, to choose his best move—whether to yield before the beast or to resist—and he was afraid. Though he would have liked to, he was not able in that situation to trust entirely to his own arms and his strength, nor did he know where to turn for help. I ran up with two excellent and well-trained dogs, and I encouraged the king by my words to put aside his fear. One of my dogs was light, quick, high-spirited, and ready to intercept the attack of the animal; unceasingly he leaped up on him from every direction and blocked him. The other dog, being strong and heavy, was competent to baffle and bring down the attacker.

(These noble dogs were a gift sent to me by our kinsman Aliso, your strong brother, Adovardo. To him they had come from the king of

---

* Alberti refers to Timur as Temir Scita. Timur did not die in 1402 but in 1405. Alberti is probably recalling, however, the catastrophic fall of another great monarch, Sultan Bayazid, who was defeated and taken captive by Timur at the battle of Angora, July 20, 1402. Gian Galeazzo died September 3.

Granada; he may have bought them from him or got them as a prize, for his great athletic skill won him the good will and affection of that king. At a certain well-known public tournament they held there, no one else could leap, fight, ride, or perform any feat of agility and strength better than he. The faster dog he called Tiger, the other, more robust, dog, was named Megastomo.)

Tiger, then, with combined caution and audacity, diverted the beast's anger and drew it on himself. While the beast fought vainly and wasted his strength on the air, Megastomo, the other dog, armed with his mighty strength and solid weight, took a deep and unshakable hold on his throat. The bear was brought down to earth so fast that it seemed to prove, as they say, that there is no animal as vulnerable in that spot as the bear. They say that a bear may even break its neck when falling on its back, like the goose, who, they say, often wrings her own neck while uprooting a plant in greedy and gluttonous haste.

The king ran the bear through with his dagger, as soon as the dog had brought him down, and so quickly finished him off. Laughing, the king then turned to me and said in Latin, "I like you, comrade in arms, you care for my safety not only on the battlefield but in the chase, too."

"I am delighted," I replied, "to have you consider me one of your own men, as I had been hoping you would. I am more pleased today with my luck than with my valor, for it has made me, as you say, your comrade in arms. It is well known, indeed, that this, the hunter's battle, is like the soldier's struggle against enemies." I had already begun to say more on this subject when a crowd of hunters appeared. Then at once I began to praise the king's valor, and to say how he alone and with his own hands had downed the great and savage beast.

The king desired my presence near him at dinner that evening, and there we went on for a long time discussing hunting. We noted that whether for birds or beasts or fish there must be men able to locate the quarry, so that one does not waste one's time; then there must be those who will block and turn the prey if it takes to flight or stands too dangerously firm. Men are needed, also, to hold it back and bring it low and subdue it, all of which clearly shows that the hunt is not only analogous to military exercise but is also a necessary and worthy occupation for princes as much as for private noblemen.

Giannozzo: What good is all this devotion and knowledge applied to the hunt—you pursue beasts, are surrounded by beasts, command and shout to beasts, and sit all the while on a beast. And if a man takes too much delight in all this, he soon becomes a beast himself. A great and useless expense, perfectly useless—you keep the house in a disordered state all year to feed animals who will serve a slight pleasure of fifteen days or so. This pleasure, anyway, can only suit people who won't work or children. What is it really but gazing at animals as they run or fly? If that is all you want, a kitten as it chases a painted butterfly or turns an egg about will perform at home thousands of prettier and stranger tricks. Outdoors you may see a wild kite fall on its prey with more cunning and often with as much zest as any trained one, and you may also see him battle in midair with another. Thus if by chance it is the sight of birds of prey you crave, you may indulge this taste in ways much less expensive, laborious, and perilous. You need not go and exhaust yourself in the heat of midsummer or in cold and snow or amid dust and sharp winds just for the sake of a little brief pleasure and useless sport. I would rather see our youth active in better ways and engaged in matters more worthy of our name.

Piero: The bird of prey is not displeasing to observe, and lovely is the flight of it as it comes down on the target. But the real pleasure is exercise —it is a delight to take the air and to relieve the soul of public responsibilities and burdensome concerns. I would add, too, that the hunt serves as a preparation, almost as a school, for military skill. One learns to make good use of the bow, the dagger, and the sword, to run upon an enemy or to stand ready and wait for him with fortitude. I cannot tell you here how closely the sport of hunting does resemble the command of arms, for that would require a long exposition and would be out of place in this talk of ours.

Lionardo: No, I think it would be to our purpose. We see how necessary the use of arms is to defend and preserve the authority and dignity of a country. We know that victory usually reinforces tranquillity, peace, and sweet friendship. If someone makes us more able to repel and punish those who attack the valued fruit of peace and all its precious rewards, how could we deny that by so doing he shows us how to live well and honorably?

Piero: As you say, the means of victory and of overcoming our enemies are probably relevant to our discussion of friendship, and, as I did say, the practice of hunting may well be of use to princes. Since these matters will be discussed elsewhere, however, I think I may skip them here.

At dinner, then, King Ladislas desired my presence in the palace among his daily companions, and he condescended to give me the power to do through him anything that I wished. Never, however, did I give anyone cause to suspect me of using Ladislas' grace and favor for any but just and worthy purposes. Even when it came to perfectly righteous causes, I asked for less than I could have obtained. I especially avoided making any use of the king's benevolence that might possibly lead anyone to suspect, in spite of everything, that I acted in weakness or let myself be corrupted. I always, for instance, refused to help a man obtain an office for which he was not thoroughly qualified by character and experience. I was never willing to get a wardship for anyone, no matter how good a friend, and no matter how well based, rich, and free of any taint of corruption he might be. For I was entirely aware that in these perilous positions, good faith and diligence are seldom and sparsely rewarded, while imprudence, inactivity, or any misfortune leads to a flood of evils and brings widespread infamy, not only on the man who holds the office, but on all his friends as well. In this and in all other situations I shunned whatever might bring me hate and envy. I avoided all ostentation and irritating display, qualities that often spring up in imprudent men along with sudden prosperity. I tended to do the opposite: I gave an easy, kind, humane reception to anyone who presented himself to me in my own house or outside it. I labored to please the eyes and ears of even the plebeian crowd in their numbers by having pleasant and genial ways.

The king loved to see his men full of high spirits, gay and active, never lethargic or idle; I therefore often took exercise in his presence, and I gently urged others to do the same, to show their powers in riding in the joust, and in dueling on foot, in fencing, jumping, and throwing spears. I tried to outdo all others not only in these activities but also in my bearing and noble style. I was willing merely to equal others in physical skill, provided I could surpass them in courtesy and loftiness of spirit. Yet, if you remember, I was never a weakling as a boy, or a laggard in the manly arts, or less able than others.

When I was with the duke, I found it burdensome and irritating always to be on the watch, to observe with infinite pains exactly what was going on and come running at once not to be late or miss out on any occasion for coming into his presence. Now with Ladislas I found it onerous to have almost no leisure and to lack any definite time to devote to my own activities and concerns. It was required of me to wait on him so much, to be nowhere but there, that I well learned the truth of the saying that the cultivation of great men's patronage is like the training of a hawk. One flight may make him wild and strange; one slight error, one mistaken word (as you literary men know by a thousand examples in books), even a single misbegotten glance alone, can be the cause of a lord's falling into a fatal passion against one whom he at first loved very much.

Lionardo: Indeed, there are numerous examples, and not obscure ones either. Cicero tells that once, when Dionysius, the king of Syracuse, was getting ready to play ball, he gave his jacket to a beloved youth to hold while he was playing. One of the boy's friends said playfully, "And what's that you're entrusting to him—your life, Dionysius?" Dionysius saw the boy smile at these words, and, for this, he had them both killed, the one for having, as he thought, shown the way to poison him, and the other for having, by his smile, consented.

Piero: For just that reason, I practiced the utmost vigilance, attention, and watchfulness in all I did. I engaged in honorable and cheerful sport and was discreet in speech and most decorous in every gesture, so that I might continue to enjoy the good graces and benevolence of Ladislas, the king. When he died,* Pope John † in Bologna, inspired by our enemies, demanded of the Albertis at his court, in no more than eight days, a loan of that enormous sum based on money deposited with our family in London, the money which you, Ricciardo, got for him before he himself expected it and before anyone else thought possible. Most of it had been sent at once by your brother, Lorenzo, in Venice. It was an incredible sum, so large that before our day no single citizen ever had so much in his private possession, for this sum was more than one thousand times eighty gold coins.

I came the fourth day after the pope asked for this money, and with great magnanimity I offered it to him and asked him to accept it. The next day it was actually handed over to him who had demanded it. I returned again to pay him a visit, and I recounted to him the many, many benefits conferred by our family on him and on other popes; for hardly anyone entered on the pontificate in our time who had no reason to congratulate himself on our generous support. I told him I could not believe that there was not some need or some hidden reason which had driven him to act against us in this way, for it represents great danger to merchants to suddenly take from them a huge sum like this. It is true, as they say, that such funds are the life blood of men who live by commerce. However, I added, we would not take great offense as long as he was

* 1414.
† John XXIII.

satisfied now, as we hoped he was. I asked him, therefore, to trust that our hearts were as affectionate toward him as ever in spite of all, though perhaps there were some who would have liked to turn him against us. These last words I uttered with the same open countenance as I had preserved through all my speech, and I accompanied my talk with such gestures as these prelates demand, almost adoring him, particularly when I said that I offered him the submission and devotion of all our Alberti family, eager to serve him in every way he might desire. He looked hard at me, and then, fixing his gaze on the ground, he clasped his hands and said that for the moment he did not deem a long answer suitable. He was well enough pleased with us, and I might return. As I did do.

He had a number of vices, first of all the most common and most notorious vice of all priests: excessive greed for money. Anything he controlled was for sale. There were many notorious simoniacs, embezzlers, and all sorts of clever rogues and scoundrels around him. He began to be fond of me, I suspect, because of the great wealth which he saw in our family. Because of this he convinced himself that I was actually the sort of man I tried to appear to him, openhanded and generous, one from whom he could hope to get copious and timely assistance.

Among his followers there was incredible strife; from hour to hour all the tempers in his household were apt to explode. Today a particular courtier could do anything—tomorrow he was excluded from all affairs. Hence from hour to hour there were universal intrigues to bring hatred and dismissal upon anyone more in favor with the pope than another. Many who saw how willingly the pope had listened to me and offered me his presence, just hoping to advance me before their particular enemies, labored to make me stand first in favor among all those near the great man. And, as you know, we become great not only through our own diligence and skill but also through the zeal and ingenuity of our supporters, whose service augments at once our authority, dignity, and power. These men, then, who preferred me to others because of their own rivalries or because of some notions of theirs about my virtue easily lifted me to a position of the greatest power and highest rank. I disliked the vices of the man and of his whole household, however, and understood only too well that the pope loved me only for what he hoped to obtain from me. I had no desire to sully my name and get some stain of infamy through too much trafficking with those scoundrels. They were men whom all good men detested and execrated. Therefore I preferred to keep aloof and remote from them. You know that intimacy with men addicted to vice always brings on disgrace and danger.

To use his patronage, however, as they say one always should make use of the friendship of priests, I was always asking him, for myself and for my kinsmen, for all those things which it was his duty to give, if not to me, to others: offices, benefices, favors. If he refused me repeatedly, I did not give up; instead I came back again with a new request. Rivals must be defeated and outdone not, as many people think, by spreading rumors and bringing envy and spite on them, but by persistence and insistence. Gossips, in fact, become suspect to princes when they do talk and hateful when they don't. We prefer to be first in virtue and merit. In order to succeed, the petitioner need only find the patron helpful once in the course of many occasions and willing, that once, to give. Things that a prince has refused you once are not therefore so completely forbidden that you may not after a while pursue them anew. I thus made him generous by the frequency of my petitions, by my copious thanks, and by my willingness to praise his own followers. What most overcame all opposition, however, was the fact that I rewarded him with gifts for every benefit received, so that no member of his court ever left me without some bounty, part of which he kept and part of which he presented to the pope.

Giannozzo: Now, that last bit of wisdom, dear Piero, that, of all your wiles, is the one I have always found best. Who is there, these days, who is himself blessed with good fortune and does not entirely withdraw, almost flee, from the friendship of the less fortunate? From them men expect nothing but trouble and expense. Who, on the other hand, will not be eager to consort with lucky and affluent men, hoping for their help in need and for their assistance in satisfying desires? We are so much inclined by nature, as it seems, to seek out and to find whatever is useful that I think we are taught by nature to take from others and to keep for ourselves—and we know well how to simulate good will or how to avoid friendship in order to suit our situation.

If priests, as you say, are the greediest of all, that does not surprise me either, for they vie with one another not to shine for their virtue and learning—there are few learned priests and less honest ones—but to outdo everyone in pomp and ostentation. They want a large number of fat and elegant horses, they want to appear in public with a huge army of well-fed retainers. And from day to day different desires arise in them, desires which are lascivious, bold, and passionate, for they have much leisure and little character. To minister to these, fortune helps them on, and so they live incontinently, caring only to satisfy their appetites and never thinking to provide for the future or to be reasonable in their expenditures. It naturally suits them, then, not to choose for their companions good men who would hesitate to carry out their ugly tasks, but to choose such as minister complacently to their lust and their vices, the fulfillment of which leads only to further criminal wishes. Such a man makes himself a veritable slave to his desires and pleads for them like a beggar; so from day to day he changes his go-betweens and procurers to suit his latest villainous demand. As a result, between the man who finds himself excluded from the solid familiarity and intimacy he thought he had yesterday and the fellow who now enjoys control of the master's thoughts and guidance of his affairs, there arises and burns a most marvelous ill will. There are always new quarrels and furious factions in the household. Everyone tries to gain the master's favor by bringing some new nourishment to feed the man's vices. He thus becomes entirely accustomed to the obscene and vile way of life he has found and entirely besieged by flatterers of the lowest and most unscrupulous sort. He is ever aroused and inflamed by some new lust and vice, the cost of which is always excessive. So his expenditures outrun the regular income of the house. He must turn elsewhere in his greed, and when it comes to providing for regular expenses—the help of his kinsmen, assistance to friends in need, keeping his family in honorable wealth and rank—he becomes inhumane, tight, tardy, and miserly.

Buto, that silly fellow I have mentioned before, here put in a word: All your reasons are summed up—*said he*—in a very brief but true and lucid saying. You'll find it the truth, for nature shows us the truth of it: "You can't pluck a hair from a shaved pate." These priests are like a lantern, when you put it on the ground it gives light to all, and, when you lift it high, the higher it goes, the more it casts useless shadows.

Then they smiled and left the table.

Carlo and I then went to our father's room to pay our respects. The others left our father Lorenzo, and then Ricciardo came in. He requested that we leave him alone with Lorenzo for a while, I think in order to make certain decisions and arrangements for the good of our whole family. We therefore returned to the room where Adovardo was engaged in conversation with Lionardo. Adovardo was answering him as follows:

Adovardo: I certainly agree, Lionardo, that the things Piero said all seemed to be wise and sound and full of prudence. His subtlety and considerable artistry were also clear to me. I don't deny that he presented the three kinds of friendship—the one based on virtue, the next on pleasure, the last on utility. But it seems to me that I want some other sort of thread and texture in talk on this subject. There is something, I don't know what it is exactly, that no ancient writer has ever been able to give me.

Lionardo: Perhaps you would have been more satisfied if Piero had not chosen a narrative mode of presentation. He might, of course, have spoken more like the scholastics, first defining the nature of friendship, then dividing it into its various kinds, and then stating within that orderly arrangement what his arguments and views were, selecting one kind of friendship for his final approval.

Adovardo: Oh, no, not at all. I like that remark of Cornelius Celsus about doctors. He preferred the doctor who manages to restore one to health and to keep one well to such as cunningly determine whether food in the stomach, according to the Hippocratic theory, is consumed by some natural heat characteristic of our system, or, as Plistonicus, the disciple of Parassagoras, thought, decays within the body, or, as Asclepiades asserted, simply passes through undigested and raw. Our case is analogous. As the doctors look for health, so the philosophers and those of us who discuss these things are seeking happiness. Happiness, moreover, is not to be had without virtue; and if virtue consists in acting virtuously, and friendship itself is one of the actions required of virtue, I shall be most pleased to hear those who will teach me about it and to praise them. First, let them tell me how I may gain a good number of friends, for it is a fact that no one is born endowed with friends as some are born endowed with riches. If one does not manage to acquire friends, one certainly will not have as many as one needs. And second, since nothing human is perfect the moment it's begun, I wish they would show me the way to make a friendship move, once it is initiated, in the direction of what they consider a good, honorable, and altogether perfect state. In the course of this process, moreover, I may find some previously unnoticed and serious fault in the man I cherish. Then let them teach me how I may skillfully loosen that friendship without breaking it entirely. And, if he mends his ways and lives honorably, I might want to recall him to his former affection for me. I should like to be as clever and knowledgeable as possible in the art of reattaching him to myself in true friendship. Considering, moreover, how fragile and unstable is anything that men undertake, be it in thought or action, I also long to know how to keep my friend persevering in good will and good faith.

Really, what is the practical use of being able to argue in debate that only friendship based on virtue is strong and enduring while friendships for utility and pleasure are transitory? Shall I find more friends, perhaps, when I have been persuaded by the philosopher Pythagoras that all things ought to be held in common by truly affectionate friends? And those I have, shall I suppose they will love me with greater faith and constancy when, from that other philosopher, Zeno, or from Aristotle, I have learned to consider a friend another self, as Zeno once called him, or to view friendship with Aristotle as a being composed of two bodies and one soul? Nor does Plato satisfy me any better when he instructs us that some friendships arise as if by nature, others through the simple and open alliance and congruence of souls, and still others only through the lesser bonds of habit, association, and continued intimacy; which three kinds of friendship he names, respectively, the natural friendship, the congruent friendship, and—because of the ancient custom of mutual entertaining of citizens from different cities—the friendship of hospitality.

I don't deny that the scholastic definitions and descriptions composed by learned men in their sheltered leisure are useful as a kind of preparation, like jousting for the use of arms. You have to live in the world, however, and deal with the actual ways and habits of men. If all you know is whether it is the mother or the father who naturally loves the children more, and whether the love of the father for his children outweighs that of the children for him, and for what reasons brothers and sisters are attached to each other, I'm afraid you end up like poor Formius, the peripatetic. He gave a long discourse on military affairs in the presence of Hannibal. Hannibal, after hearing him out, remarked that he had seen a good deal, but nothing sillier than this fellow who apparently believed that one could do on the field in the presence of an enemy just what one could think of while arguing in the schools. You know the truth—how can anyone dream that mere simplicity and goodness will get him friends, or even acquaintances not actually harmful and annoying? The world is so full of human variety, differences of opinion, changes of heart, perversity of customs, ambiguity, diversity, and obscurity of values. The world is amply supplied with fraudulent, false, perfidious, bold, audacious, and rapacious men. Everything in the world is profoundly unsure. One has to be far-seeing, alert, and careful in the face of fraud, traps, and betrayals. To deal with human wickedness in all its boldness, daring, and greed one must be able to remain constant, temperate, and full of inner strength. These are the qualities I would like to see actually practiced by a man whose friendship I hoped to gain and to enjoy. These are qualities not just to be learnedly categorized and almost diagrammed. So there it is; I want to be instructed in this sense concerning friendship, how to obtain it, increase it, diminish it, recover it, and make it permanent.

Lionardo: The order you specify, Adovardo, I think would be highly approved by learned men, for it is perfectly consonant with nature. But I also find it hard to believe that you are displeased with the ancient writers for setting out according to their own principles and methods, that true friendship is nothing but a combining together of all our human and divine concerns, reaching agreement and loving one another with entire good will and perfect charity. Nor could you be dissatisfied with their proofs that this true friendship can occur only among good men, since wicked men are always hateful and burdensome to each other. Ever full of boredom or of unbridled license, they are unsuited to enjoy friendship with other men. Then the ancient writers set forth the differences among various sorts of friendship, and which sort is solid and true, and what are the best and most holy laws for its proper existence. It is a rule of theirs, you know, that one must first judge to what extent a certain person is capable of friendship and not begin to love a man you do not know to be faithful and good. We should not be too precipitous in loving at first, but should sustain the onslaught of attraction. All our feelings, they say, should be strengthened and tempered with prudence and modesty. Then, when we have yielded ourselves to affection, let there be no falsehood between us, no simulation, nothing dishonorable, only true and willing service and ready help at all times. Let our actions be guided and limited not by ambition or greed, but only by true, constant, and unfaltering virtue. If, in fact, you want the questions you have asked to be answered in the order you have imposed on them, I think you will find plenty in the ancient writers to satisfy you on every point.

Adovardo: I won't deny, Lionardo, the usefulness of the old writers' counsels. Yet I cannot agree that there is much written on this problem and the art of resolving it. Today, as you know, we have of our own writers only Cicero and an occasional letter of Seneca and not much more on the subject; among the Greeks we have Aristotle and Lucian. I speak no ill of these, but I doubt that anyone but me would praise them for their treatment of this subject. I am one who holds any writer in reverence and admiration. They say that virtue is the bond and the best source of friendship, and that friendship flourishes and brings forth good fruit where there is good will, agreement on goals, and frequent association. They say that virtue leads to an honorable friendship, and frequent meeting gives pleasure, while mutual service creates a near certainty of mutual affection. You, who have some experience, certainly knew such things, which are neither very subtle nor very practical in their application, long before you ever read them written anywhere. Who in fact is so foolish and completely unintelligent about everything that he does not know benefits received and the zealous and assiduous pursuit of things that please us are likely to make people well liked and appreciated?

But not every man who is well read knows how to show his virtue in such a temperate and worthy form as to win him good will and friendship. Nor will such an academic type know just how and with how much zeal, effort, and service he can touch this or that kind of mind at a given place and time, so as to win ready acceptance. That is the kind of knowledge I call necessary. I think you won't deny that I am right. It is not the kind of knowledge one can acquire in solitude, from silent and motionless books. One has to learn it in the public marketplace, at the theater, and in people's homes, through another kind of diligence and experience.

I have not found it so easy to know who those good people are who love only virtue. It is not always equally easy for me to show by my service and favor the good will I wish to show to particular persons. Mere zeal and continual converse do not always carry us to the point where we can cull the fruits of friendship. How rarely indeed do parity and congruence of souls correspond to the ancient saying of our poet, Ennius: "we find our sure friends when our fortune is unsure." I'm telling you, Lionardo, it may not be so easy as some guileless people think to get friends. What a lot of work is involved! It goes beyond knowing such things as whether friendship was invented to supply our need, or whether we ought to feel toward our friends that which they feel toward us, or whether friendship ought to be applied to any end but true and virtuous love.

Lionardo: You talk, Adovardo, as though you had not found many, many good counsels and useful illustrations of this matter in all the writers. For not philosophers only, but all the historians are full of excellent teaching applicable to all kinds of friendship. I cannot think you would put their examples below those you could draw from the ordinary crowd and the masses. I really don't think you will find less good sense and knowledge of life among historians than among any ordinary persons, however clever, that you might choose. If it is age and experience that make men wise, history, as you know, covers not only more than one lifetime but more than one century. If we gain knowledge and astuteness through having heard, seen, and experienced many things, history both sees and knows more causes and effects, and more remarkable ones, of greater authority and eminence than any *pater familias* you might meet, however bent on gathering wisdom.

In short, once we have learned that all our labors will not profit us unless we observe the philosophers' precepts and warnings to choose only virtuous and diligent friends, we can easily gather from historians and from other literature as well the sort of craft and skill you have been teaching us. The philosophers' precepts, moreover, if they should prove of little help in the forming of friendships, at least do not hurt you in the observance and certainly do harm you in the breach.

Adovardo: I am surprised that you ask me to draw lessons for the pursuit of friendship from the historians, who usually talk only of public disturbances, the overthrow of republics, the inconstancy and fickleness of fortune. I suppose you can forge the bonds of friendship out of the quarrels which divided the Carthaginians and Romans in their desire each to obtain the island of Sicily? I suppose you could compose from their tricks and onslaughts an art suited to give me tranquil and happy amity and union of hearts? I shall laugh if you really claim to demonstrate with those massacres and by those devastations of territory how I may enjoy the benefits of contented friendship.

Lionardo: Yet there are innumerable illustrations and remarks to be found in the historians and philosophers which are suited to help us find friends. There are remarks that are a joy to read, most worthy of remembrance, truly authoritative, and by no means to be ignored or disdained. The mother of Alexander of Macedon, Olympia, used to write to him urging him to strive to gain friends by gifts, benefits, and by the kind of works which would redound to his glory and spread his fame. And it is one of the first notions to be found in all the Stoic philosophers that there is nothing more likely to make a man well loved than virtue and an honorable character. Thus Theseus, the conqueror of the Marathonian bull, was impelled to admire Hercules by his fame and high repute. Themistocles, Plutarch says, gained great good will among his own people because when he held office he was a just and severe judge.

Aulus Vitellius, the man who succeeded Silvius in the Roman principate, became a favorite of the emperor, Suetonius tells us, because he was highly skilled in the reading of auguries; and the same person was no less well liked by Claudius because he played checkers extremely well. Octavian liked Maecenas because he found him silent and discreet; he liked Agrippa because he saw his fortitude under all sorts of strain. Cato observed that his country neighbor Valerius Flaccus was very diligent in the cultivation of his fields. It was an occupation of which Cato was extremely fond, and so he became his friend. Thus did virtue serve these persons, and they gained by the appearance of zeal in honorable and worthy pursuits.

As to the usefulness of benefits and gifts, everyone knows how much they help, isn't that so? Titus Quintius Flaminius by his decrees freed the province of Asia from the many false usurous bonds that oppressed it. He got so popular with all the inhabitants of that province, they say, that the loud welcome and acclaim he received in the theaters deafened and stupefied the birds and made them fall out of the sky on the crowd. What is there that gifts cannot do? They can win you new friends, certainly, but they can also reconcile and recall even men filled with serious malice and hardened hate against you. The family of the Fabians in Rome, at a time when they were rather out of favor with the people, took in a great many of the wounded after that battle against the Etruscans where the consul Fabius was killed. There they nursed them and recovered by this action all their former popularity. The Senate was at one time enormously hated by the people and faced grave revolts, but it made a decree that a salary should be paid to Roman citizens in the army. The richest men of Italy joined in this action. And so those who had hated them before were recalled by this benefit to favor and peaceful friendship.

Not only man is tamed by gifts, so are animals. Aulus Gellius says in a memorable tale that a certain Androdorus,* the slave of a noble Roman who was a consul in Africa, fled from his master into the desert. There in a cave, where he took shelter and hid, he found a lion suffering from a thorn in his paw and cured him. For this benefit there was such an alliance formed between those two that they lived in perfect harmony for three whole years. In gratitude for the kindness received, the lion sometimes brought the man a part of his prey, which Androdorus cooked in the heat of the sun at midday. Thus he was fed and survived. It happened

---

* Androcles.

that the lion was captured and taken to Rome, which forced the man to flee. Once he left his lair, he was seized by the army of the man whose fugitive slave he was. Then, for his contumacy, he was sentenced to be thrown to the beasts, a death to which serious criminals were then condemned. But a miracle happened. His old friend the lion no sooner saw Androdorus then he practically took him in his arms and protected him from the other wild beasts. That was a sight that moved the multitude, and so both slave and lion were restored to liberty. They were such good friends, moreover, that they say when the two went out in the streets, Androdorus led the lion by a light bridle as if on a leash through all the streets of Rome. People said, "Here is the man who is friends with a lion and the lion who offered hospitality to a man."

Seneca, too, writes of a marvelous and incredible spectacle he saw of the same kind. The good writers, including Pliny, remind us how that serpent in Egypt, accustomed to feed at the table of a certain man, when one of his little serpents had bitten and killed the son of the man, recognized that this was a breach of friendship and himself killed his son to revenge the wrong, thus depriving himself of his dear child. And not only that, but he then had the courage to return under that roof where he had lived in such intimacy and where his own offspring had committed such an act of ingratitude.

The divine mind of Titus, according to Suetonius and Eutropius, recognized the value of gifts for gaining friends, so much so that in the evening, when he was left to himself, he would sorrow whenever he found that on that day he had neither promised nor given anything to somebody.

You will also see great good will arise among those who enjoy pleasurable and joyous conversation together. Plato says that men are caught with pleasure, like fish with a hook. They write that Perseus so liked the generous visage of Theseus that he instantly made friends with him. Likewise did Theseus when he saw the style and the beauty of Pirithous. Pisistratus was dear to Solon and, some say, Alcibiades to Socrates, for his handsome appearance. Marcus Antonius gained a good deal of favor by talking of love with young men and serving the passions of lovers. Sulla, as Sallust tells us, was better liked by his army because he allowed them to be lascivious in Asia beyond what ancient Roman severity allowed. And I could give you innumerable other stories and sayings which could serve as excellent models and allow you to extract most useful precepts for the acquisition of friends. The man who knows all this and is able to win friends on such occasions and by such means will certainly also be able to renew and to increase at will the great benevolence and solid favor he wants. To maintain these I suppose there is nothing better than frequent intercourse, happy, honorable, and substantial—with some practical usefulness to it. As to dissolving friendships, who would deny that lack of contact is the most applicable means. Nothing so thoroughly cancels out even the strongest impression as absence.

Adovardo: Ah, Lionardo, what a mass of further information would be needed before one could really discuss this matter in its breadth and extent. It is as though some student had heard from the astronomers that Mars disposes the force of armies and the outcome of battles, Mercury establishes the various branches of knowledge and governs the subtlety of minds and marvelous skills, Jove controls ceremonies and the souls of religious men, the sun reigns over worldly offices and principalities, the moon precipitates journeys and the fluctuations of spirit among women and mobs, Saturn weighs down and slows our mental processes and undertakings—and so he would know the character and power of each. But if he did not know how to evaluate their effect according to their place in the sky and their elevation, and what favorable or unfavorable effect their rays have on each other, and how their conjunctions are able to produce good or ill fortune, surely that student would be no astrologer. The mere recognition of those bare principles is indispensable to any understanding of the art, but even with them you have only just entered the domain of other, almost innumerable laws necessary if you would foresee and understand the things which the sky tends to produce. Likewise, these very useful and numerous examples and sayings, which you say are so amply provided by the best authors, do not give us all the help we need.

It occurs to me, too, in conjunction with our subject and inquiry, that sometimes I have felt I was viewing not only the causes which give rise to friendship, but the actual method, almost the laws of its formation. I have observed that friendship is born either by our diligence or by the action of others who, by almost inviting us to do so lead us to ally ourselves to them with good will and eager service to their honor and their needs. I have noticed that if one would be invited to this state, it helps to know how to present oneself as honorable, modest, pleasant, friendly, joyful, temperate, conscientious, kind, and as lively of spirit as constant, as well as illustrious in name and fame. I have seen how much it attracts a man if we appear noble and good to him, almost a refuge and haven where he may find good counsel, immediate action, prompt help, and true consideration for his every concern, from a mind that accepts ample responsibility diligently. Liberality, frequent attendance, munificence, gratitude, good faith, piety, a general good hope and expectation of our character on the part of the public, these things are the best intermediaries of friendship.

I have found, too, that we must know diverse arts, must have a supple spirit, must show no little discretion as well as assiduity, if we would attach the spirit of men to ourselves. Nothing is more volatile, light, easily blown about by the slightest wind. A little spark may start a great fire of hatred in a man; a little gleam of virtue may cause him to love us. One must act like a man reaching first to the outermost leaf of a branch, then seizing a stronger twig, then the branch itself which he can bend, so as to pick the fruits. So must one deal with human minds and spirits, not hoping to trap them in one gesture but first holding out some reward, then proceeding with deliberation. Yesterday you greeted him, and that was enough to give him the sense of your noble presence and pleasant manner. Thanks to this he has judged you not ill mannered or inexperienced. Today you may sow in him the seed of some hope, some desire to see you again tomorrow. And there is almost no one who will not find the time long waiting for the day when you said you would see him, not only because then you will give him or tell him something that interests him but because he wants then to be asked for help in some concern of yours that you have not yet mentioned. Somehow, I don't know why, we are all by nature enormously curious and eager to know everything. There is hardly anyone who will not want to be with you often if you are a person who deals honorably and who gives occasion for decent pleasure and laughter.

I made up my mind, however, that I need not always engage in this contest in every group where I might find myself being tested. I am one of those, however, as I frankly admit, who wants to be well liked by both the good and the not-so-good. In fact, the hatred of any man may harm me, while the good will of anyone leads eventually to the fulfillment of our needs. There is no harm, either, in dealing with the blows received from vicious and utterly wicked men by using the help of men who are not themselves the best, but who will share the risks of defense or vengeance. Yet I would always as far as possible avoid intercourse and familiarity with bad and unscrupulous men. There I agree with the philosophers, who say that there can only be friendship among good men.

Who can love others more than himself? But wicked men do not love themselves. They are always troubled and unhappy, now thinking on their past crimes, now turning over some new criminal plan, now considering and realizing how empty they are of excellence. Filled with vices, hating other men, unloved by God, they live in misery. To this you must add that the friendship of wicked men leads to all sorts of trouble, risks, difficulties, and burdensome anxieties. In the end you must either fall into infamy along with your friend or depart from him as an enemy. I shun men who are not good, therefore, and am ready to accept the friendship of all those who seem to me good men.

There are many signs by which I am able to discern good from not good men: first of all the name and general fame of a man is enough evidence to indicate to me how much affection I ought to bestow on a man. Also it has always been the clearest sign of true temperance if a man abstains from pleasures, devotes himself with labor, application, and diligence to those things that are most praiseworthy and not least fatiguing. To know who is good, moreover, and to join many good men to oneself in friendship, what doubt can there be that it is necessary not to remain in solitude but to mingle in the midst of men? I am not praising hereby the man who is equally accessible to all; I do think it wrong not to preserve one's dignity. It is a mistake to apply either severity or affability where and when these are not suitable. Some men irritate people by their aloofness, others displease because they behave like public welcomers, greeting this man, kissing that one, smiling at the next, and presenting altogether too bland, flattering, and servile an appearance as they precipitate themselves to please all who happen to be there. We prefer to show modesty in all our actions. We shall not act so as to lose our dignity and authority in the hope of winning favor, for dignity and authority are two things that always serve the cause of friendship, that are hard to acquire and easy to lose. One frivolous act, one unconsidered word, cancel out the good reputation we have won. Let us therefore, in everything we do, serve the public eye, for it is our task to please the public if we hope to draw an abundance of friends to ourselves, whom we shall choose from the public.

But who can say where there is more diversity, in men's faces or in their hearts? You shall see some who are dignified in manner, temperate in words, slow to reply, severe in judgment, inclined to get angry in argument, proud in competition—these are the common vices of men who are rich and prosperous through fortune. Others are gay, jolly, happy, humorous; others are pacific, reticent, taciturn, humble, full of shame; others are querulous, bold, thoughtless, whimsical, impulsive, and willful. Some, as one of the poet Plautus' characters remarks, are of a double or multiple nature, not only in their mind and heart but in every reply, act, and word that they offer, so that you find it hard to know whether they tend to friendship or to enmity. Such is the variety and corruption of nature among mortals. Nor was Theophrastus wrong, that ancient philosopher of antiquity who had reached the age of ninety and wondered how it could be that the Greeks, all born under one sky, raised according to the same system, and educated by the same discipline and customs, were actually so very different in character. As a result of this variety, some men, apparently to praise you, mention things which are rather blameworthy and to be deprecated than to be praised, yet they do it in so blameless a way that you cannot openly express your displeasure. Others are thoroughly ambiguous in the meaning of everything they do. Others are stubborn and arrogant. Others are treacherous and untrustworthy. They openly praise and applaud you and yield you the place of honor but actually want to raise themselves above you and to make you obedient and subservient to them. So you shall find hardly anyone exists who has not some signal defect of character. In their philosophy of life rare indeed are such as can preserve in words and wishes and deeds the mediocrity praised by the peripatetics, so as to run to no kind of excess, to lean neither toward too much nor toward too little.

I won't deny, however, that virtue helps enormously to make us acceptable and well liked by everyone, since we are all by nature inclined to like virtuous men, and the praises men give them move us strongly to appreciate and to revere them. No one will deny that a man of virtue deserves praise, hence favor and good will. But then I must also say that every difference of life, of customs, habits, age, and occupation, troubles the relationships of men. Such difference impedes the process described by Empedocles, by which love allows the spirits of two persons to run together and unite, like water and milk. Any resemblance, I would say, greatly attracts men and invites them to love. That famous historical character, the Athenian Timon, a bitter and hard man, wanted to make friends with Alcibiades, whose company he said would please him—for it seemed to him this audacious and overstimulated youth would cause many people trouble and disaster. Apemantus [?] too loved a strange man similar to himself. And it is said that to gain the love of barbarians,

Alexander dressed in their kind of scarves and garments. Marcus Cato reminds us how, to gain the affection of his soldiers, he wanted to possess nothing that would make him different from them.

Even as a boy, not so well learned but well taught by nature, I realized that any resemblance among men, even if not praiseworthy, will tend to make mortals of the same sort friends, and now I know it from all these examples. During my first years in Genoa I found this very helpful wisdom, for, having arrived there friendless and without acquaintances, I pretended to be in love with a young girl distinguished among the ladies for her beauty and sensibility. By right of this, I plunged into the company of other noble youths dedicated at that age to the indulgence of love. Among them I gained contacts and friends who are still useful to me and to my kin to this very day.

But some indeed are so prone and so inclined by nature to make friends that the least sign of excellence or of similar interests arouses love and brings out their good will. Others, on the contrary, are slow and restrained in affection. The old, even if similar to yourself in disposition and interests, will yet prove slower and more deliberate than young people in contracting new friendships. Perhaps they are not to be blamed either, since they have experienced in the course of many years that some go to a lot of trouble and cunningly bargain to form friendships only to exploit them and live off the labor and fortune of others. There is hardly anyone who will rush to form a new friendship with you unless he expects that it will be useful to him somehow and bring some hoped for reward. Young people almost all enjoy gathering new affection, and there are not a few poor people of unstable fortune who by artifice make themselves your servants and offer themselves diligently, almost enticing you to like them. Since this is how things are, varied arts, varied maneuvers, are required of you.

Not only are the ears, as Zeno the philosopher said, the best trap for capturing human hearts—by which I take it he meant eloquence, or perhaps the good fame and high commendation with which we are first presented. Charm and personal attractiveness, a cultured way of life, worthy ways and habits suggesting humaneness and readiness for friendship, these are no less valuable nets. You cannot help pleasing men if your every act, word, deed, garment, and bearing show that you are a modest person, will behaved, and graced with virtue. It will happen but seldom then that new groups of people will not come to you every day wanting to become acquainted with you and to frequent your company. If, as Cicero wrote to his brother, the face and visage be the door of our spirit and the entrance thereto, let it never fail to be open to all, liberal and public of spirit. The erudite will come to you, those who know all the subtlest truths and most difficult arts. They will want you as a witness and proclaimer of their fame and excellence. Those who labor at commerce and merchandising will also wish to acquire your useful acquaintance. To wealthy young men who live in splendid style the great problem is to find something agreeable to do in the evening; these will not be the last to grasp at your kindness and pleasing cultivation. With each of these you must remember to imitate Alcibiades, who in Sparta, the land of thrift, of laborious exercises, of great competition for glory, was frugal, rugged, and unlettered; in Ionia delicate and luxurious; in Thrace he learned to drink hard and enjoy himself with those people. He knew so well how to adapt himself to the models set before him that when he was in Persia, a foreign land full of pomp and delighting in show, he surpassed Tissaphernes the king in his haughtiness of manner and magnificent display.

But to adapt quickly to a situation and to make friends it is necessary to study the gestures, words, customs, and conversation of others. One must learn what pleases and what saddens each one, what moves him to anger, to laughter, to talk, and to silence. Truly to know the emotions, to recognize the inclinations of people's temperament and character, one must not lack a special kind of excellent cleverness which is rare in the world. One must be able to tell various true or pretended stories, concerning the method and art of a lover managing his affairs, concerning the diligence, zeal, and eagerness which another applies to gain, how much care, labor, and love another devotes to learning and the study of letters or to the military occupations, or concerning some other actions and concerns such as you think apply to the one listening to you. And while you tell this tale, you must not show your own cleverness or fine eloquence, but tell it in a simple plain way, noting all his expressions, his gestures, and every remark by which he shows what he approves and what he condemns.

Brutus and Cassius, plotting to avenge the liberty of their country, which Gaius Caesar had occupied with arms, perhaps discussed in public questions of this sort—as whether it would be praiseworthy to imperil the Senate in order to benefit the people, or whether civil war would be worse for citizens of the country than tyranny, and thus through arguing they understood that to Statilius, the epicure, and to Favonius, the imitator of Cato, they could communicate but little, nor could they commit their safety to the loyalty and friendship of these men.

The prudence of your ancestor, Battista, of Messer Benedetto Alberti, who was a most cultivated man, was on this level. He sent a certain young man to the western regions to join the companies and engage in their vast business affairs. This was a young man of modest visage, zealous in his work, properly restrained in his conduct of life, in whom, as far as he knew, there was no visible vice. Yet for this very reason, Messer Benedetto wondered if there were not some great fault in this young man, something so serious and horrible that he was especially careful to hide it. He had no doubt that every man, be he the best and most holy in the world—since we are all terrestial creatures and almost constrained to pursue our will and appetite with more intensity than to obey reason with true judgment and integrity—bears some fault and defect. Watching this young man very carefully, therefore, and pondering on his worth, he just once saw him at table after dinner, playing with the bread crumbs on the table in the manner of a man handling dice. He immediately ordered his son Messer Andrea, a young knight who, were he alive today and had kept his characteristic ways and studies, would enjoy no less authority and fame than his father, to tempt the young man first to play at checkers, chess, and similar games which are not dishonorable, and then to try other games, which are more notorious and evil. Thus did he discover that this was not a person to whom he should entrust his wealth and his affairs. Such wiliness is no small advantage if a man would discover even the hidden life and character of others.

When you do know the nature and the habits of those you propose to take for friends and to draw closer to yourself, it is important to be as diligent as Cataline. There was a clever man, a real artist in this respect, who would give to this man a sparrow hawk, to that one weapons, to a third a slave boy, and always just what the person wanted. Often, too, I have seen great good will develop among men who had never seen each other at all, because one had defended the dignity, reputation, and good name of the other against slanderers and detractors. When we have helped a man's friends and agents by our deeds, our counsels and support, and have assisted them in becoming more useful or more admirable to him, when we have seconded their hopes and desires, we may hope for his benevolence.

But really, I am making a fool of myself here, talking to you as if I could instruct you in the gaining of friends, when you are a man who, I know, has always won the love of all men. I don't know how I embarked on this course, and perhaps I pursued this discussion too boldly. It deserved, as I now realize, a more deliberate and erudite style of speech, which I admit is beyond me. What can I say, Lionardo? These remarks are enough, and, if a great store of further precepts is needed to fill out each point, you have those you said were sufficient in themselves to cover the whole subject. You only asserted, which I do not deny is true, that the useful, the honorable, and the pleasurable give rise to friendship and cause it to develop. The man skillful in building new relationships of benevolence toward himself will also know enough to maintain them, to rekindle them when they are dead, and to increase their intensity at will.

Lionardo: Now don't dodge our request with clever tricks, Adovardo. Don't refuse to give Battista and Carlo here the benefit of your completed thought. They, too, long to be endowed with friends as you are. You in no way fall short as a teacher. Your talk as far as you've gone has truly been delightful and rich. You have in fact persuaded me that there is a better hope of learning the art of friendship in living conversation than in books and through scholarship, much as I formerly admired that method.

If you do refuse to gratify our wishes and petitions now, and to satisfy our needs, if you do harden yourself against us now, you contradict your own precepts concerning always trying to gain men's favor and good will. If so, you may be sure we will believe nothing of what you have said. Unless you have decided your thoughts on this subject are mere trivia, then it must be that you have preferred to be loved for your kindness by strangers rather than by your own kin. You'll have proved that you do not have toward us the good will and kindness which others find in you.

Adovardo: I do care to preserve the affection of others but I also cherish as always the love of my own family. If that love were not increased by my merit from day to day, I should count it a disgrace. I have held back here, however, because I would have preferred to offer you some more prepared speech. All that I have been saying seems to me lacking in order. I would have liked to build it up more logically.

Lionardo: What caviler could have found fault with your system so far, Adovardo? First you told us friendship is obtained through our own efforts and those of others. To this you attached the consideration of such acts as put us in demand and bring us favor and good will. You discussed the methods of initiating friendship, and you distinguished among the sorts of persons who are easier or more difficult to get to know and to win to friendship. Here you gave us some clear and unmistakable signs. Then you enabled us wisely to scrutinize the souls of men, and finally you started to discuss the way a better and more solid friendship may be built up on the foundations once these are laid. All this makes a coherent line of argument and a noble structure.

Go on, now, as you were doing, and let your teaching, which I find very valuable and which I know is absent from our books, go on showing us how to increase the number of our friends. Let us then reward your perseverance in teaching by our readiness to learn. If you don't continue, not knowing how to fulfill this duty imposed on us by our love for you, we shall fail to do so. We admit no excuse. We are eager to hear what you have to say. You have spoken of the beginnings of friendship, now tell us how friendship increases and is perfected. Continue.

Adovardo: I have often observed, both among our own citizens and elsewhere, the following trick which men used to gain a large following and, by their favor and support, to climb to great heights and be feared for their power. When these men found that certain persons resisted their blandishments and refused to become intimate with them, they got these people involved in some quarrel or grave and fatal feud or somehow entangled in bitter trouble. Then those who had previously refused to give their friendship freely would find themselves forced by need and by the snare prepared for them to seek their way out of trouble by begging and committing themselves fully to those whom they now recognized as their masters. I would not do this. Nor am I among those who, to increase the appreciation of their kindness, keep you waiting unnecessarily for their help. That, too, would be against our precepts for friendship, for by refusing to do you a favor when asked, I should do you a disservice to gain your affection. I think my present way does not displease you, for I have not made it my aim to act like those who hold back precious stones and will hardly show them, trying to increase their price. But the trouble is I can't imagine you telling the world that I, a man of genius, have discovered new facts in the realm of friendship, things never before known or written about. That idea would make everyone of you, my attentive listeners, laugh. There is no one with a smattering of education who would not reproach me with arrogance for this, and with disdaining the wisdom and writings of our ancestors, who have so long been admired by all men.

Lionardo: I am sure Battista and Carlo here would laugh indeed if, after I told you we wanted to hear what you had to say and would not listen to any excuse, you were now to escape by this trick and not provide us with the teaching we longed and hoped for. In such an informal discussion surely it will be enough if you just help us as we beg of you to do. You ought to realize now, I think, that it is up to you to prove to us that you really don't, as you said, want to make us wait a long time for your kindness.

Adovardo: You win. Listen to me then. The next thing is to see by what means and in what manner a friendship may be increased and made perfect. Then we must ask, if something disturbs the course of the affectionate relationship, what considerations are essential in that situation. Then we shall speak about the ways of restoring a friendship. Then I shall tell you a few devices not known to everyone, by which one may govern relations with both fellow citizens and outsiders in such a way that, as you shall see, one may preserve all the favor and good will which one has first called into being and then cultivated. You shall also hear a little about the way men filled with good will and ardent love should conduct themselves.

These may all be excellent and wise words, if we begin, perhaps, by distinguishing those men most worthy of our zealous efforts to gain their good will and win their friendship. Some people might speak at great length on just this point, and would show off their ingenuity by contriving a great multiplicity of questions: whether rich men make better friends than less fortunate ones; which is the more loyal, a friend who has called upon you in his need or you, who have been generous with him; whether prudent men are slower than foolish ones in forming intimate and close friendships; whether virtuous men love others more than they are loved. And I could go on listing a lot of points like this, but I wonder how useful these questions are really. They might delight the vanity of some people, it is true, who love to shine in scholastic disputations. To us, however, let it suffice to proceed according to the ancient poet, Valerius Martiallis, who wrote the following epigram.

> If you long, perhaps, to be well loved
> Since I see you surrounded by friends,
> Let me, Rufus, also be permitted to join them.
> And do not disdain me because I am new;

All your old friends were once new ones.
Look at newcomers and when you see them,
Think if they might make good old friends.

So, to answer this whole question in brief, this is what I would advise: fortunate and affluent men are indeed extremely useful friends, not so much because they will help you with their wealth and power directly but because, as I have found by experience when I have tried in every country always to become a friend of the highest ranking citizens, they open the way to acquaintance with all lesser and ordinary persons. The latter try to show approval by their benevolence and reverence toward anyone on whom their superior bestows a smile and a willing ear. Men of letters, furthermore, since they long for fame and reputation, will be sure to prove very amiable and generous of their friendship when they meet a man of worth. They consider intense popularity and popularity with many people not very different from the honor they seek. They view a wide acquaintance as something closely related to the fame and repute they pursue. The best persons, however, to give you true friendship and simple affection are the ones who have reciprocated their older friendships well and constantly. They are people who spare no trouble for the sake of a friend, who offer to bear trouble, expense, and injury for his sake, and who never in any danger or difficulty forget the loyalty and duty they owe to him. These are also diligent, zealous, and ingenious in the constant pursuit and cultivation of any advantage, praise, honor, authority, and fame that may come to the man they have undertaken to love. These, it is true, are also few and far between, but who would not rather have two or even one such true friend than a whole pack of false and frivolous ordinary ones?

Perhaps it is the same here as in the other matters that have been discussed—activities which men pursue, property, responsibilities, and worthy works—too many close connections prove hard for a good man to live up to adequately. Thus perhaps it is not admirable in forming ties of affection if one links oneself to a great number of people. The ancient people of Scythia, we hear, had friendships sworn in blood, for, you remember, they were very warlike men and needed the best of friendships to help them in battle. These men used to shed blood by cutting their finger, and the ancient authors admire the spirit of those two or at most three friends, who, having thus dipped the point of a sword in each other's blood and drunk of it together, promised never to betray each other in danger or in any circumstance. The same authors condemn men who would ally themselves with a larger number of such sworn brothers and consider them no better than public prostitutes. Aristotle has an admirable comment on this matter: a private home is not suited to contain thousands of men, and a mere ten or twenty will not be a sufficient number for a city, and likewise ought there to be a correct and definite number of friends suitable for friendship. Do you think we should consider how great a number is neither too heavy nor too feeble?

Lionardo: Now who would refuse to be loved by all men? Who does not thoroughly enjoy finding that he has an almost infinite number of friends? I have always admired that holy and divine precept our priests give us that tells us to love our neighbor as ourselves: that is the procedure of charity which would commend all men to you.

Adovardo: I thank you for your remark, which leads me not to omit here some very lofty considerations. Therefore, now, not to show off my erudition before you, Lionardo, but to clarify my position as much as seems needful to me, I shall briefly review this subject from the beginning. This will, at the same time, clear the path to what I wish to say concerning the cultivation and perfection of friendship. It is called *amicizia* because it is the one experience which requires the affection of soul called *amore.* By the strength of that affection every honorable advantage, joy, and praise of the one you love delights you. So we must investigate whence this affection springs and how, and what it is.

It quite often happens to me that I long for the good fortune and happiness of someone I have never seen, but of whom I have heard that he is learned, good, and pursues excellence. This affection of mine I think you would not call friendship, but rather good will. Likewise not infrequently you may have encountered a person in your circle or your household who was so zealous and attentive in his conduct toward you that you might easily have thought of him as your friend, if only there had been loyalty and comprehensive good will in him. We would not call a temple or basilica perfect if its structure lacked a roof to cover those who enter and to protect them from sun and rain, or if it lacked a porch which served partly to keep out the wind, partly to keep the place separate from other public and profane places. Indeed, perhaps even if it lacked proper ornamentation, it would not be a perfect or finished edifice. Likewise a friendship can never be called perfect and complete if it lacks something. It is not true friendship if the friends do not mutually feel good faith and firm and simple affection of soul, entirely excluding and preventing any suspicion and hate that could in any way trouble their sweet concord and union. I would not call it perfect friendship either if it were not full of the delight of good character and habits.

The love of these things, as we all know, must not only be felt by one but understood and returned by the other. Why? Because, although I may be, and indeed am, eager to be of use to you, and you zealous to serve my advantage and honor, yet it will not be true of us that I can consider you my friend, or that you see me as one who truly loves you and whom you trust, unless you first know what we can hope and expect from each other. This is a kind of knowledge which can only be had by seeing each other and by listening and so to speak experiencing each other's affection. This frequent and close acquaintance, is it the very force and sinews of friendship? No, of course not. Why? Because, as you can see every day, many greet us, attend on us, frequently help us, sometimes indeed give us support and fulfill the duties of friendship, yet we know they have less affection toward us than they pretend. We find that neither affection nor daily familiarity alone constitute complete friendship, but that friendship is rooted in affection. As the chick is hatched out of the egg where it was kept, so love when it has been conceived in the soul takes heart and steps out into the light and common awareness of those who love. This happens when it has been well discerned through seeing each other and through familiarity. Where assiduous care is lacking, however, the warm beginning and vital intensity is later lost or aborted. Affection in friendship, if not diligently nourished, perishes. If the conversation and truthful communication between friends lacks the ardor of affection, how shall the spoiled or empty egg hatch? In such a case, assiduous care will be in vain.

What shall we say? This, then—that affection joined to familiarity constitutes true and perfect friendship? We shall not. Why not? Don't you know that not every sort of familiar acquaintance nor every sort of affection of spirit that is kindled brings true friendship into life? I hope to understand more clearly what this perfect friendship is, and what sort of intimacy and benevolence produces it.

Now I want you, Battista and Carlo, to listen to what follows here. I am repeating for you, not for Lionardo who is a learned man, these principles drawn from the fount of philosophy. I say that the men we find disposed to show us good will and to give us loyal and ready service are of various kinds. Some are inclined to do so because perhaps they think we are excellent, prudent, and wise, so that we merit and they are obliged to give us reverence and to wish us good fortune and every sort of happiness.

Others are generous with us because they expect and hope that our kind favor will bring them assistance in their need, assistance and support in their necessity. Another sort are inclined to feel affection toward us because joy and merriment fill them through our presence. We cast out all their heaviness of heart. We soothe their heavy cares and painful thoughts by our sweet humor, joyfulness, and jokes. I think there is hardly a bond between men's souls which is not essentially one of these three. As you see, these bonds depend on joy and pleasure, or usefulness and reward, or honor, virtue, and excellence of character. All these friends hope for our good fortune and increase. All further our cause.

Yet they do not all have the same end or cause for wishing you happy. The pleasure-bound lovers do not minister and serve you with all that they have for the sake of another, but for the sake of their own satisfaction. Those who are drawn by gifts and the utility which they have found in you or hope to find likewise wish you good and copious fortune in order to benefit from it themselves, not because they want only to see you happy. But no love is greater than that of the person who is not moved by some lovely and desired thing obtained or hoped for from you, or by some benefit which your generosity provides or promises him, but who reveres and honors you—who prizes and delights in your character and in your honorable conduct. Not even these friends will be yours in a lasting and constant way unless your affection was gradually established and developed in practical, pleasant, and honorable intimacy. There are plenty of joy- and pleasure-seeking friends, and a good number who are interested in you for the sake of some personal advantage. Friends who not only pursue our advantage and happiness where they may hope for a reward for their service and loyalty, but who rejoice in our good beyond their own, such friends are naturally rare. Far rarer, however, are the most constant and best friends of all.

You should not really count as a friend any man who is not as close to you and deeply attached through converse with you as he possibly can be. With pleasure-seeking and greedy friends, no perfect good will, based on daily intercourse, is possible. It is a fact everyone knows and rediscovers every day that riches, beauty, power, prosperity, and other graces and gifts of fortune are passing and fragile delights. Good will forged of such weak and perishable stuff can have no constancy or firmness. A man may cultivate the soil around an olive tree to give it a fresh bed, or he may diligently prop up the vine with its husband, the oak; yet this is not affection but the desire to get all possible advantage out of his labor and expense. It's the same in the world, thanks to the corrupt and decadent ways of men. People are, as we know, widely versed in the art of pretending friendship with their words, their faces, and their actions, chiefly in order to reward others for service and gifts. There is hardly a well-laid and sumptuous table but plenty of the people there, filling your household and your daily life, are not friends but false and fraudulent flatterers. I can only advise you to keep them at as great a distance as you can.

There are those, on the other hand, who clearly admire your character and your habits, who respond to you more with feelings than with words, and who would rather increase your honor, your excellence, and your good name than cover you with smiles and blandishments. These you should accept as your chosen intimates and try to keep always by your side. Do not doubt it, virtue always adorns an excellent friendship. Virtue is a holy thing and eternally blesses with the brightness and splendor of fame whoever possesses it. If your friendship was born of virtue and confirmed by constancy, it will be everlasting between you and very happy. You may say truly virtuous men to delight in our virtue are rare, while for men who are not themselves virtuous, virtue is no attraction. True enough. This is what should force you to the conclusion that there is only a small number of men to whom we should open our whole heart, mind, and life and whom we should try by all possible ways and attractions and solicitude to win to our side. For only the few who are truly good can be true and lasting friends.

So we have said now who are the people most worthy of our affection and what is their number. There remains the other point we set out to clarify: how exactly friendship between ourselves and those we have chosen can be encouraged to develop well. But I don't want to be lengthier on this subject, Lionardo, than you were expecting. I felt I had to explain the point to these listeners, who are not as learned as you are. From now on I shall be brief. But what is it, Lionardo, that weighed on your spirit just now and made you sigh, as though some sadness had entered your mind?

Lionardo: On the contrary, Adovardo, what I gather from what you have said makes me very happy about what I think is probably coming next. At the same time it is true that I do grieve, for certain members of our own Alberti family, it seems, may be such that the excellent ideas you have been expressing so well would leave them cold and disdainful. If they were not so thoughtless, credulous, precipitous, and stubborn in the

pursuit of every whim, perhaps they would not elevate every presumptuous stranger who causes them a moment's laughter. They would not prize
such persons above the most modest and decent of their own kin, who are
only too loving and reverent, as they know full well. I have no doubt that
if certain people listened to you, they would be less lavish and prodigal in
their gifts to those who do not merit it.

It also seems clear to me, from what Adovardo says, that the man who
makes friends in masses ends up living alone in his old age, abandoned
also by those whom he always rejected with cruelty and lack of family
feeling. I can only expect to see the man who persists in that way of life,
insulting his own kin and loving lascivious men, end in disgrace. By good
men he will be condemned, and even by those flatterers who used to hang
around him he will be despised and held in contempt. Who indeed but
this supremely foolish creature could fail to recognize the danger and the
impediment of dishonest and dishonorable friends, whatever the state of
his fortunes. Greedy, lascivious, and reckless, they will do nothing for you
in time of adversity, and if you are lifted to high places by fortune, they
will bring infamy and hate your way. But go on, Adovardo, God forbid
our family should fall into such misfortune and distress.

Adovardo: Ah me, it is a fortunate person who when he is flooded with
wealth and abundance knows how to give his favor to loyalty, constancy,
and honor rather than to the frivolous flattery and to the false obsequiousness of importunate and corrupt scoundrels. But let us hope for
better things for our family, as long as life is granted to Lorenzo and to
ourselves.

The greatest friendship, as I have been saying, must lack nothing; if
necessary parts are missing, it cannot be called complete. What the
necessary attributes of friendship are, we have already made clear: a true,
simple, and open affection, pleasant intimacy and converse in which are
honorably shared the interests, opinions, and fortunes of both friends,
and, to cement all this, every kind of ready service. If a man desires the
increase of a friendship, we conclude, he must direct its path toward
perfection. Perfect it will be when it is maintained primarily neither by its
utility nor by the pleasure it provides, but only by the shared pursuit of
virtue. Do you agree?

Lionardo: I agree.

Adovardo: My first duty, then, is to see that anyone whose friendship I
should like to win knows that only virtue can attract my heart and will.
Second, I must not tolerate in any friend of mine the blemish of vice or of

any shameful thing. I must long with all my heart for him to achieve every excellence and noble grace so that our friendship, heightened from day to day by our mutual pursuit of excellence, may grow and flourish. Our habit of seeing each other frequently, based on worthy lives, will further strengthen our friendship and will make it strong enough to withstand any suspicion or the inclination to gradual oblivion.

Lionardo: Yes, but who is so modest and so pliable that he delights in being made better by anyone else? I can't think of anyone who would really be grateful to his friend for pointing out some fault the friend might see in him, for nobody really minds his own vices much.

Adovardo: You do admit that a man full of vices cannot really be accounted a friend?

Lionardo: And if I do?

Adovardo: I'll tell you after you have answered me this: which do you think is better, to withdraw one's affection or to try to improve the person you care for?

Lionardo: If I saw no way of improving him without arousing hatred, I would rather save what good will he might bear me. The fact does seem to be, as they say, that service wins friends and truth generates hatred.

Adovardo: As if there weren't many ways of correcting a man's conduct by the words one uses in talking with him. If a person knows you are entirely loyal and really love him, hardly anyone, I think, would be so intemperate and full of self-indulgence and petulance that he would not be influenced. If he sees that you, a serious and consistent man, show disgust at the behavior of lascivious people and repulsion from bestial ones, he will want to seem as different as possible from those whom you chide severely and vividly condemn. If it does happen that you have to correct your friend, how can a good man shun the opportunity to make someone he loves a better citizen. All he has to do is speak wisely and temperately, without bitterness, as best he can. I have no doubt, however, that if a man tries to protect his friend from shame and disgrace by timely words of prudence and charity, his friend will love him more for this than for keeping quiet.

Of course if you are sure he has such a hard head that, as you suggest, there is nothing you could do to make him more worthy of your friendship, you will not be able to attract him to some virtue beyond his capacity. Yet such improvement would, as I say, permit a better and, indeed, a most perfect friendship between you. If, however, you really could not with all your zeal make the man you care for become a praiseworthy one, and if all your diligence cannot separate him from his shameful vice so that friendship would be possible, then I think you would act most prudently to cut him off entirely from yourself. Otherwise you let him hurt your name and fame and be in effect your enemy. If we would not seek the friendship of a man who would harm and diminish our possessions, the same certainly applies to one who would take away the most precious thing we have, our name, our fame, our authority among men. That is what threatens us when men who are full of vice remain our friends and intimates. It may be you should feel more repugnance for such a man than for an open enemy. There will be room elsewhere to discuss at greater length the harm that friendship and intimacy with scoundrels brings down on you.

Now our next problem is how to dissolve our friendship with this sort of person without falling into some kind of trouble. Since one can rarely give up knowing such people without kindling hatred in them, we shall also look into the methods of combatting hatred. It is a matter I mentioned earlier which should be third on our agenda. We have stated, then, how friendship is acquired, and in what way and by what means and with whom—for they must be persons suited to enjoy true friendship—we may hope to bring a true and perfect friendship to fruition. Now we shall consider the method by which friendship is dissolved and the way enmity may be endured. Does that seem to you a sensible way for me to proceed?

Lionardo: It does.

Adovardo: Listen, then. To me there is always something reprehensible in someone showing hate for a person he formerly loved. It reflects too much inconstancy, a truly effeminate trait. It seems to show an odiously irresponsible spirit to be unable to go on loving a person you once thought worthy of your love. That is the way it is: who can help feeling critical of a man who either at first chose a friend imprudently and unthinkingly allowed himself to love an unworthy person, or later was so light and inconstant that he did not continue in a manly way to show the prescribed constancy in perpetuating the friendship he had initiated? Is anyone so stupid that he does not count a friend as one of his finest and dearest possessions? What small or light thing could move him, if to lose a friend did not truly grieve him?

So what can we say? And yet it does not take a much stronger reason to make you destroy a friendship yourself than others mention when they try to persuade you to give one up. I think we should agree here and now among ourselves that if a man were perfectly wise, he would not ever stop loving someone once he had declared himself his friend. I confess, however, that not all mortals deserve to be inscribed in the ranks of the perfectly wise, while all men, as if by nature, seem to want friends and to be prone to form friendships. And I shall assert to you what you yourself would say, that things often do happen to make a good and honorable man, one who loves a good name and high praise, one who is attached to virtue and to his country, feel that he would prefer to have one whom he loves be less close to him than formerly. When that happens it is not wrong in a wise and temperate manner to loosen the ties of friendship.

First of all, then, we must ascertain for what reasons it becomes permissible to view as a mere stranger one who was formerly a most intimate friend. This means we must recall what we said above, that friendship arises from affection—honorable acquaintance having kindled in our hearts good will toward one who seems to deserve it. Anyone who is essentially reasonable can hardly help finding dishonorable and wicked men repugnant. If, moreover, a person feels drawn to another for the satisfaction of some dishonorable wish, he does not, indeed, love him, but only wishes to see him happy and fortunate for the sake of some personal advantage of his own. All this, which I have summed up most briefly here, proves that true affection is necessarily based on honor and is inseparable from virtue. When, on the other hand, we are drawn to those who do deserve it, different little fires and sparks of love enter our minds and kindle greater flames from day to day as acquaintance and intimacy feed the fire with zealous and eager kindness and the open exchange of affection. If virtue, indeed, is the source of affection, and no one should doubt that virtue is a very holy and sacred thing, it does not offend me to believe also that affection is something like virtue itself, something holy and sacred. Now it cannot be that religion does not encompass virtue. There has never been a religious man who did not first love virtue, nor will you ever find a virtuous man who is not deeply religious. So, without offense, let us place righteous affection among the holy and sacred things.

Now I think we may properly draw an analogy here with marriage. The priests say that in that relationship there are two essential bonds: one is the bond of two souls that seek to be virtuously united in one. This, they clearly prove, is a divine thing—though their arguments would be too long to set forth here and not particularly relevant either. This bond, as they assert, is not for us mortals to break. The other bond that unites two persons in marriage is the work of procreation, and if an impediment appears in this connection which is serious enough so that any wise person might, after thinking it over, decide to avoid such relations, then we are permitted to sever this bond. Likewise in friendship one cannot avoid the sense that it is a matter of piety always to preserve one's affection, to sustain it as long as possible. It is the duty of humanity, and still demanded by its uncorrupted continuing essence, that we love any man who shares life with us. I admit, however, that a man who has the vices and conduct of an animal can no longer be considered a man, but only a monster.

It remains our obligation not to hate anyone who has been even more than a fellow man to us, who has been linked to us by the bond of affection which we have just called sacred. But if intimacy causes any real distress such as, even under pressure, a good and wise man would not tolerate, I do not deny you the freedom to end that part of the relationship in accordance with rational considerations. The only condition is that with the end of actual intimacy you still preserve your good will in a spirit of honor and piety. I do think that it is against religion and contrary to your moral obligations ever to burst into anger on account of some offense, to undertake revenge of some kind, to break faith with the person, or to betray any secret which most sacred affection caused him, as it were, to deposit with you. Such a trust must always be honored and a secret remain a secret with you. Trust and confidences are part of the precious friendship which once existed between you, though it no longer exists. One may hope that it will be restored; it is indeed a good and worthy deed to attempt to restore it. Even if there is no chance of restoring the friendship, however, I must condemn the man who would do perfidious harm to his former friend. I think it the same as the act of one who, to harm an enemy, would injure a loyal friend.

The Assyrian Gobyas, in Xenophon, told Cyrus, the king of the Persians, that the reason he lived in exile from his own country was his inability to tolerate the presence in his kingdom of a man who had killed his own dear son. He could, in fact, have killed this man, but he would not even do him any injury, because he has been the close friend of his father. Cicero, speaking in the Senate, inveighed greatly against Mark Anthony, because, counter to every moral dictate of civilized life, he had published some private letters formerly received from Cicero. Nor is it right, because of some offense received, to make public past conversations with the man who was your friend. I think when they thus assert certain obligations as due to the past friendship, they mean to affirm that these are continuing obligations due to virtue and to the sweetness of former association. If I have convinced you of these things, which I have stated very briefly, and therefore perhaps obscurely, then, Lionardo, the question is when we have the right to end all this, and under what circumstances we ought to end or somewhat to diminish a formerly happy friendship and give up the gentle and delightful habits of affection.

Lionardo: Now who would need more convincing on a point which no man of good education doubts, namely that love combined with virtue is to be regarded as a high and sacred thing. After all, who could fail to render tribute, as you suggest, to former and so to speak exhausted friendship? We are obliged, after all, to preserve some faith and to fulfill the duties of honor even toward our enemies. Who could deny that breaking faith does more harm to the man who thus falls into wicked ways than to the one who is hit by misfortune due to treachery. That point is proved by the same arguments which show that vice is more damaging to him who harbors it than poverty or any sort of pain.

Perhaps this is the place to demonstrate, however, what disadvantages and troubles are serious enough to give good men justification for dissolving a friendship. I wonder if you will support the common view that money is practically the first consideration in human affairs and most to be valued. I wonder whether you would agree with those rather shrewd characters who, as soon as they see a friend pressed by need, suspect that they will be asked for help and promptly block off all access to themselves to one who had put some hope in them. They then accuse the times, say they are having a lot of unexpected difficulties, and pretend to be in debt. If you do approve the subterfuges of such people, I shall not admire you for it. Still more strongly would I differ from anyone who saw no harm in the practice of so many men one sees, men who, when they are asked for help, find it most convenient to free themselves by offending and alienating their old friend in some way and leaving him insulted.

Adovardo: How disgusting! And how true. Nothing is further from the mind of a just and good man than to see no evil in such vile and ugly cunning. It is altogether foreign to one who deserves and who seeks real friends. Does not the ancient opinion of some philosophers run that friendship was invented precisely so that we might assist one another in our ever recurring needs and wants? Doesn't that help to persuade us that it is the duty of friendship to assist a friend in need? Men are always praising persons of such fine and moral disposition that they do not wait to be asked or begged but gladly and quickly, in a liberal spirit, offer a friend whatever he needs and more. Anyone humane and reasonable is repelled by the churlish character who, in order to save the whole of his little hoard, lets his life be somehow shameful and contemptible. The truly virtuous and liberal man counts it a part of his good fortune to have an opportunity gladly to distribute his gifts. If these things are so, to whom should we be more pleased to give than to our friends? Where is avarice more shameful than when it is shown toward those with whom they say we ought to hold all things in common? So how could I possibly put among serious grievances this true and worthy use of liberality, namely helping to supply the necessities of those who hope in me and love me? Why, men still praise certain persons who exposed their very lives in order to fulfill their whole duty to friendship. They say, too, that a true friend will not spare property or labor or his own person in order to benefit the one he loves.

Lionardo: What then are the heavy burdens which we may refuse to carry?

Adovardo: Does it seem a heavy burden to lose one's property for one's friend's sake?

Lionardo: To many it does.

Adovardo: Do grief and misery seem heavy if these keep a friend happy and content?

Lionardo: They do, to many.

Adovardo: Does it seem hard to expose oneself to fatal risks for the safety of a friend?

Lionardo: Hard? And how!

Adovardo: Yet how many gladly venture on the stormy seas, and willingly on land risk death in war, in order to gather riches?

Lionardo: Many do.

Adovardo: I don't know about other people, but I myself would certainly risk much wealth in the hope of gaining honor.

Lionardo: And we like you, I assure you, are of the number that thirsts eagerly for praise.

Adovardo: And what do you think about other men?

Lionardo: I think hardly anyone not altogether barbarous would hesitate to be prodigal for the sake of praise and honor.

Adovardo: If that is our opinion, we shall say that, in the hope of praise and fame, we do not much care for money.

Lionardo: Agreed, certainly.

Adovadro: Anything else is negligible compared to a bad name.

Lionardo: It seems true.

Adovardo: So we may call a bad name a heavy burden.

Lionardo: We think so.

Adovardo: And not to fall into ill repute, we shall practice the wiles of the man we were just talking about. We shall close every access to ourselves, placing prudence and honor on guard.

Lionardo: I admire you. It seems to me, then, that this is your answer: if our friend, by his vices, imperils our reputation, we recognize the evil of this thing. We may to keep from getting some sort of bad name segregate ourselves from him and try to put plenty of distance between us.

Adovardo: That's what I meant. Nonetheless, not every sort of vice seems to me to merit the destruction of a friendship. There is an old proverb: "If you cannot tolerate a fault in your friend, the fault is yours."

Lionardo: Yet I think perhaps it is a wise saying that goes, "He who tolerates his friend's vice by his silence makes the vice his own."

Adovardo: Look how hard I've been trying to be brief and perhaps arguing this question in too compressed a way. I shall not go on at length, therefore, to explicate these two sayings and to decide which is the better. Here is the reasonable formula I myself like to apply: when it comes to the faults that anyone may have, faults that do no harm to anyone but the man himself, like drinking, lechery, and such pleasures, I think if your admonitions don't seem to help, the saying of the common people is right: "He's your friend, take him as he is." If he harbors more serious vices, however, of the sort that may bring disgrace upon you, like abetting a thief, sheltering a traitor to one's country, giving encouragement to a pirate, we want no part of such serious crimes. Do you agree?

Lionardo: Heartily.

Adovardo: Now we have seen the reasons that suffice or do not suffice to make us dissolve a friendship. And we have also seen that it is only the active relations, not the good will, that we have a right to end. Now we must consider the method of dissolving such an intimacy. The word "dissolve" itself suggests that what is wanted here is not, as they say, to tear the bonds that unite you, but to untie them knot by knot. When I consider this problem of thinning out the frequent contacts and lessening the intimacy between people, I think it is excellent to imitate the good father of a family who realizes one day that he is overburdened with expenses. He does not cut down the family budget completely in one day, lest he cause general astonishment. In the course of time, instead, he sends away the groom and keeps only one pair of horses, another day he dismisses some servants whose services are expendable. He eventually sends away even members of the family to engage in this or that distant enterprise. Livy tells us that Gaius Marcus Rutilius found out about a number of persons in his army who had decided to invade Capua, a fruitful and most abundant country. Rutilius hereupon pretended that he suspected nothing, but at various times sent the leaders of the conspiracy, one after the other, to different places on pretended errands of great importance. He could not, I think, have simply exterminated the lot of them at once without causing violent dissension and danger. It's like trying to put out a great fire in a fireplace where too much wood has been set aflame. Rather than flooding the fireplace, you would do well to pick out one log after another and lay it in water. This puts the fire out faster, expends less labor, less water, and less smoke, and does not splash water and dirt all over the floor. Besides, you can keep as much fire and as many logs going as you want.

Friendship is the same sort of thing. One day you may give up the weapons, horses, hawks, and dogs for which a certain man has eagerly sought out your companionship. Later you may gradually give him less support and assistance in other matters than you used to do. As time goes by you turn your activities in new directions, until he dissociates himself from you almost of his own volition, and with no offense taken. You can understand that a strong affection once kindled is not suddenly extinguishable by the cessation of all social contact. That would inevitably produce clouds of emotional turbulence and more than a little spilling over of resentment. That's why I admire anyone who knows how to quench the fire while saving a few logs where good will still glows and may endure—I don't know why—a long time even without further contact to feed it.

Discontinuing one aspect of the friendship after another, we do much as architects do when they build a tower. First they let the foundations settle, then raise the walls to a certain point, then wait for them—as they put it—to get their teeth. After that they go on building safely on top of all this and finish the edifice. If they had labored in one span of time and without interruptions, however, the first foundations on the earth would surely have loosened, the weight of the superstructure would have further cracked them apart, and the whole structure would finally have caved in and crumbled to earth. We should likewise reduce the relationship first by a reduction of contact, then by cautiously making other breaks, and perhaps end by not producing enmity or new, more serious troubles. I have seen men too suddenly and abruptly excluded think themselves so deeply insulted that they did not feel obliged to stop at anything to get revenge.

Lionardo: It is contrary to reason for such a sudden hatred to spring up unless some great offense occurred. Why else should I suddenly close my door to one who just before had access to the innermost recesses of my being. But some people are by nature so ready to fly into an indignant rage and so spiteful in their holding of grudges that for the slightest offense they will become your deadly enemies. It is fair to say of these persons that the slightest ripple upsets the frail craft.

Adovardo: Fair enough, and the more we know they are this kind of demanding people, the more cautiously we must proceed so that they cannot make enemies of us even if they want to. Yet I could not blame a person who would proudly choose to throw off an insolent person at once rather than tolerate vileness close to him and practically encourage behavior that disgraces him.

Lionardo: I am fully persuaded by your arguments, yet I suspect you may find many people would rather shelter a perfidious traitor than send him off to malign them publicly elsewhere. You don't want to keep a wild beast chained up in your house and feed it, as they say, but you also don't like to set it free to roam hungry through the streets. That was a point made by Philip of Macedon to his son Alexander when the latter, with the encouragement of his friends, sent away a carping and spiteful attendant. Philip said it was not the best idea thus to give him a reason for running around speaking evil where people did not know his character.

Adovardo: I don't think a man of real virtue and of upright spirit would, out of respect for the vanity of others, allow himself to seem either excessively timid or not sufficiently interested in being good rather than seeming so. You know that a man of spirit would rather be excellent than just maintain a good façade. Nor will a good man doubt, I think, that his reputation is bright and strong enough to countervail the insinuations and attacks of one malicious person. Only men of bad character are afraid that someone who knows will, as you say, dare tell the world about his vices.

Lionardo: Isn't it possible that false calumniators will be believed?

Adovardo: It certainly is. As they say, once you have heard something, you can't unhear it. Men don't demand that what they hear be true, but only that it be probable. As to what is probable, they consult their other experience of life and human character.

Lionardo: Then what will a good and cultivated person do? Will he perhaps just ignore the troublesome pest, or will he attempt, as many do, to harm him in his turn and so to blunt and bridle his garrulous loose tongue?

Adovardo: You are compelling me to talk about things that I have been willing to omit. I wanted to run quickly and succinctly through this material, fulfilling this task you imposed on me of describing my views on friendship. Now you are drawing me into a discussion of enmity. You know it is enmity that demands of us the discipline and method needed to endure injuries or to obtain revenge.

Some injuries strike our person, others endanger us, as we think, by harming our possessions. Among our possessions we may count particularly our fame, our dignity, our name, and the authority we exercise. These are precious and invaluable adornments by which we arrive at happiness and glory among men. Some people make the mistake of viewing as harmful and dangerous what they ought to ignore as unimportant. They involve themselves in a fight with unworthy opponents. What sensible person engaged in speaking publicly on high topics, demonstrating his genius and his eloquence, would take for a personal enemy the ass that happened to bray nearby? Would he plan a revenge on this intruder? Or at the Lupercalian games described by Plutarch, when the noble and politically active young men ran naked through the streets and made the multitude yield them a path by blows—can you imagine one foolish enough to stop fighting as he ran in order to quiet a dog that barked at his heels? That's what it is like when a man whose life is full of virtue and who is engaged in noble actions, one who is winning real glory, pays excessive attention to the voice of some brutish critic. That's what it is like for a man engaged in the pursuit of glory by great deeds to interrupt everything in order to occupy himself with the refutation of a loud-mouthed and base-hearted calumniator. Our real business is always to exhibit by the very excellence of our conduct that such persons are liars and frauds.

Pyrrhus, the king of the Epirotes, asked certain young men whether they had, as he had been told, spoken slanders about him while in their cups. To this they replied, "We did, a good deal—and had we been drunker still, we would have said even sillier things." I do think he laughed. Philip, the father of Alexander of Macedon, on the other hand, said to the Athenian orators: "I thank you for maligning me. I owe it to you that I have become a better man from day to day, always striving by word and deed to prove you liars." His son Alexander, too, replied to an accusation from a man who was always speaking ill of him: "It is only proper for a king to do good and to hear evil." But if kings, who have the power to avenge insults and to strike heavily the insolence of their disloyal subjects, are admired for paying small attention instead, I think it is clear that any good man is blameless if he likewise ignores those whom, moreover, he could not punish without serious danger to himself.

Lionardo: This is the lesson I conclude that we may draw: namely, we should not take the backbiting and slander of irresponsible men as a serious affront to provoke us to enmity and vengeance. . . . They say that of two who had spoken ill of him [Alexander], he condemned the one whose character was grave and responsible, but left unpunished the fool who had never been able to hold his tongue or tempered his words. Now it seems that if someone responsible and mature should spread some calumny to undermine our fame and reputation, then perhaps we should take it seriously.

Adovardo: But what responsible man does not scorn to invent truths? There is nothing more contrary to a responsible and mature citizen's character than this kind of loose talk. It's disgraceful and it's below a real man. This is a kind of folly we should take trouble to avoid! Can you imagine any greater madness than to exhibit yourself to the world as a vicious, cowardly, and shameful creature? What disgusting malice, for no personal advantage and at great risk to yourself, to injure an innocent man. Can you think of a vice abominable enough to equal it? Thievery, larceny, rapine at least contribute something to the material well-being of the one who commits them, and thus have some excuse. The evilspeaker gets nothing but hatred and blame. I avoid such a man like the poisonous pest he is. It is contemptible and absolutely intolerable for a man to seek his vengeance, even for a grave offense, by words, let alone by falsehoods. To show boldness in chatter only is the feminine way. It is appropriate to creatures lacking any kind of spiritual fortitude. Cyrus, king of the Persians, killed with a dagger thrust the young man in his army he heard making ugly remarks about Alexander, their enemy. "I feed you to fight with your sword against Alexander," he said, "not with vicious stories." Now what kind of man could it be who would not regret his own vileness, seeing, in contrast to his own words, the clear and obvious virtues of the man he had reviled?

Lionardo: There are many people considered wise these days who view as among the gravest injuries ever done them any words that lack respect and reverence. They think that the man who offends them in this way is a capital enemy and spare no means to avenge themselves. They say, and you yourself just approved the view a short time ago, that nothing is so highly to be prized as fame, and that words can fly from place to place and do such damage that no arrow of Jove is as bad. They aptly cite the ancient opinion of Zeno: "If I care nothing for the evil spoken of me, I shall not hear the praises either."

Another ancient philosopher, Chilon, also impresses them with his ideas—this is the one who expired with joy when he saw his son crowned victor at the Olympic games. He once made the remark that three things are the most difficult in the world: to keep secrets, to make good use of leisure, and to know how to tolerate injuries. They tend to agree with Coriolanus, who declared the proper actions of a great soul and of fortitude were self-discipline, strength of will, superiority to all men, refusal to be subjected to anyone. They also find no fault with Alcibiades for his response when, greatly offended against by his own countrymen, he fled on that account to the Lacedaemonians. He would act in such a way on the battlefield that they would realize he was still alive—so he said and so he did. They like the notion of the poet Publius: "Accept an injury and you invite another." They believe in the necessity of meeting injuries with force, and they like to cite the words of Heraclitus to their purpose where he says: "Injuries must be canceled out." This kind of people also approve the saying: "If you tolerate the offense, you favor the unjust man." And they praise Agathocles, who, when he had conquered a city and taken it, sold many of his own men for the bad words they had uttered against him while fighting. When someone asked him, "Oh little potter," for his father, as you know, was a master maker of the clay vessels known as *figuli,* "how are you paying these soldiers of yours?" Agathocles only answered, "I have conquered them." When he sold them he added, "If you do not show humility in the future, I shall accuse you to your masters." Isocrates, writing to Demonicus, declared that one should not fail in good will to one's friends or in hatred to one's enemies. And so there are many more they could cite who put revenge among the highest glories of a virile and heroic heart. In addition they point out that no family will be much honored if it does not know how to avenge injuries and to make itself feared.

Adovardo: If those people were not excessively proud and all too violent, they would see more clearly what enmity really is and to what extent a good man may legitimately seek revenge. They would realize first of all, I think, what a terrible thing enmity is and that one should strive by all means to avoid it. The ancients used to say that the amatory passion known as love is a thing easily experienced if you want it, but not so easily gotten rid of. We can surely say the same here of enmity. It is easy enough to start, but it can't be ended without great trouble and danger. Enmity is defined as a deep-seated and serious hatred. We may, perhaps, say that hatred originates in envy—the vice of a man who cannot bear to see people enjoying good things which he thinks undeserved. Envy usually arises as a result of our ambition and our by no means retiring character, for we like to surpass others and perhaps act proudly and even ungraciously toward those who surround us. They in their turn, from envying us, turn to hating us profoundly. Some would conclude that enmity arises, therefore, through our own fault. Yet I have often seen good men hated.

Aristophanes the poet was an enemy to Socrates and wrote a comedy directed against this very good and holy man. Plato the philosopher and Xenophon the orator, Aeschines and Aristippus, the friends of Socrates, were great enemies to each other. Cato, the excellent citizen and holy guardian of the republic, was accused by his enemies of no less than fifty capital crimes. We read how he stood on trial at the age of eighty and made the comment that it was hard for him to plead for his life now with a new and unfamiliar generation of citizens when he had lived so long among their fathers.

We also read, in Aulus Gellius and others, that there have been a certain number of persons who suddenly shifted from enmity to unexpected friendship. This is an experience which may make some people doubt that these intense passions spring up as a result of our efforts. They may seem, in fact, to manifest the power of fate and of the stars. They say that Aristides, from earliest childhood as if by some trait of his innate disposition, felt a deadly hatred for Themistocles, the son of Neocles. Aratus of Sicyon intensely and actively hated any tyrant, as if by his very nature. Yet just as a priest had once predicted of him when he found two gall bladders in the entrails of the victim, he became closely allied with a former archenemy. It happened, as though prompted by the fates, that this Aratus became the close friend of Antigonus the tyrant. Once, indeed, as he and Antigonus lay under one cover to keep out the cold, he smilingly told him the story of the prediction, and he was very pleased that the gods had ordained it thus. We read also that as if by destiny and through heavenly decrees, Africanus and Gracchus, Lepidus and Flaccus, without intermediaries, transformed their feuds into alliances.

So let us not try to argue here about the ultimate causes and, as they say, the elements of enmity. Whether enmity springs from a defect of our own character or from the malice of others, or arises by the ordained plan of heaven, I do see that if a man is my enemy, he will do in all things the opposite of what my friend will do. The man who loves me will wish me well and will grieve for my sorrows, seeking and delighting in my good. My enemy desires my unhappiness and suffering, rejoices at my every misfortune, pursues and enjoys whatever disturbs and disrupts my honorable enterprises and the growth of my fame. My friend will be pleased to see me active and happy. It will be a delight to him to discuss with me those things which are of use to me, which give us both pleasure and which tend to the fulfillment of my wishes and the improvement of my character. My enemy, on the other hand, becomes upset when he sees me. He only hopes and attempts to say and do things in my presence which will offend me, show contempt, make my mind depressed and anxious, cause me to suffer and to grieve. My friend tells me all his secrets, keeps mine very secret whether he is near me or not, keeps my welfare in mind, and wishes deeply to benefit me. My very health and life are a burden to my enemy. We may say that if friendship is a union of hearts which makes men hold all human and divine things in common, enmity, on the other hand, is the entire alienation and opposition of minds and wills.

Clearly if someone has an enemy in this sense, I cannot blame him for wishing in all reasonableness and wisdom to strike back against the offenses done him rather than to endure everything out of indolence or cowardice. Yet I shall continue to condemn excessive violence or bitterness of feeling in the pursuit of revenge. Any outburst of wrath and quarreling that brings subsequent trouble and disgrace seems to me unworthy of a great soul and a real man. That is not revenge, indeed, but the very fulfillment and accomplishment of the precise wishes and hopes of our enemies, since they wish us every evil. Some people say that anger is the means of putting strength into action. Pythagoras and quite a number of other philosophers, however, deny that a wise man is ever kindled to anger, whether against free man or slave. I might cite Architas the Tarentine or Plato and others highly praised in the historians, who all preferred never to act in anger. I shall only say that it is not the action of a constant and responsible man or a sign of mature and well-considered judgment to embark on some sort of violence out of anger.

"There is always an opportunity for revenge," Quintus Catulus said to Gaius Piso, "if you wait long enough." In our Etruria, too, there is a proverb: "No weapon outdoes a stalk of straw split by arrows while you wait." I can't admire people who, even for a just cause, utter excited and threatening speeches and embark without forethought on an unconsidered course of action. They seem like that ancient Bactrian proverb which Corabes the Persian mentioned to his host, Darius: "The scared dog barks more than the fierce one." They say, too, that deep waters are quieter than shallow ones. So men of resolution with minds guided by deep thought are more dangerous to their enemies in their silence than if they utter threats. I think the indignation of true men is like a bow: the harder it is to bend by anger and the greater the force of the offense required to bend it, the harder the blow when they do strike back.

Many people will disagree strongly with me here. They think it high spirited to keep up a fight, once it is on, with blood and spirit. They say it is a sign of strength to refuse to overlook an insult. They agree with Coriolanus: when he was wounded in battle and his friends asked him to retire behind the lines and tend to his injuries, Coriolanus said, "When you're winning, you don't get tired." Still better do they like the reply of the Romans to the ambassadors of the Volsci: "You were first to have recourse to arms; we, however, will be the last to set them down." Yet I don't believe in any sort of dissension, particularly when it is going to do harm to the man who embarks on a feud. Pyrrhus, when he had lost many of his friends in a victorious battle, said, "one more victory over the Romans, and we shall all be dead." It is a heavy victory that brings us harm, and not a desirable one.

Who could approve of that prefect Butes who was besieged by Cimon in Thrace and out of stubborness set fire to the earth to perish in the flames with many noble Persian princes. I won't mention those Talanians, of whom Sallust tells, who were pressed by Metellus, and therefore destroyed themselves with all their possessions by fire. The Numantians did the same thing when overcome by Scipio, as did the famous Gauls in the foothills of the Alps when they were defeated by Marius. There were, likewise, the women of the Ambronitians, who dashed their children's heads on the rocks and killed themselves upon their bodies. There were also the companions of Joshua of Jerusalem who were besieged in a cave and slew one another by lot.

The Lycians, whom Brutus destroyed, had been hunted down and besieged at Xanthus, but were still stubborn. First they set fire to the siege machinery the Romans had placed around them, and then, seeing the flames blowing back and catching their own houses even toward the center of their city, they almost seemed to rejoice in their calamity. Old and young, men and women of every age, they ran out and ferociously fought off the Romans, who out of pity wanted to help them put out the enormous and extensive fire. The obstinacy and pride of those Lycians, however, as they tell us, made them even spread the fire with their own hands. They were pleased all to perish and become ashes together with their city.

There have indeed been so many stubborn and merciless souls who preferred to lose their life rather than be defeated that it would take too long to go on mentioning them and reproving them for it here. In all cases I should deny that this was true manliness and resolution, for all were so afraid of losing what they had that they preferred to lose everything in bitter and stubborn and perfectly fruitless opposition. As to the notion that, as they claimed, they preferred death to slavery, this only shows that they knew nothing of true fortitude. I should not care to listen to men who tried to convince me that the nobility of a strong spirit does not lie in being able to bear every sorrow and every blow that fortune deals.

This discussion, however, does not pertain to our subject or to the closely woven brevity I have tried to maintain. Let me just say this: no contention pleases me, especially where there is more danger in the struggle for victory than reward in the victory. I shall never see anything but folly in a man's wanting to resist an enemy who is stronger than himself. In a wise man the hope of victory, moreover, will never be inflated by his longing for a fight. I notice that the bull, the horse, and other beasts can rarely be provoked to a fight until they feel a blow. I am resolved always to praise the man who, even when he does fight, wants chiefly to keep his name and fame free of any dishonor or blame.

I don't think one is always justified in fighting and in unleashing great and bitter hatred. Alexander, the son of Philip of Macedon, was encouraged by his father to compete in those contests they called the Olympic games, but he refused to do so because there were no peers for him to contend with. Cato is praised particularly because of his behavior toward Scipio, as well as for the rest of his conduct. For Scipio, being his junior, resented him, but Cato treated him with no more severity than was usual toward a boy still young and immature. I certainly think, as Cicero said, that the disposition of the magnanimous man is merciful, not at all hard and obstinate. You ought to realize that inability to put away hatred is the result either of fear or of a rigid and boorish character. If people think you cannot put away or forget an enmity, it sometimes happens that they become your deadly and merciless enemies for this very reason. Almost all men look upon one who is excessively resentful as a mad monster, for he burns with hatred and only dreams of revenge. Yet, as Cicero says, we are by our very nature made to meet necessities and to repel danger. Unless we are declared enemies, I don't know why, we will even come to the aid of people quite unrelated to ourselves and act like ardent friends in a moment of need.

Who can help loathing the cruel peoples who once lived beyond the Nomads, men who drank the blood of a wounded enemy? The Zelons used the skulls of their dead enemies as dishes. The Scythians whom Herodotus describes sacrificed one of every ten captured enemies instead of a sheep. They allowed only such as carried the head of a slain foe to participate in their feast. Of the skins of their enemies, they fashioned quivers for their arrows and other things. I can see your disgust when I merely describe them. Always shun every sort of cruelty therefore. If it does come about that one must avenge oneself with harsh deeds, at least if one has the wisdom one can always use temperate words. One can show by one's manner that it is not the wish to enjoy revenge but only the injury wrought by one's enemy which has forced one to it. Marcus Tully, after the death of the conspirators led by Cataline, gave him up to the people, but all he said was, "His life is done." Phocion refused to show pleasure at the death of his enemy Philip, and to the friends who encouraged him to make a sacrifice to the gods on this occasion he replied that it by no means suits a king to celebrate calamities that befall mortal men.

I won't omit three precepts which I should like to see always uppermost in the minds of men who fight. First, you should remember that you are nothing more than a mortal man exposed to the chances of fortune. Second, you must remember that your enemy, however wicked, is a man. Not only the bull and the lion, the bear and the wild pig, who can all bring a man down by their strength, have horns and tusks and claws to hurt you—even a mouse or any small animal defends itself, as Brasidas remarked when his finger was bitten. The third precept is this: always believe that human minds can change. It can easily happen that each of the enemies grows tired of living under the burdens and in the everlasting intense anxiety which enmity imposes on him. If, as Bias, one of the seven sages, says—the opinion is also ascribed to the poet Publius—we should conduct our friendships as though we might one day cease to be friends, let us also conduct our enmities as though we might one day cease to be odious and harmful to to each other. This is what I think of enmity, unless you want more.

Lionardo: Surely these are excellent precepts. I am happy with both your wealth of ancient opinions and examples and with the extremely compressed form of your rhetoric. You would not want a much more expansive and ample style. Accept our thanks, Adovardo. You have told us how to endure enmities without disgrace, a thing perhaps few people know how to do. If, as we have now learned how to conduct a fight, we had learned also how to win when we contend with our enemies, there would be nothing left to be desired on this subject.

One might, perhaps, just add the point that great harm can come from not showing open enmity to one who secretly offends us. If he is known to be no friend, men will give less credence to his empty ranting and his calumnies and all such ways of secretly harming and injuring a man. One might, for this reason, be persuaded that it is better to pursue enmity to the point where no more could be done by the most enthusiastic, spirited, and bellicose fighter. One who did this, however, might not be dealing with his enemy in the manner you propose, as though he could possibly cease sometime to be odious to the man who at present hates him. I take your advice to mean something else, namely that we should never in hatred perpetrate something which, if the feud should end, would leave ineradicable memories of wickedness and terrible cruelty.

Adovardo: That was indeed my opinion, Lionardo. I say that if you get into a fight to vindicate yourself, you will find it hard to have an enemy who can harm you less than you can harm him or would be willing to. If he is unable to harm you much, there are only two possible reasons for it. One is that you have armed yourself with vigilance, foresight, and extreme cunning rather than with rage, indignation, and the sword. Nothing should be lacking that might be needed for your fullest defense, for they say that to violence there is no answer but more violence. The other way is to disarm him entirely of every instrument and of all strength to hurt you with. I shall indicate to you at once what these means are and how they are found. Not only sword and arrow are such means, but also supporters, allies, opportunities, devices, traps, all things that may some-how serve to bring disaster upon you. Our task, then, is to get these means, if we can, out of his hands.

If a man is not underhanded or treacherous in the way he does this, but fights in an open and just way, no one will ever blame him for a manly and spirited opposition, nor will anyone fail to excuse him if he gives like for like—not hate for hate—but violence for violence and indignation for offenses. Let us act accordingly, then. Let us remove his weapons and so prepare ourselves that he can harm neither our person nor our possessions. Above all let us keep our name unblemished, for that has always been the prime and most valued possession of a wise man.

Lionardo: I am satisfied. But to arrange for him not to wish to harm us is perhaps more difficult. Therefore when we have made sure he is not able to hurt us, what else remains but to press home our victory?

Adovardo: Don't you know the two kinds of good and glorious victory? The first was described by Diogenes, who when he was asked how one can do an enemy most harm replied "by living honorably and spending your energy in worthwhile ways." Have no doubt of it, the man who hates to see your well planted and cultivated garden and who grieves to see you dressed in joyful, splendid garments, surrounded by friends, healthy, and thriving will grieve most of all when he sees you living in a cultivated way, graced with virtue, spoken of with noble words and high praises, a man free of any taint. As to the other way, it is, as I have said, to try if possible to make him less desirous to refuse your friendship. Who can deny the completeness and glory of such a victory, to accomplish the honorable, felicitous, and praiseworthy feat of killing hate and enmity itself at one blow, and to acquire a new friend?

Lionardo: Now who do you think will be so wise and learned in these arts that he can do what you propose? Do you think, perhaps, that if some of us have been listening carefully and remember all that you have said so far, and are willing to follow your good counsels as set forth here, we will not still find it impossible, by sheer cleverness, to escape being hated? Look, Adovardo, to make the heart of a man already passionately opposed to you become well disposed, you need new and more powerful means. You need more than what you have been showing us may effectively win over a new acquaintance without preconceptions. It is a hard thing to give up anger without first seeking revenge. Any man who has been angered will judge his own cause to be just. He will therefore claim the right to fight for justice.

Adovardo: Kindness, benevolence, liberality, and such virtues, provided one does not falsify or merely pretend to them, enable us to create friendships. Do not deny, Lionardo, that they may make even hard and bitter hearts calm themselves and return to their former good will. If a benefit from one who neither could nor should harm us is a welcome thing, who could possibly deny that one owes real gratitude to a person who could and perhaps should be harshly vindictive but prefers to be kind and generous? This, I think, any man of discretion would view as a double gift, a benefit from one who was ready to harm you but who decided not to be troublesome and severe but kind and accommodating. Such kindness, such magnanimity is worthy of a soul fit to command other men. He is doubly generous, first because he does not harm you, second because he gives you a gift and a reward. Who could help loving a man thus born to glory and deserving of immortality? Whose character would be so egregiously treacherous as to fail to commend such a man to perpetual honor, a man whose kindness released his enemy from fear and anxiety, grievous burdens in themselves, and whose noble liberality recalled his enemy to sweet and happy friendship?

Who, desiring the peace and tranquillity all men long for and praise, could stupidly think that while he suffers hate and contumely and pursues vengeance he can ever be secure? Who is so foolish as not to know that injuries do not dissolve enmity but only greatly intensify hate? Can you find a wise man who would seek vengeance except in the hope of making his enemies cease offending him so much? Now Thales of Miletus may be as wise as they think when, in reply to the question, "What alleviates the burden of sorrow in our life?" he says, "Seeing our enemy worse off than we are." But a sensible person, not being a perfect fool, tries to avoid a life of anxiety concerning feuds and therefore can hardly help doing all he can to mitigate ill will or at least to escape intensified hate. Once a man begins to seek more carefully, moreover, he is sure to find a number of excellent ways and means to soften even rude and harsh spirits.

Good words, they say, are the best medicine for evil deeds. It is written that a certain woman by the name of Rome set fire to the ships of the Trojans just to end the tedium of sailing. Thereupon, as some say, they soon built the city of Rome. The women begged pardon and used humble words to pacify their husbands, whose just anger they had aroused and who were ready to punish them. Cyrus, according to Xenophon, was called into the presence of Cyaxares and had a conversation with him where they discussed and cleared away all the causes of their enmity. They came out of the conversation friends. Alcibiades, by the use of flattery and blandishments, pacified and reconciled the angry Tissaphernes, who had, because of his jealousy of Alcibiades, left the Lacedaemonians, an enemy to the very name of Greeks. There were the Heraclians, as Justin tells us, who cleverly made friends of their enemy Lammacus and his army by the use of benefits and gifts. If their oppressors now became their friends they thought this the best indemnity for the damages done them in war.

I would certainly declare, in short, that if a feud was not begun by our fault nor offenses avenged with harshness or bitterness on our part, we should not find it too difficult, by bowing and yielding to the other's anger, to soften any enemy in the world. To be freed from anxiety and to escape hatred, to obtain a new friend as well, makes it consonant with your dignity thus to bow and to be kind and gentle. Wishing to continue a quarrel or a feud when you could be done with it is not only pride and sourness but intolerable folly. As Zeno used to remark, lupins are a harsh and bitter fruit until soaked in water; then they become soft and sweet. Human hearts, too, though the flames of anger and indignation may harden them and fill them with bitterness, are helped and mollified, in good time anyway, if we show a desire for friendship. If we give men reason for it, they will become softer and more tractable. It is a good idea to be the first to confess a misdeed to one who is close to you, for he will listen with a more temperate mind to you, who speak with gentleness and mitigate the facts with excuses, than to a gossip or talebearer. If you have perhaps committed some fault, you are more likely to gain his pardon if his anger is still fresh and has not been allowed to harden with time.

Lionardo: I agree. But I also recall the remark of Plutarch, that Dionysius pretended to be reconciled to Dion, and so lured Dion into his fortress by himself. There he confronted him with the letter he had written to the Athenians and commanded the sailors to carry him away to Italy. Perhaps they are not wrong when they say "never trust a former enemy." It is as if they were warning you that once a man had been your enemy he would never become a true friend. I think from your remarks, however, that this does not apply to those who are able wholly to leave hatred and the evils of enmity behind them and to transform all their feelings into affection.

Adovardo: So it is, for hatred is called the poison of friendship and the very blood of enmity. Nothing in enmity is so painful as the very hatred itself, a pestilent thing and one feared by every man of discretion. It does not cease to gnaw at the mind of whoever harbors it. It acts like a true poison, constantly corroding and spoiling every innermost thought and good idea. Seen in another person, too, one knows what a rabid and dangerous thing hatred is for its objects. Remember that hatred causes those whom you need in daily life and even your own kin to desert you, while it kindles in the hearts of strangers the desire to do you harm and cunningly to persecute you. Robberies, murders, subversion of states, treachery, conspiracies, every evil springs from hatred. As the fig tree growing in the cracks of ancient marble temples was at first so small you might have dug it out with your nails, yet when it grew was able to dislodge great rocks and to overturn the whole edifice, so hatred was easy to extirpate at the start, but in the long period of its growth and toughening it destroyed every rational harmony in life, every power of thought in the mind. Ultimately the mind is so ruined that it accepts any cruelty and inhumanity as long as it seems likely to bring revenge and satisfaction.

Let us therefore exercise every care and solicitude in the effort to fight this poisonous evil in ourselves and in others. This is certainly necessary if we aspire to be good constructors and preservers of friendship. If one would preserve friendship, one must diligently imitate the doctors, who study health and its preservation by first examining the sources of various diseases and then, having found that heavy food, indigestion, cold, fatigue, or grief or other conditions may exist, tell us to avoid them in order to continue in good health. I think in thus seeking to preserve friendship it would be no error to investigate the causes of enmity and then to struggle vigorously to oppose these and not to let them get in our way.

Lionardo: We agree that this is a matter for investigation. Perhaps we already have the answer, however, in the few words you said before, when you seemed to reason step by step that hatred springs from envy and enmity from hatred.

Adovardo: Agreed. But let us now take up our system for the preservation of friendship, the fifth question we proposed to handle. We have seen the birth, growth, dissolution, and recovery of friendship and found enmity to be its contrary. We have observed the first elements of friendship to be affection expressed and increased through familiar contact and converse involving mutual service and good will. Perhaps we may say that malevolence expressed and increased by contact involving offenses and insults is the fundamental principal of enmity, the contrary of friendship. If you grant me this point, I shall tell you how to prevent envy, from which arises malevolence, the contrary of affection. This will be a very useful thing for you to know and perhaps something you have not heard before.

Lionardo: Reason and affection alike forbid us to disagree with you. Go on.

Adovardo: I shall try to obey you, but not to be verbose. There are some prosperous men and men of means who show off their riches more than others do, and one sees them proudly flaunting the gifts of fortune. They are splendid and sumptuous in dress, with great retinues, a multitude of daily guests, and all sorts of ostentation. The more immoderately they indulge this tendency, the more many people wish to see their fortunes decline and their situation become less favorable. Some, I have observed, actually lead criminally licentious lives, without a care for law or for the opinion of better men, and without respect for their place in the hearts of their fellow citizens. This makes their presence a burden to all their fellow citizens. There are others, and quite a lot of them too, who whether from ambition to stand first in honor or for some other reason show dislike toward anyone who labors hard, perhaps pursues the noble arts with zealous study, and devotes himself to arduous and worthwhile things which win him a good name. I have noted that practically any sort of competition leads to hard feelings, for each desires the fulfillment of his own ambition and considers himself offended by anyone who gets in his way.

We seem, then, to have found three causes of malevolence: first, it is directed against ostentatious men, also against wicked men, and also against those whom we want to equal or surpass. (I grant that there are some men so malevolent and bitter by nature that everything good that happens to others makes them sad.) Which of these is most harmful to the preservation of friendship I shall not discuss—perhaps all of them are less than helpful. I also see that it is not always the vices of others but sometimes our own that cause hatred and enmity to take root. I think it is easier to educate ourselves than others. Let us, then, appear such that no one's eyes or ears may be troubled by any sort of ostentation on our part, nor by any arrogance of gesture or of word. Virgil used to admire his Maecenas because "You, who could do anything, would, as far as one could see, never do anyone any harm." There was an ancient saying much repeated by the philosophers: "The more you can do, the less you ought to wish to." If one observes this rule in one's own case, one learns that to restrain one's will does not diminish one's fortune but does increase one's honor and good name among men, things more precious than wealth.

Plato the philosopher wrote to the Syracusan Dion, "And be aware, therefore, O Dion, that good will is a great help in everything, while pride leaves a man solitary and bereft of friends." The haughty man is no pleasure to those among whom he lives, and less still to others. Hence Aristotle's comment: "Since we rarely love a man who is no pleasure to us, the proud man, being unpleasant, will be unloved." We often find even a small act of pride offensive from a man we dislike. So we should realize that if we indulge in certain immodest mannerisms, they may generate grave hatred of us in those who thus see us as puffed up with fatuous conceit. Sallust tells how Jemalus came to bear a deep hatred toward his brother, Aterbal, because of the latter's gesture of pride in sitting down at a higher place. Gracchus, when he returned from Carthage, took a house again near the market of the poor artisans, to show he was not better than other men and had not become attached to pomp and circumstance. So let us too calculate and control ourselves, and let us show no outward sign of pride.

Of course we must far more obviously shun licentiousness and immorality in word or deed. Our duty is to find no fault, to praise only those who merit it, and to make ourselves, as it were, the heralds and promulgators of our friends' virtues. Let us make sure many people bear witness at the same time to their excellence and to our benevolence. Isocrates wrote to Demonicus that the beginning of good will was praise and the beginning of malevolence was finding fault. So let us be careful not to show disapproval by word or gesture. Let us try, saving our dignity, to be sure even the least of men feel we have no taste for pomp and vain ostentation and that all appreciate our courtesy and kindness, which will tend to make us popular. As Laelius said to Cicero that he had never in any way offended Scipio or ever received any offense from him, let us too avoid appearing in any way unpleasant or ungracious to those whose favor we wish to keep.

It may be that some whom we would like to consider well disposed toward us harbor an unfortunate haughtiness of temperament or burn with an immodest and rather unreasonable greed for even more praise and admiration than they deserve. Some may be hard and solitary by nature. Such people we may try to keep in a good state of mind by our gentleness and pleasant speech, though we shall not fall into flattery or obsequiousness. These remain unworthy of a noble spirit. Let us act like Alcibiades who, as they say, could imitate the chameleon, an animal which according to reports is able to vary its color to suit its environment. With melancholy men we will be rather austere, with liberal men magnanimous. In general, as Cicero said to his brother, let us suit our expression, countenance, words, and gestures to men's desires. Laberius the poet remarked that on a road where the fatigue of walking makes almost everyone sad and heavy, one cheerful companion is like a vehicle and lifts one out of one's weariness. Cato used to say that the dinner or the feast where men are more delighted by the talk and the spirit than with the fare is the right place to foster friendship. Paulus Aemilius said a well-prepared feast was the work of a noble spirit, not unlike the commanding of an army, but with a very different outcome, for the one labor makes you feared and the other arouses and preserves affection. Nothing, as Aristotle said, is so natural to friends as living together.

Everything must be done in its proper time, however, and managed in an orderly way. Men's souls, which are by nature particularly inflammable, kindle suddenly in hatred and wrath and break abruptly away from affection. It is good to realize that just as we are not always in a good mood and do not always persevere in our good intentions, others too have changes of feeling and are drawn in new directions according to the moment. It matters for the future of any relationship, as Tully said to Decius Brutus, what were its first beginnings and what persons were involved, as it were, in opening the doors. Just as the man who comes to call on us at a bad moment annoys us, so a letter or greeting may offend us if it is inopportune. Cyrus, as Xenophon writes, used to find out by means of his servant Sacca whether Antiages, his uncle, was happy or sad —only then would he decide whether to go and see him. Isocrates, writing to Demonicus, reminds him how easily one can get too much of anything. He says that for this reason he would rarely invite his friends. We do not praise the wisdom of those who give daily feasts and live in an unordered luxury. Nor do we always approve of parsimony and silence. Suetonius writes that Caesar was invited by a friend and found that the dinner had been too modest. As he left he made the remark, "I hadn't thought of myself as that close a friend of yours."

It does happen occasionally that a very close friend, impelled by change of fortune or by other circumstances, takes on new habits and develops new aspirations. These may even destroy your affection. Some rise in rank and come to enjoy high authority, whereupon they may grow insolent and contemptuous toward their less powerful friends. Some, it may be, fall into adversity and are broken by poverty. Sometimes these may yield to despair, and filled with suspiciousness they may act boorish toward us. Their conduct may no longer befit men of honorable character, but be reduced to baseness. I think there is some aptness in the remark that one owes reverence to a friend whose position one would honor and respect anyway if one did not know him personally. I also think that no man of humane and moral character would willingly fail an affectionate friend in his hopes and needs. It is not charitable, I think, not to want to give faithful counsel, devoted help, honorable aid, sincere, zealous, and prompt assistance to raise the spirits of one who is fond of you, to lift him out of his depression, to content him more fully even than he has thought of asking. No one would deny that friendship involves working for common advantages; it is further asserted that all that friends have should be held in common. The opinion of the philosopher Epicurus is generally accepted that friendship is an honorable association of wills. Who, if this is so, would not want to eliminate from a friendship any distress of either friend, as a personal burden. We should not forget the reflection of Demetrius, son of Phanostratus: "A true friend in good fortune comes to you only when called, but in adversity he comes running on his own to help you." Chilon the philosopher thought a friend should be more eager to share your hardships than to enjoy your prosperity with you.

It may indeed happen that your friend asks something of you that is not honorable and says as Blosius, the friend of Gracchus, did that there should be no limit to your willingness to help a friend. Aristotle, however, in refutation of certain opinions of his master, Plato, said one should love one's friend, but truth more. We, too, should serve the friend who loves us, but consider honor our best friend. Indeed I cannot quite understand how one who wants to see my honor impaired can really be a friend. When Pericles' friend asked him to give false testimony, he replied, "As far as the altar, I shall obey you, the altar being the spot where his oath would have to be given. Chilon the philosopher once consciously gave some bad advice in order to protect his friend, but he suffered to the end of his days from an uncertainty whether he had merited praise or blame. Antigonus had a dream in which he saw Mithridates mowing down golden grain, and thereupon he called his son, Demetrius, swore him to secrecy, and plotted with him to kill Mithridates. Demetrius called Mithridates and talked to him of other things, but at the same time, as they walked on the shore, he wrote with a stick in the sand, "Flee!" Mithridates understood and took the advice.

You can see clearly enough that where a useful and honest way exists, even if it involves danger, we should not wait to be asked for help, but it does us credit to come unasked. With prudence and proper caution we should confront our own and the other's danger. As to base actions, however, I think it is clear that our duty is to shun them. It may also happen, and come between us and one who says he loves us, that he puts some political advantage above our affection. If a man is like that, let us imitate Pedaretus the Lacedaemonian, who was refused an office that he asked for; he turned away without showing any disappointment and only said he was happy to discover that his fatherland apparently contained so many virtuous citizens to whom, rather than to himself, the republic might be entrusted. We may make Crassus our model, for he said he could tolerate without disquiet the many people who surpassed him in fortune's gifts, but he grieved if anyone outdid him in gaining the prizes which one wins by one's own efforts, such as virtue and a knowledge of things worth knowing.

When we compete for such prizes as the favor and grace the people can bestow, I think it is hardly right once engaged in the contest to think our own judgment less fallible than public opinion. If we have taken the position that those who confer the dignity are competent and are guided by reason and thought, it is a matter of honor and a sign of self-discipline to accept their judgment. If, on the other hand, you think the judges incompetent or ignorant, you have only yourself to blame for having submitted yourself to them.

Sometimes too it happens that your friends quarrel among themselves, and when you favor one, the other begins to consider you his enemy. The result may even be that neither side likes you as well as before. Livy the historian tells us that at one time, when the Roman plebs were fighting with the patricians over the question of debts and of usurious rates of interest, they asked the support and assistance of the consul Servilius. They begged him earnestly to care for their welfare and to help relieve them of their heavy burdens. The consul took a middle position and negotiated, but he found no favor with the Senate, which was very unsympathetic to this cause, nor did he keep the favor of the plebs, for they thought he was yielding to the Senate. It ended in his being considered by the patriciate too soft toward the people and really an ambitious demagogue, while the plebs declared he was deceitful and treacherous. Soon he was hated by both parties.

On this point I like the conduct of Caesar, who found Crassus and Pompey engaged in quarreling and decided to win the friendship of both and increase his own power by means of their favor. He undertook to arrange an alliance and agreement between the two leaders. Thus it became possible for Caesar himself to enter the entourage of each and to be seen working zealously in their service. Plato wrote to Dion, "I will be the middleman you want, yes, if you find yourself engaged in a quarrel, and I shall try to reconcile and pacify you. If the fighting is based on real hatred, however, I would rather one of you sought another arbitrator."

As Aristotle the philosopher lay dying at the age of sixty-two, he was asked by his disciples to pronounce one of them his successor as teacher of the others (two of them were Theophrastus of Lesbos and Menedemus of Rhodes). Aristotle was silent for some time. When some, who were concerned over the problem, repeated their question, he demanded that they find some wine good for his health. They brought him the best wines of Rhodes and Lesbos. He tasted the one and showed that he liked it. He tasted the second, and said, "This one, too, pleases me." Thus they understood that he liked both Theophrastus of Lesbos and Menedemus of Rhodes. They praised his decision not only because it was in itself a judicious one but also because he showed such modesty in the way he expressed it. He wanted, even after his death, to keep the love of all of them.

Pomponius Atticus saw his country torn by the wars of Cinna and realized that he could not go on in the enjoyment of his position unless he gave his support to one of quarreling parties. Therefore, as they tell us, he separated himself from the conflict by going away to Athens. There he pursued his studies and made himself extremely popular with the Athenians, largely because he lived as though a commoner among the commoners, yet was also equal to the leading citizens. It counted in his favor, too, that he learned to speak the Greek language as well as if he had been born and raised in Athens, which may be why he was called Atticus. Sulla, one of the chiefs in the civil war, since he admired him and prized his noble character, asked him to join in the leadership of his armies. "Don't ask me, I pray you," Atticus replied, "to fight now against those whose ally against you I might have become had I not avoided that by abandoning Italy." Sulla praised his answer. Atticus also excused himself from the wars of Caesar and Pompey, saying he was too old and would be useless on campaigns. For this reason, even though he helped the friends of Pompey with money, he was not badly received in the end by Caesar, the victor.

Tiro, the most educated slave of Cicero, writes a story concerning Pompey's building of a temple to the Goddess of Victory in Rome, where he wanted to inscribe his honorable titles. A quarrel arose among the literary men consulted as to how to write one title, *"tertium consul."* or *"tertio c."* This quarrel was submitted to the judgment of Marcus Tully, who, to satisfy all parties, prudently recommended they write just the first three letters, *"ter."* Chilon the philosopher too, as Laertius Diogenes tells us, was called on to arbitrate between two friends. To avoid offending one or the other, he persuaded them to take the case elsewhere. Camillus the dictator once got the siege of the fortress of the Veii to the point where he could have burst into it by an underground passage and taken their very rich country. Though he had such a great victory in his hand, however, he did not want to cause resentment in the Senate by giving the great prize over to his armies to sack; nor did he want to fall into disfavor with the people in general by letting all the booty fall into the public coffers. So he wrote to the Senate for orders. Thus did all these men manage to avoid offending the feelings of the people around them.

You see how I have strained my wits to be brief. I could have added more points which are not irrelevant, but I would have overextended my talk. One reminder I must not omit: I want you all to remember that nothing is so valuable at every stage of friendship as benefits bestowed. On these—since on friendship nothing now remains to be said, I think—I shall give Battista and Carlo some pithy epigrams which they who are of the age of study may wish to memorize.

Lionardo: Do not put a stop to this compressed teaching of yours. It was all so rich in excellent ideas and in splendid examples that I found more and more things as I listened that I wanted to note down or to single out for praise. You have delighted me, Adovardo, entirely and excessively delighted me. But I won't agree that you have finished or that you have now said enough to cover the subject of friendship.

Adovardo: We discussed by what arts it may be acquired, increased, diminished, and for what reasons it may be renewed. Then we discoursed on the labors one may justifiably undertake to preserve it. What more do you want?

Lionardo: Nothing, if all these were fully explained, and they were. But see, this is what I hope for from you now. Piero taught us how to acquire favor at the court of princes. By you we have been instructed in every other problem of winning love. If now someone who was himself a prince were to ask you, most excellent master of friendships, to teach him what almost no prince seems to know by himself, that is how to make himself loved, I think it would be foreign to your amiable nature to refuse him this valuable service.

Adovardo: O most fortunate prince who should thus desire to win affection and to be less feared than loved! This is something they could all do by one action, and that a highly pleasurable one. Yet they neglect this means to acquire immortal love and admiration.

Lionardo: I am waiting to hear what that one action is.

Adovardo: What is Carlo saying?

Lionardo: He says Messer Antonio Alberti has arrived to greet Lorenzo.

Adovardo: Well, then——I'll answer you tomorrow.

INDEX